TOKYO TARAREBA GIRLS

4

AKIKO HIGASHIMURA

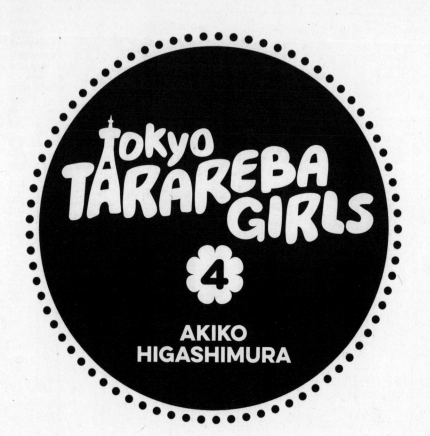

TODAY'S RECOMMENDATIONS

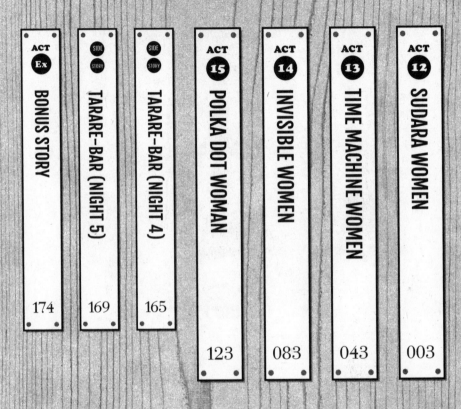

ACT 12 SUDARA WOMEN

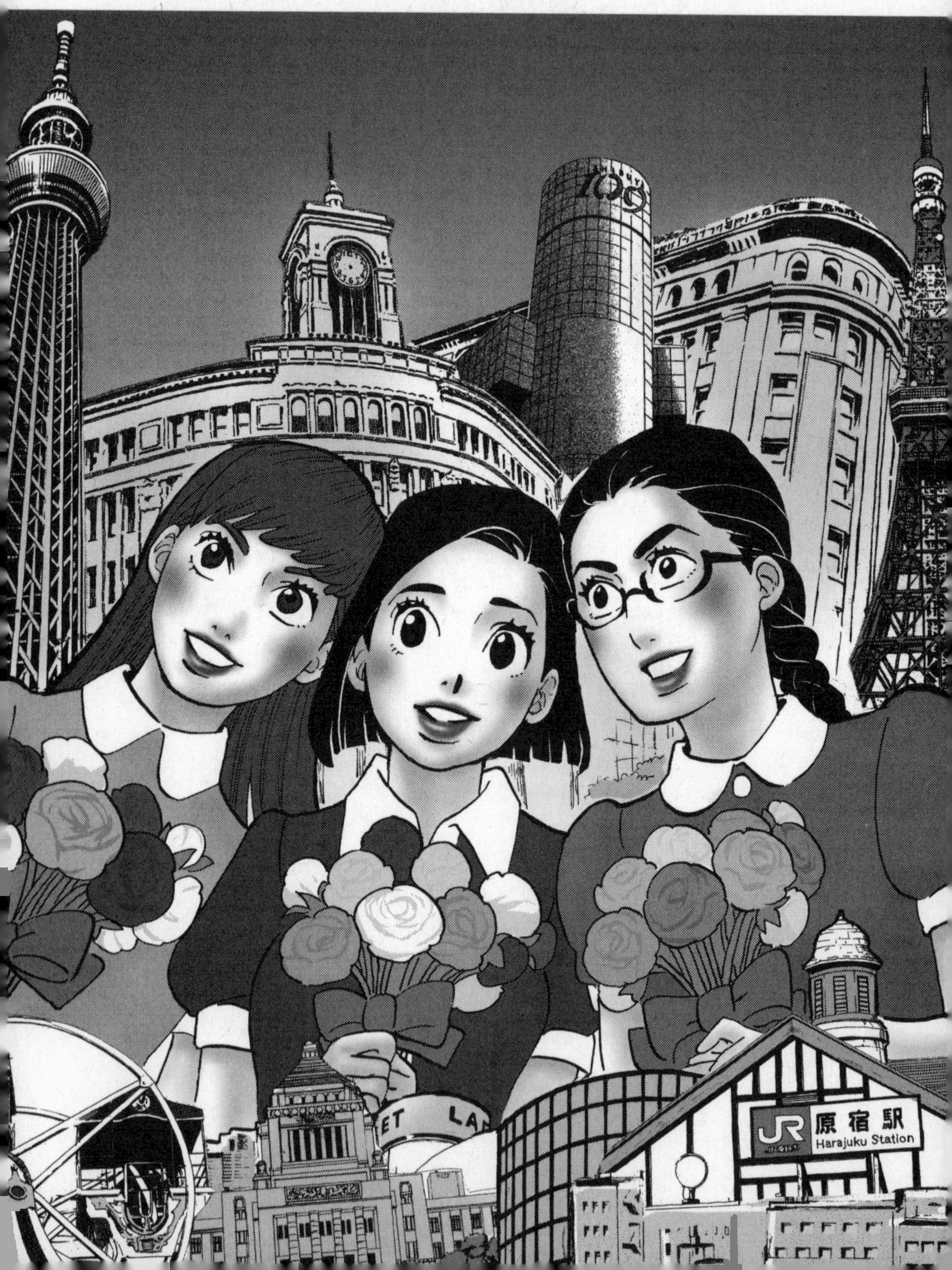
109
原宿駅
Harajuku Station

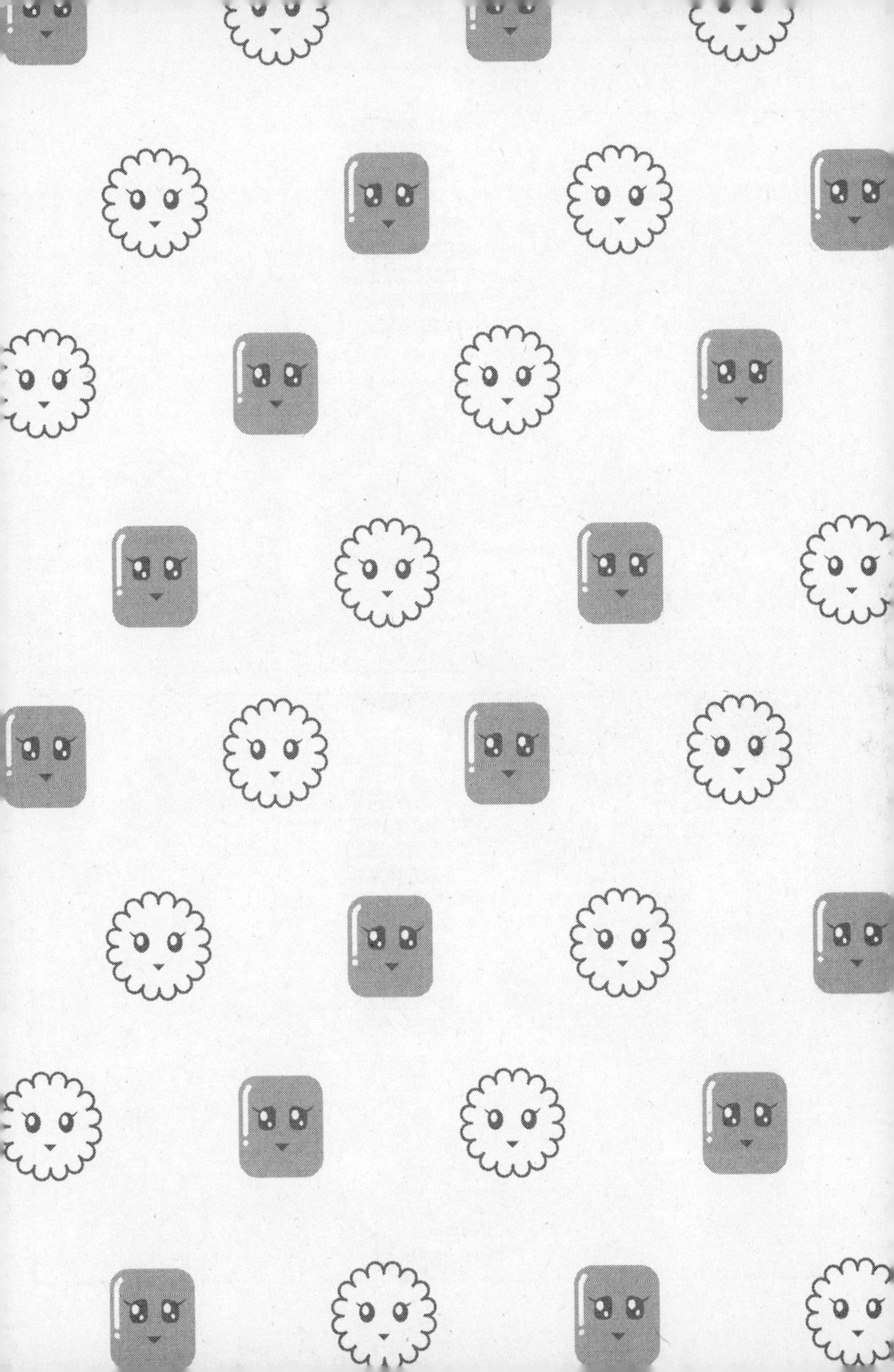

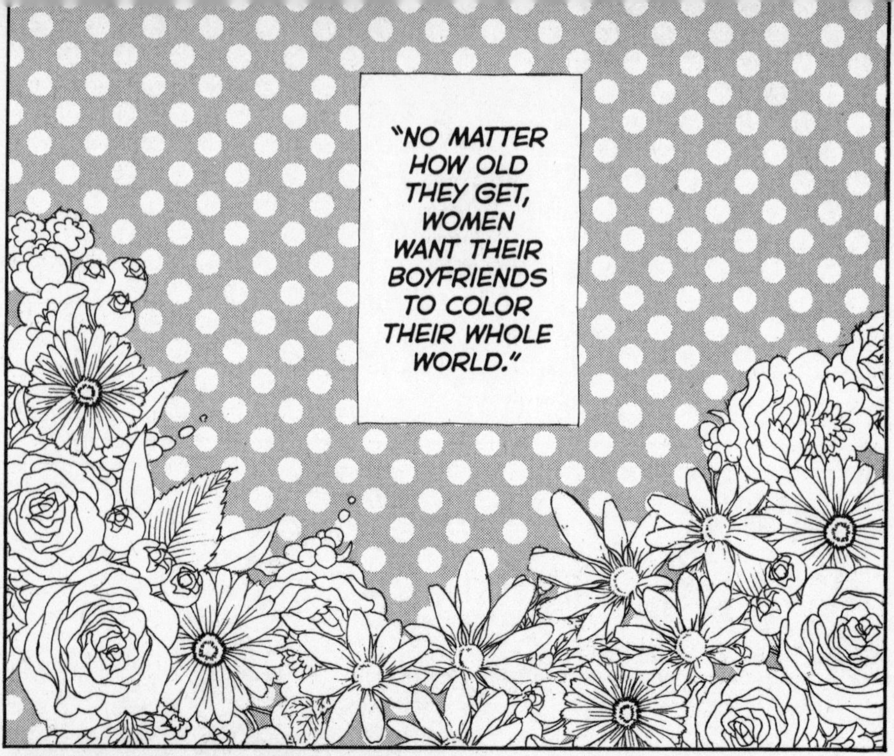
"NO MATTER HOW OLD THEY GET, WOMEN WANT THEIR BOYFRIENDS TO COLOR THEIR WHOLE WORLD."

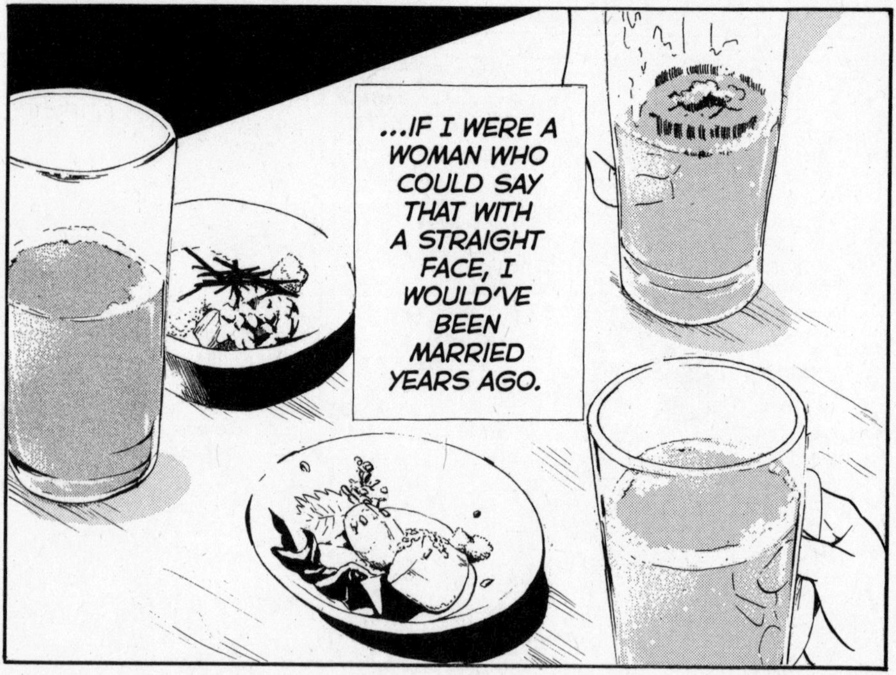
...IF I WERE A WOMAN WHO COULD SAY THAT WITH A STRAIGHT FACE, I WOULD'VE BEEN MARRIED YEARS AGO.

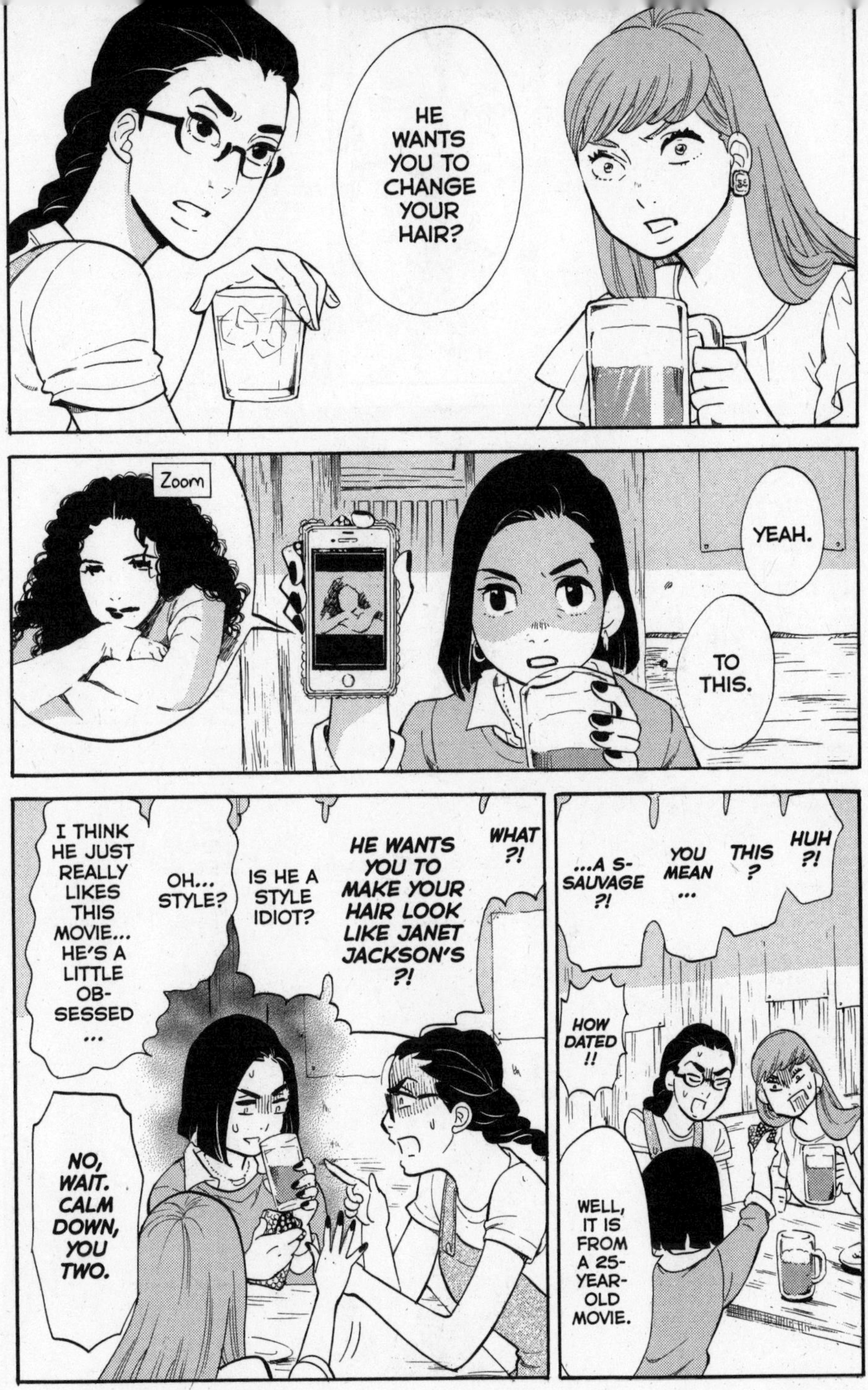
HE WANTS YOU TO CHANGE YOUR HAIR?
YEAH.
TO THIS.
Zoom
HUH ?!
THIS ?
YOU MEAN ...
...A S-SAUVAGE ?!
HOW DATED !!
WELL, IT IS FROM A 25-YEAR-OLD MOVIE.
WHAT ?!
HE WANTS YOU TO MAKE YOUR HAIR LOOK LIKE JANET JACKSON'S ?!
IS HE A STYLE IDIOT?
OH... STYLE?
I THINK HE JUST REALLY LIKES THIS MOVIE... HE'S A LITTLE OBSESSED ...
NO, WAIT. CALM DOWN, YOU TWO.

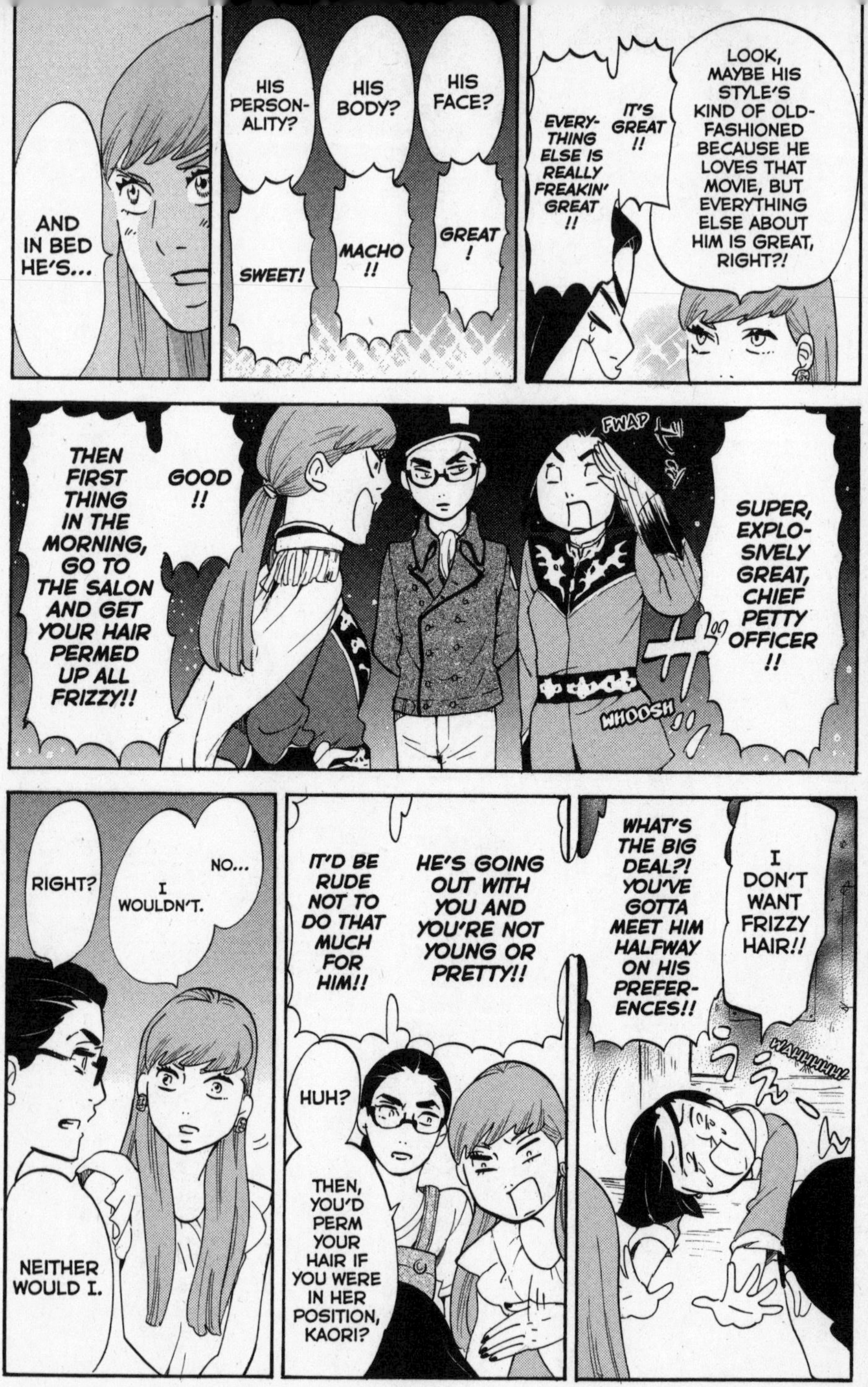
LOOK, MAYBE HIS STYLE'S KIND OF OLD-FASHIONED BECAUSE HE LOVES THAT MOVIE, BUT EVERYTHING ELSE ABOUT HIM IS GREAT, RIGHT?!
IT'S GREAT !!
EVERYTHING ELSE IS REALLY FREAKIN' GREAT !!
HIS FACE?
GREAT !
HIS BODY?
MACHO !!
HIS PERSONALITY?
SWEET!
AND IN BED HE'S...
FWAP
SUPER, EXPLOSIVELY GREAT, CHIEF PETTY OFFICER !!
WHOOSH
GOOD !!
THEN FIRST THING IN THE MORNING, GO TO THE SALON AND GET YOUR HAIR PERMED UP ALL FRIZZY!!
I DON'T WANT FRIZZY HAIR!!
WHAT'S THE BIG DEAL?! YOU'VE GOTTA MEET HIM HALFWAY ON HIS PREFERENCES!!
HE'S GOING OUT WITH YOU AND YOU'RE NOT YOUNG OR PRETTY!!
IT'D BE RUDE NOT TO DO THAT MUCH FOR HIM!!
HUH?
THEN, YOU'D PERM YOUR HAIR IF YOU WERE IN HER POSITION, KAORI?
NO...
I WOULDN'T.
RIGHT?
NEITHER WOULD I.

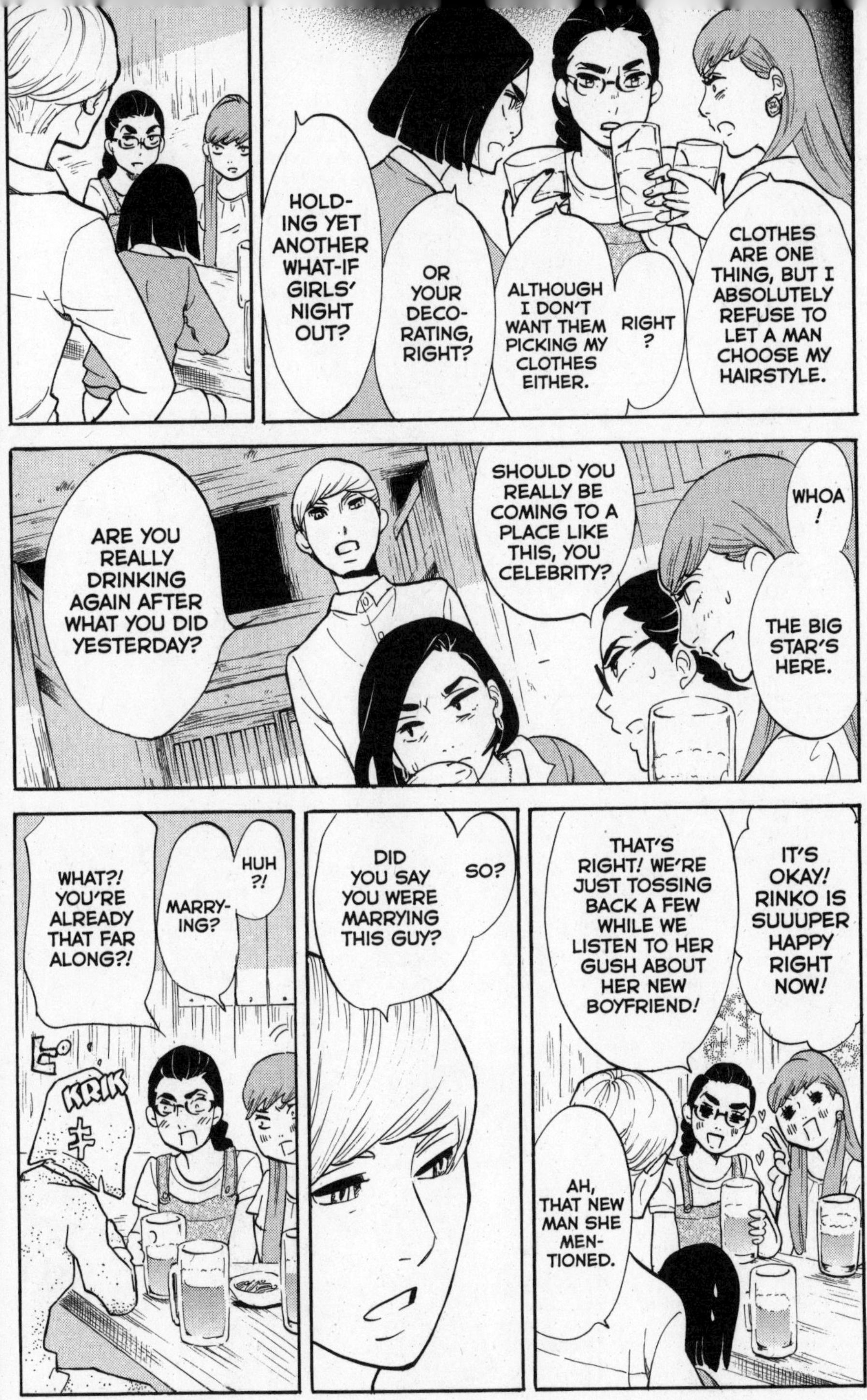
CLOTHES ARE ONE THING, BUT I ABSOLUTELY REFUSE TO LET A MAN CHOOSE MY HAIRSTYLE.
RIGHT?
ALTHOUGH I DON'T WANT THEM PICKING MY CLOTHES EITHER.
OR YOUR DECORATING, RIGHT?
HOLDING YET ANOTHER WHAT-IF GIRLS' NIGHT OUT?
WHOA!
THE BIG STAR'S HERE.
SHOULD YOU REALLY BE COMING TO A PLACE LIKE THIS, YOU CELEBRITY?
ARE YOU REALLY DRINKING AGAIN AFTER WHAT YOU DID YESTERDAY?
IT'S OKAY! RINKO IS SUUUPER HAPPY RIGHT NOW!
THAT'S RIGHT! WE'RE JUST TOSSING BACK A FEW WHILE WE LISTEN TO HER GUSH ABOUT HER NEW BOYFRIEND!
AH, THAT NEW MAN SHE MENTIONED.
SO?
DID YOU SAY YOU WERE MARRYING THIS GUY?
HUH?!
MARRYING?
WHAT?! YOU'RE ALREADY THAT FAR ALONG?!
KRIK

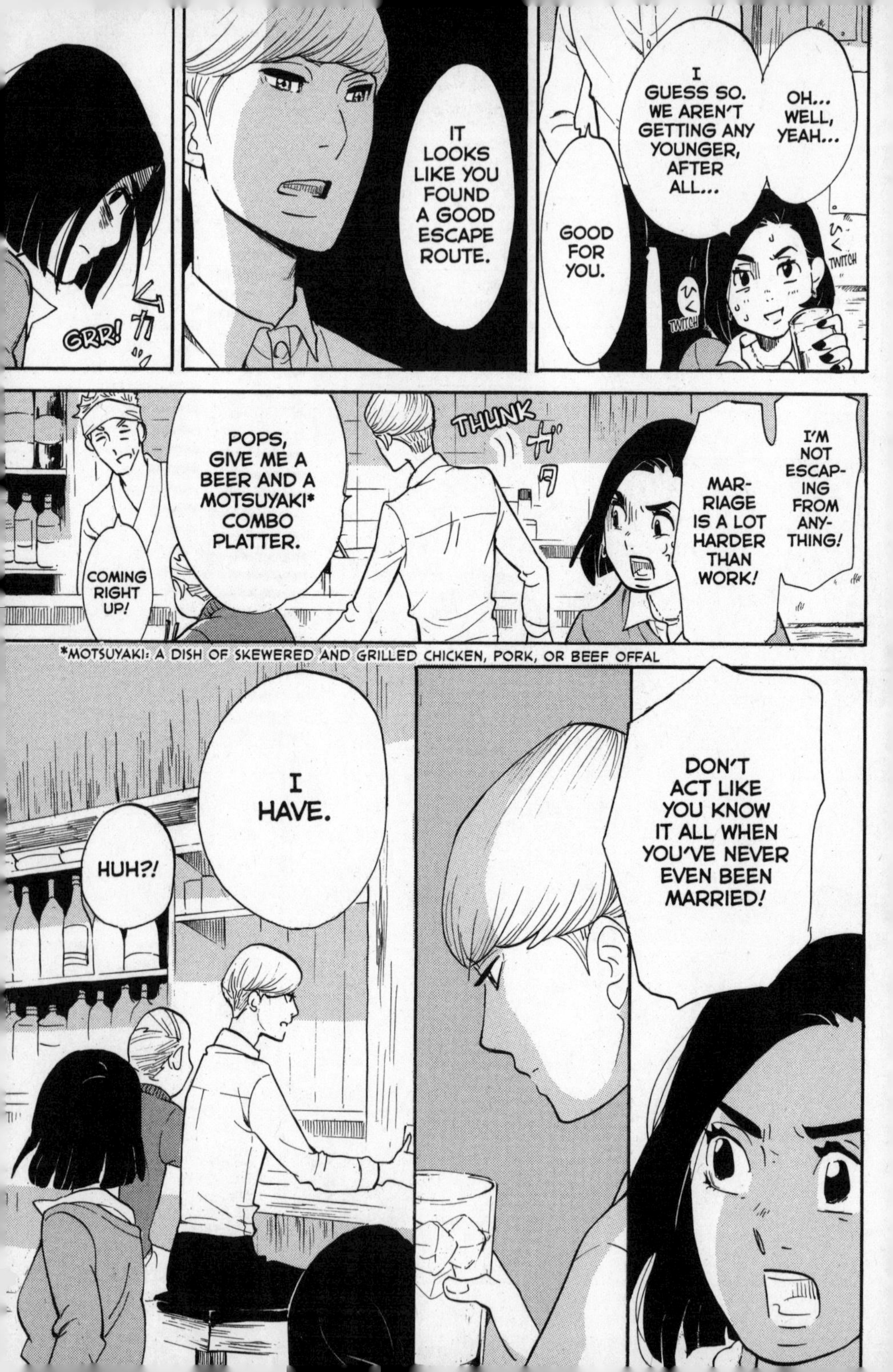
OH... WELL, YEAH...
I GUESS SO. WE AREN'T GETTING ANY YOUNGER, AFTER ALL...
GOOD FOR YOU.
TWITCH
TWITCH
IT LOOKS LIKE YOU FOUND A GOOD ESCAPE ROUTE.
GRR!
I'M NOT ESCAPING FROM ANYTHING!
MARRIAGE IS A LOT HARDER THAN WORK!
THUNK
POPS, GIVE ME A BEER AND A MOTSUYAKI* COMBO PLATTER.
COMING RIGHT UP!
*MOTSUYAKI: A DISH OF SKEWERED AND GRILLED CHICKEN, PORK, OR BEEF OFFAL
DON'T ACT LIKE YOU KNOW IT ALL WHEN YOU'VE NEVER EVEN BEEN MARRIED!
I HAVE.
HUH?!

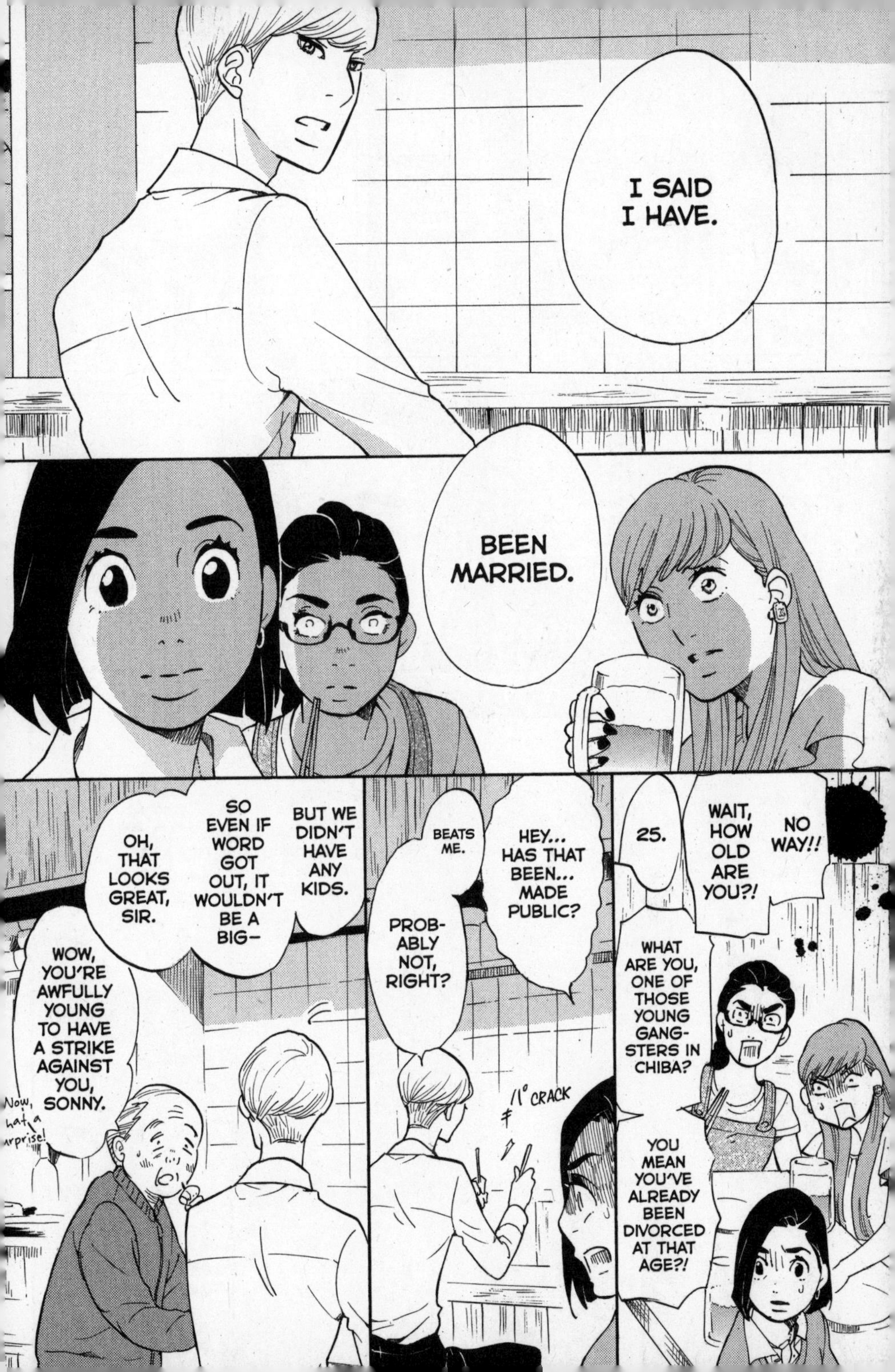
I SAID I HAVE.
BEEN MARRIED.
NO WAY!!
WAIT, HOW OLD ARE YOU?!
25.
WHAT ARE YOU, ONE OF THOSE YOUNG GANG-STERS IN CHIBA?
YOU MEAN YOU'VE ALREADY BEEN DIVORCED AT THAT AGE?!
HEY... HAS THAT BEEN... MADE PUBLIC?
BEATS ME.
PROB-ABLY NOT, RIGHT?
CRACK
BUT WE DIDN'T HAVE ANY KIDS.
SO EVEN IF WORD GOT OUT, IT WOULDN'T BE A BIG—
OH, THAT LOOKS GREAT, SIR.
WOW, YOU'RE AWFULLY YOUNG TO HAVE A STRIKE AGAINST YOU, SONNY.

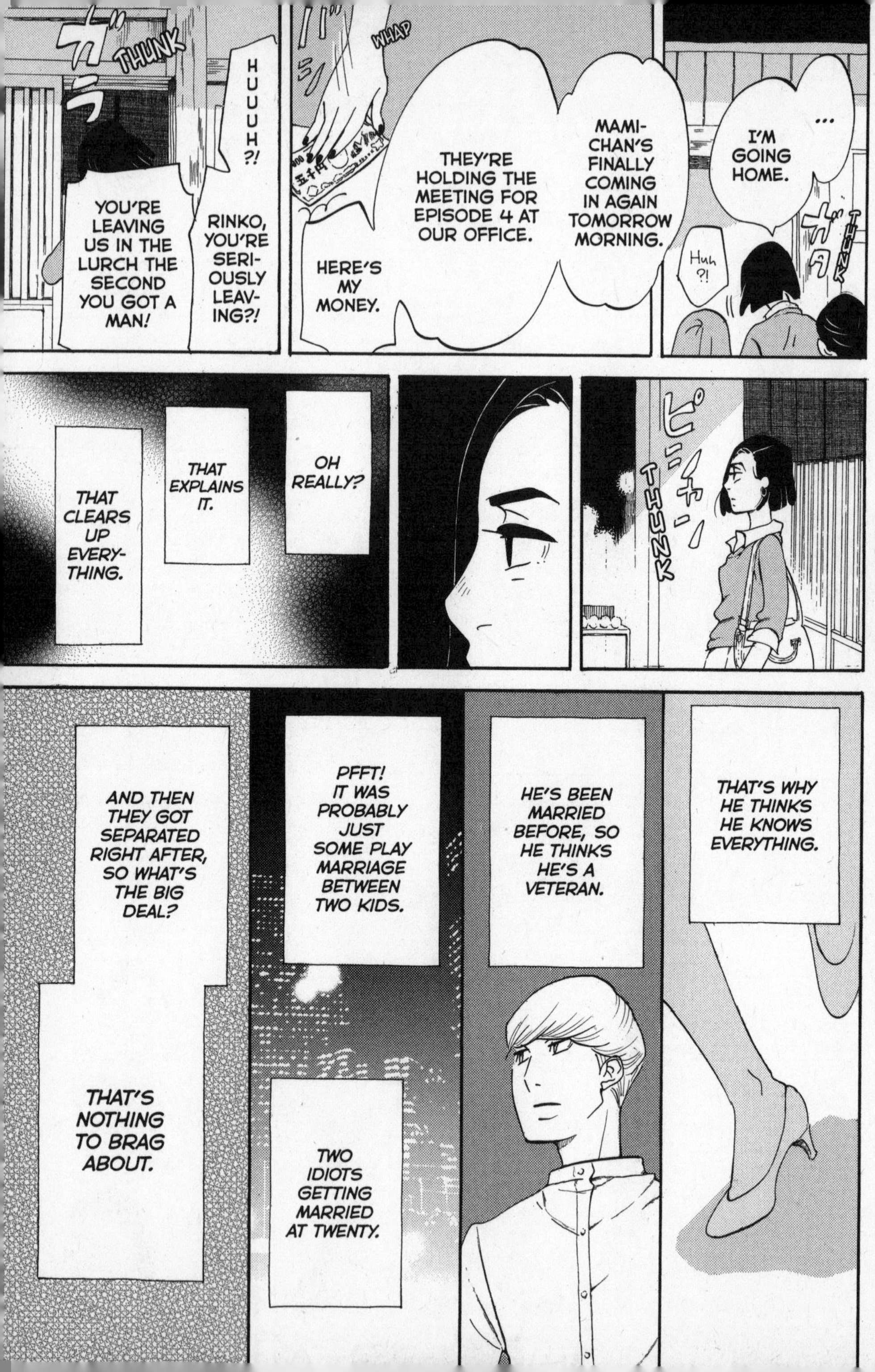
...
I'M GOING HOME.
THUNK
Huh ?!
MAMI-CHAN'S FINALLY COMING IN AGAIN TOMORROW MORNING.
THEY'RE HOLDING THE MEETING FOR EPISODE 4 AT OUR OFFICE.
WHAP
HERE'S MY MONEY.
HUUUUH?!
RINKO, YOU'RE SERIOUSLY LEAVING?!
THUNK
YOU'RE LEAVING US IN THE LURCH THE SECOND YOU GOT A MAN!
THUNK
OH REALLY?
THAT EXPLAINS IT.
THAT CLEARS UP EVERYTHING.
THAT'S WHY HE THINKS HE KNOWS EVERYTHING.
HE'S BEEN MARRIED BEFORE, SO HE THINKS HE'S A VETERAN.
PFFT! IT WAS PROBABLY JUST SOME PLAY MARRIAGE BETWEEN TWO KIDS.
TWO IDIOTS GETTING MARRIED AT TWENTY.
AND THEN THEY GOT SEPARATED RIGHT AFTER, SO WHAT'S THE BIG DEAL?
THAT'S NOTHING TO BRAG ABOUT.

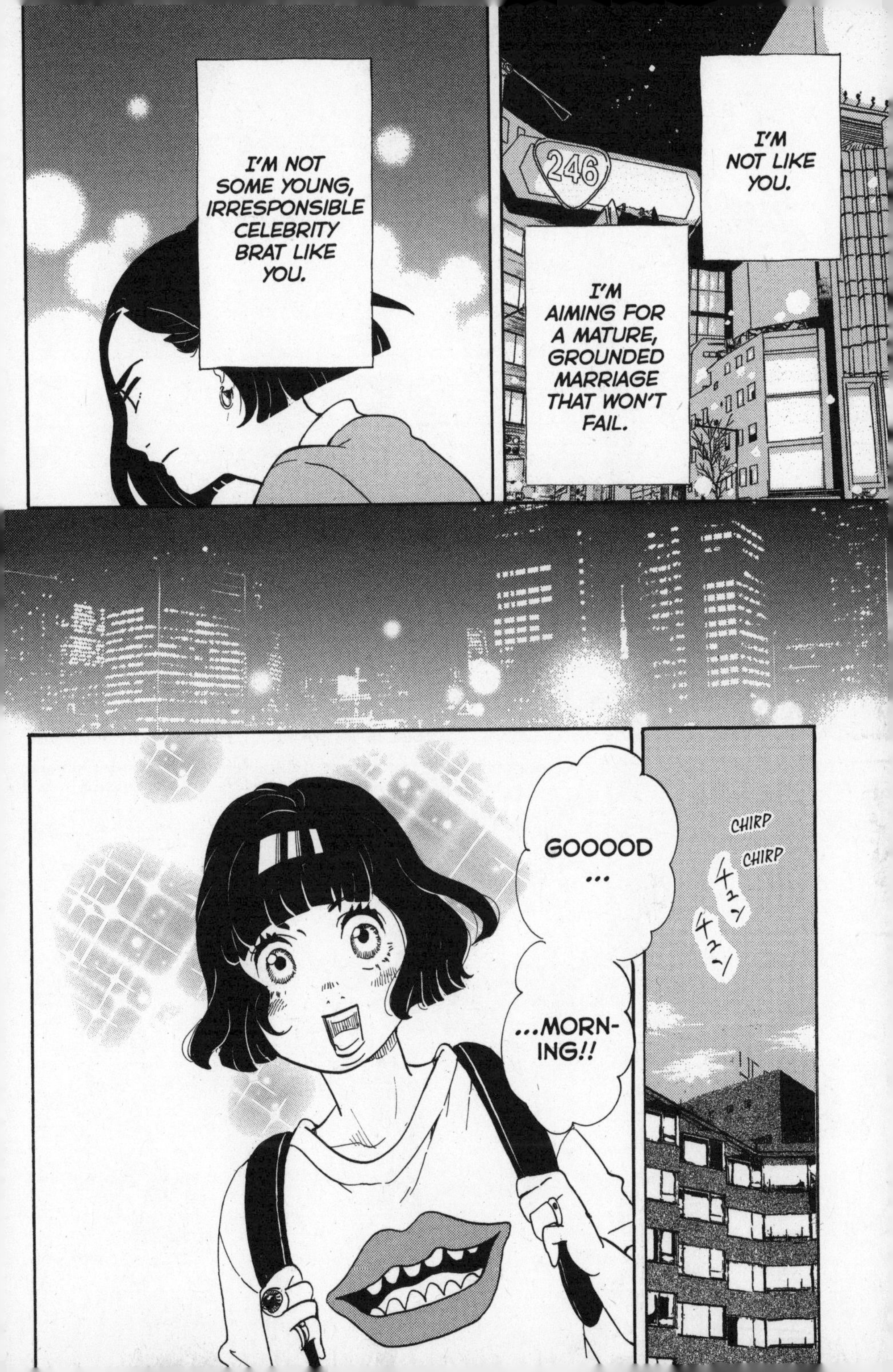
246
I'M NOT LIKE YOU.
I'M AIMING FOR A MATURE, GROUNDED MARRIAGE THAT WON'T FAIL.
I'M NOT SOME YOUNG, IRRESPONSIBLE CELEBRITY BRAT LIKE YOU.
CHIRP
CHIRP
GOOOOD ...
...MORN-ING!!

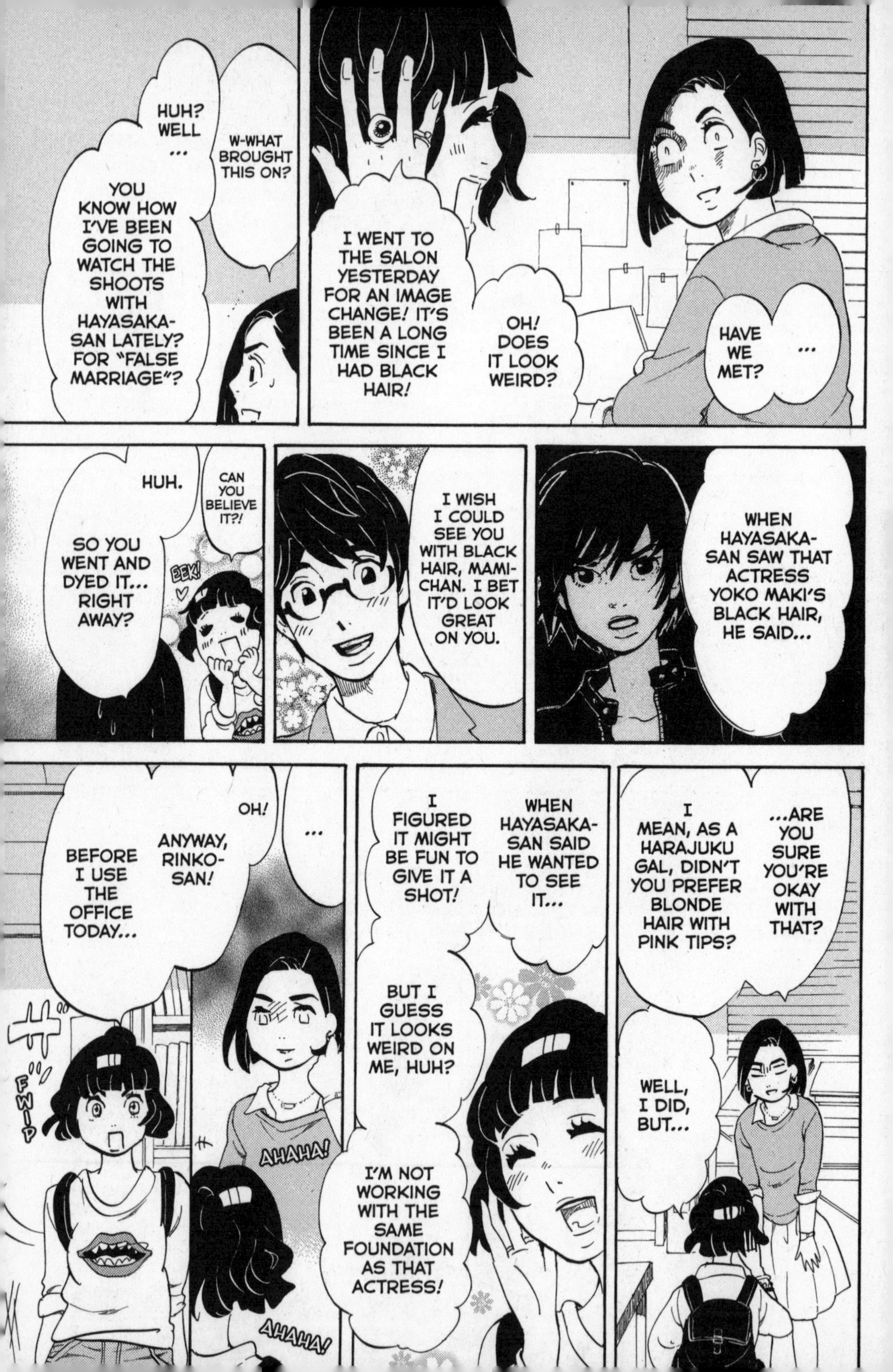
HAVE WE MET? ...
I WENT TO THE SALON YESTERDAY FOR AN IMAGE CHANGE! IT'S BEEN A LONG TIME SINCE I HAD BLACK HAIR!
OH! DOES IT LOOK WEIRD?
W-WHAT BROUGHT THIS ON?
HUH? WELL ...
YOU KNOW HOW I'VE BEEN GOING TO WATCH THE SHOOTS WITH HAYASAKA-SAN LATELY? FOR "FALSE MARRIAGE"?
WHEN HAYASAKA-SAN SAW THAT ACTRESS YOKO MAKI'S BLACK HAIR, HE SAID...
I WISH I COULD SEE YOU WITH BLACK HAIR, MAMI-CHAN. I BET IT'D LOOK GREAT ON YOU.
CAN YOU BELIEVE IT?!
EEK!
HUH.
SO YOU WENT AND DYED IT... RIGHT AWAY?
...ARE YOU SURE YOU'RE OKAY WITH THAT?
I MEAN, AS A HARAJUKU GAL, DIDN'T YOU PREFER BLONDE HAIR WITH PINK TIPS?
WELL, I DID, BUT...
WHEN HAYASAKA-SAN SAID HE WANTED TO SEE IT...
I FIGURED IT MIGHT BE FUN TO GIVE IT A SHOT!
BUT I GUESS IT LOOKS WEIRD ON ME, HUH?
I'M NOT WORKING WITH THE SAME FOUNDATION AS THAT ACTRESS!
AHAHA!
AHAHA!
...
OH!
ANYWAY, RINKO-SAN!
BEFORE I USE THE OFFICE TODAY...
FWIP

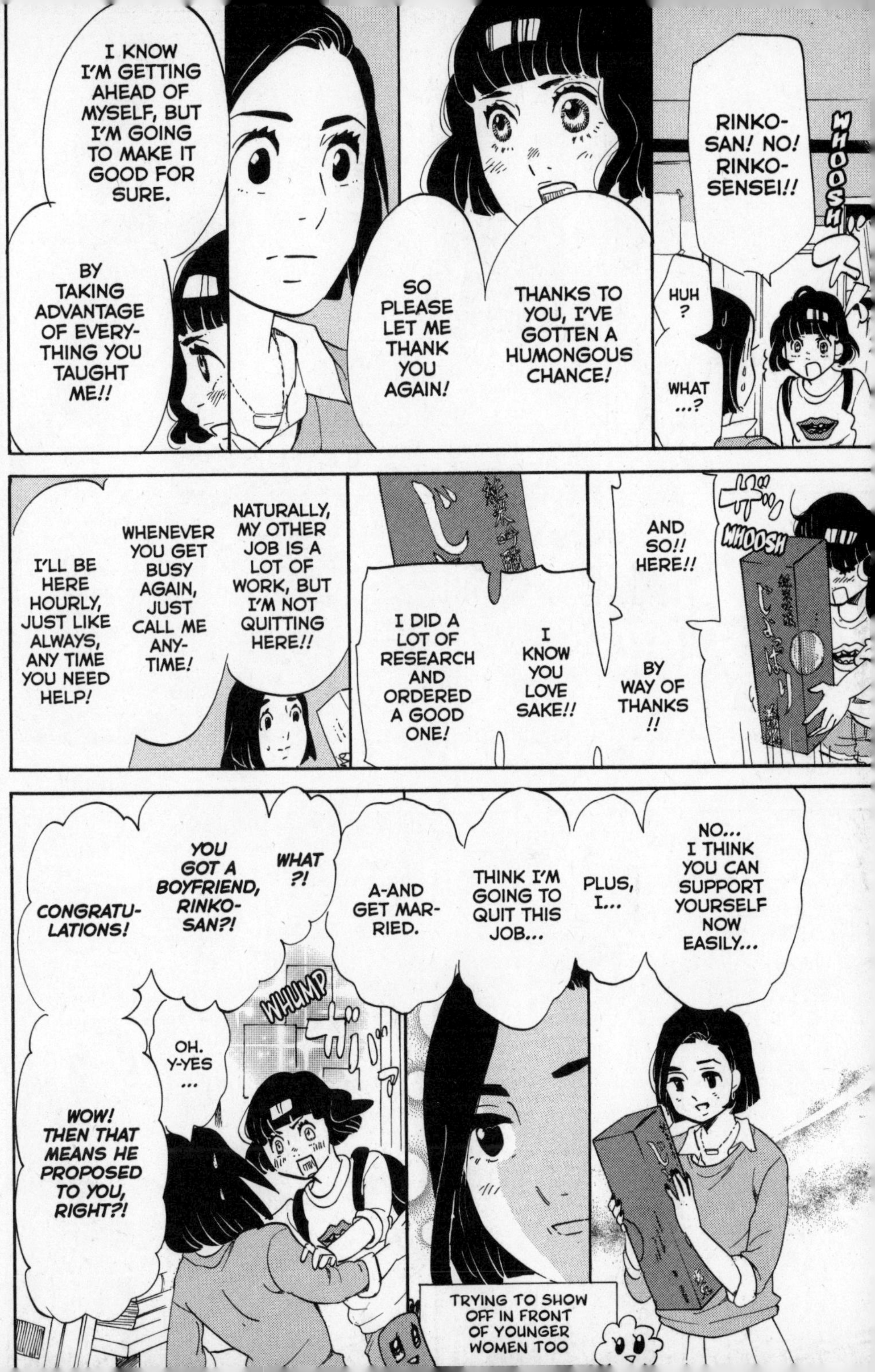
RINKO-SAN! NO! RINKO-SENSEI!!
WHOOSH
HUH?
WHAT...?
THANKS TO YOU, I'VE GOTTEN A HUMONGOUS CHANCE!
SO PLEASE LET ME THANK YOU AGAIN!
I KNOW I'M GETTING AHEAD OF MYSELF, BUT I'M GOING TO MAKE IT GOOD FOR SURE.
BY TAKING ADVANTAGE OF EVERYTHING YOU TAUGHT ME!!
WHOOSH
AND SO!! HERE!!
BY WAY OF THANKS!!
I KNOW YOU LOVE SAKE!!
I DID A LOT OF RESEARCH AND ORDERED A GOOD ONE!
NATURALLY, MY OTHER JOB IS A LOT OF WORK, BUT I'M NOT QUITTING HERE!!
WHENEVER YOU GET BUSY AGAIN, JUST CALL ME ANYTIME!
I'LL BE HERE HOURLY, JUST LIKE ALWAYS, ANY TIME YOU NEED HELP!
NO... I THINK YOU CAN SUPPORT YOURSELF NOW EASILY...
PLUS, I...
THINK I'M GOING TO QUIT THIS JOB...
A-AND GET MARRIED.
TRYING TO SHOW OFF IN FRONT OF YOUNGER WOMEN TOO
WHAT?!
YOU GOT A BOYFRIEND, RINKO-SAN?!
CONGRATULATIONS!
WHUMP
OH. Y-YES...
WOW! THEN THAT MEANS HE PROPOSED TO YOU, RIGHT?!

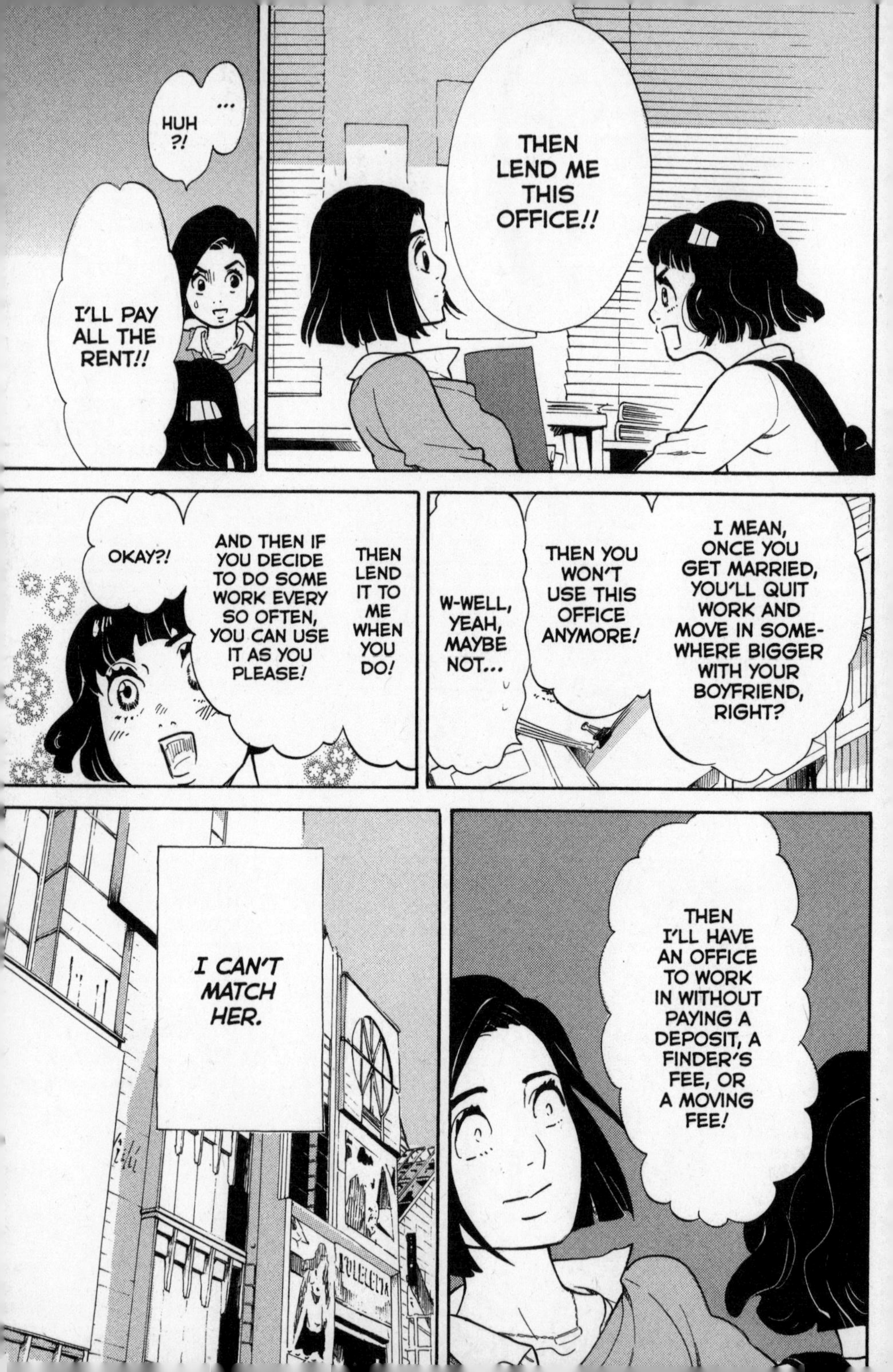
THEN LEND ME THIS OFFICE!!
... HUH?!
I'LL PAY ALL THE RENT!!
I MEAN, ONCE YOU GET MARRIED, YOU'LL QUIT WORK AND MOVE IN SOMEWHERE BIGGER WITH YOUR BOYFRIEND, RIGHT?
THEN YOU WON'T USE THIS OFFICE ANYMORE!
W-WELL, YEAH, MAYBE NOT...
THEN LEND IT TO ME WHEN YOU DO!
AND THEN IF YOU DECIDE TO DO SOME WORK EVERY SO OFTEN, YOU CAN USE IT AS YOU PLEASE!
OKAY?!
THEN I'LL HAVE AN OFFICE TO WORK IN WITHOUT PAYING A DEPOSIT, A FINDER'S FEE, OR A MOVING FEE!
I CAN'T MATCH HER.

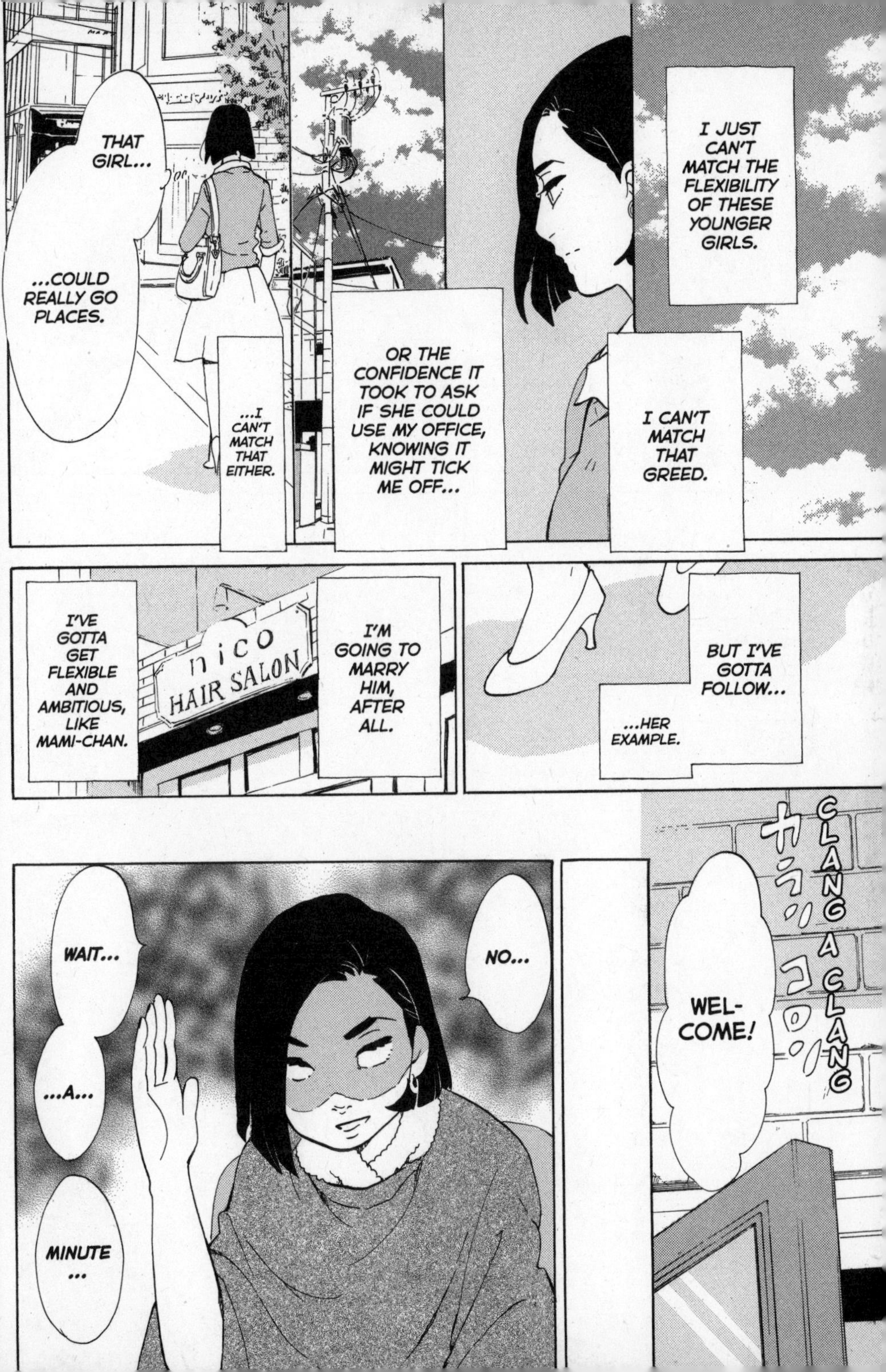
I JUST CAN'T MATCH THE FLEXIBILITY OF THESE YOUNGER GIRLS.
I CAN'T MATCH THAT GREED.
OR THE CONFIDENCE IT TOOK TO ASK IF SHE COULD USE MY OFFICE, KNOWING IT MIGHT TICK ME OFF...
...I CAN'T MATCH THAT EITHER.
THAT GIRL...
...COULD REALLY GO PLACES.
BUT I'VE GOTTA FOLLOW...
...HER EXAMPLE.
I'M GOING TO MARRY HIM, AFTER ALL.
nico HAIR SALON
I'VE GOTTA GET FLEXIBLE AND AMBITIOUS, LIKE MAMI-CHAN.
カランコロン
CLANG A CLANG
WEL-COME!
NO...
WAIT...
...A...
MINUTE ...

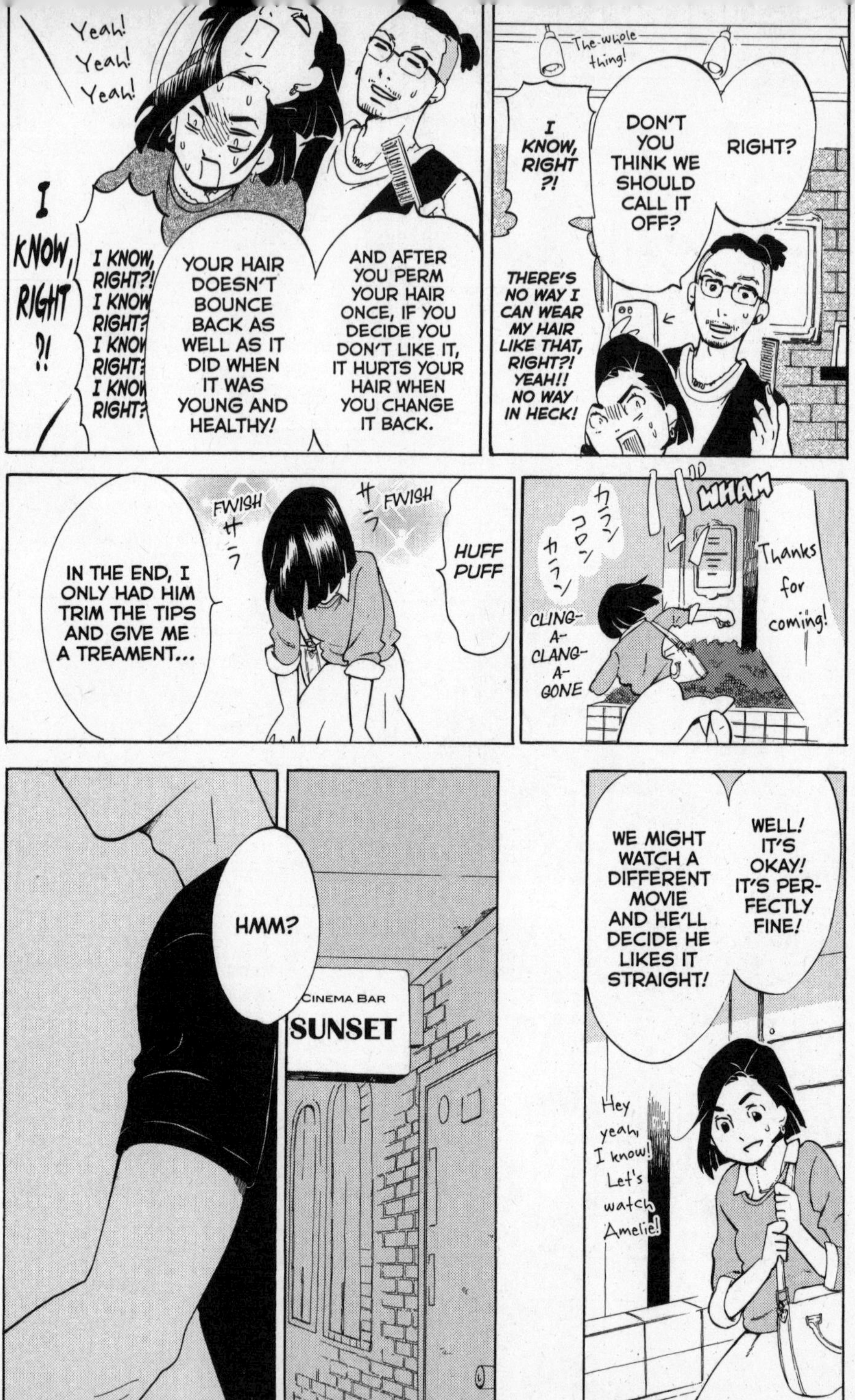
The whole thing!
RIGHT?
DON'T YOU THINK WE SHOULD CALL IT OFF?
I KNOW, RIGHT?!
THERE'S NO WAY I CAN WEAR MY HAIR LIKE THAT, RIGHT?! YEAH!! NO WAY IN HECK!
Yeah! Yeah! Yeah!
AND AFTER YOU PERM YOUR HAIR ONCE, IF YOU DECIDE YOU DON'T LIKE IT, IT HURTS YOUR HAIR WHEN YOU CHANGE IT BACK.
YOUR HAIR DOESN'T BOUNCE BACK AS WELL AS IT DID WHEN IT WAS YOUNG AND HEALTHY!
I KNOW, RIGHT?! I KNOW RIGHT? I KNOW RIGHT? I KNOW RIGHT?
I KNOW, RIGHT?!
WHAM
カラン コロン カラン
CLING-A-CLANG-A-GONE
Thanks for coming!
HUFF PUFF
サラ FWISH
FWISH サラ
IN THE END, I ONLY HAD HIM TRIM THE TIPS AND GIVE ME A TREAMENT...
WELL! IT'S OKAY! IT'S PER-FECTLY FINE!
WE MIGHT WATCH A DIFFERENT MOVIE AND HE'LL DECIDE HE LIKES IT STRAIGHT!
Hey yeah, I know! Let's watch Amelie!
CINEMA BAR
SUNSET
HMM?

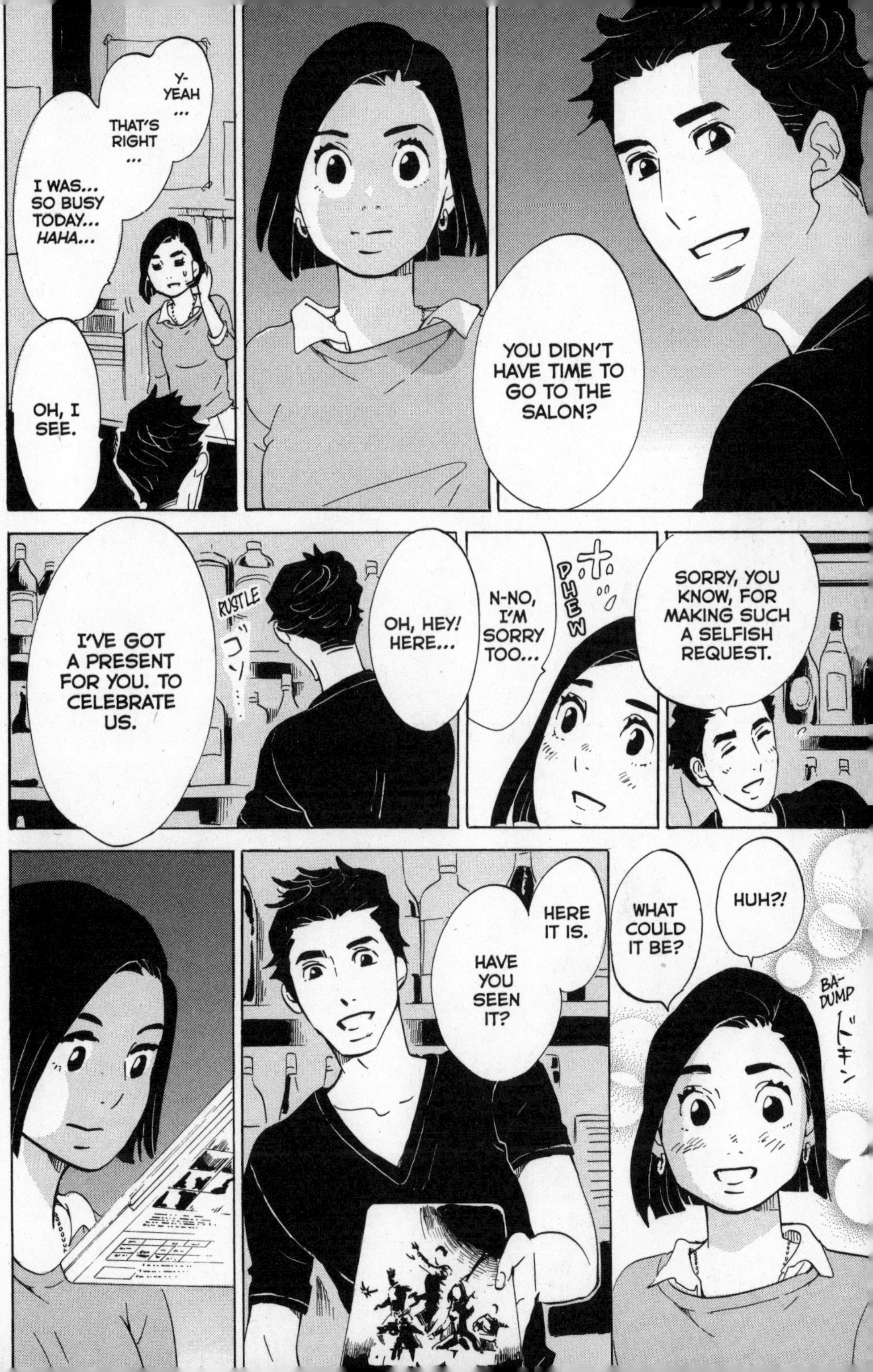

YOU DIDN'T HAVE TIME TO GO TO THE SALON?
Y-YEAH... THAT'S RIGHT...
I WAS... SO BUSY TODAY... *HAHA*...
OH, I SEE.
SORRY, YOU KNOW, FOR MAKING SUCH A SELFISH REQUEST.
PHEW
N-NO, I'M SORRY TOO...
OH, HEY! HERE...
RUSTLE
I'VE GOT A PRESENT FOR YOU. TO CELEBRATE US.
HUH?!
WHAT COULD IT BE?
BA-DUMP
ドキン
HERE IT IS.
HAVE YOU SEEN IT?

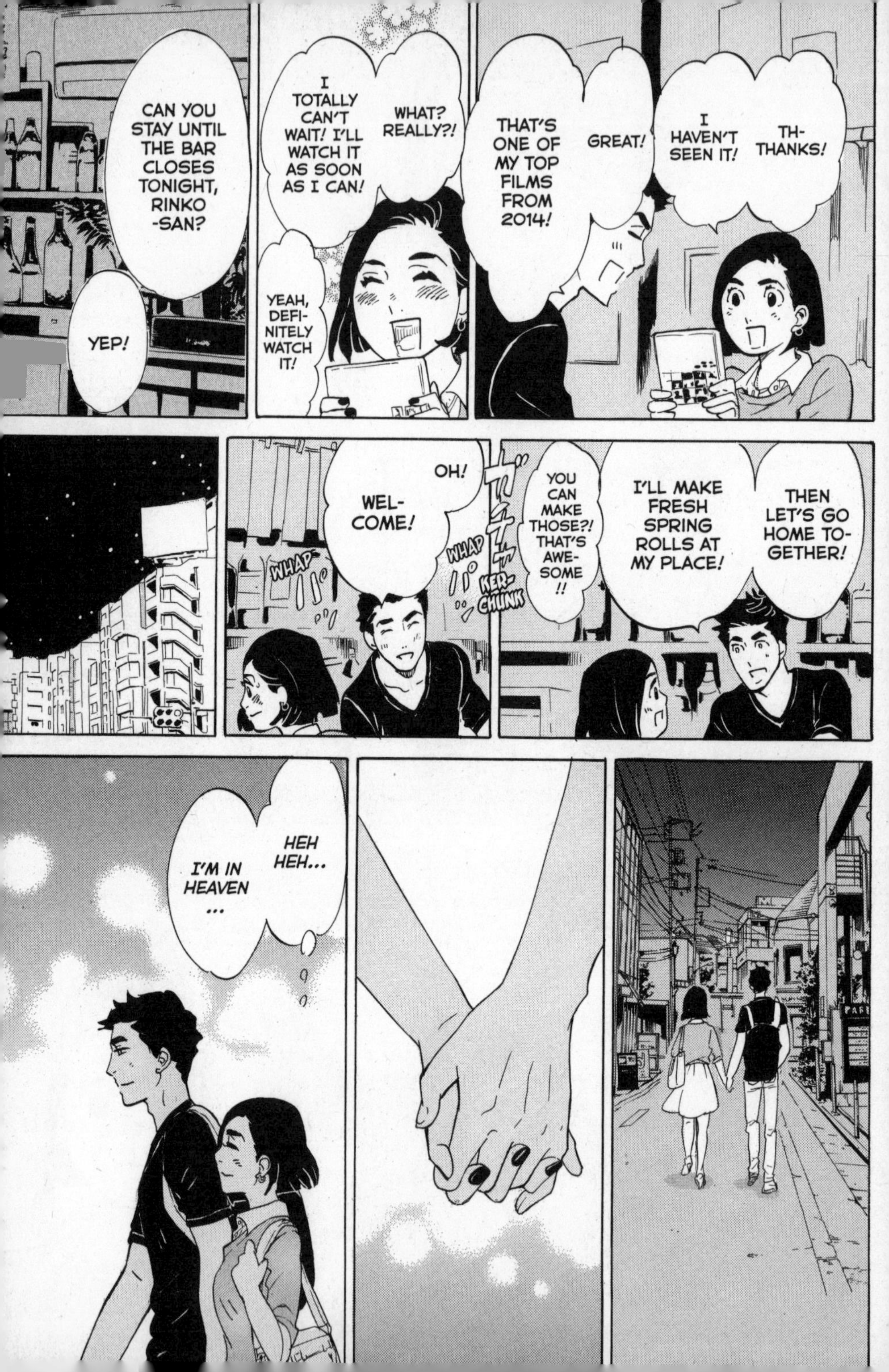
TH-THANKS!
I HAVEN'T SEEN IT!
GREAT!
THAT'S ONE OF MY TOP FILMS FROM 2014!
WHAT? REALLY?!
I TOTALLY CAN'T WAIT! I'LL WATCH IT AS SOON AS I CAN!
YEAH, DEFINITELY WATCH IT!
CAN YOU STAY UNTIL THE BAR CLOSES TONIGHT, RINKO-SAN?
YEP!
THEN LET'S GO HOME TOGETHER!
I'LL MAKE FRESH SPRING ROLLS AT MY PLACE!
YOU CAN MAKE THOSE?! THAT'S AWESOME!!
KER-CHUNK
WHAP
OH!
WELCOME!
WHAP
HEH HEH...
I'M IN HEAVEN...

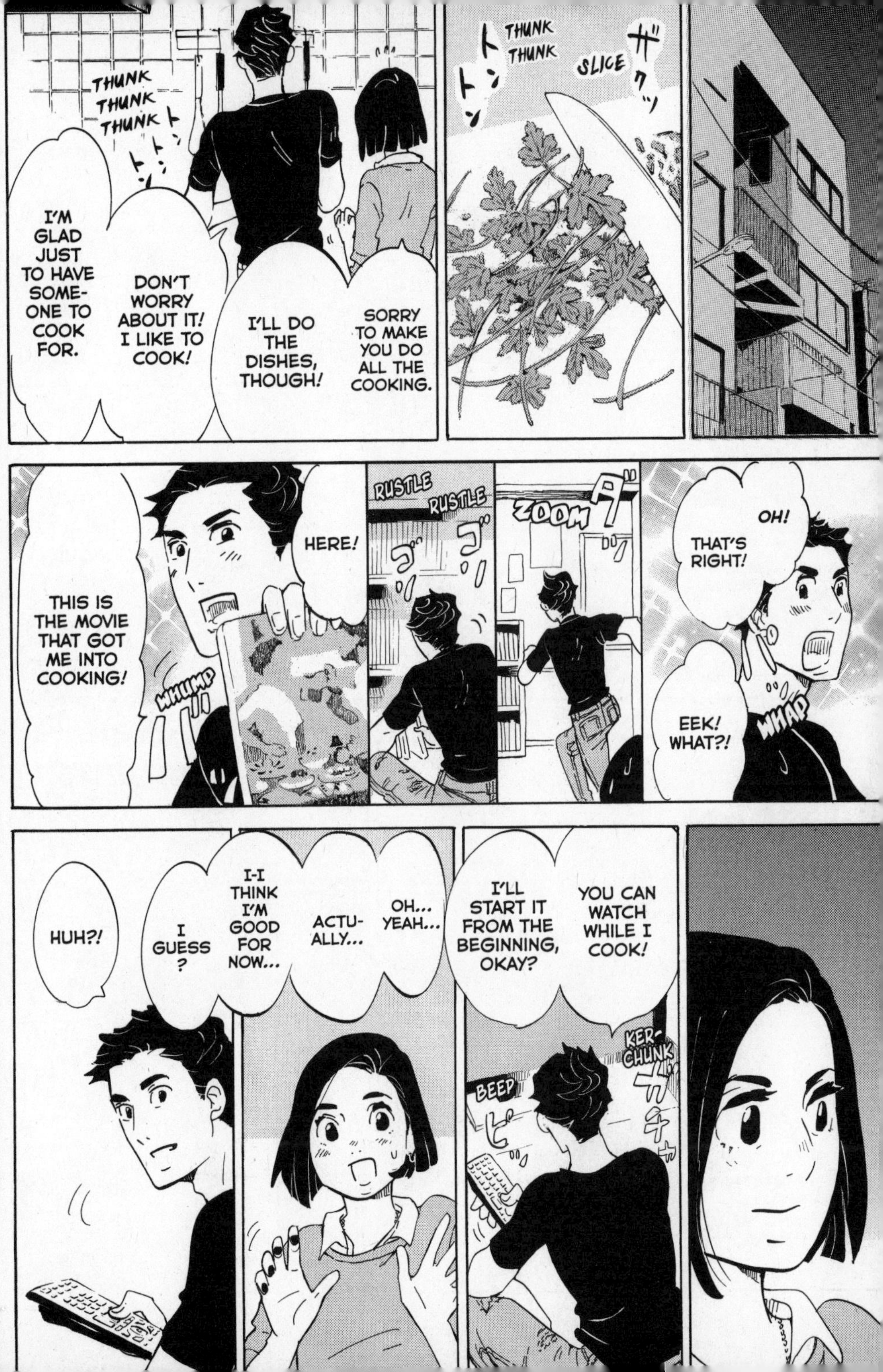
THUNK THUNK
トントン
SLICE
ザクッ
SORRY TO MAKE YOU DO ALL THE COOKING.
I'LL DO THE DISHES, THOUGH!
DON'T WORRY ABOUT IT! I LIKE TO COOK!
I'M GLAD JUST TO HAVE SOME-ONE TO COOK FOR.
THUNK THUNK THUNK
OH!
THAT'S RIGHT!
EEK! WHAT?!
WHAP
ZOOM
RUSTLE RUSTLE
HERE!
THIS IS THE MOVIE THAT GOT ME INTO COOKING!
WHUMP
YOU CAN WATCH WHILE I COOK!
I'LL START IT FROM THE BEGINNING, OKAY?
KER-CHUNK
BEEP
OH... YEAH...
ACTU-ALLY...
I-I THINK I'M GOOD FOR NOW...
I GUESS?
HUH?!

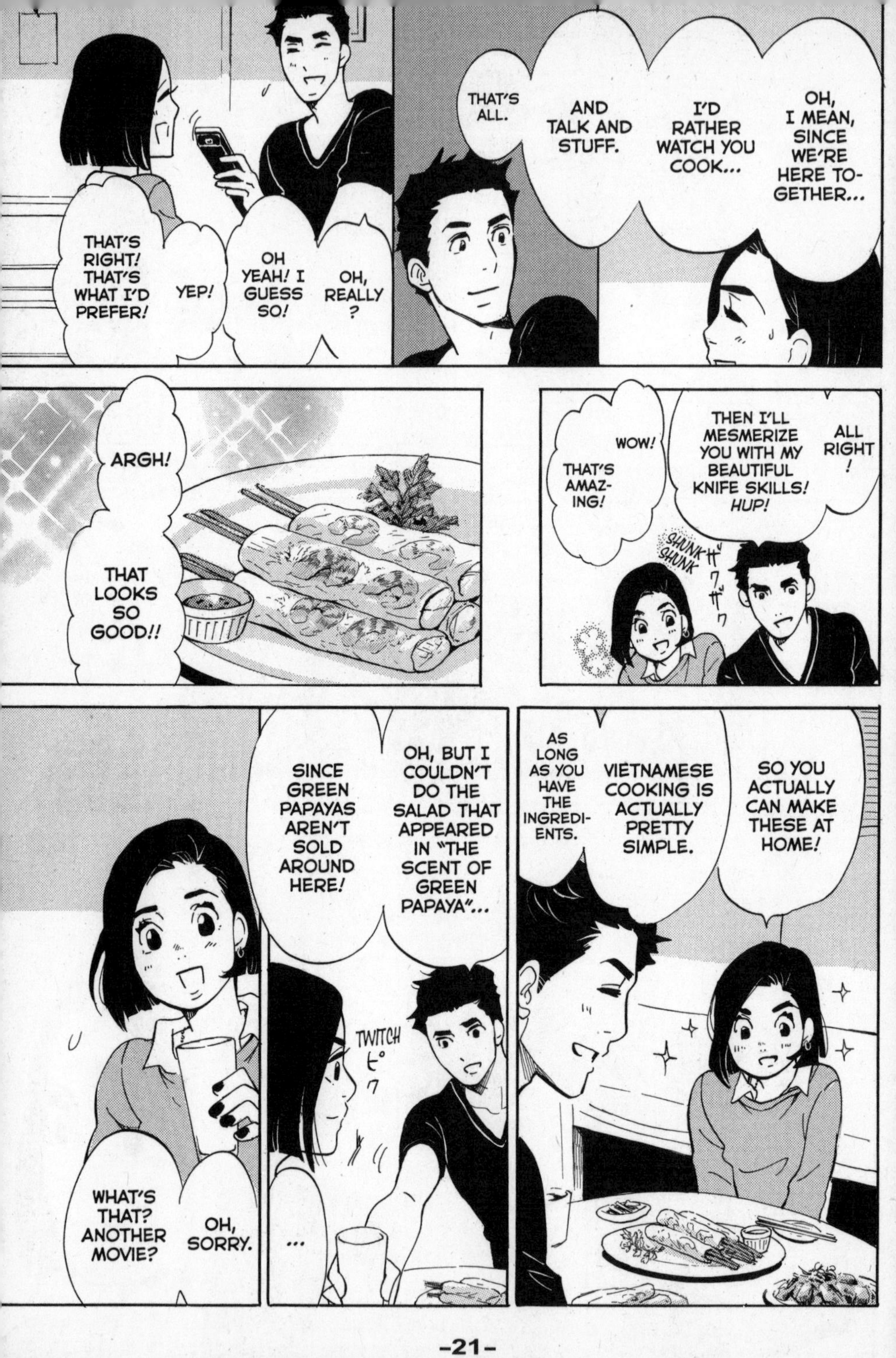
OH, I MEAN, SINCE WE'RE HERE TO-GETHER...
I'D RATHER WATCH YOU COOK...
AND TALK AND STUFF.
THAT'S ALL.
OH, REALLY?
OH YEAH! I GUESS SO!
YEP!
THAT'S RIGHT! THAT'S WHAT I'D PREFER!
ALL RIGHT!
THEN I'LL MESMERIZE YOU WITH MY BEAUTIFUL KNIFE SKILLS! HUP!
SHUNK SHUNK
WOW!
THAT'S AMAZ-ING!
ARGH!
THAT LOOKS SO GOOD!!
SO YOU ACTUALLY CAN MAKE THESE AT HOME!
VIETNAMESE COOKING IS ACTUALLY PRETTY SIMPLE.
AS LONG AS YOU HAVE THE INGREDI-ENTS.
OH, BUT I COULDN'T DO THE SALAD THAT APPEARED IN "THE SCENT OF GREEN PAPAYA"...
SINCE GREEN PAPAYAS AREN'T SOLD AROUND HERE!
TWITCH
...
OH, SORRY.
WHAT'S THAT? ANOTHER MOVIE?

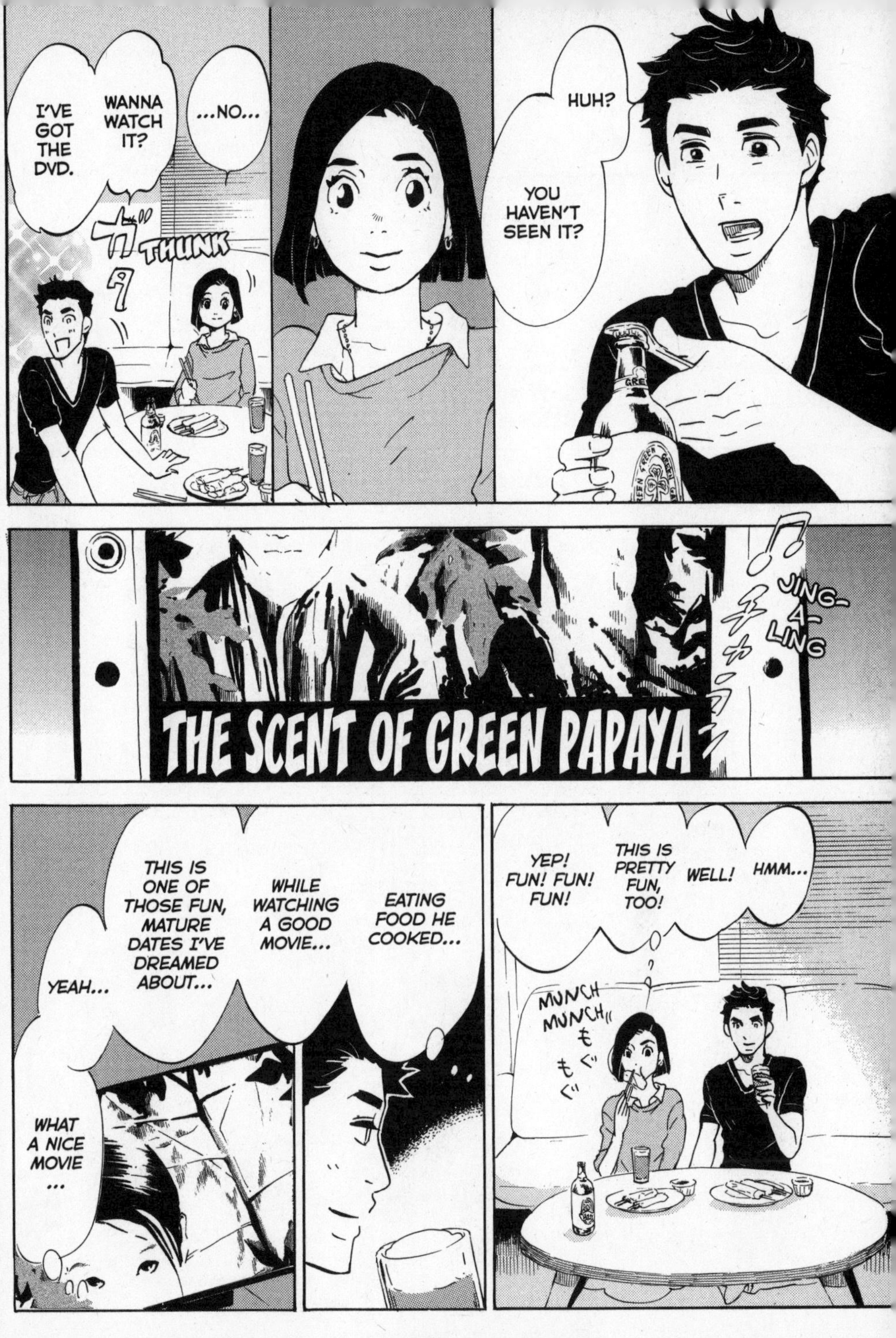
HUH?
YOU HAVEN'T SEEN IT?
...NO...
WANNA WATCH IT?
I'VE GOT THE DVD.
THUNK
JING-A-LING
THE SCENT OF GREEN PAPAYA
HMM...
WELL!
THIS IS PRETTY FUN, TOO!
YEP! FUN! FUN! FUN!
MUNCH MUNCH
EATING FOOD HE COOKED...
WHILE WATCHING A GOOD MOVIE...
THIS IS ONE OF THOSE FUN, MATURE DATES I'VE DREAMED ABOUT...
YEAH...
WHAT A NICE MOVIE...

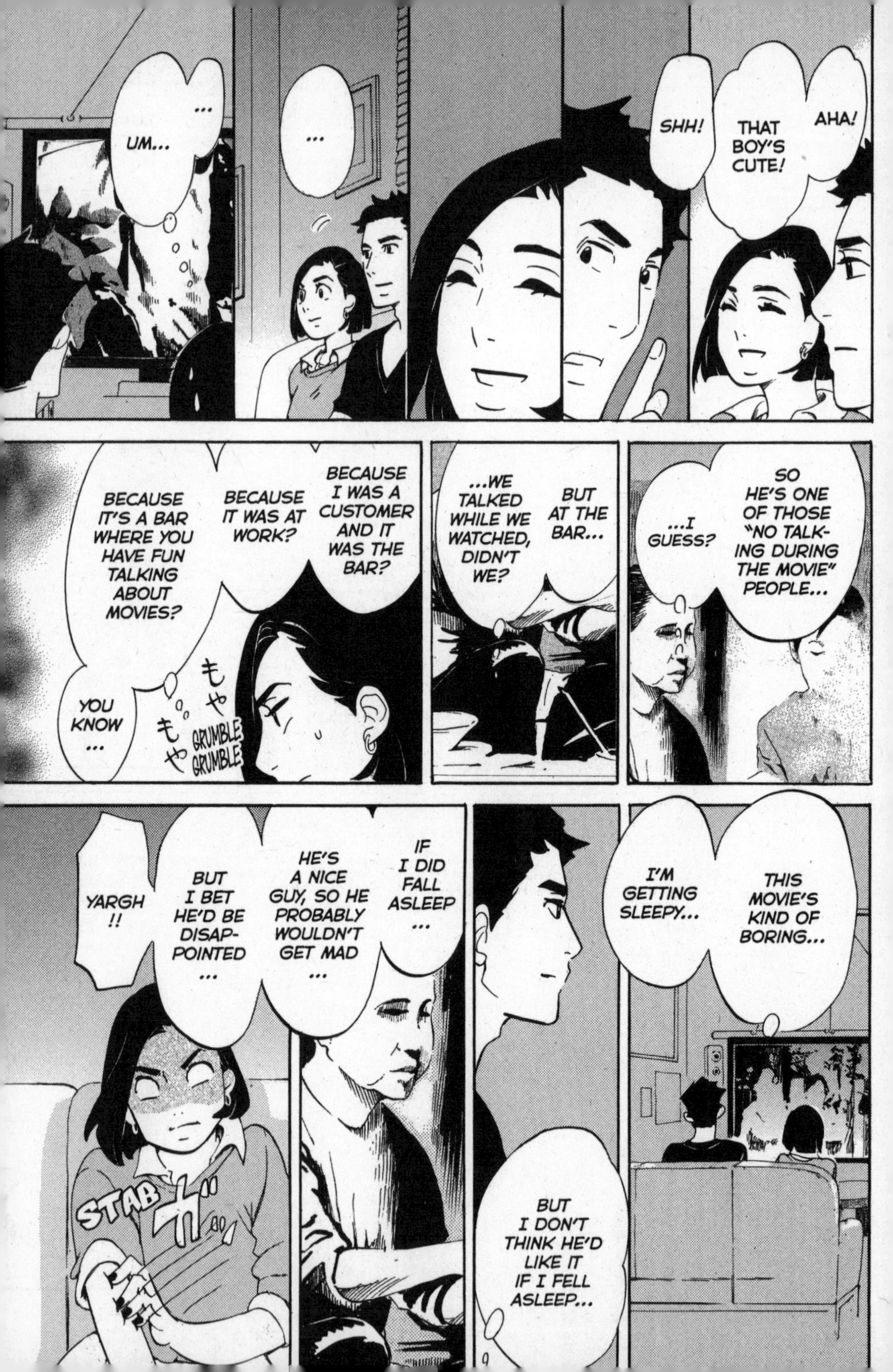

AHA!
THAT BOY'S CUTE!
SHH!
...
...
UM...
SO HE'S ONE OF THOSE "NO TALKING DURING THE MOVIE" PEOPLE...
...I GUESS?
BUT AT THE BAR...
...WE TALKED WHILE WE WATCHED, DIDN'T WE?
BECAUSE I WAS A CUSTOMER AND IT WAS THE BAR?
BECAUSE IT WAS AT WORK?
BECAUSE IT'S A BAR WHERE YOU HAVE FUN TALKING ABOUT MOVIES?
YOU KNOW...
もやもや
GRUMBLE GRUMBLE
THIS MOVIE'S KIND OF BORING...
I'M GETTING SLEEPY...
BUT I DON'T THINK HE'D LIKE IT IF I FELL ASLEEP...
IF I DID FALL ASLEEP...
HE'S A NICE GUY, SO HE PROBABLY WOULDN'T GET MAD...
BUT I BET HE'D BE DISAPPOINTED...
YARGH!!
STAB

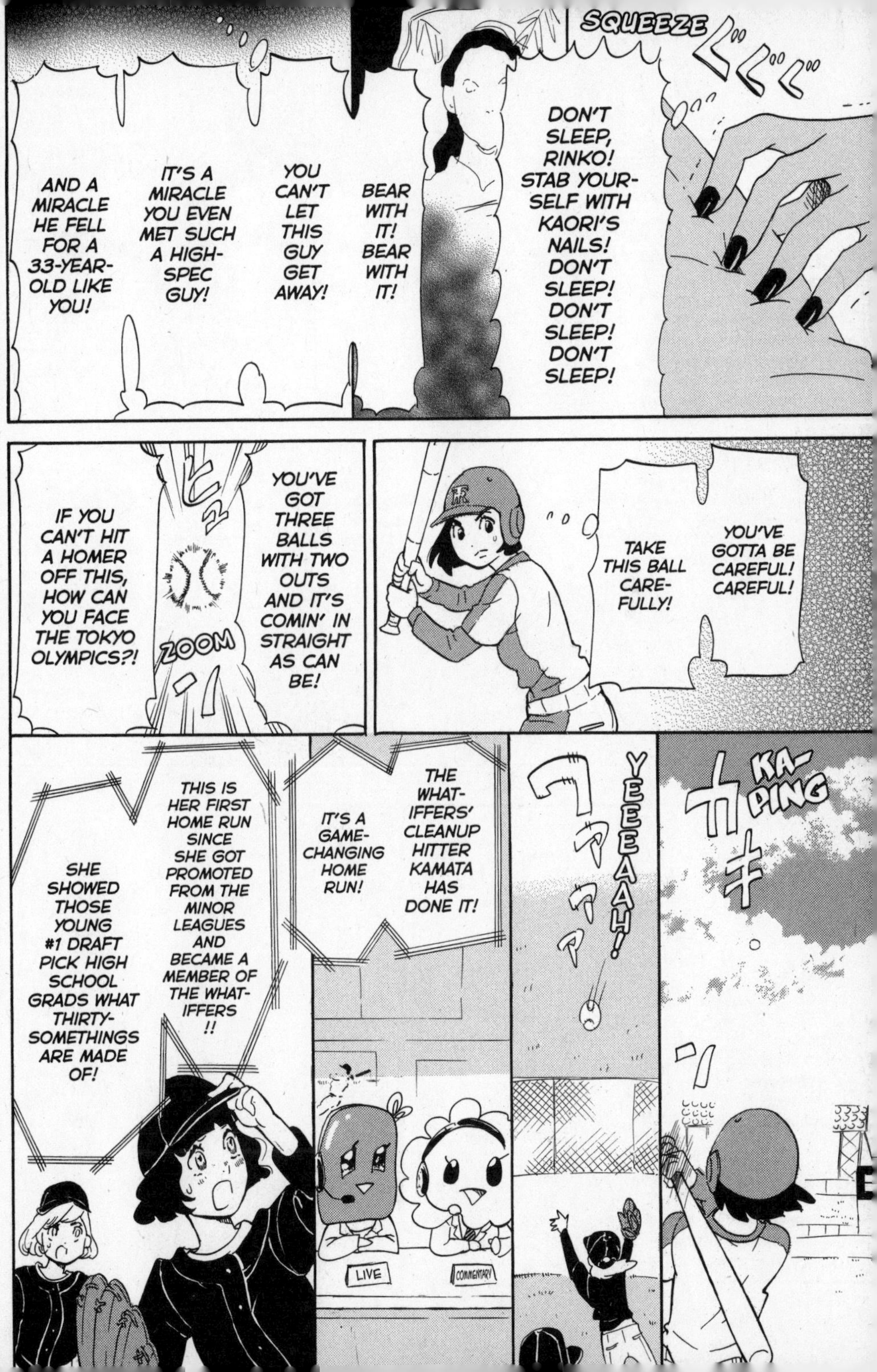

SQUEEZE
DON'T SLEEP, RINKO! STAB YOURSELF WITH KAORI'S NAILS! DON'T SLEEP! DON'T SLEEP! DON'T SLEEP!
BEAR WITH IT! BEAR WITH IT!
YOU CAN'T LET THIS GUY GET AWAY!
IT'S A MIRACLE YOU EVEN MET SUCH A HIGH-SPEC GUY!
AND A MIRACLE HE FELL FOR A 33-YEAR-OLD LIKE YOU!
YOU'VE GOTTA BE CAREFUL! CAREFUL!
TAKE THIS BALL CAREFULLY!
YOU'VE GOT THREE BALLS WITH TWO OUTS AND IT'S COMIN' IN STRAIGHT AS CAN BE!
ZOOM
IF YOU CAN'T HIT A HOMER OFF THIS, HOW CAN YOU FACE THE TOKYO OLYMPICS?!
KA-PING
YEEEAAH!
THE WHATIFFERS' CLEANUP HITTER KAMATA HAS DONE IT!
IT'S A GAME-CHANGING HOME RUN!
LIVE
COMMENTARY
THIS IS HER FIRST HOME RUN SINCE SHE GOT PROMOTED FROM THE MINOR LEAGUES AND BECAME A MEMBER OF THE WHATIFFERS !!
SHE SHOWED THOSE YOUNG #1 DRAFT PICK HIGH SCHOOL GRADS WHAT THIRTY-SOMETHINGS ARE MADE OF!

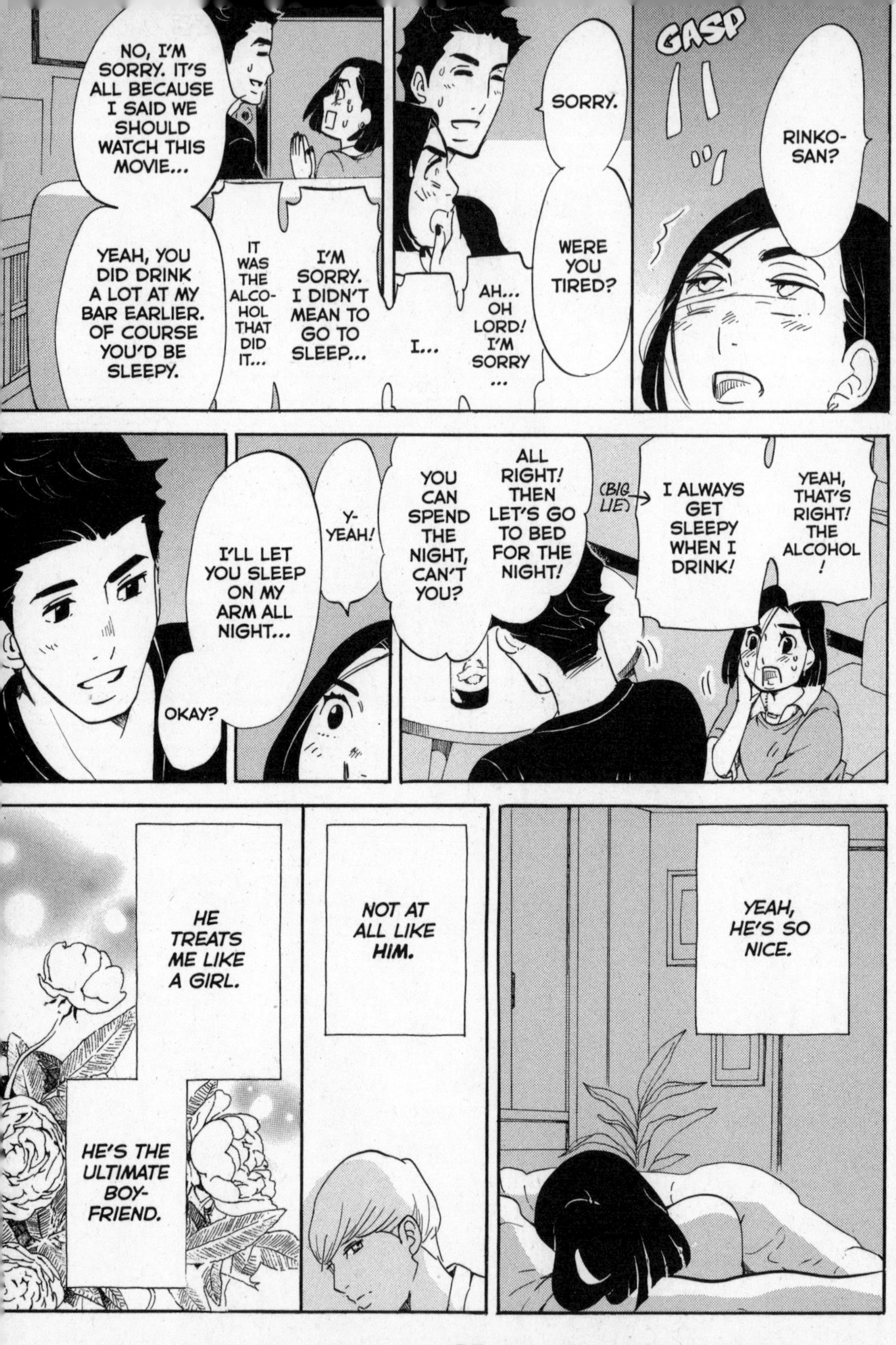
GASP
RINKO-SAN?
SORRY.
WERE YOU TIRED?
AH... OH LORD! I'M SORRY...
I...
I'M SORRY. I DIDN'T MEAN TO GO TO SLEEP...
NO, I'M SORRY. IT'S ALL BECAUSE I SAID WE SHOULD WATCH THIS MOVIE...
YEAH, YOU DID DRINK A LOT AT MY BAR EARLIER. OF COURSE YOU'D BE SLEEPY.
IT WAS THE ALCOHOL THAT DID IT...
YEAH, THAT'S RIGHT! THE ALCOHOL!
I ALWAYS GET SLEEPY WHEN I DRINK!
(BIG LIE)
ALL RIGHT! THEN LET'S GO TO BED FOR THE NIGHT!
YOU CAN SPEND THE NIGHT, CAN'T YOU?
Y-YEAH!
I'LL LET YOU SLEEP ON MY ARM ALL NIGHT...
OKAY?
YEAH, HE'S SO NICE.
NOT AT ALL LIKE HIM.
HE TREATS ME LIKE A GIRL.
HE'S THE ULTIMATE BOY-FRIEND.

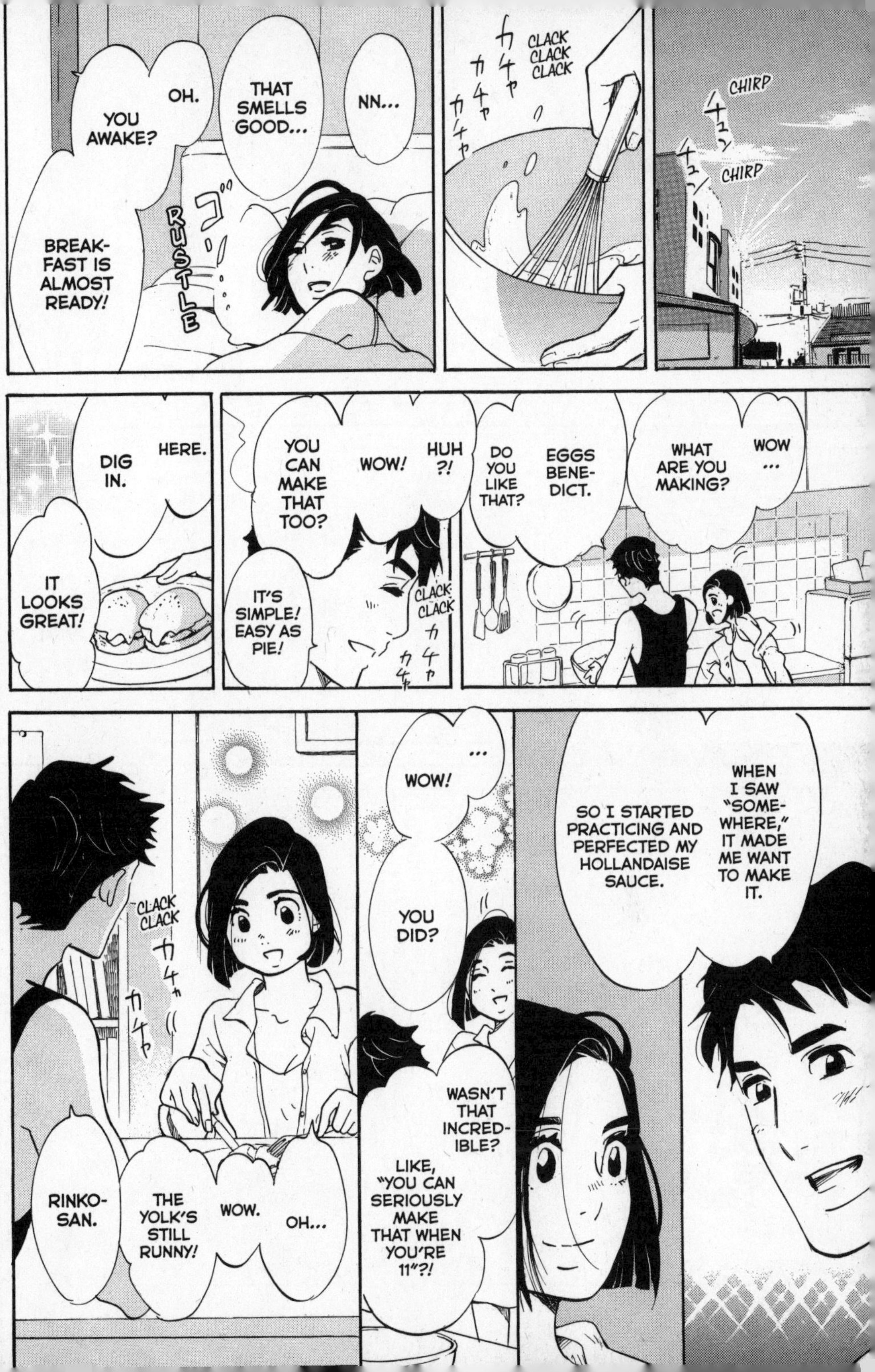
CHIRP
チュン
CHIRP
チュン
CLACK CLACK CLACK
カチャカチャカチャ
NN...
THAT SMELLS GOOD...
OH.
YOU AWAKE?
RUSTLE
ゴソ
BREAKFAST IS ALMOST READY!
WOW...
WHAT ARE YOU MAKING?
EGGS BENEDICT.
DO YOU LIKE THAT?
HUH?!
WOW!
YOU CAN MAKE THAT TOO?
CLACK CLACK
カチャカチャ
IT'S SIMPLE! EASY AS PIE!
HERE.
DIG IN.
IT LOOKS GREAT!
WHEN I SAW "SOMEWHERE," IT MADE ME WANT TO MAKE IT.
SO I STARTED PRACTICING AND PERFECTED MY HOLLANDAISE SAUCE.
...
WOW!
YOU DID?
WASN'T THAT INCREDIBLE?
LIKE, "YOU CAN SERIOUSLY MAKE THAT WHEN YOU'RE 11"?!
CLACK CLACK
カチャカチャ
OH...
WOW.
THE YOLK'S STILL RUNNY!
RINKO-SAN.

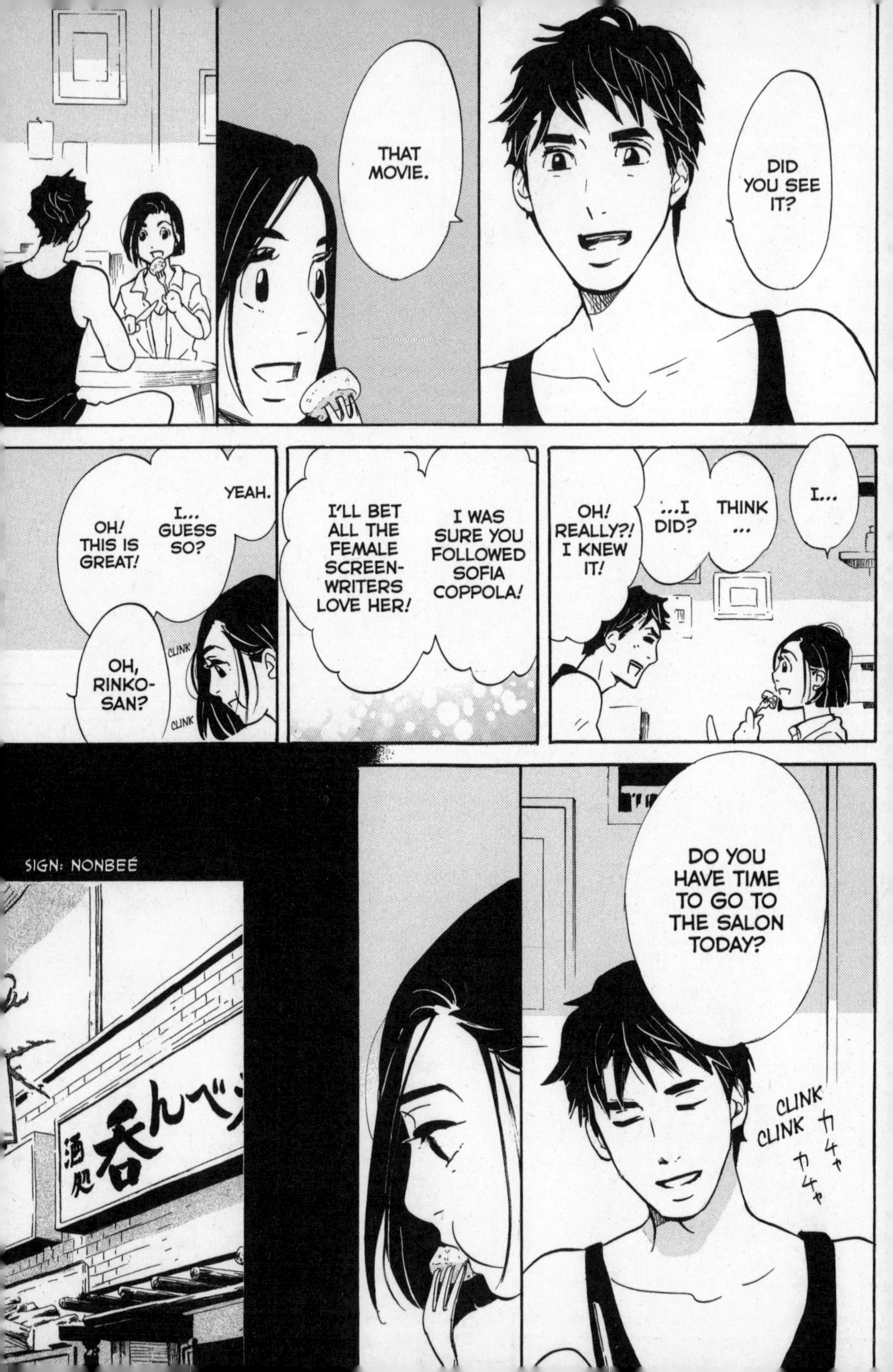
DID YOU SEE IT?
THAT MOVIE.
I...
THINK ...
...I DID?
OH! REALLY?! I KNEW IT!
I WAS SURE YOU FOLLOWED SOFIA COPPOLA!
I'LL BET ALL THE FEMALE SCREEN-WRITERS LOVE HER!
YEAH.
I... GUESS SO?
OH! THIS IS GREAT!
CLINK
OH, RINKO-SAN?
CLINK
DO YOU HAVE TIME TO GO TO THE SALON TODAY?
CLINK CLINK
カチャ カチャ
SIGN: NONBEÉ
酒処 呑んべ

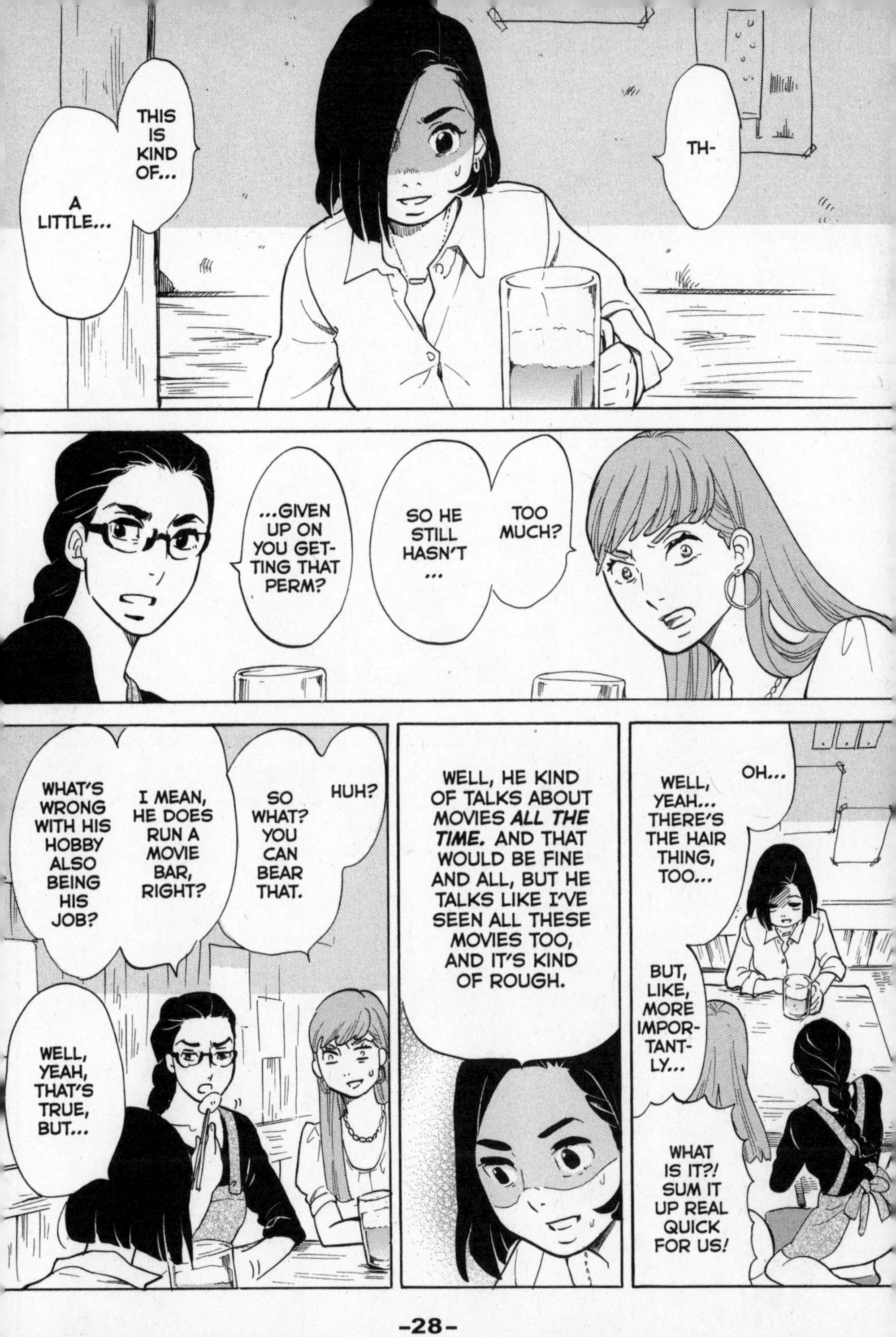
TH-
THIS IS KIND OF...
A LITTLE...
TOO MUCH?
SO HE STILL HASN'T ...
...GIVEN UP ON YOU GETTING THAT PERM?
OH...
WELL, YEAH... THERE'S THE HAIR THING, TOO...
BUT, LIKE, MORE IMPORTANTLY...
WHAT IS IT?! SUM IT UP REAL QUICK FOR US!
WELL, HE KIND OF TALKS ABOUT MOVIES *ALL THE TIME.* AND THAT WOULD BE FINE AND ALL, BUT HE TALKS LIKE I'VE SEEN ALL THESE MOVIES TOO, AND IT'S KIND OF ROUGH.
HUH?
SO WHAT? YOU CAN BEAR THAT.
I MEAN, HE DOES RUN A MOVIE BAR, RIGHT?
WHAT'S WRONG WITH HIS HOBBY ALSO BEING HIS JOB?
WELL, YEAH, THAT'S TRUE, BUT...

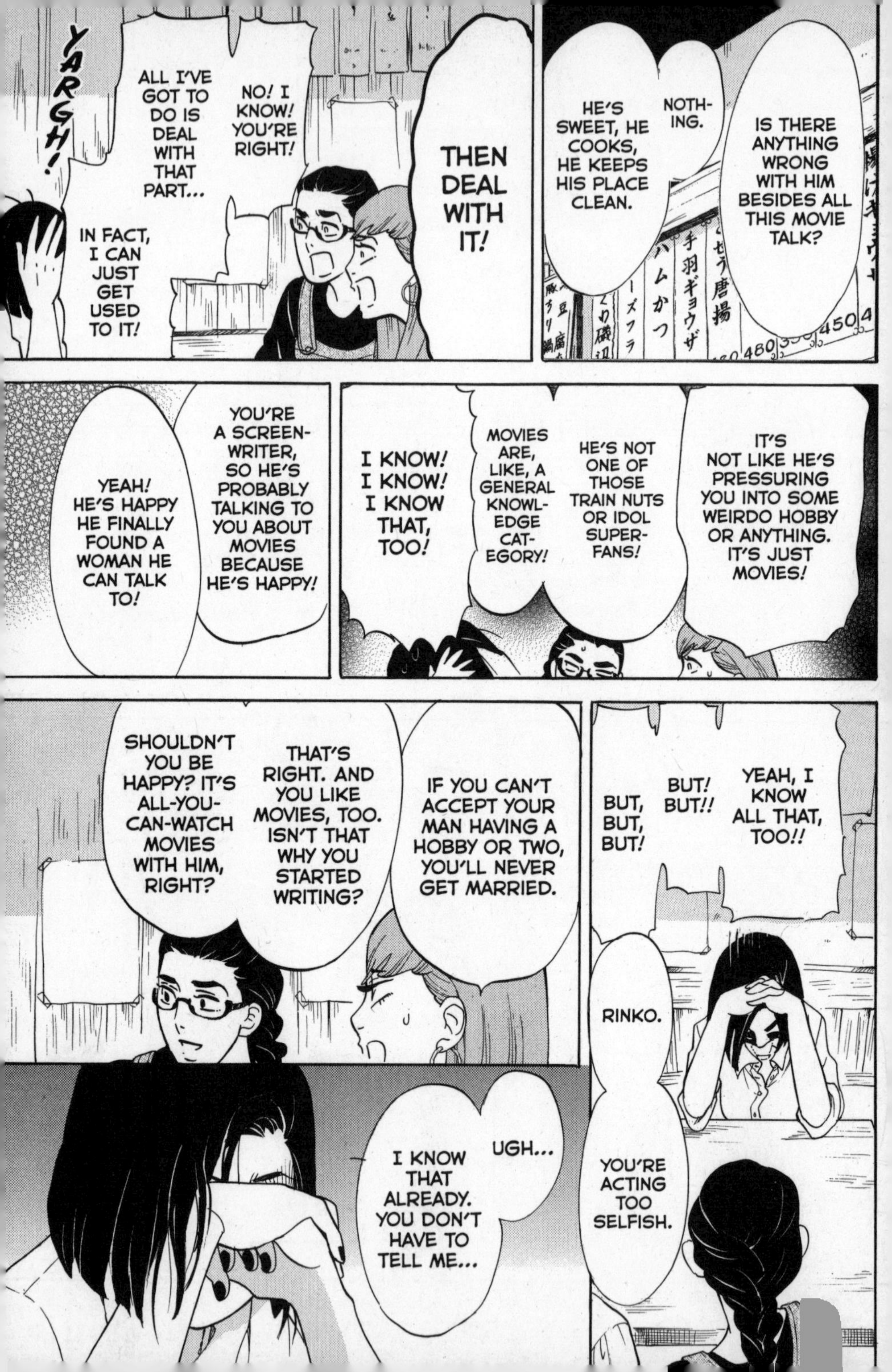
IS THERE ANYTHING WRONG WITH HIM BESIDES ALL THIS MOVIE TALK?
NOTH-ING.
HE'S SWEET, HE COOKS, HE KEEPS HIS PLACE CLEAN.
手羽ギョウザ
ハムかつ
450
480
THEN DEAL WITH IT!
NO! I KNOW! YOU'RE RIGHT!
ALL I'VE GOT TO DO IS DEAL WITH THAT PART...
YARGH!
IN FACT, I CAN JUST GET USED TO IT!
IT'S NOT LIKE HE'S PRESSURING YOU INTO SOME WEIRDO HOBBY OR ANYTHING. IT'S JUST MOVIES!
HE'S NOT ONE OF THOSE TRAIN NUTS OR IDOL SUPER-FANS!
MOVIES ARE, LIKE, A GENERAL KNOWL-EDGE CAT-EGORY!
I KNOW! I KNOW! I KNOW THAT, TOO!
YOU'RE A SCREEN-WRITER, SO HE'S PROBABLY TALKING TO YOU ABOUT MOVIES BECAUSE HE'S HAPPY!
YEAH! HE'S HAPPY HE FINALLY FOUND A WOMAN HE CAN TALK TO!
YEAH, I KNOW ALL THAT, TOO!!
BUT! BUT!!
BUT, BUT, BUT!
RINKO.
YOU'RE ACTING TOO SELFISH.
IF YOU CAN'T ACCEPT YOUR MAN HAVING A HOBBY OR TWO, YOU'LL NEVER GET MARRIED.
THAT'S RIGHT. AND YOU LIKE MOVIES, TOO. ISN'T THAT WHY YOU STARTED WRITING?
SHOULDN'T YOU BE HAPPY? IT'S ALL-YOU-CAN-WATCH MOVIES WITH HIM, RIGHT?
UGH...
I KNOW THAT ALREADY. YOU DON'T HAVE TO TELL ME...

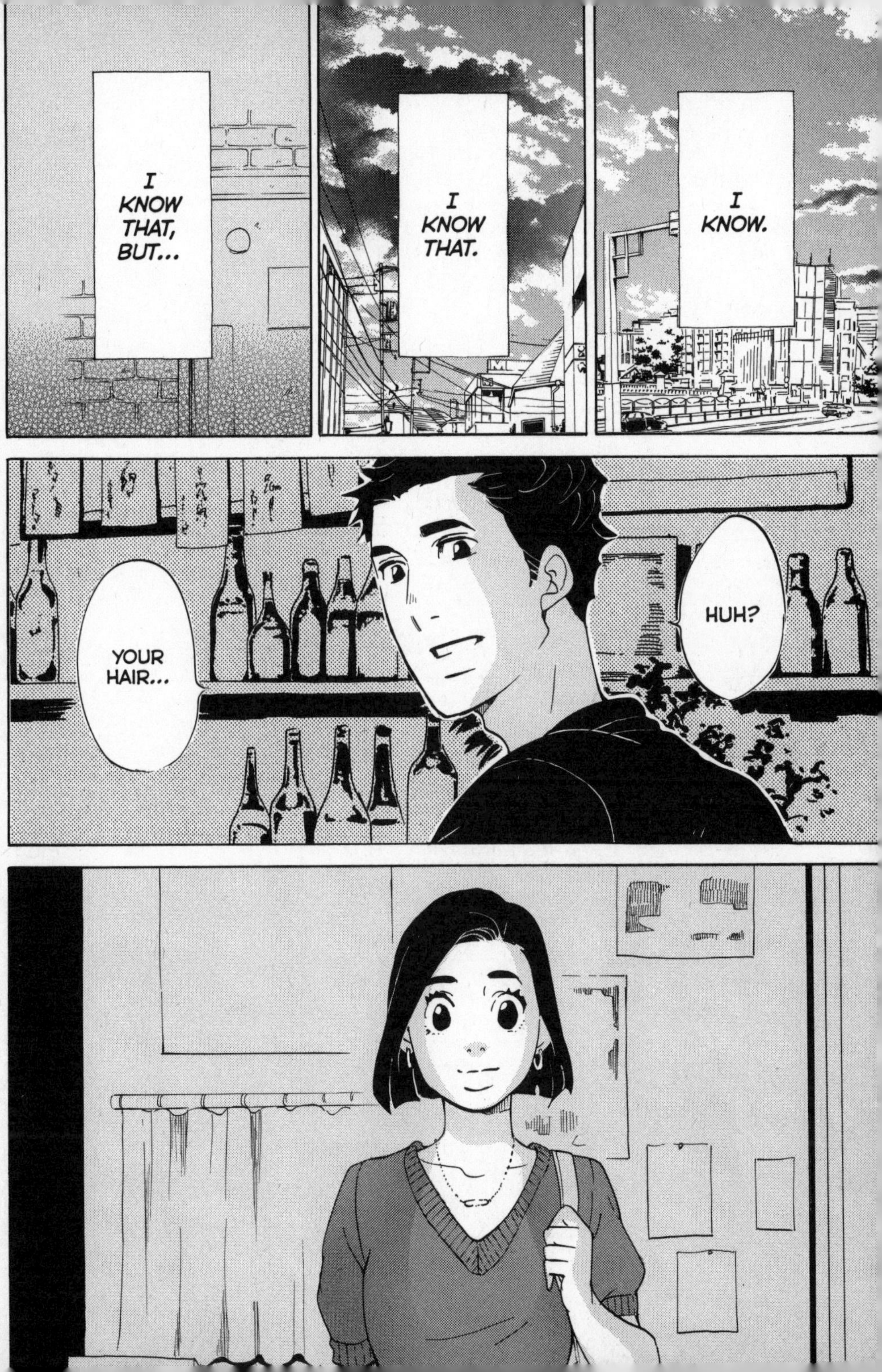
I KNOW.
I KNOW THAT.
I KNOW THAT, BUT...
HUH?
YOUR HAIR...

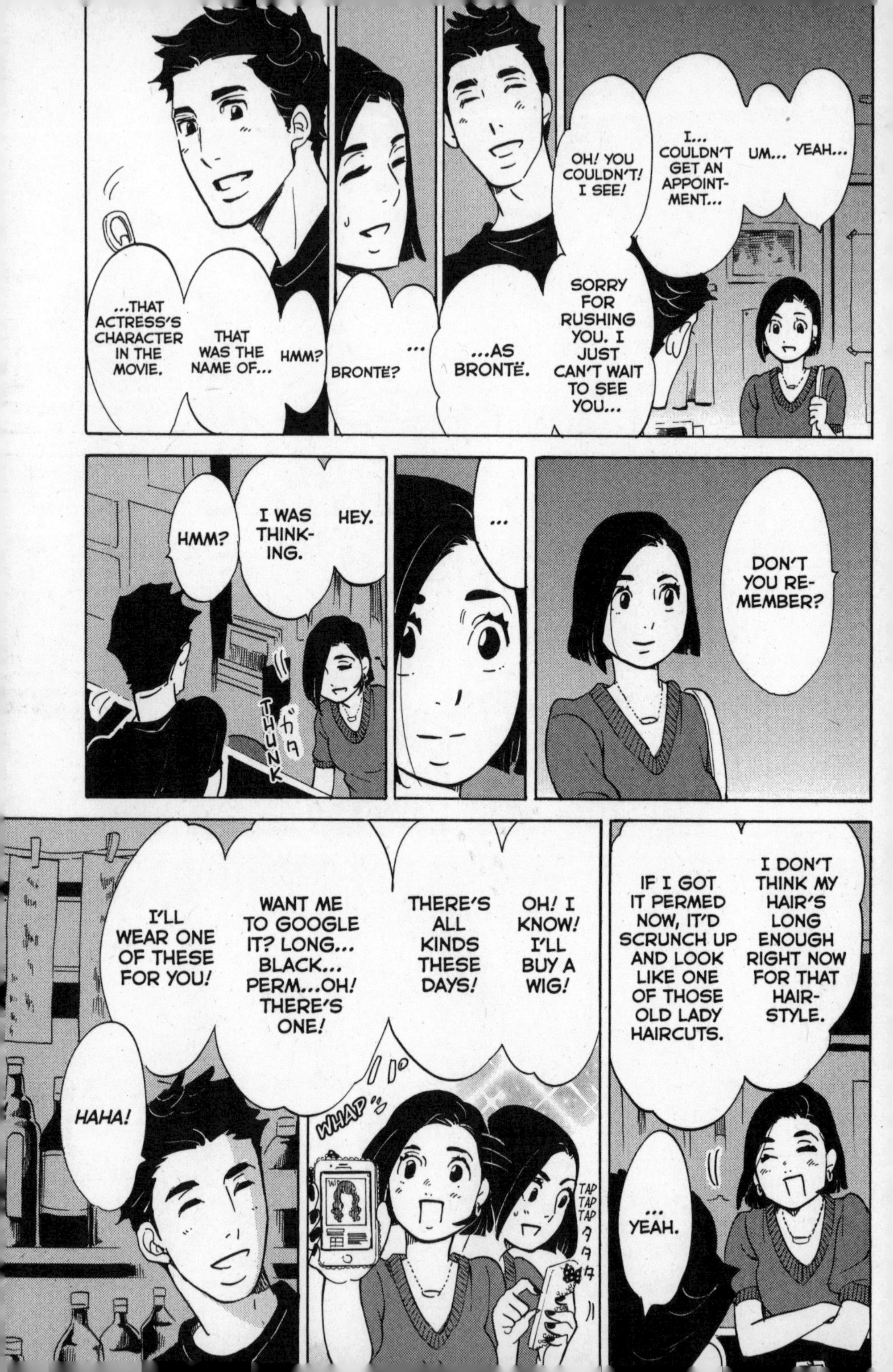
UM... YEAH...
I... COULDN'T GET AN APPOINT-MENT...
OH! YOU COULDN'T! I SEE!
SORRY FOR RUSHING YOU. I JUST CAN'T WAIT TO SEE YOU...
...AS BRONTË.
...
BRONTË?
HMM?
THAT WAS THE NAME OF...
...THAT ACTRESS'S CHARACTER IN THE MOVIE.
DON'T YOU RE-MEMBER?
...
HEY.
I WAS THINK-ING.
HMM?
ガタ
THUNK
I DON'T THINK MY HAIR'S LONG ENOUGH RIGHT NOW FOR THAT HAIR-STYLE.
IF I GOT IT PERMED NOW, IT'D SCRUNCH UP AND LOOK LIKE ONE OF THOSE OLD LADY HAIRCUTS.
... YEAH.
OH! I KNOW! I'LL BUY A WIG!
THERE'S ALL KINDS THESE DAYS!
WANT ME TO GOOGLE IT? LONG... BLACK... PERM...OH! THERE'S ONE!
TAP TAP TAP
タタタ
WHAP
I'LL WEAR ONE OF THESE FOR YOU!
HAHA!

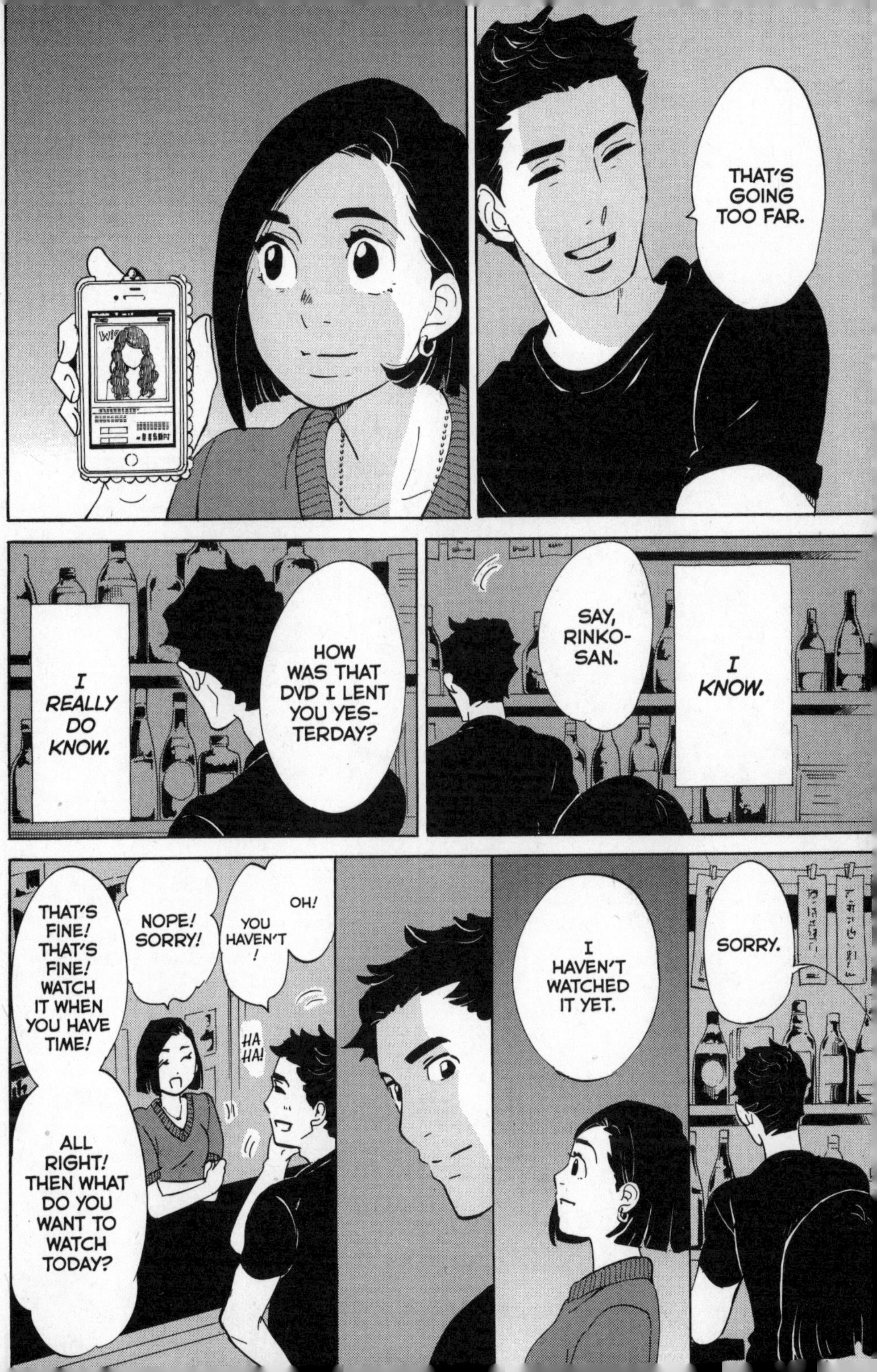
THAT'S GOING TOO FAR.
I KNOW.
SAY, RINKO-SAN.
HOW WAS THAT DVD I LENT YOU YES-TERDAY?
I REALLY DO KNOW.
SORRY.
I HAVEN'T WATCHED IT YET.
OH!
YOU HAVEN'T!
NOPE! SORRY!
HA HA!
THAT'S FINE! THAT'S FINE! WATCH IT WHEN YOU HAVE TIME!
ALL RIGHT! THEN WHAT DO YOU WANT TO WATCH TODAY?

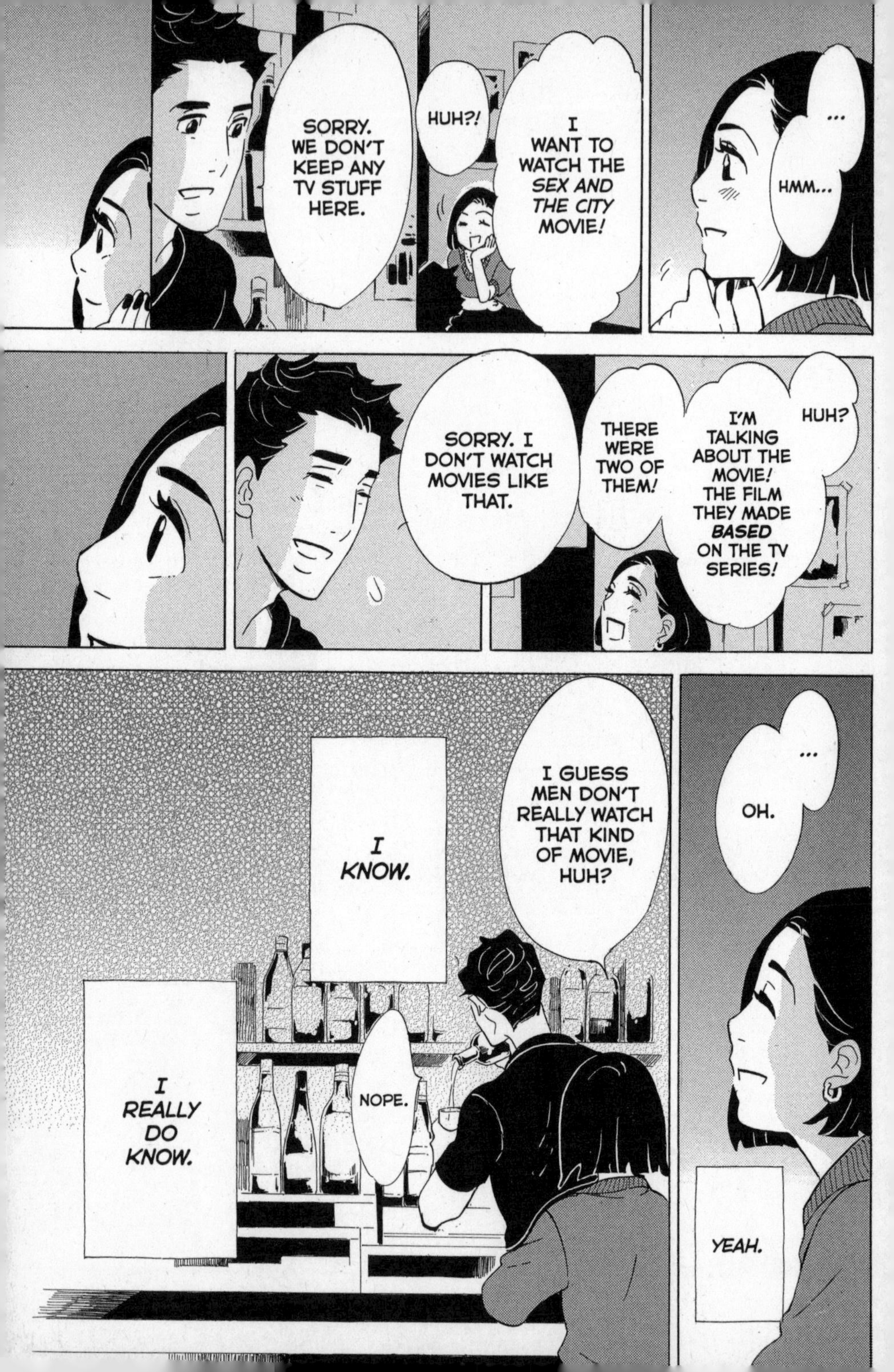
...
HMM...
I WANT TO WATCH THE SEX AND THE CITY MOVIE!
HUH?!
SORRY. WE DON'T KEEP ANY TV STUFF HERE.
HUH?
I'M TALKING ABOUT THE MOVIE! THE FILM THEY MADE BASED ON THE TV SERIES!
THERE WERE TWO OF THEM!
SORRY. I DON'T WATCH MOVIES LIKE THAT.
...
OH.
YEAH.
I GUESS MEN DON'T REALLY WATCH THAT KIND OF MOVIE, HUH?
I KNOW.
NOPE.
I REALLY DO KNOW.

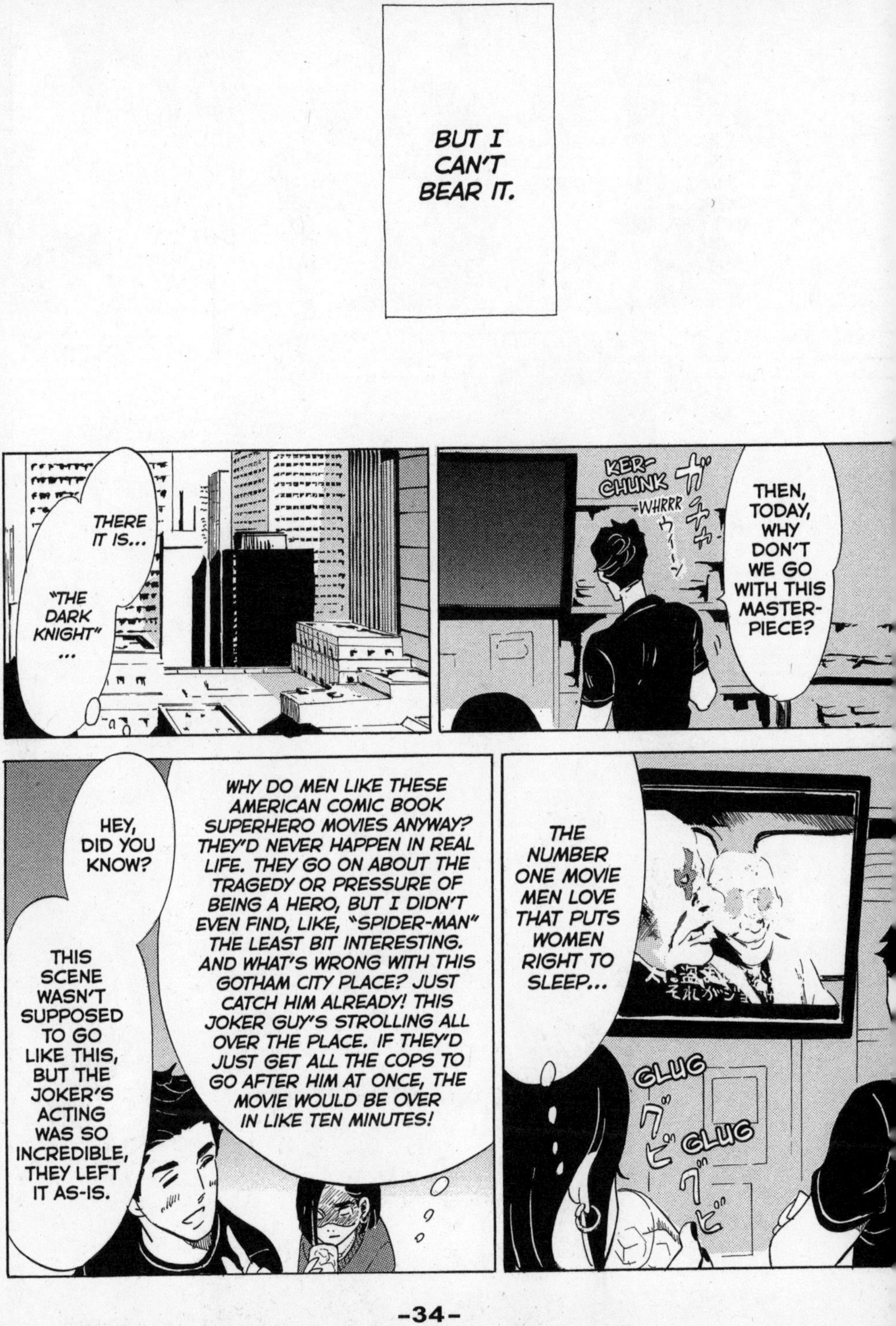
BUT I CAN'T BEAR IT.
KER-CHUNK
ガチャ
WHRRR
ウィーン
THEN, TODAY, WHY DON'T WE GO WITH THIS MASTER-PIECE?
THERE IT IS...
"THE DARK KNIGHT" ...
THE NUMBER ONE MOVIE MEN LOVE THAT PUTS WOMEN RIGHT TO SLEEP...
GLUG
GLUG
WHY DO MEN LIKE THESE AMERICAN COMIC BOOK SUPERHERO MOVIES ANYWAY? THEY'D NEVER HAPPEN IN REAL LIFE. THEY GO ON ABOUT THE TRAGEDY OR PRESSURE OF BEING A HERO, BUT I DIDN'T EVEN FIND, LIKE, "SPIDER-MAN" THE LEAST BIT INTERESTING. AND WHAT'S WRONG WITH THIS GOTHAM CITY PLACE? JUST CATCH HIM ALREADY! THIS JOKER GUY'S STROLLING ALL OVER THE PLACE. IF THEY'D JUST GET ALL THE COPS TO GO AFTER HIM AT ONCE, THE MOVIE WOULD BE OVER IN LIKE TEN MINUTES!
HEY, DID YOU KNOW?
THIS SCENE WASN'T SUPPOSED TO GO LIKE THIS, BUT THE JOKER'S ACTING WAS SO INCREDIBLE, THEY LEFT IT AS-IS.

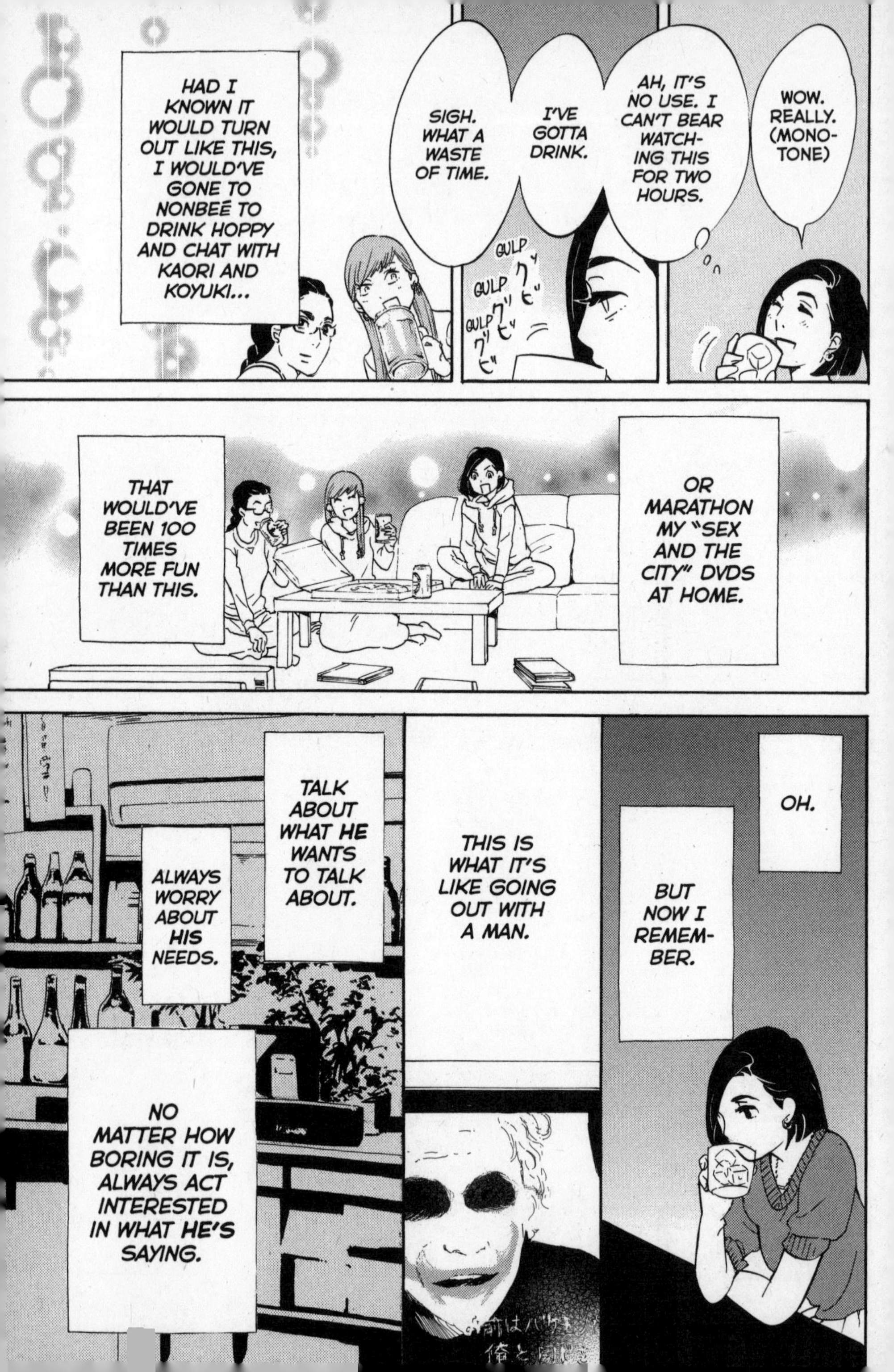
WOW. REALLY. (MONO-TONE)
AH, IT'S NO USE. I CAN'T BEAR WATCH-ING THIS FOR TWO HOURS.
I'VE GOTTA DRINK.
SIGH. WHAT A WASTE OF TIME.
GULP
GULP
GULP
HAD I KNOWN IT WOULD TURN OUT LIKE THIS, I WOULD'VE GONE TO NONBEÉ TO DRINK HOPPY AND CHAT WITH KAORI AND KOYUKI...
OR MARATHON MY "SEX AND THE CITY" DVDS AT HOME.
THAT WOULD'VE BEEN 100 TIMES MORE FUN THAN THIS.
OH.
BUT NOW I REMEM-BER.
THIS IS WHAT IT'S LIKE GOING OUT WITH A MAN.
TALK ABOUT WHAT HE WANTS TO TALK ABOUT.
ALWAYS WORRY ABOUT HIS NEEDS.
NO MATTER HOW BORING IT IS, ALWAYS ACT INTERESTED IN WHAT HE'S SAYING.

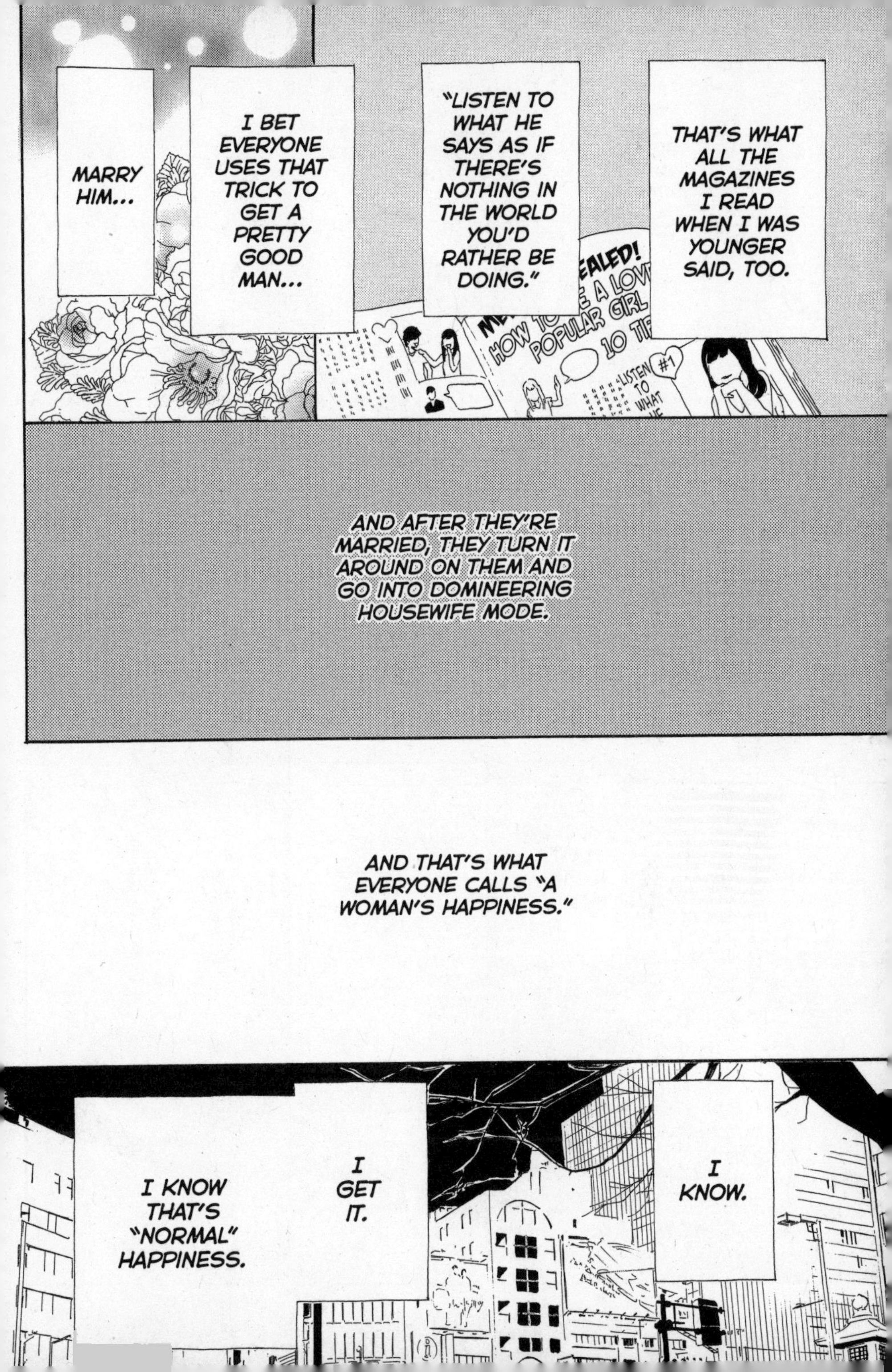

THAT'S WHAT ALL THE MAGAZINES I READ WHEN I WAS YOUNGER SAID, TOO.
#1
LISTEN TO WHAT
"LISTEN TO WHAT HE SAYS AS IF THERE'S NOTHING IN THE WORLD YOU'D RATHER BE DOING."
I BET EVERYONE USES THAT TRICK TO GET A PRETTY GOOD MAN...
MARRY HIM...
AND AFTER THEY'RE MARRIED, THEY TURN IT AROUND ON THEM AND GO INTO DOMINEERING HOUSEWIFE MODE.
AND THAT'S WHAT EVERYONE CALLS "A WOMAN'S HAPPINESS."
I KNOW.
I GET IT.
I KNOW THAT'S "NORMAL" HAPPINESS.

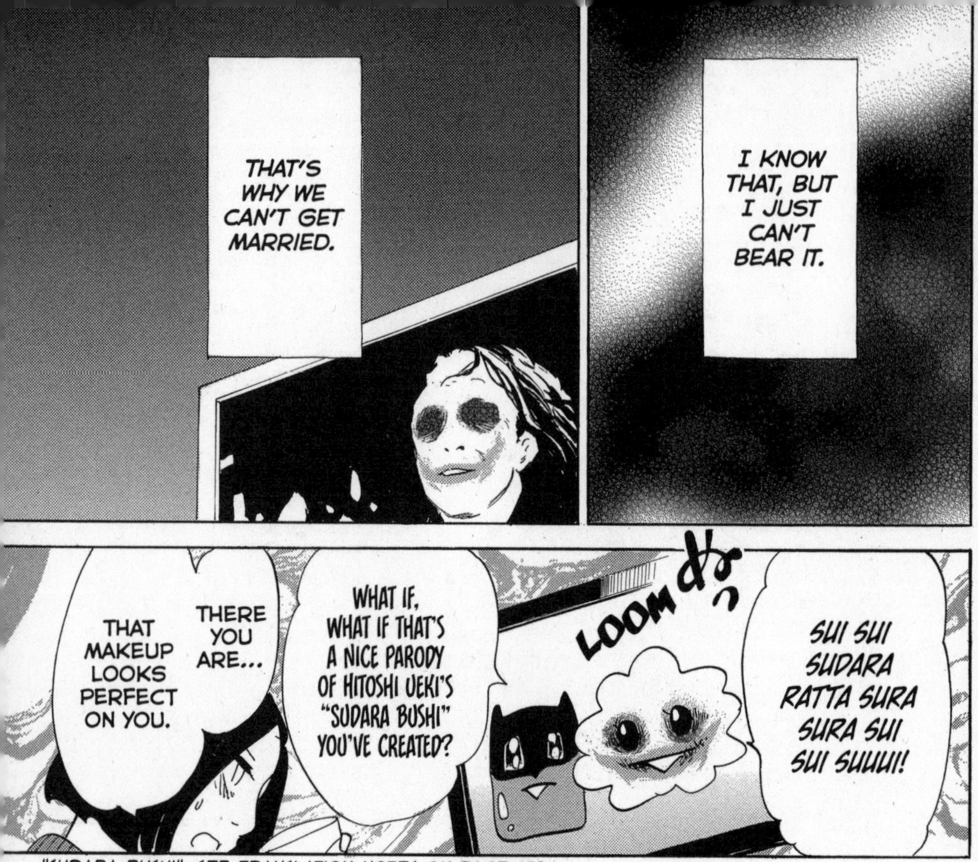
I KNOW THAT, BUT I JUST CAN'T BEAR IT.
THAT'S WHY WE CAN'T GET MARRIED.
SUI SUI SUDARA RATTA SURA SURA SUI SUI SUUUI!
LOOM
WHAT IF, WHAT IF THAT'S A NICE PARODY OF HITOSHI UEKI'S "SUDARA BUSHI" YOU'VE CREATED?
THERE YOU ARE...
THAT MAKEUP LOOKS PERFECT ON YOU.

"SUDARA BUSHI": SEE TRANSLATION NOTES ON PAGE 173.

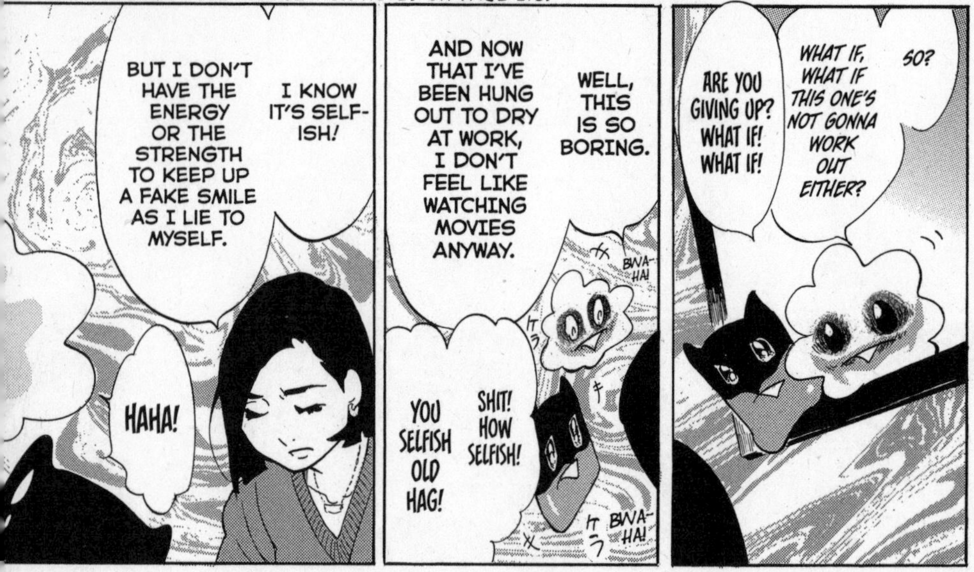
SO?
WHAT IF, WHAT IF THIS ONE'S NOT GONNA WORK OUT EITHER?
ARE YOU GIVING UP? WHAT IF! WHAT IF!
WELL, THIS IS SO BORING.
AND NOW THAT I'VE BEEN HUNG OUT TO DRY AT WORK, I DON'T FEEL LIKE WATCHING MOVIES ANYWAY.
BWA-HA!
SHIT! HOW SELFISH!
YOU SELFISH OLD HAG!
BWA-HA!
I KNOW IT'S SELF-ISH!
BUT I DON'T HAVE THE ENERGY OR THE STRENGTH TO KEEP UP A FAKE SMILE AS I LIE TO MYSELF.
HAHA!

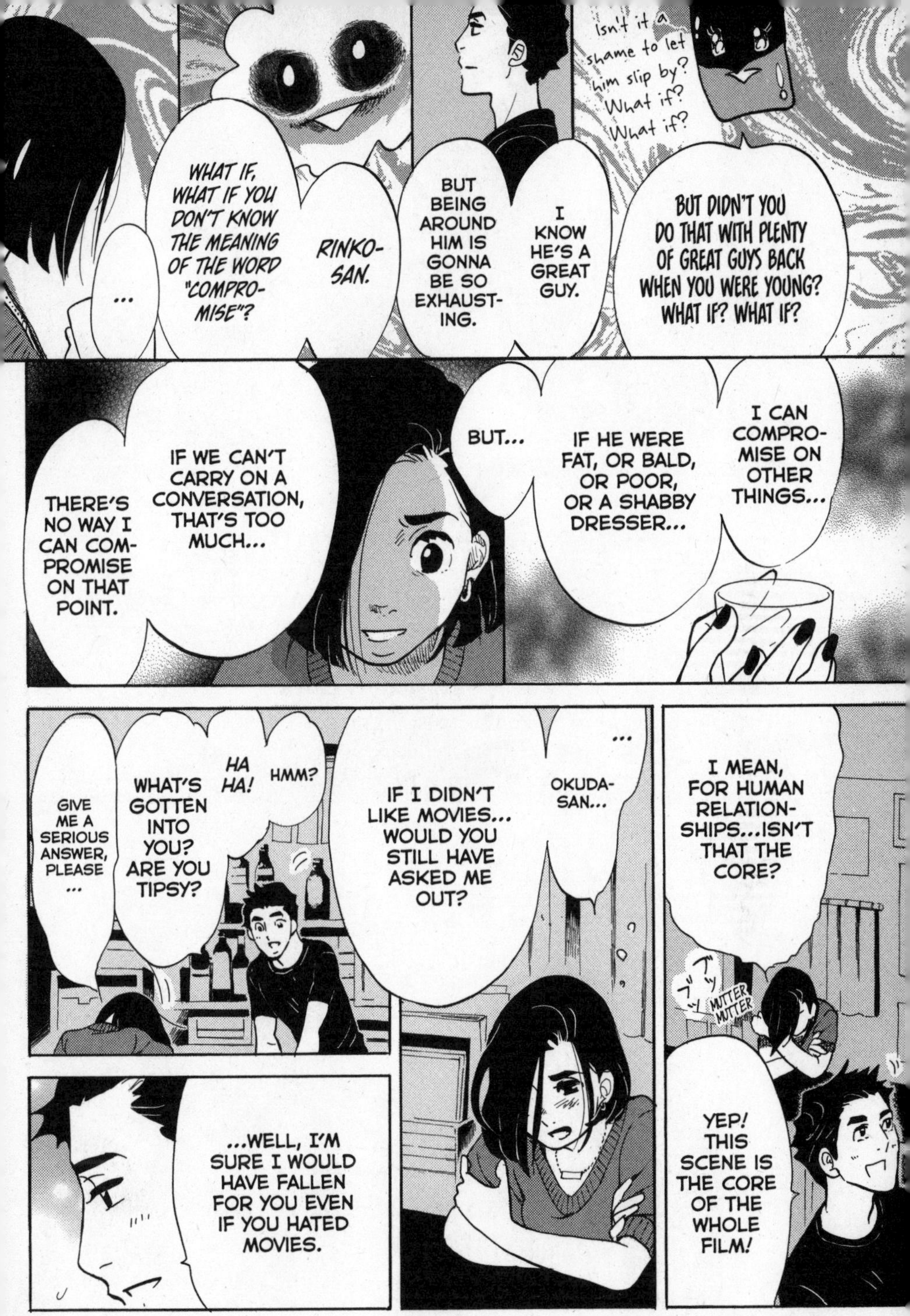
Isn't it a shame to let him slip by? What if? What if?
BUT DIDN'T YOU DO THAT WITH PLENTY OF GREAT GUYS BACK WHEN YOU WERE YOUNG? WHAT IF? WHAT IF?
I KNOW HE'S A GREAT GUY.
BUT BEING AROUND HIM IS GONNA BE SO EXHAUSTING.
RINKO-SAN.
WHAT IF, WHAT IF YOU DON'T KNOW THE MEANING OF THE WORD "COMPROMISE"?
...
I CAN COMPROMISE ON OTHER THINGS...
IF HE WERE FAT, OR BALD, OR POOR, OR A SHABBY DRESSER...
BUT...
IF WE CAN'T CARRY ON A CONVERSATION, THAT'S TOO MUCH...
THERE'S NO WAY I CAN COMPROMISE ON THAT POINT.
I MEAN, FOR HUMAN RELATIONSHIPS...ISN'T THAT THE CORE?
MUTTER MUTTER
YEP! THIS SCENE IS THE CORE OF THE WHOLE FILM!
...
OKUDA-SAN...
IF I DIDN'T LIKE MOVIES... WOULD YOU STILL HAVE ASKED ME OUT?
HMM?
HA HA!
WHAT'S GOTTEN INTO YOU? ARE YOU TIPSY?
GIVE ME A SERIOUS ANSWER, PLEASE...
...WELL, I'M SURE I WOULD HAVE FALLEN FOR YOU EVEN IF YOU HATED MOVIES.

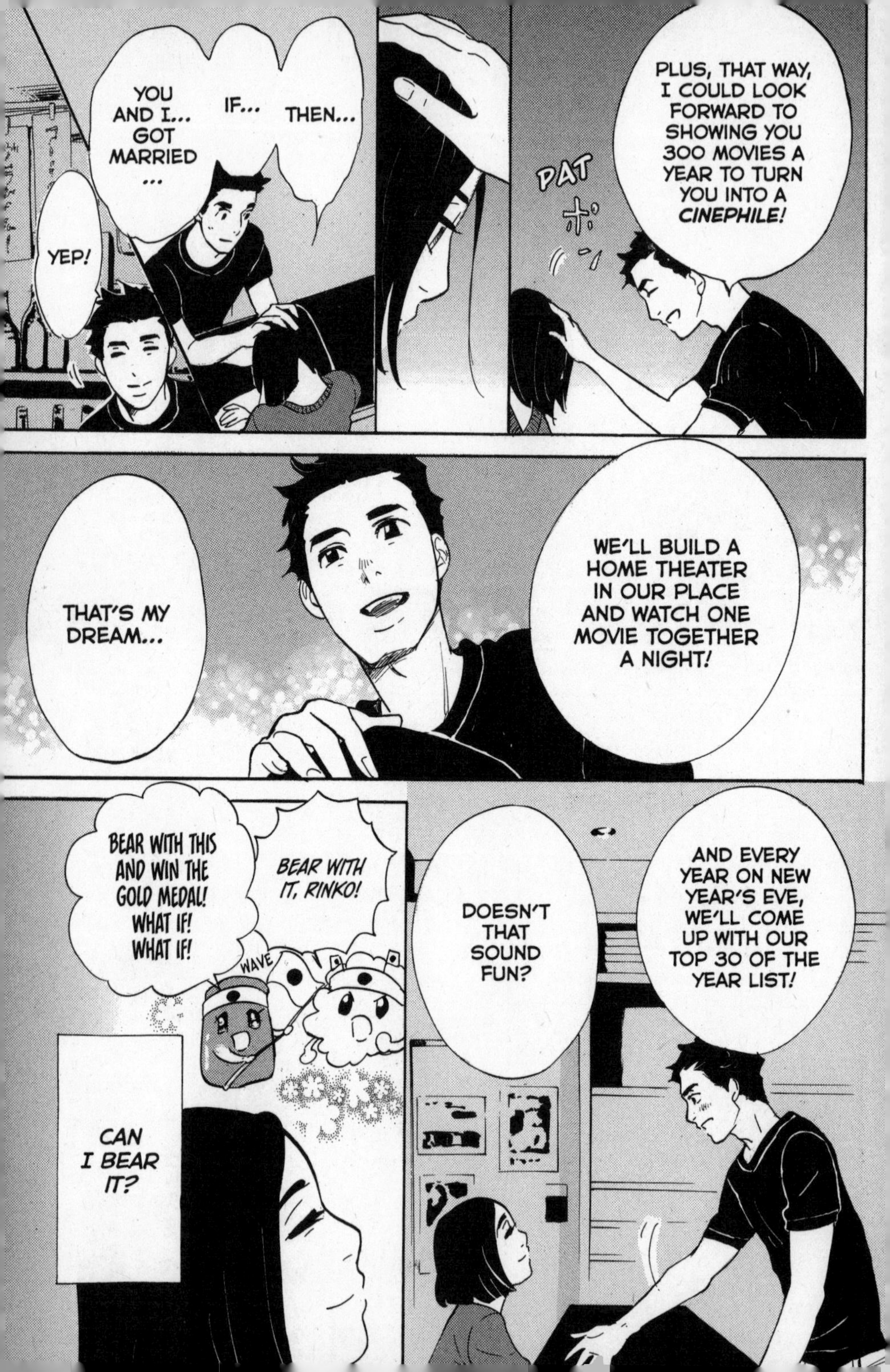
PLUS, THAT WAY, I COULD LOOK FORWARD TO SHOWING YOU 300 MOVIES A YEAR TO TURN YOU INTO A *CINEPHILE!*
PAT
YOU AND I... GOT MARRIED ... IF... THEN...
YEP!
WE'LL BUILD A HOME THEATER IN OUR PLACE AND WATCH ONE MOVIE TOGETHER A NIGHT!
THAT'S MY DREAM...
AND EVERY YEAR ON NEW YEAR'S EVE, WE'LL COME UP WITH OUR TOP 30 OF THE YEAR LIST!
DOESN'T THAT SOUND FUN?
BEAR WITH IT, RINKO!
BEAR WITH THIS AND WIN THE GOLD MEDAL! WHAT IF! WHAT IF!
WAVE
CAN I BEAR IT?

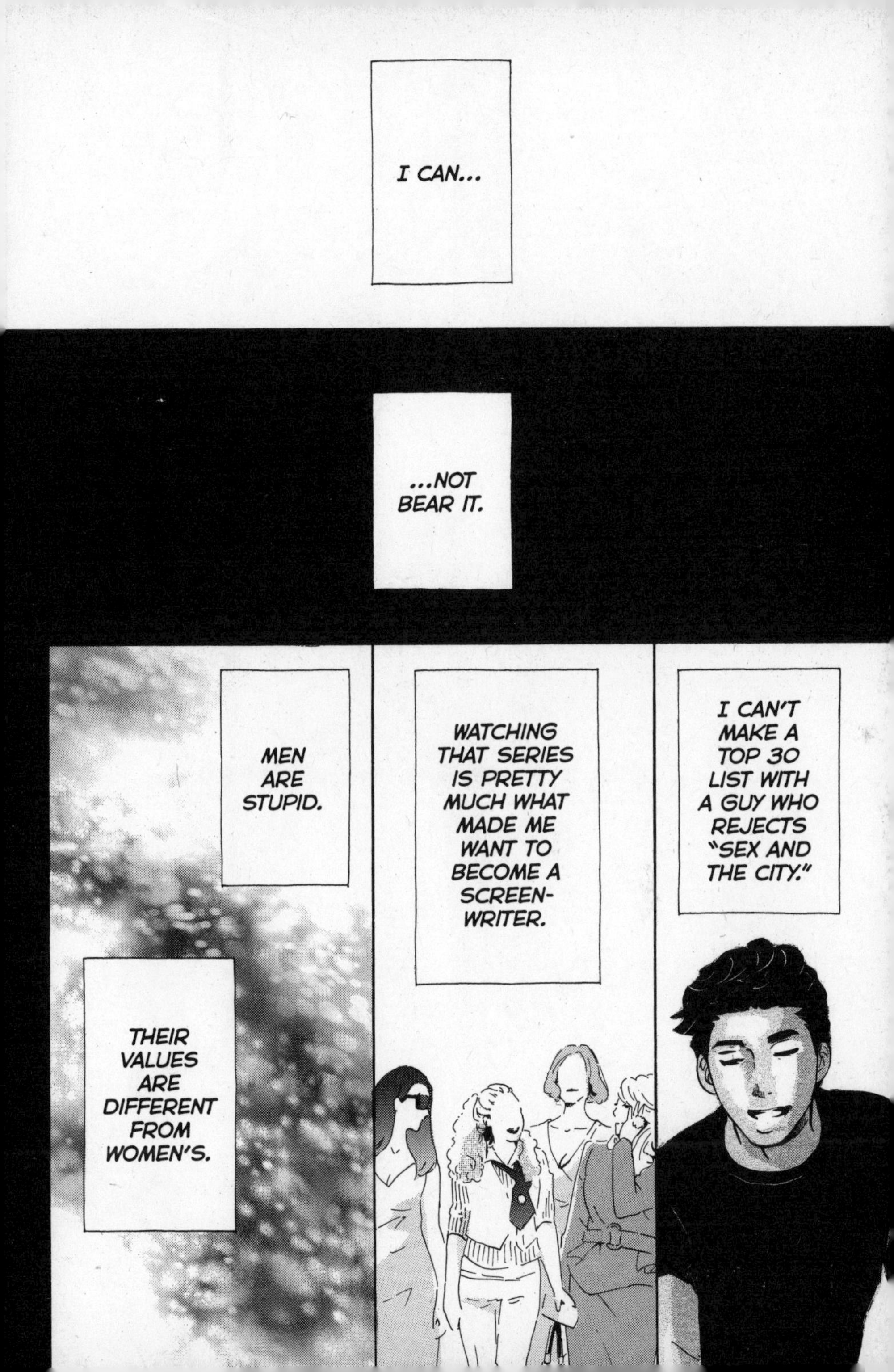
I CAN...
...NOT BEAR IT.
I CAN'T MAKE A TOP 30 LIST WITH A GUY WHO REJECTS "SEX AND THE CITY."
WATCHING THAT SERIES IS PRETTY MUCH WHAT MADE ME WANT TO BECOME A SCREEN-WRITER.
MEN ARE STUPID.
THEIR VALUES ARE DIFFERENT FROM WOMEN'S.

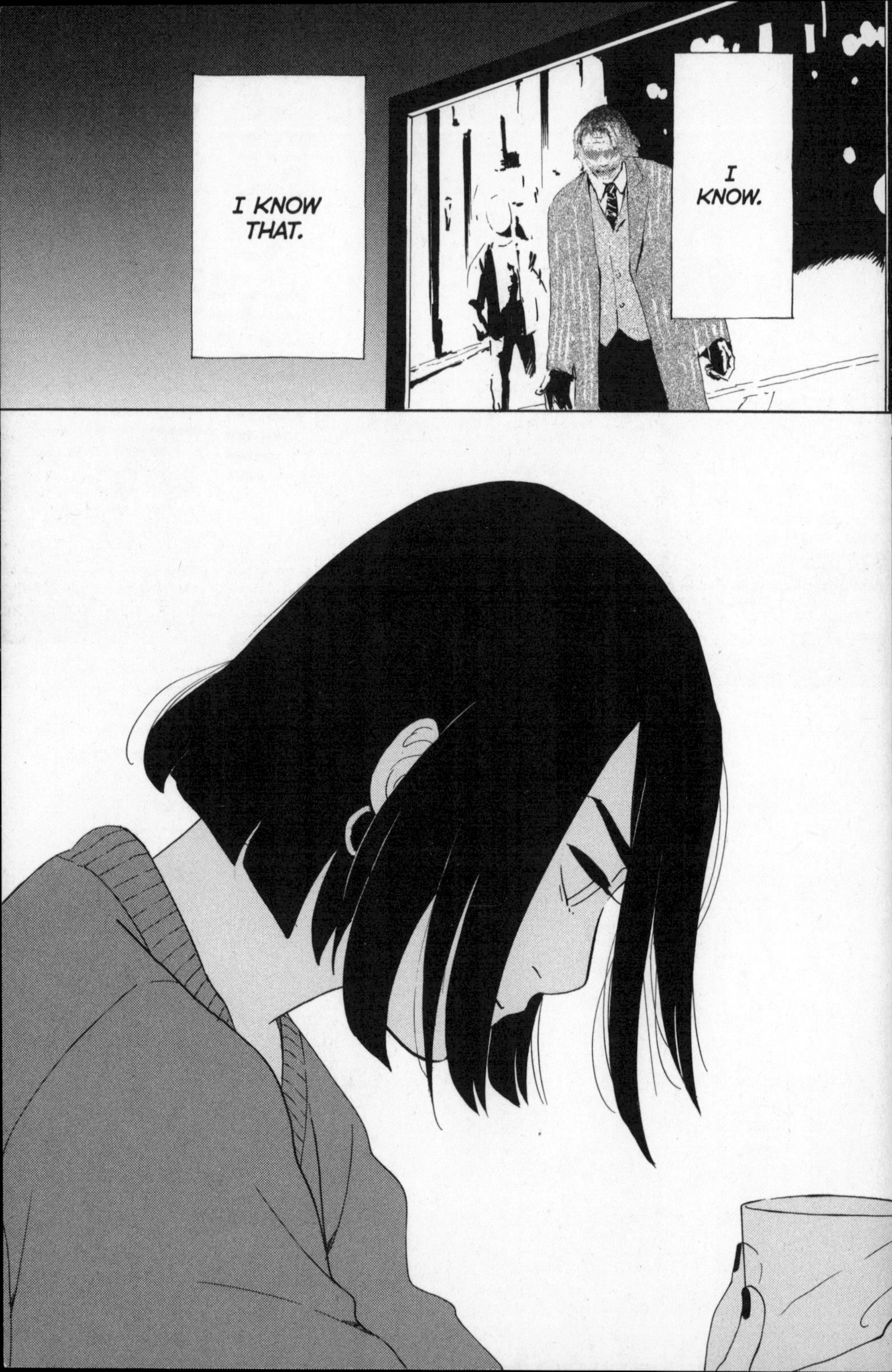
I KNOW.
I KNOW THAT.

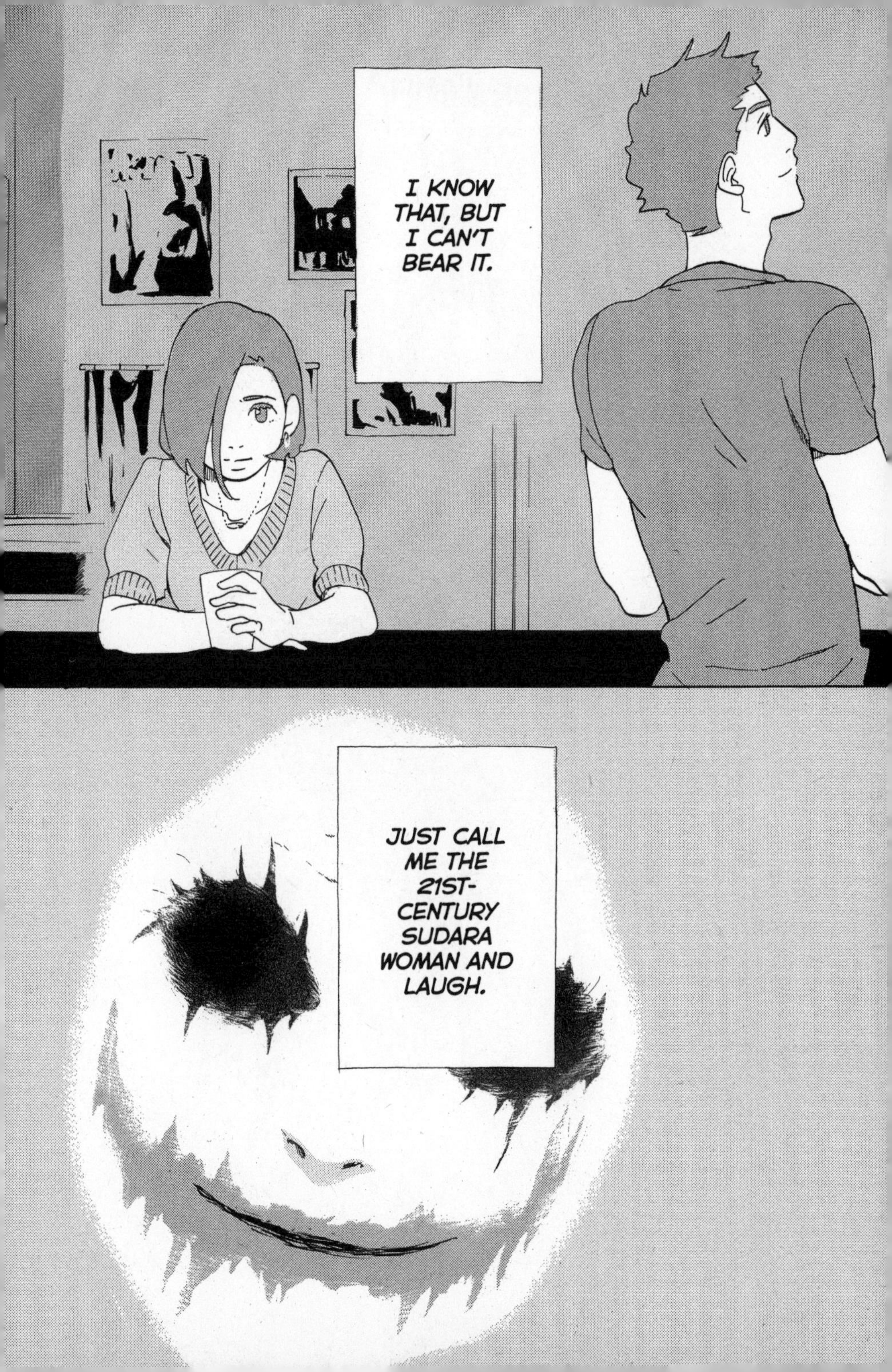
I KNOW THAT, BUT I CAN'T BEAR IT.
JUST CALL ME THE 21ST-CENTURY SUDARA WOMAN AND LAUGH.

ACT 13 TIME MACHINE WOMEN

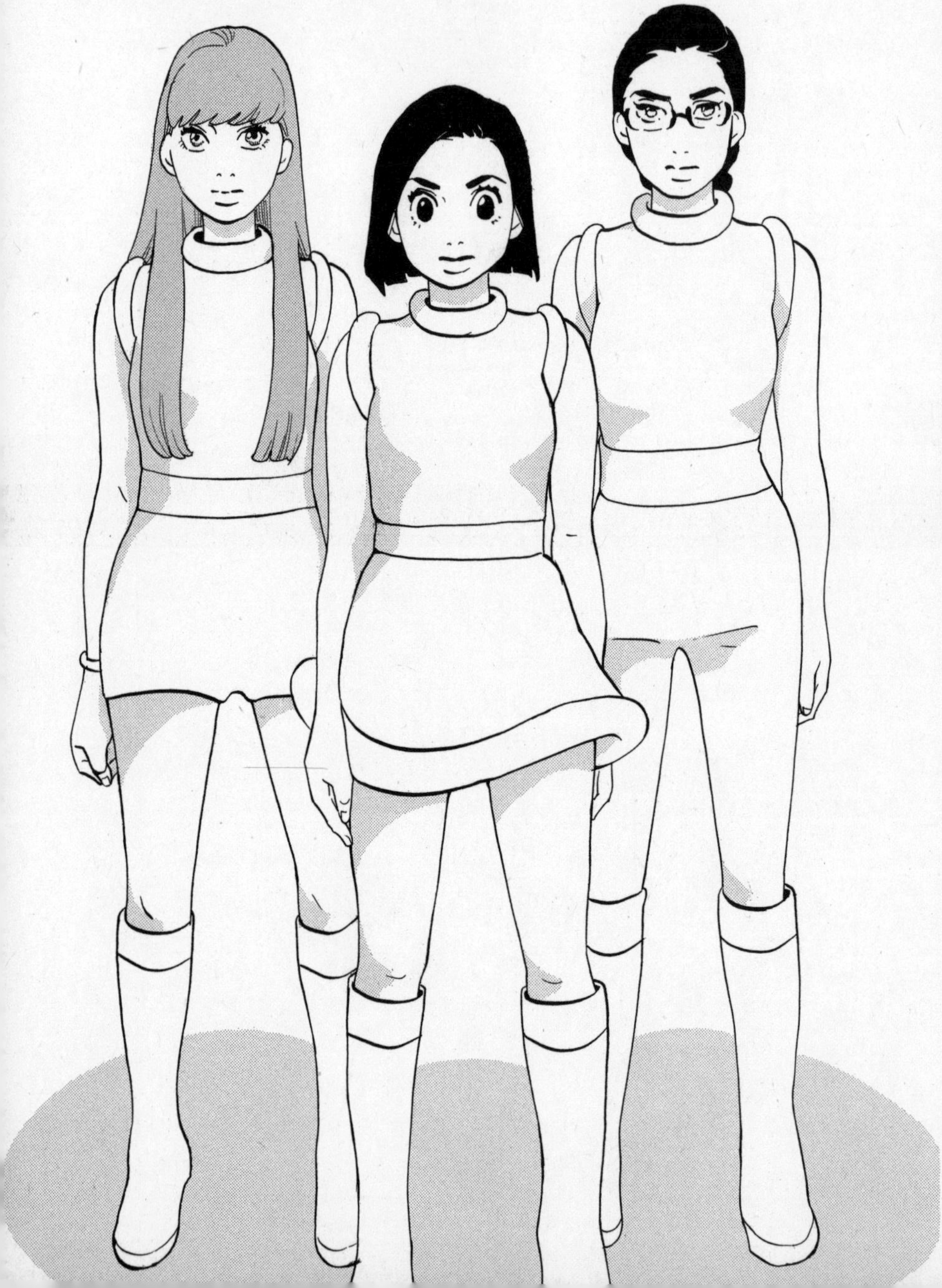

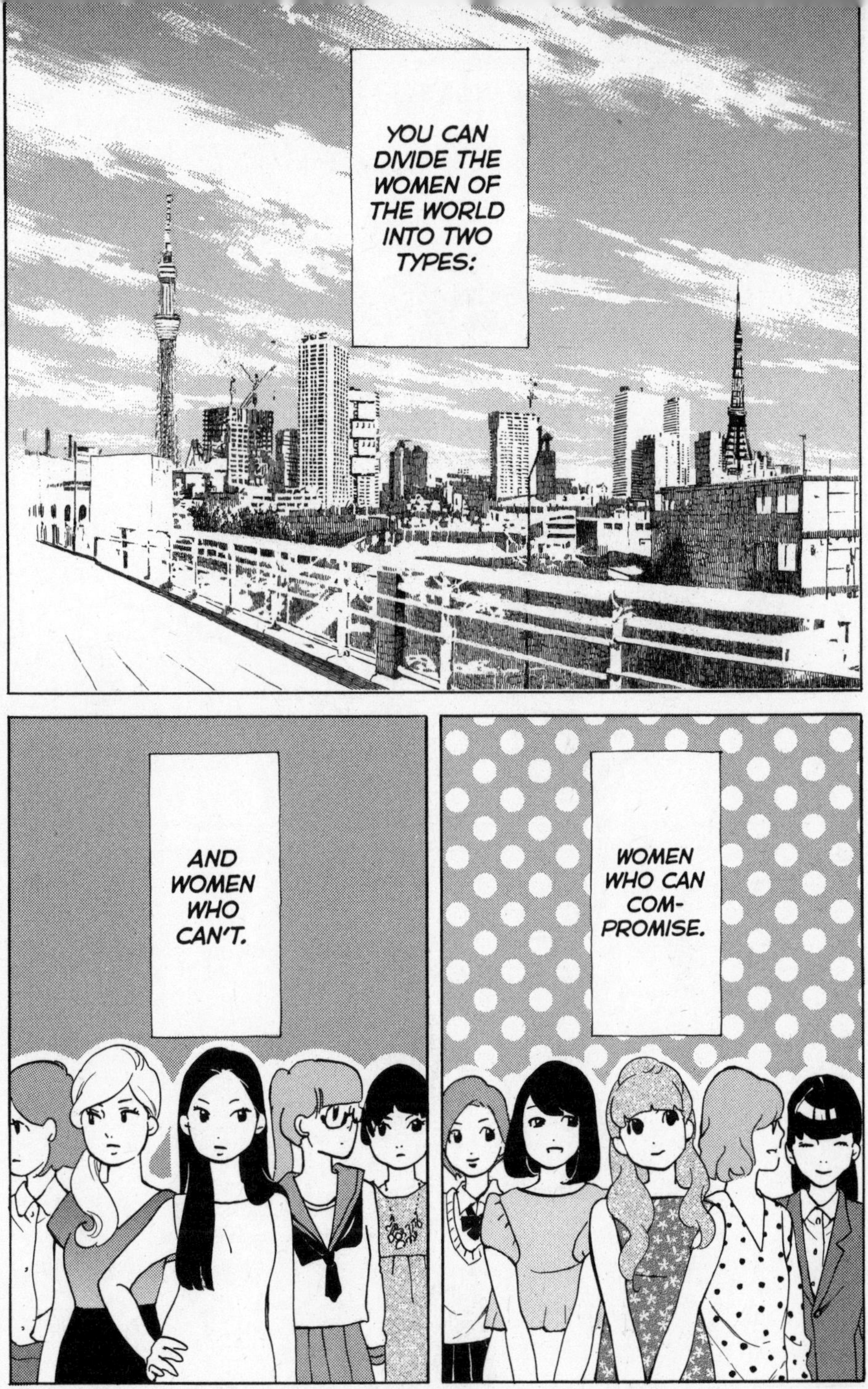
YOU CAN DIVIDE THE WOMEN OF THE WORLD INTO TWO TYPES:
WOMEN WHO CAN COM-PROMISE.
AND WOMEN WHO CAN'T.

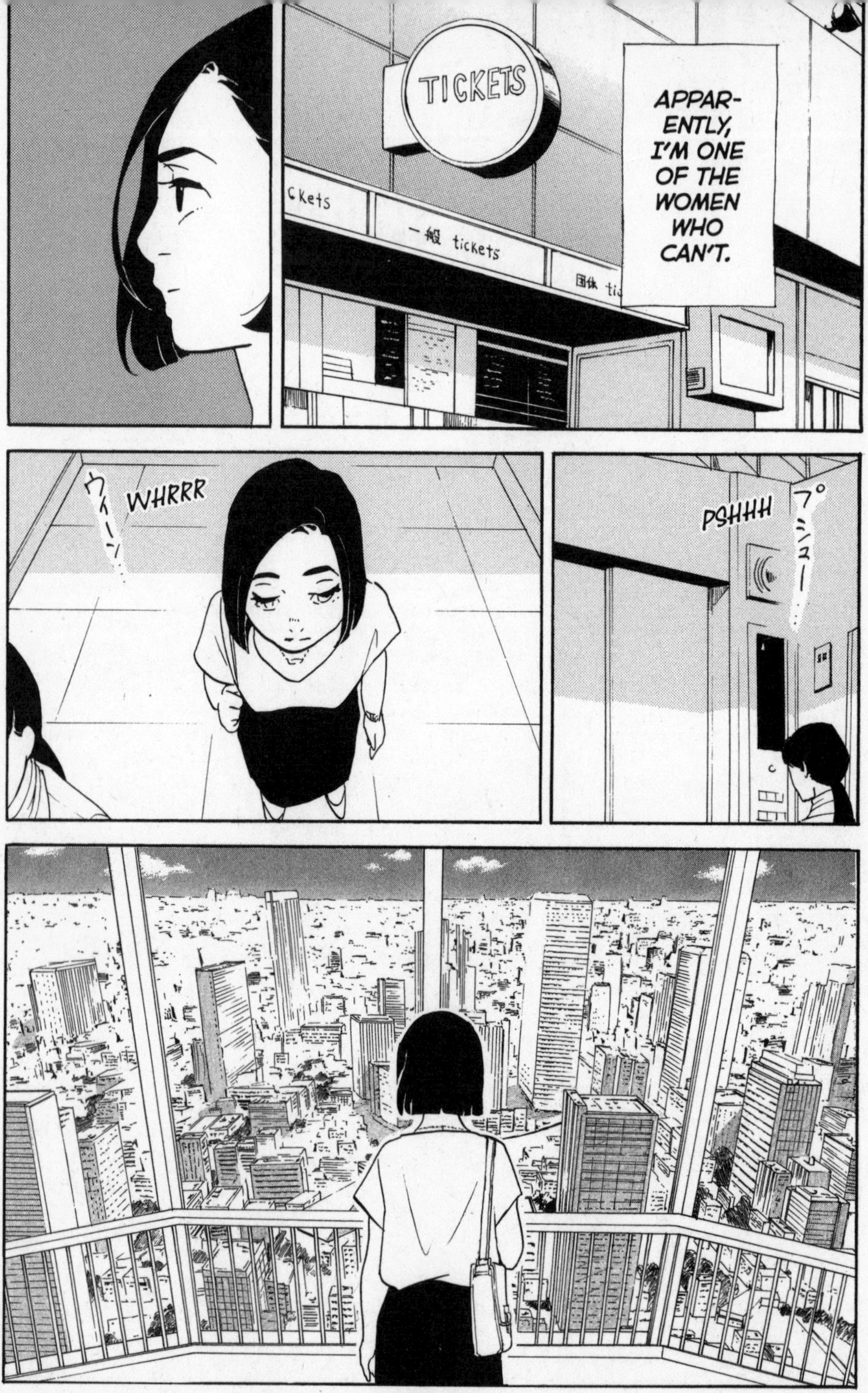
TICKETS
ckets
一般 tickets
APPARENTLY, I'M ONE OF THE WOMEN WHO CAN'T.
PSHHH
プシュー
WHRRR
ウィーン

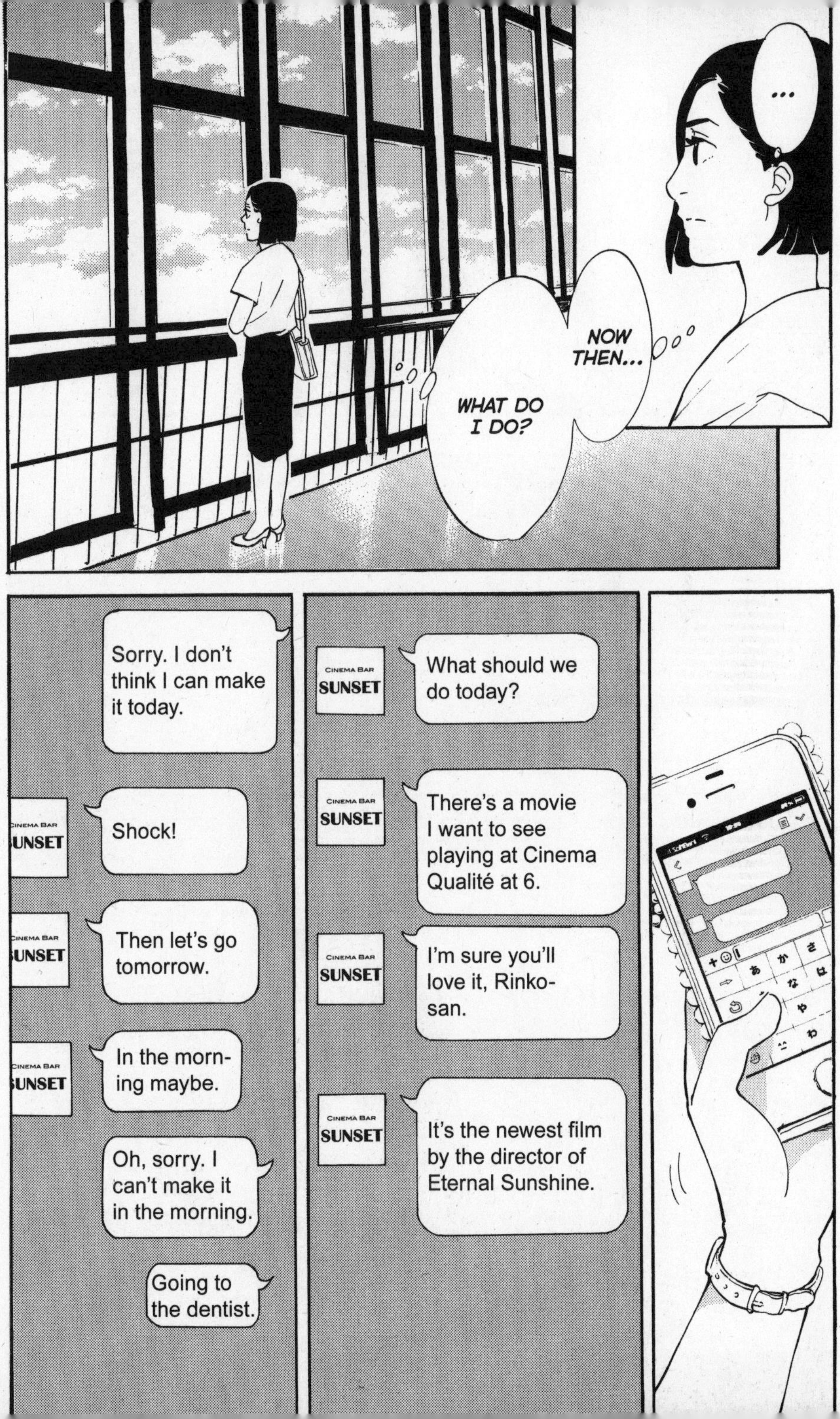
...
NOW THEN...
WHAT DO I DO?
CINEMA BAR SUNSET
What should we do today?
CINEMA BAR SUNSET
There's a movie I want to see playing at Cinema Qualité at 6.
CINEMA BAR SUNSET
I'm sure you'll love it, Rinko-san.
CINEMA BAR SUNSET
It's the newest film by the director of Eternal Sunshine.
Sorry. I don't think I can make it today.
CINEMA BAR SUNSET
Shock!
CINEMA BAR SUNSET
Then let's go tomorrow.
CINEMA BAR SUNSET
In the morning maybe.
Oh, sorry. I can't make it in the morning.
Going to the dentist.

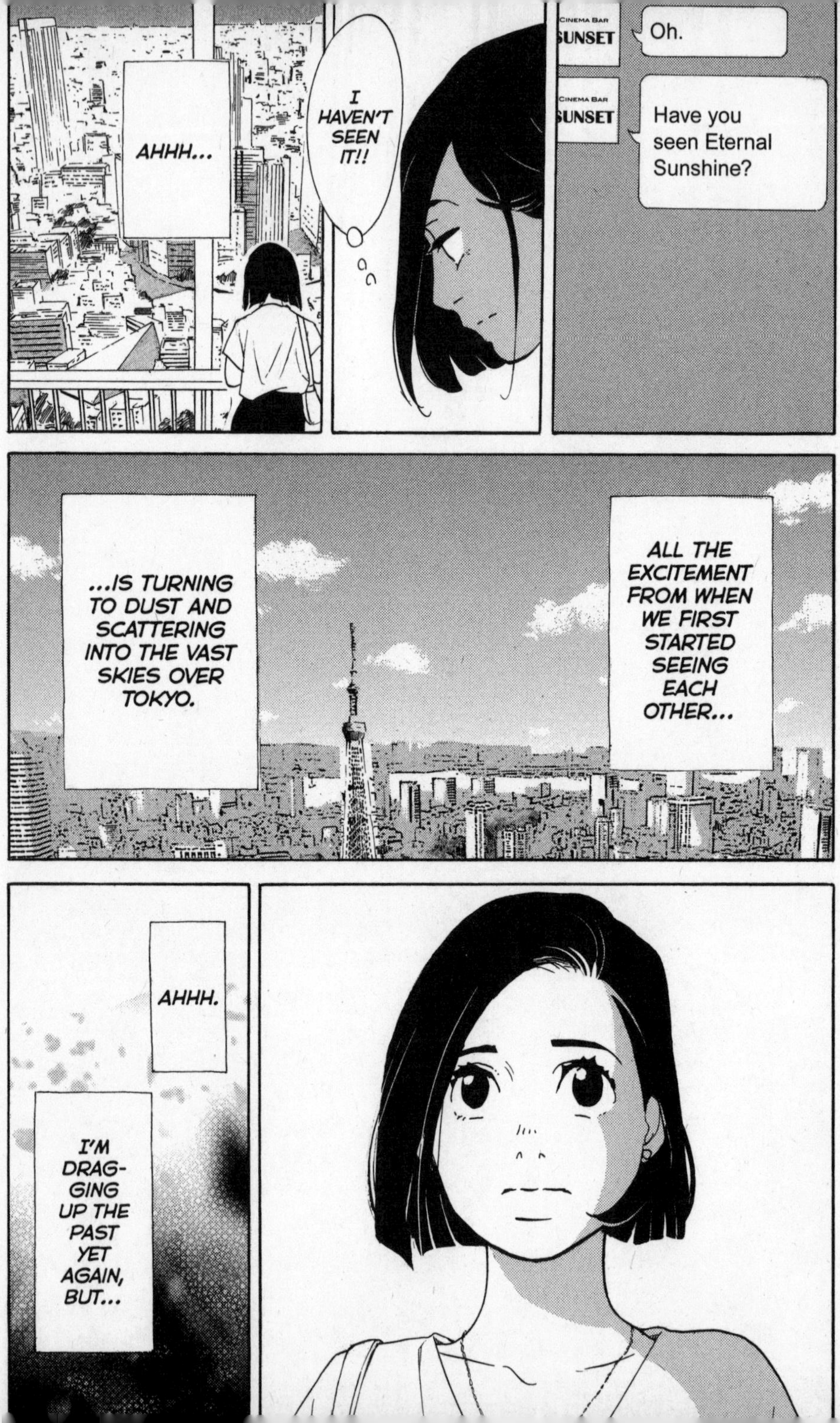

CINEMA BAR SUNSET
Oh.
CINEMA BAR SUNSET
Have you seen Eternal Sunshine?
I HAVEN'T SEEN IT!!
AHHH...
ALL THE EXCITEMENT FROM WHEN WE FIRST STARTED SEEING EACH OTHER...
...IS TURNING TO DUST AND SCATTERING INTO THE VAST SKIES OVER TOKYO.
AHHH.
I'M DRAG-GING UP THE PAST YET AGAIN, BUT...

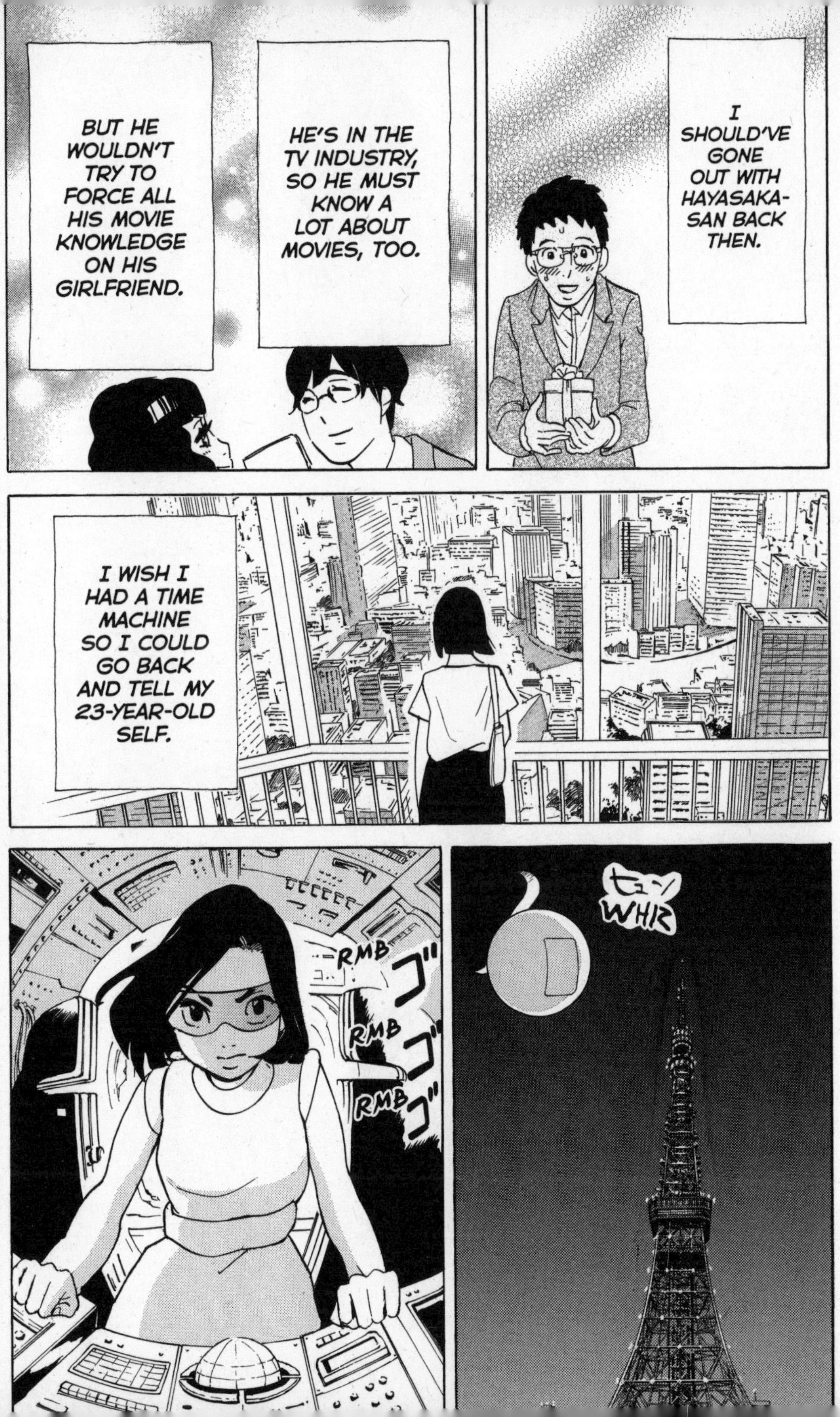
I SHOULD'VE GONE OUT WITH HAYASAKA-SAN BACK THEN.
HE'S IN THE TV INDUSTRY, SO HE MUST KNOW A LOT ABOUT MOVIES, TOO.
BUT HE WOULDN'T TRY TO FORCE ALL HIS MOVIE KNOWLEDGE ON HIS GIRLFRIEND.
I WISH I HAD A TIME MACHINE SO I COULD GO BACK AND TELL MY 23-YEAR-OLD SELF.
ヒュン
WHIR
RMB
ゴ
RMB
ゴ
RMB
ゴ

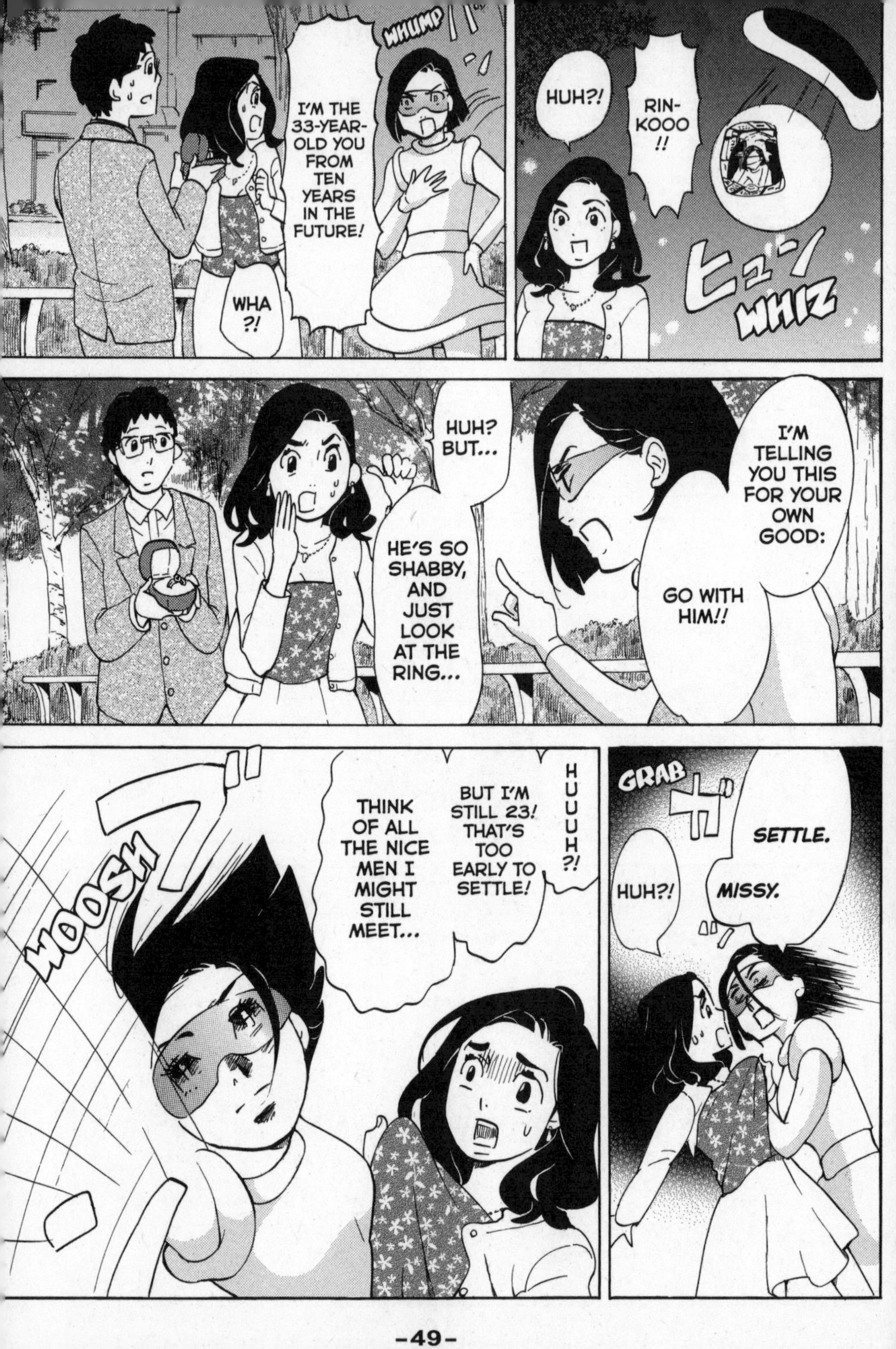
RIN-KOOO!!
HUH?!
ヒューン
WHIZ
WHUMP
I'M THE 33-YEAR-OLD YOU FROM TEN YEARS IN THE FUTURE!
WHA?!
I'M TELLING YOU THIS FOR YOUR OWN GOOD:
GO WITH HIM!!
HUH? BUT...
HE'S SO SHABBY, AND JUST LOOK AT THE RING...
SETTLE.
MISSY.
GRAB
HUH?!
HUUUH?!
BUT I'M STILL 23! THAT'S TOO EARLY TO SETTLE!
THINK OF ALL THE NICE MEN I MIGHT STILL MEET...
WOOSH

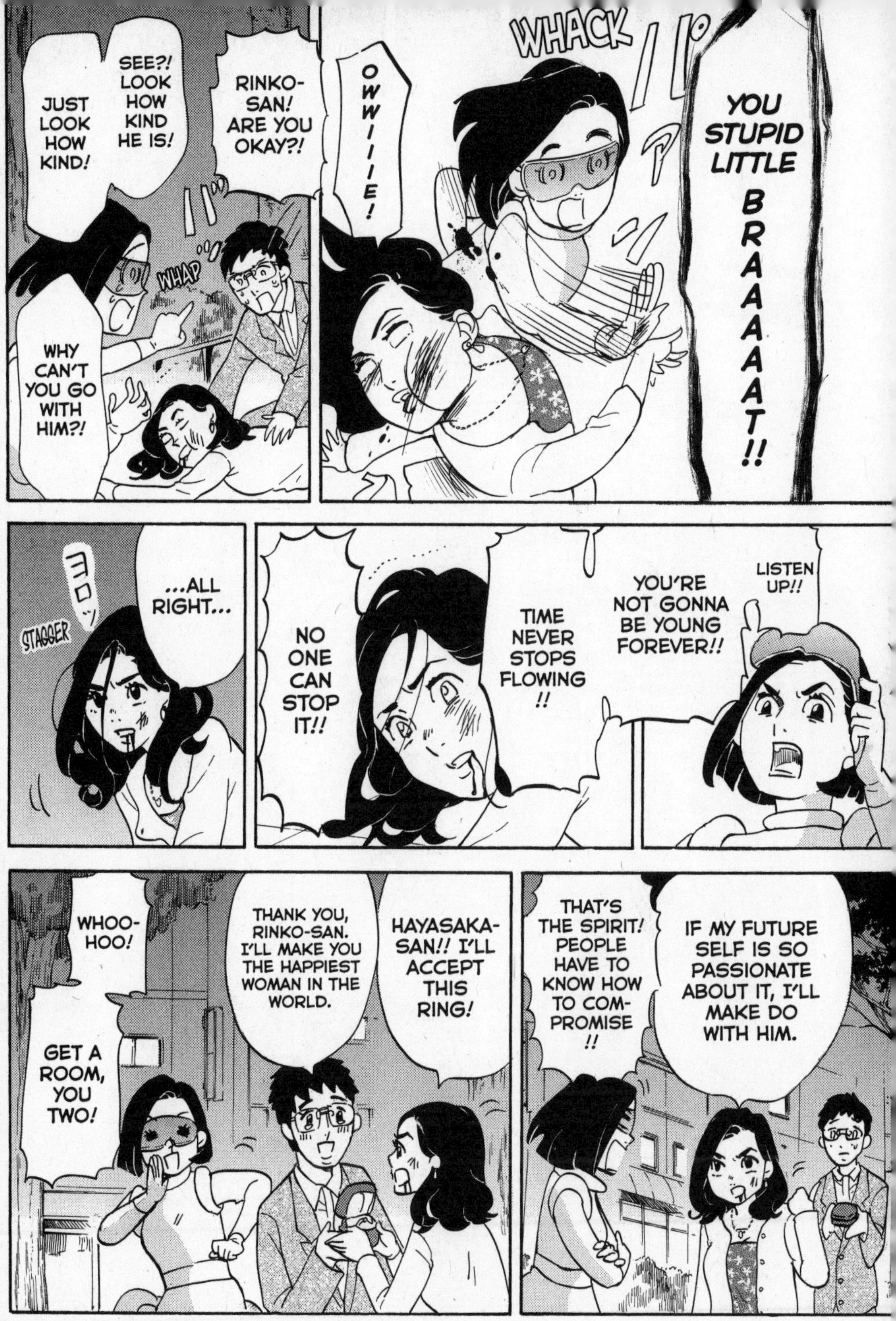
WHACK
YOU STUPID LITTLE BRAAAAAT!!
OWWIIIIE!
RINKO-SAN! ARE YOU OKAY?!
SEE?! LOOK HOW KIND HE IS!
JUST LOOK HOW KIND!
WHAP
WHY CAN'T YOU GO WITH HIM?!
LISTEN UP!!
YOU'RE NOT GONNA BE YOUNG FOREVER!!
TIME NEVER STOPS FLOWING!!
NO ONE CAN STOP IT!!
...ALL RIGHT...
ヨロッ
STAGGER
IF MY FUTURE SELF IS SO PASSIONATE ABOUT IT, I'LL MAKE DO WITH HIM.
THAT'S THE SPIRIT! PEOPLE HAVE TO KNOW HOW TO COM-PROMISE!!
HAYASAKA-SAN!! I'LL ACCEPT THIS RING!
THANK YOU, RINKO-SAN. I'LL MAKE YOU THE HAPPIEST WOMAN IN THE WORLD.
WHOO-HOO!
GET A ROOM, YOU TWO!

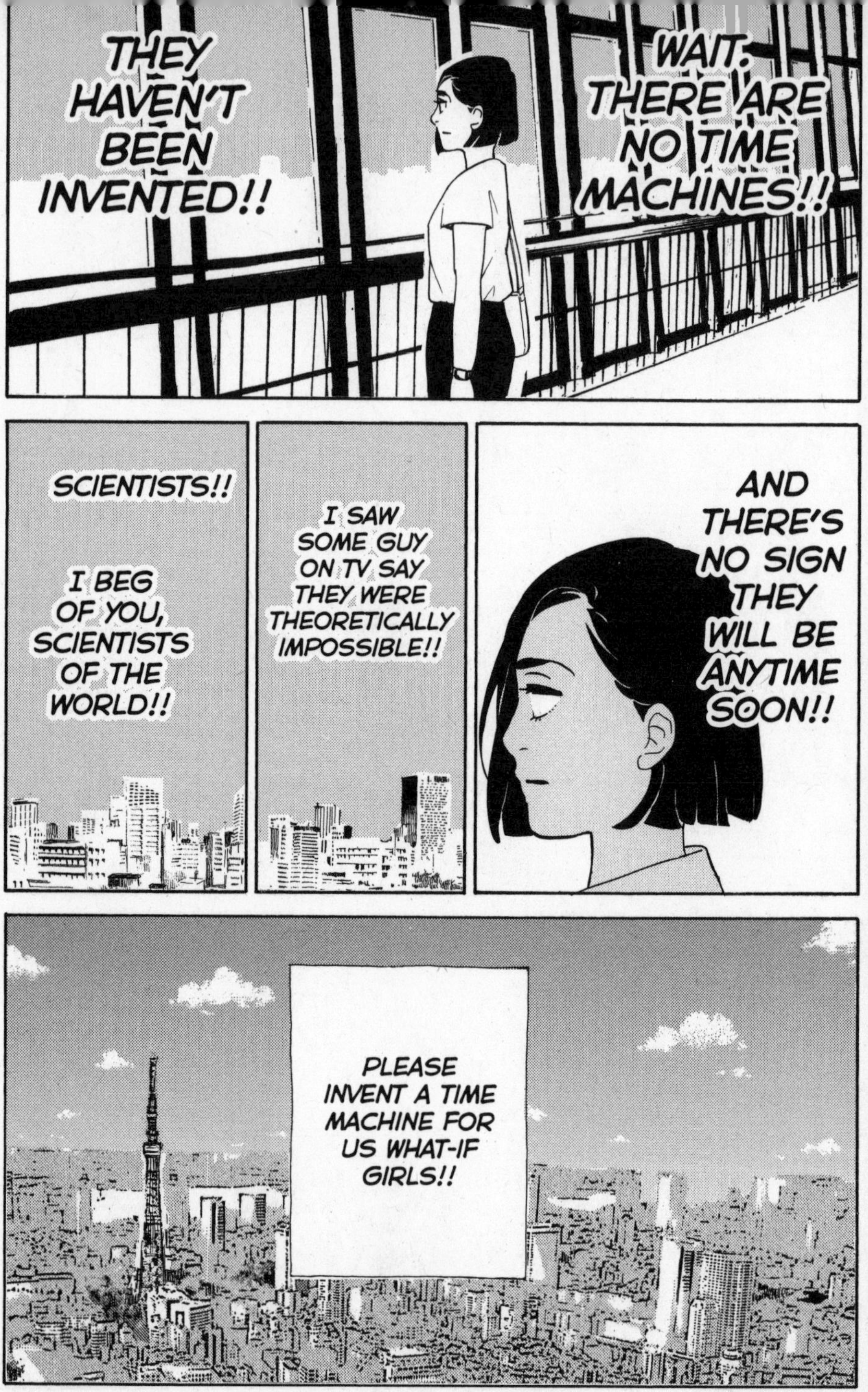
WAIT. THERE ARE NO TIME MACHINES!!
THEY HAVEN'T BEEN INVENTED!!
AND THERE'S NO SIGN THEY WILL BE ANYTIME SOON!!
I SAW SOME GUY ON TV SAY THEY WERE THEORETICALLY IMPOSSIBLE!!
SCIENTISTS!!
I BEG OF YOU, SCIENTISTS OF THE WORLD!!
PLEASE INVENT A TIME MACHINE FOR US WHAT-IF GIRLS!!

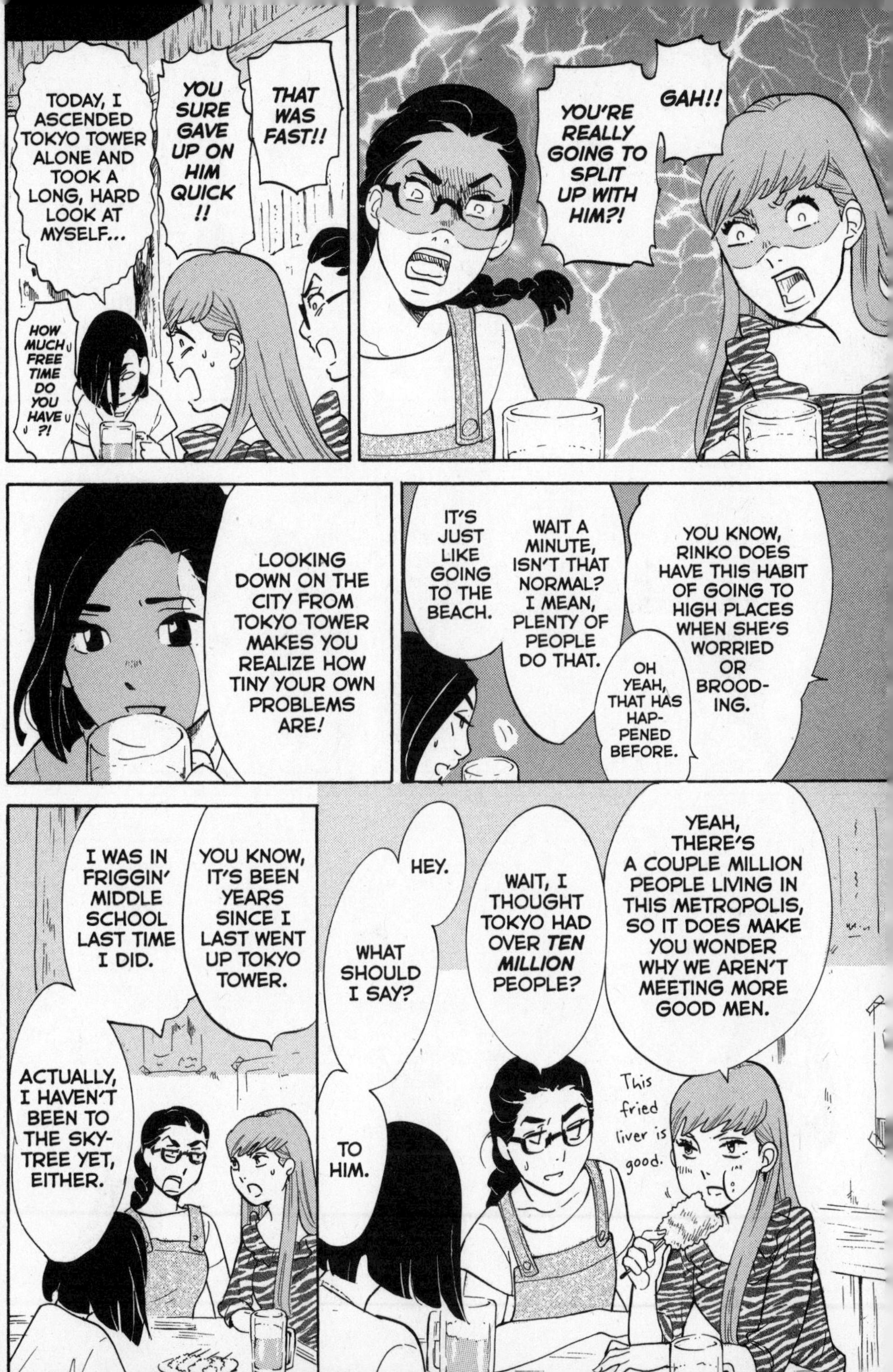
GAH!!
YOU'RE REALLY GOING TO SPLIT UP WITH HIM?!
THAT WAS FAST!!
YOU SURE GAVE UP ON HIM QUICK!!
TODAY, I ASCENDED TOKYO TOWER ALONE AND TOOK A LONG, HARD LOOK AT MYSELF...
HOW MUCH FREE TIME DO YOU HAVE?!
YOU KNOW, RINKO DOES HAVE THIS HABIT OF GOING TO HIGH PLACES WHEN SHE'S WORRIED OR BROOD-ING.
OH YEAH, THAT HAS HAP-PENED BEFORE.
WAIT A MINUTE, ISN'T THAT NORMAL? I MEAN, PLENTY OF PEOPLE DO THAT.
IT'S JUST LIKE GOING TO THE BEACH.
LOOKING DOWN ON THE CITY FROM TOKYO TOWER MAKES YOU REALIZE HOW TINY YOUR OWN PROBLEMS ARE!
YEAH, THERE'S A COUPLE MILLION PEOPLE LIVING IN THIS METROPOLIS, SO IT DOES MAKE YOU WONDER WHY WE AREN'T MEETING MORE GOOD MEN.
This fried liver is good.
WAIT, I THOUGHT TOKYO HAD OVER *TEN MILLION* PEOPLE?
HEY.
WHAT SHOULD I SAY?
TO HIM.
YOU KNOW, IT'S BEEN YEARS SINCE I LAST WENT UP TOKYO TOWER.
I WAS IN FRIGGIN' MIDDLE SCHOOL LAST TIME I DID.
ACTUALLY, I HAVEN'T BEEN TO THE SKY-TREE YET, EITHER.

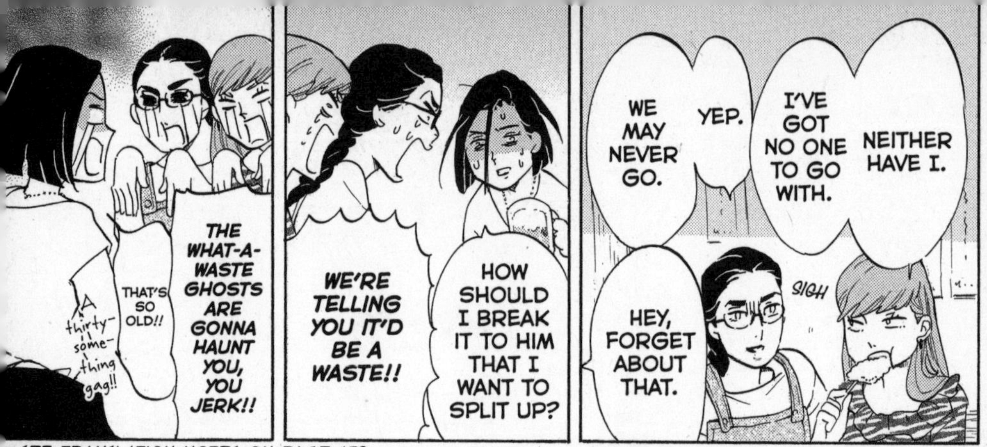
NEITHER HAVE I.
I'VE GOT NO ONE TO GO WITH.
YEP.
WE MAY NEVER GO.
SIGH
HEY, FORGET ABOUT THAT.
HOW SHOULD I BREAK IT TO HIM THAT I WANT TO SPLIT UP?
WE'RE TELLING YOU IT'D BE A WASTE!!
THE WHAT-A-WASTE GHOSTS ARE GONNA HAUNT YOU, YOU JERK!!
THAT'S SO OLD!!
A thirty-something gag!!

SEE TRANSLATION NOTES ON PAGE 173.

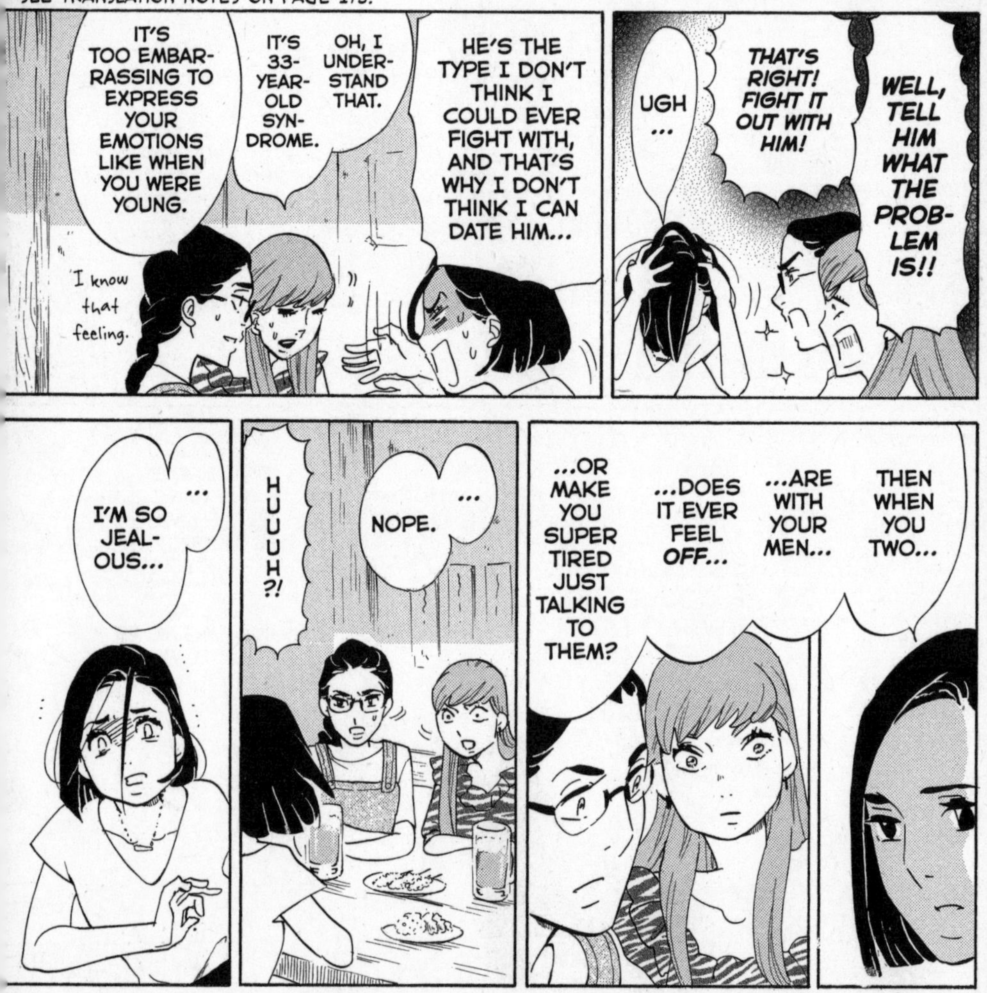
WELL, TELL HIM WHAT THE PROB-LEM IS!!
THAT'S RIGHT! FIGHT IT OUT WITH HIM!
UGH...
HE'S THE TYPE I DON'T THINK I COULD EVER FIGHT WITH, AND THAT'S WHY I DON'T THINK I CAN DATE HIM...
OH, I UNDER-STAND THAT.
IT'S 33-YEAR-OLD SYN-DROME.
IT'S TOO EMBAR-RASSING TO EXPRESS YOUR EMOTIONS LIKE WHEN YOU WERE YOUNG.
I know that feeling.
THEN WHEN YOU TWO...
...ARE WITH YOUR MEN...
...DOES IT EVER FEEL OFF...
...OR MAKE YOU SUPER TIRED JUST TALKING TO THEM?
...
NOPE.
HUUUH?!
...
I'M SO JEAL-OUS...

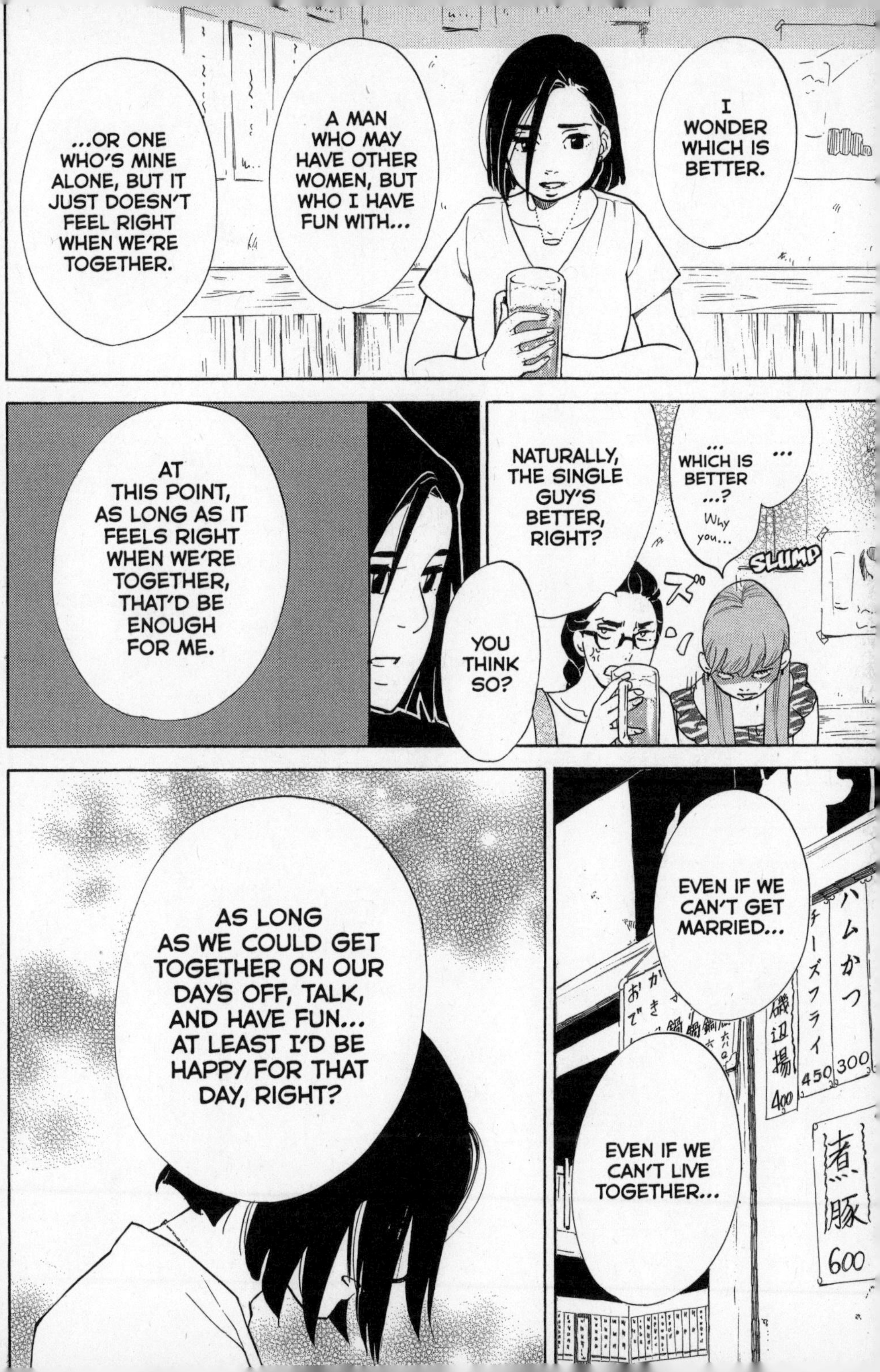
I WONDER WHICH IS BETTER.
A MAN WHO MAY HAVE OTHER WOMEN, BUT WHO I HAVE FUN WITH...
...OR ONE WHO'S MINE ALONE, BUT IT JUST DOESN'T FEEL RIGHT WHEN WE'RE TOGETHER.
...
...WHICH IS BETTER ...?
Why you...
SLUMP
ズ
NATURALLY, THE SINGLE GUY'S BETTER, RIGHT?
YOU THINK SO?
AT THIS POINT, AS LONG AS IT FEELS RIGHT WHEN WE'RE TOGETHER, THAT'D BE ENOUGH FOR ME.
EVEN IF WE CAN'T GET MARRIED...
ハムかつ 300
チーズフライ 450
磯辺揚 400
煮豚 600
EVEN IF WE CAN'T LIVE TOGETHER...
AS LONG AS WE COULD GET TOGETHER ON OUR DAYS OFF, TALK, AND HAVE FUN... AT LEAST I'D BE HAPPY FOR THAT DAY, RIGHT?

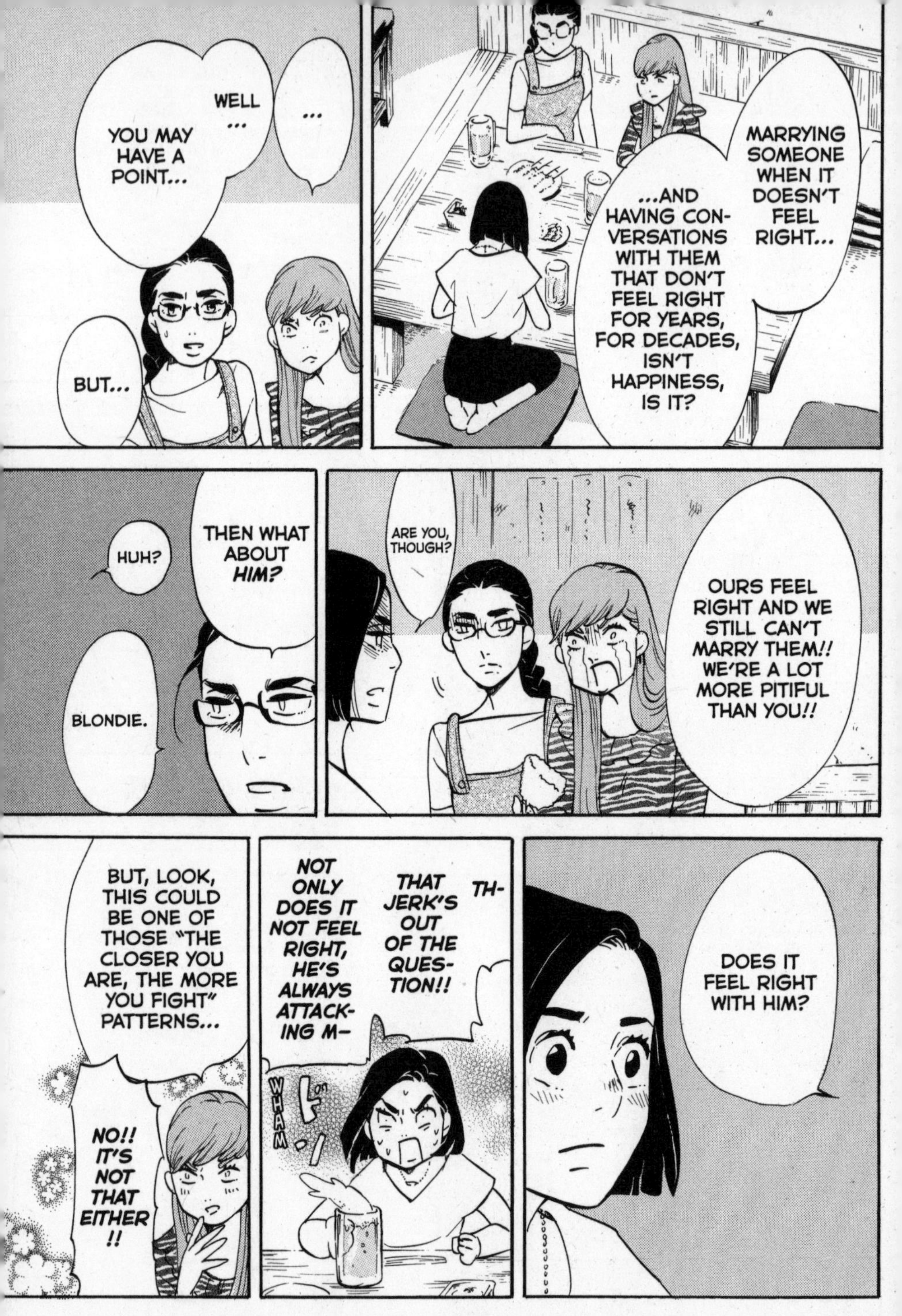
MARRYING SOMEONE WHEN IT DOESN'T FEEL RIGHT...
...AND HAVING CON-VERSATIONS WITH THEM THAT DON'T FEEL RIGHT FOR YEARS, FOR DECADES, ISN'T HAPPINESS, IS IT?
...
WELL ...
YOU MAY HAVE A POINT...
BUT...
OURS FEEL RIGHT AND WE STILL CAN'T MARRY THEM!! WE'RE A LOT MORE PITIFUL THAN YOU!!
ARE YOU, THOUGH?
THEN WHAT ABOUT *HIM?*
HUH?
BLONDIE.
DOES IT FEEL RIGHT WITH HIM?
TH-
THAT JERK'S OUT OF THE QUES-TION!!
NOT ONLY DOES IT NOT FEEL RIGHT, HE'S ALWAYS ATTACK-ING M-
WHAM
BUT, LOOK, THIS COULD BE ONE OF THOSE "THE CLOSER YOU ARE, THE MORE YOU FIGHT" PATTERNS...
NO!! IT'S NOT THAT EITHER !!

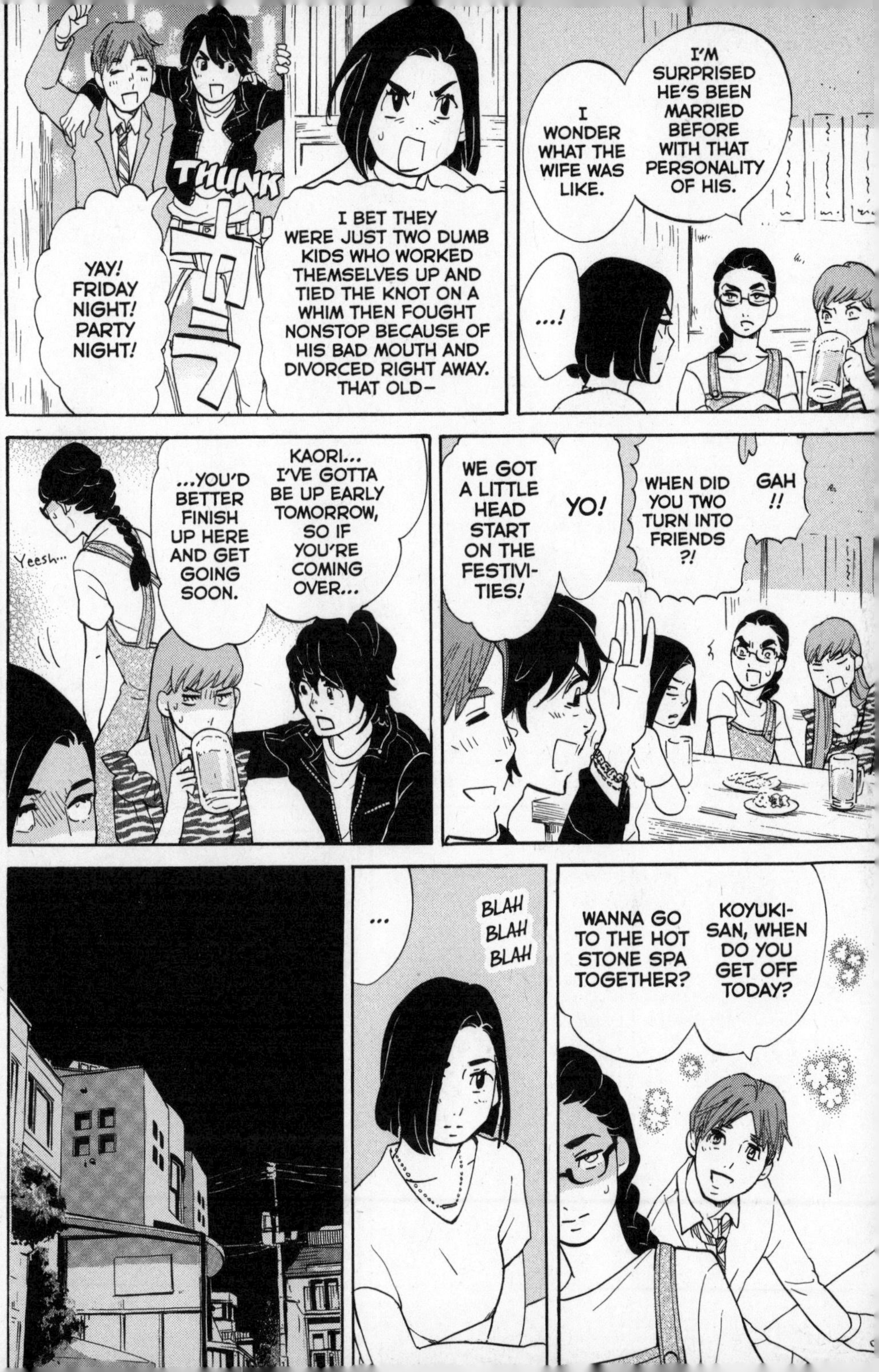
I'M SURPRISED HE'S BEEN MARRIED BEFORE WITH THAT PERSONALITY OF HIS.
I WONDER WHAT THE WIFE WAS LIKE.
...!
I BET THEY WERE JUST TWO DUMB KIDS WHO WORKED THEMSELVES UP AND TIED THE KNOT ON A WHIM THEN FOUGHT NONSTOP BECAUSE OF HIS BAD MOUTH AND DIVORCED RIGHT AWAY. THAT OLD—
THUNK
YAY! FRIDAY NIGHT! PARTY NIGHT!
GAH !!
WHEN DID YOU TWO TURN INTO FRIENDS ?!
YO!
WE GOT A LITTLE HEAD START ON THE FESTIVITIES!
KAORI... I'VE GOTTA BE UP EARLY TOMORROW, SO IF YOU'RE COMING OVER...
...YOU'D BETTER FINISH UP HERE AND GET GOING SOON.
Yeesh...
KOYUKI-SAN, WHEN DO YOU GET OFF TODAY?
WANNA GO TO THE HOT STONE SPA TOGETHER?
BLAH BLAH BLAH
...

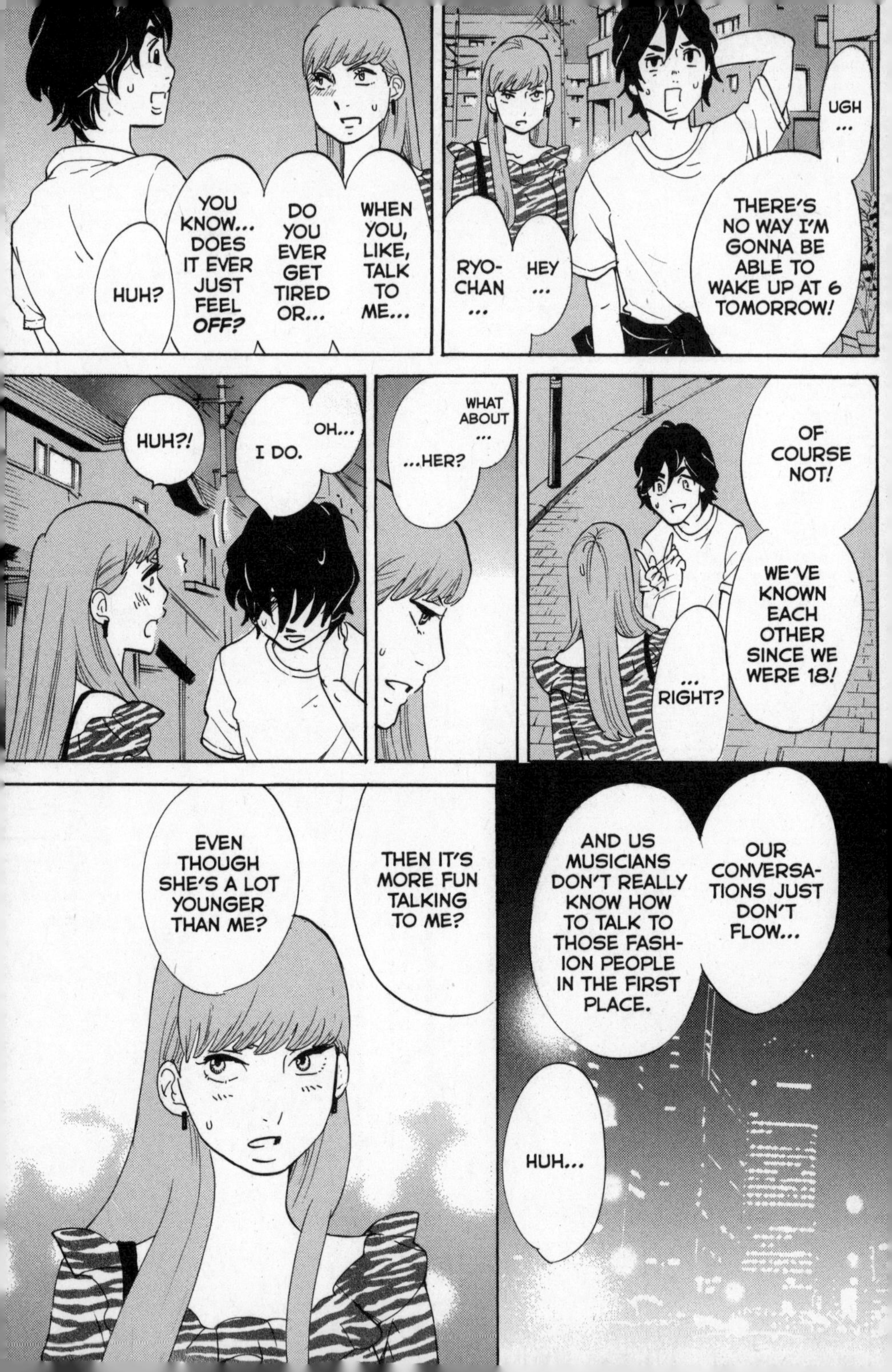
UGH ...
THERE'S NO WAY I'M GONNA BE ABLE TO WAKE UP AT 6 TOMORROW!
HEY ...
RYO-CHAN ...
WHEN YOU, LIKE, TALK TO ME...
DO YOU EVER GET TIRED OR...
YOU KNOW... DOES IT EVER JUST FEEL *OFF?*
HUH?
OF COURSE NOT!
WE'VE KNOWN EACH OTHER SINCE WE WERE 18!
... RIGHT?
WHAT ABOUT ...
...HER?
OH... I DO.
HUH?!
OUR CONVERSA-TIONS JUST DON'T FLOW...
AND US MUSICIANS DON'T REALLY KNOW HOW TO TALK TO THOSE FASH-ION PEOPLE IN THE FIRST PLACE.
HUH...
THEN IT'S MORE FUN TALKING TO ME?
EVEN THOUGH SHE'S A LOT YOUNGER THAN ME?

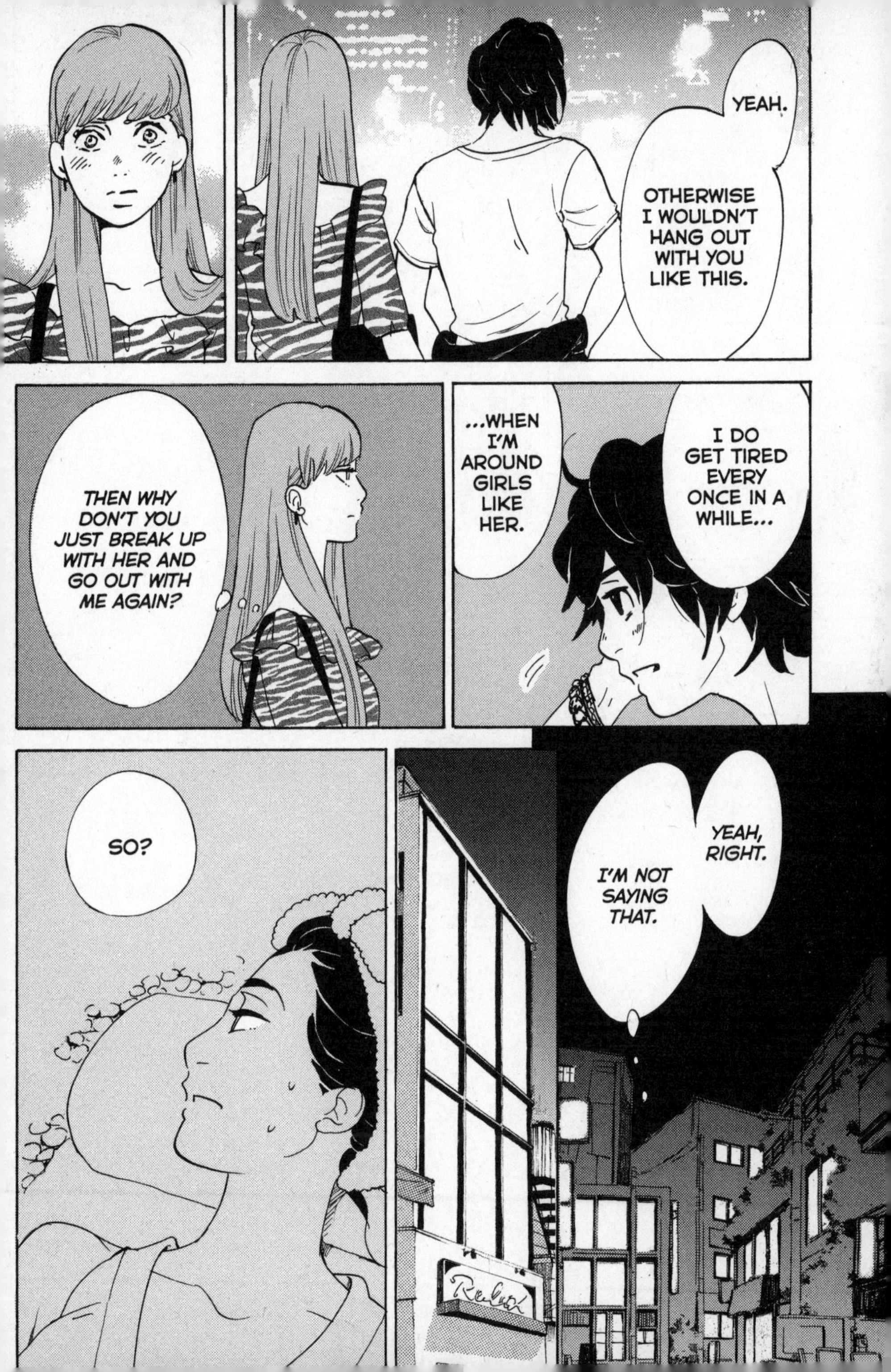
YEAH.
OTHERWISE I WOULDN'T HANG OUT WITH YOU LIKE THIS.
I DO GET TIRED EVERY ONCE IN A WHILE...
...WHEN I'M AROUND GIRLS LIKE HER.
THEN WHY DON'T YOU JUST BREAK UP WITH HER AND GO OUT WITH ME AGAIN?
YEAH, RIGHT.
I'M NOT SAYING THAT.
SO?

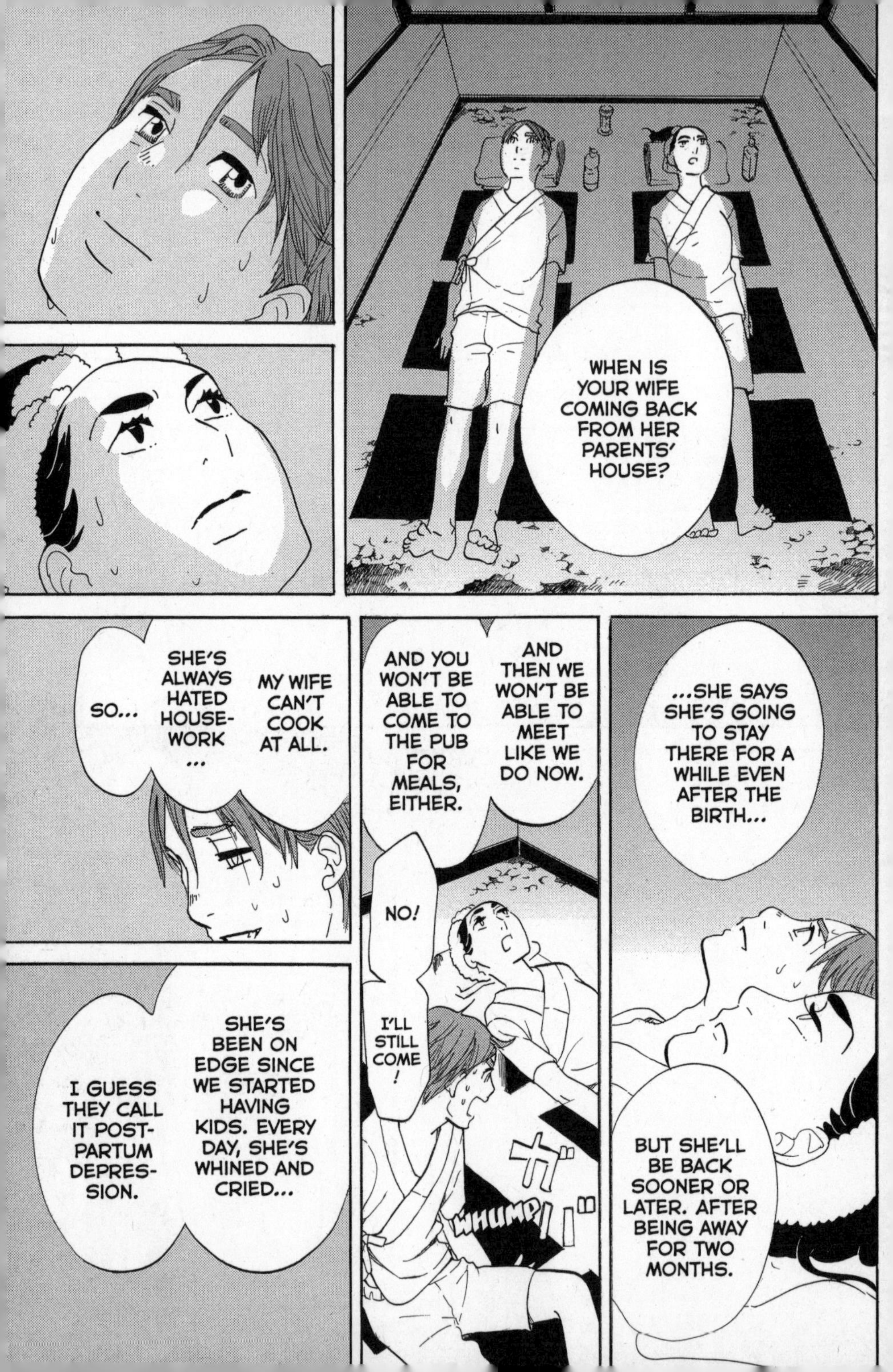
WHEN IS YOUR WIFE COMING BACK FROM HER PARENTS' HOUSE?
...SHE SAYS SHE'S GOING TO STAY THERE FOR A WHILE EVEN AFTER THE BIRTH...
BUT SHE'LL BE BACK SOONER OR LATER. AFTER BEING AWAY FOR TWO MONTHS.
AND THEN WE WON'T BE ABLE TO MEET LIKE WE DO NOW.
AND YOU WON'T BE ABLE TO COME TO THE PUB FOR MEALS, EITHER.
NO!
I'LL STILL COME!
WHUMP!
MY WIFE CAN'T COOK AT ALL.
SHE'S ALWAYS HATED HOUSE-WORK...
SO...
SHE'S BEEN ON EDGE SINCE WE STARTED HAVING KIDS. EVERY DAY, SHE'S WHINED AND CRIED...
I GUESS THEY CALL IT POST-PARTUM DEPRES-SION.

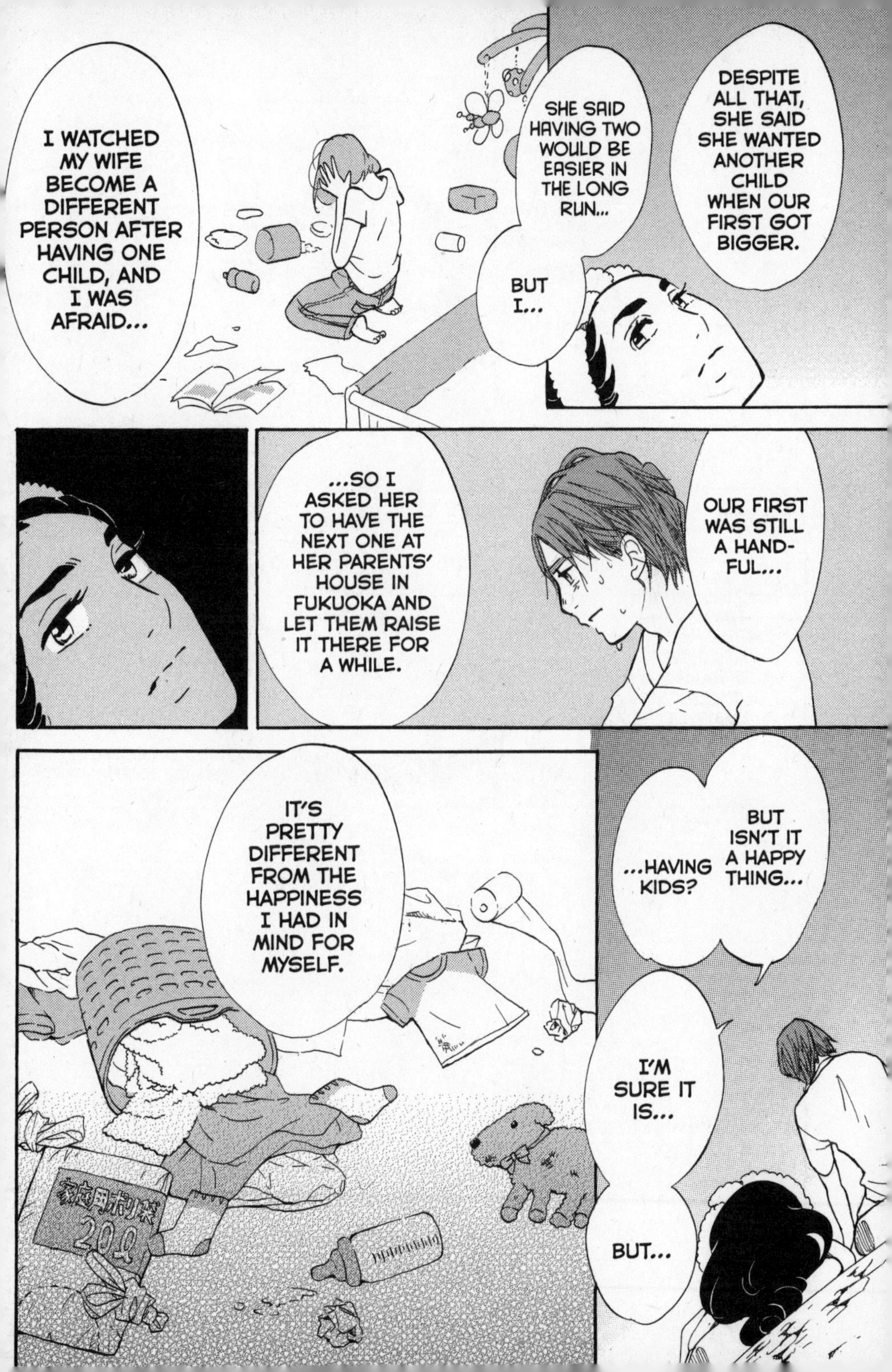
DESPITE ALL THAT, SHE SAID SHE WANTED ANOTHER CHILD WHEN OUR FIRST GOT BIGGER.
SHE SAID HAVING TWO WOULD BE EASIER IN THE LONG RUN...
BUT I...
I WATCHED MY WIFE BECOME A DIFFERENT PERSON AFTER HAVING ONE CHILD, AND I WAS AFRAID...
OUR FIRST WAS STILL A HAND-FUL...
...SO I ASKED HER TO HAVE THE NEXT ONE AT HER PARENTS' HOUSE IN FUKUOKA AND LET THEM RAISE IT THERE FOR A WHILE.
BUT ISN'T IT A HAPPY THING...
...HAVING KIDS?
I'M SURE IT IS...
BUT...
IT'S PRETTY DIFFERENT FROM THE HAPPINESS I HAD IN MIND FOR MYSELF.
家庭用ポリ袋

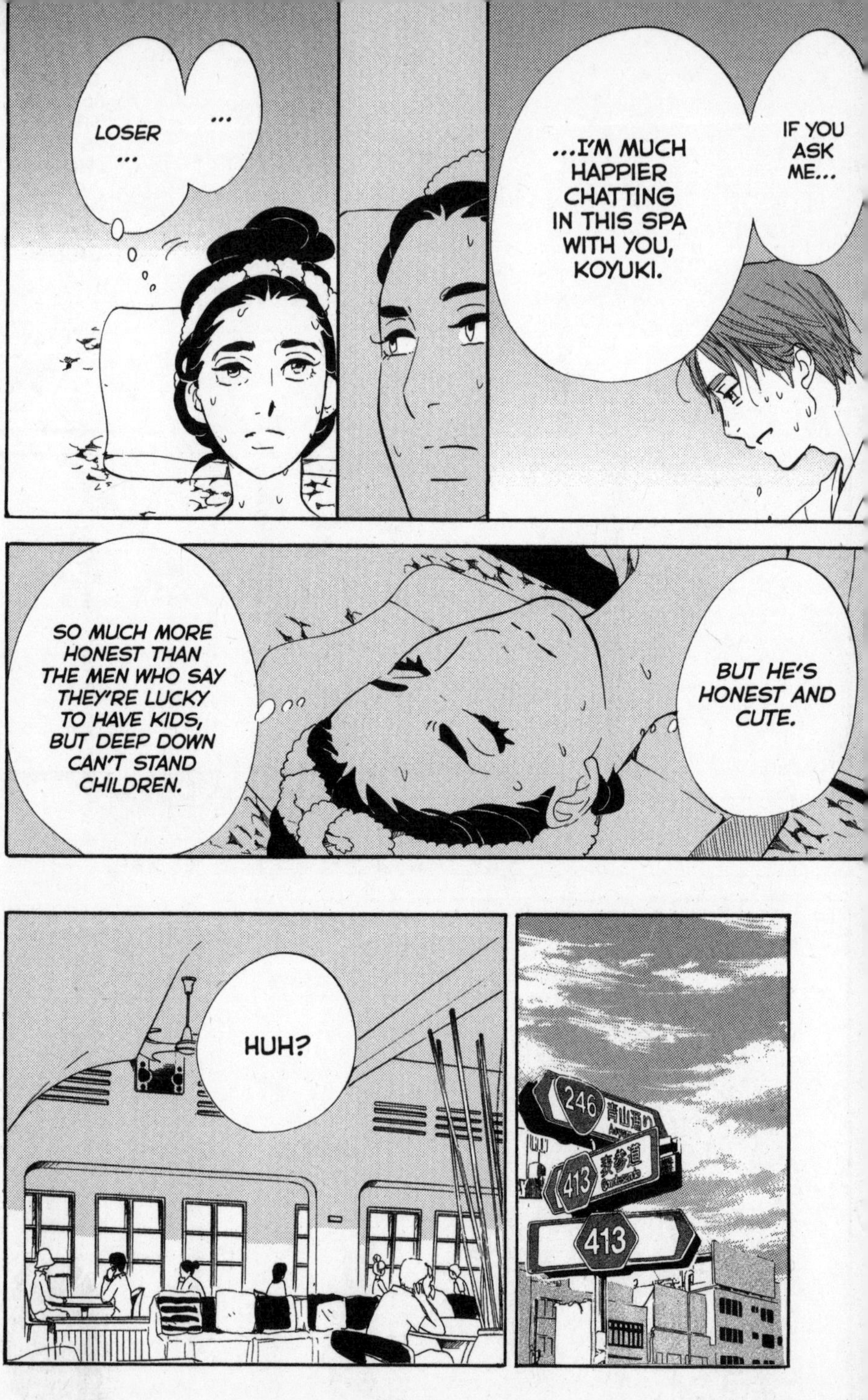
IF YOU ASK ME...
...I'M MUCH HAPPIER CHATTING IN THIS SPA WITH YOU, KOYUKI.
...
LOSER ...
BUT HE'S HONEST AND CUTE.
SO MUCH MORE HONEST THAN THE MEN WHO SAY THEY'RE LUCKY TO HAVE KIDS, BUT DEEP DOWN CAN'T STAND CHILDREN.
246
青山通り
413
表参道
413
HUH?

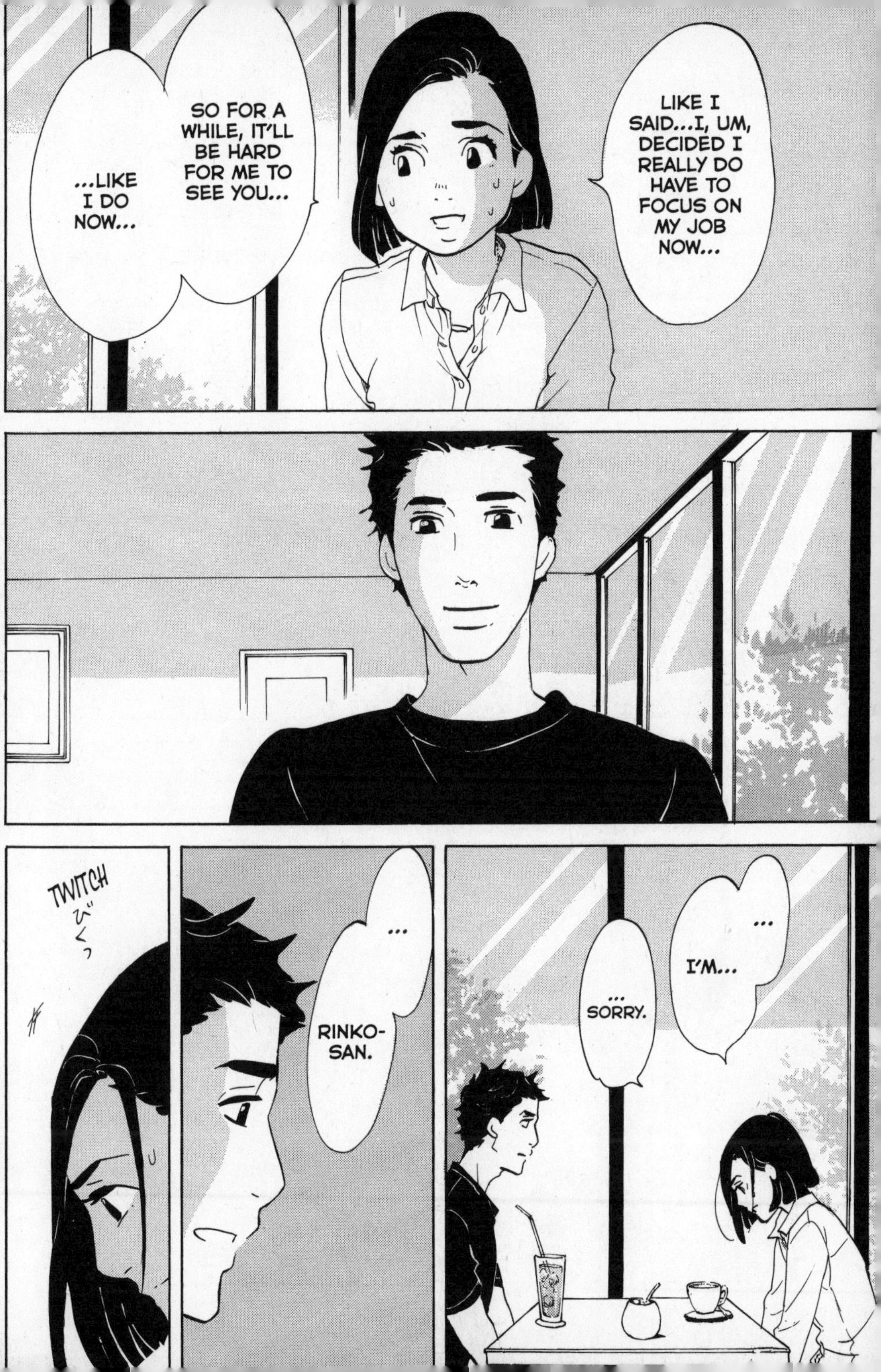
LIKE I SAID...I, UM, DECIDED I REALLY DO HAVE TO FOCUS ON MY JOB NOW...
SO FOR A WHILE, IT'LL BE HARD FOR ME TO SEE YOU...
...LIKE I DO NOW...
... I'M...
... SORRY.
... RINKO-SAN.
TWITCH
びくっ

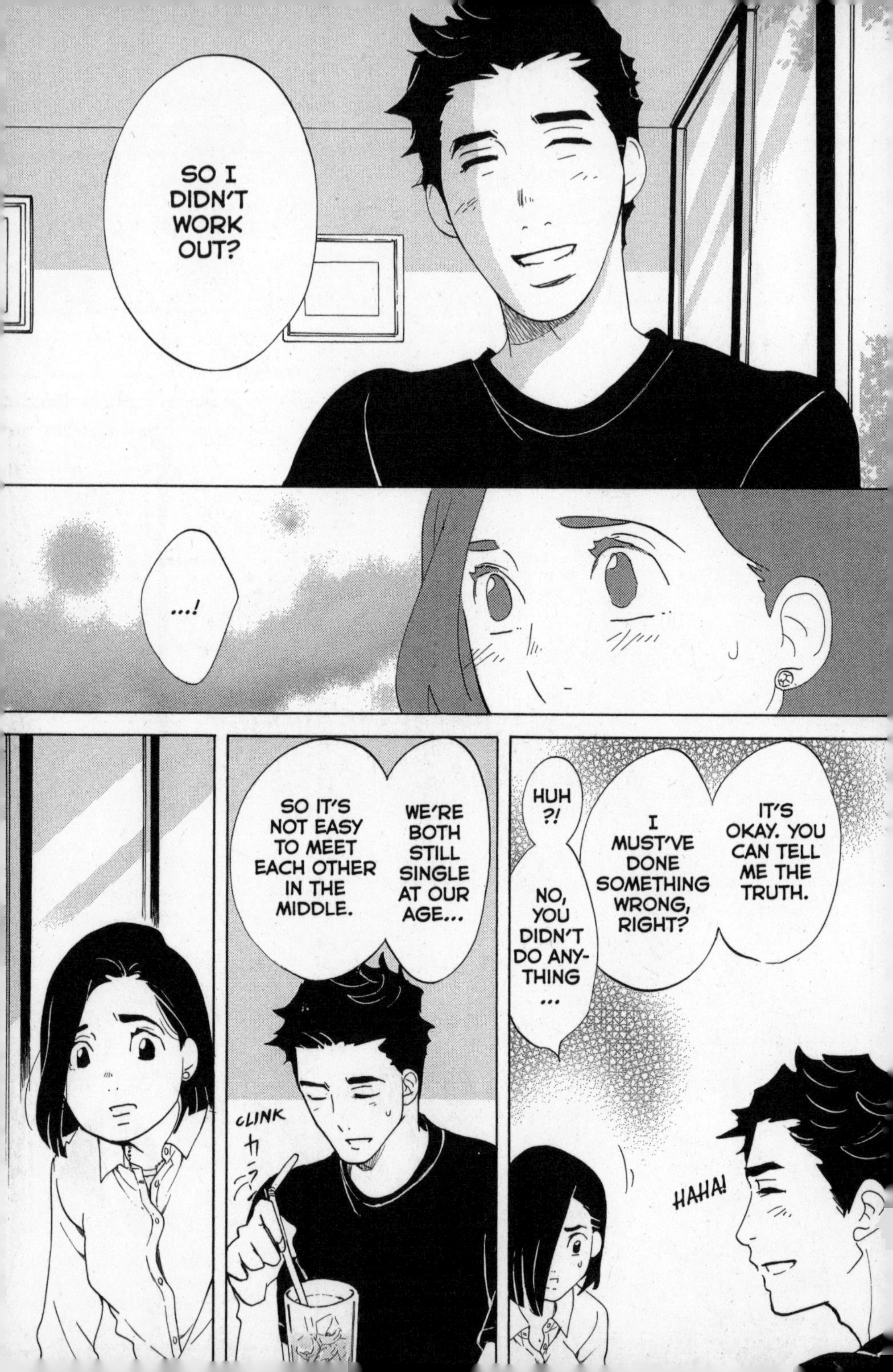
SO I DIDN'T WORK OUT?
...!
IT'S OKAY. YOU CAN TELL ME THE TRUTH.
I MUST'VE DONE SOMETHING WRONG, RIGHT?
HUH ?!
NO, YOU DIDN'T DO ANY-THING ...
HAHA!
WE'RE BOTH STILL SINGLE AT OUR AGE...
SO IT'S NOT EASY TO MEET EACH OTHER IN THE MIDDLE.
CLINK
カラ

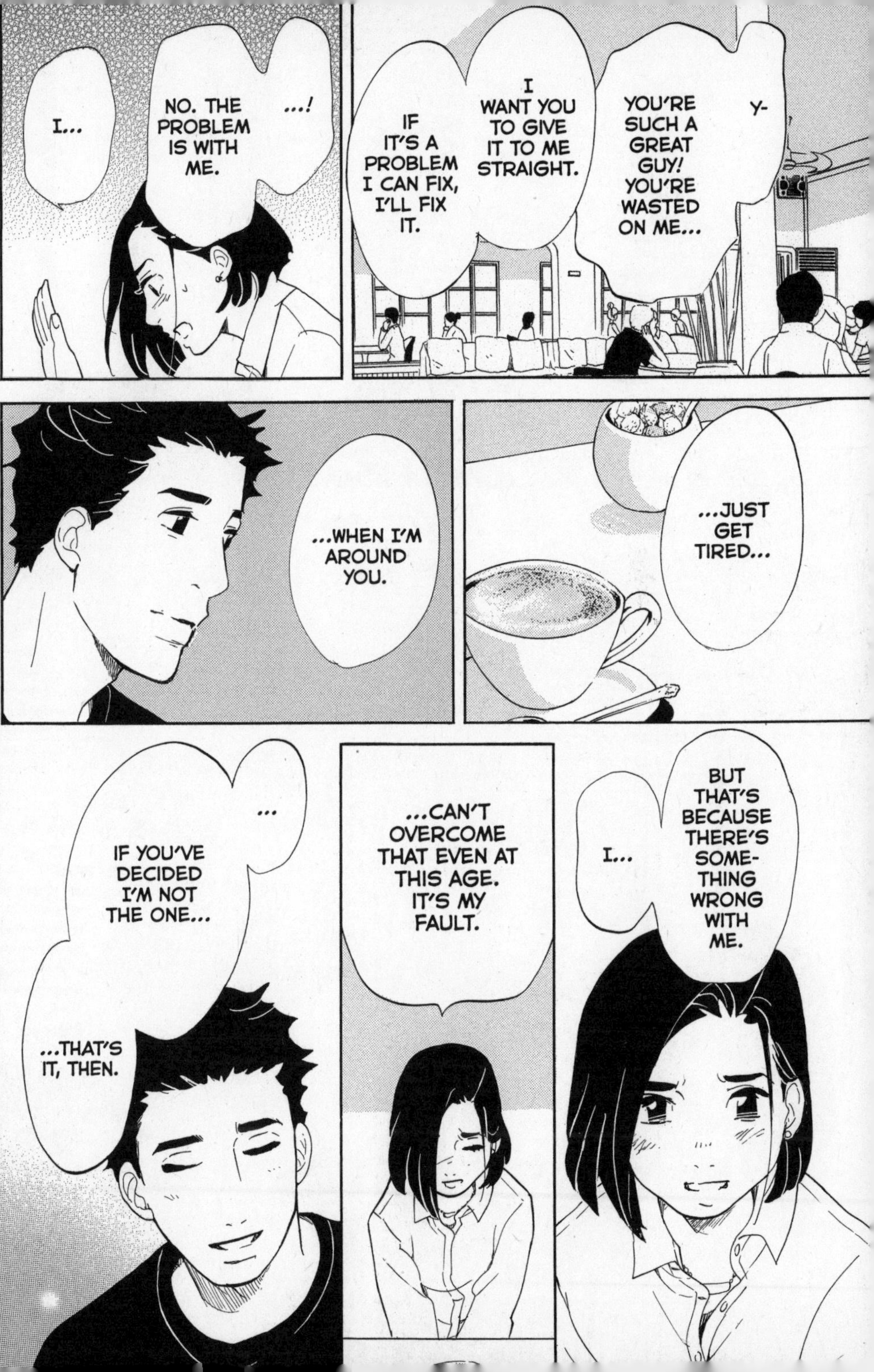
Y-
YOU'RE SUCH A GREAT GUY! YOU'RE WASTED ON ME...
I WANT YOU TO GIVE IT TO ME STRAIGHT.
IF IT'S A PROBLEM I CAN FIX, I'LL FIX IT.
...!
NO. THE PROBLEM IS WITH ME.
I...
...JUST GET TIRED...
...WHEN I'M AROUND YOU.
BUT THAT'S BECAUSE THERE'S SOME-THING WRONG WITH ME.
I...
...CAN'T OVERCOME THAT EVEN AT THIS AGE. IT'S MY FAULT.
...
IF YOU'VE DECIDED I'M NOT THE ONE...
...THAT'S IT, THEN.

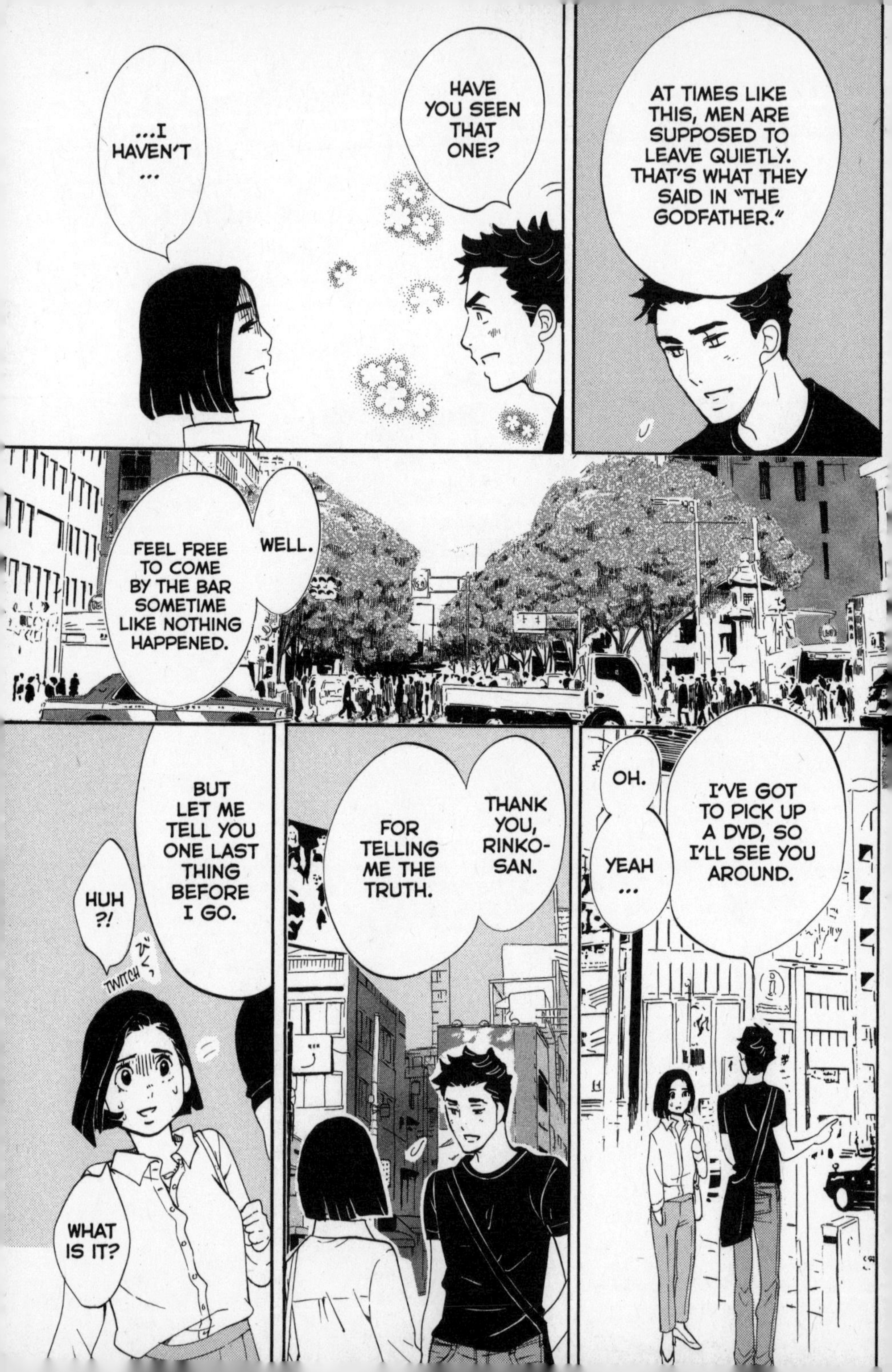
AT TIMES LIKE THIS, MEN ARE SUPPOSED TO LEAVE QUIETLY. THAT'S WHAT THEY SAID IN "THE GODFATHER."
HAVE YOU SEEN THAT ONE?
...I HAVEN'T ...
WELL.
FEEL FREE TO COME BY THE BAR SOMETIME LIKE NOTHING HAPPENED.
I'VE GOT TO PICK UP A DVD, SO I'LL SEE YOU AROUND.
OH.
YEAH ...
THANK YOU, RINKO-SAN.
FOR TELLING ME THE TRUTH.
BUT LET ME TELL YOU ONE LAST THING BEFORE I GO.
HUH ?!
TWITCH
WHAT IS IT?

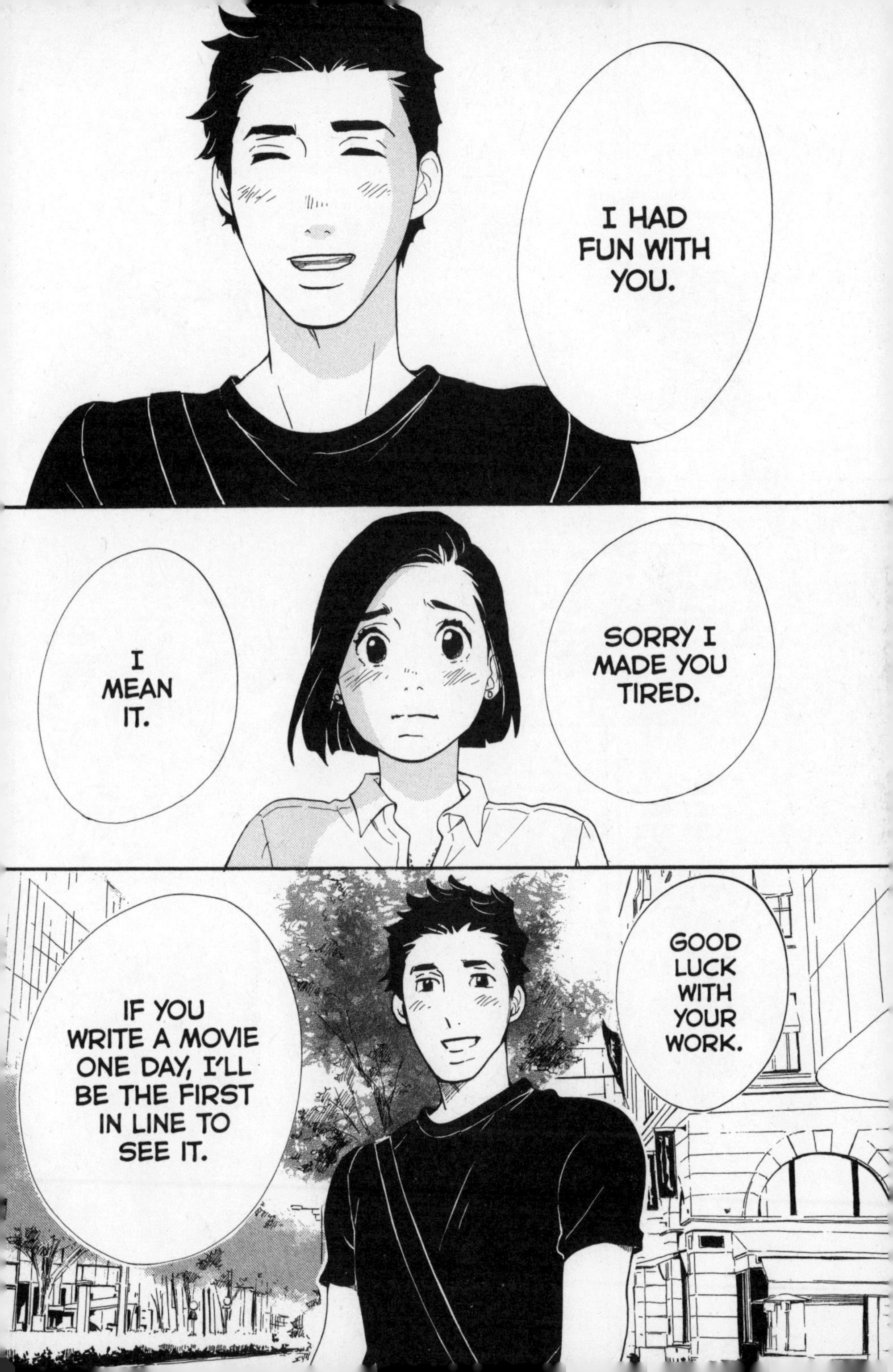
I HAD FUN WITH YOU.
SORRY I MADE YOU TIRED.
I MEAN IT.
GOOD LUCK WITH YOUR WORK.
IF YOU WRITE A MOVIE ONE DAY, I'LL BE THE FIRST IN LINE TO SEE IT.

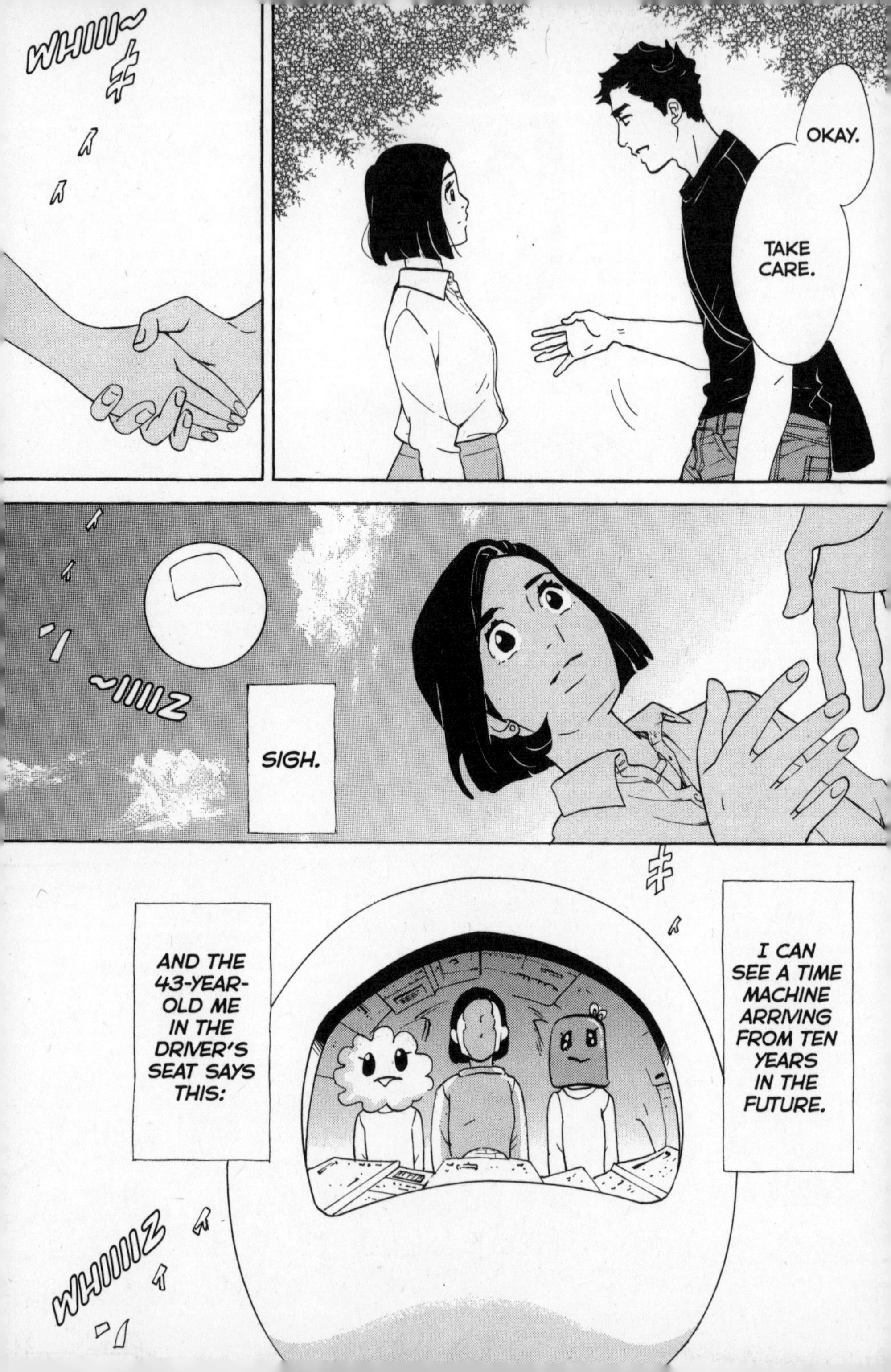
OKAY.
TAKE CARE.
WHIIII~
SIGH.
~IIIIZ
I CAN SEE A TIME MACHINE ARRIVING FROM TEN YEARS IN THE FUTURE.
AND THE 43-YEAR-OLD ME IN THE DRIVER'S SEAT SAYS THIS:
WHIIIIZ

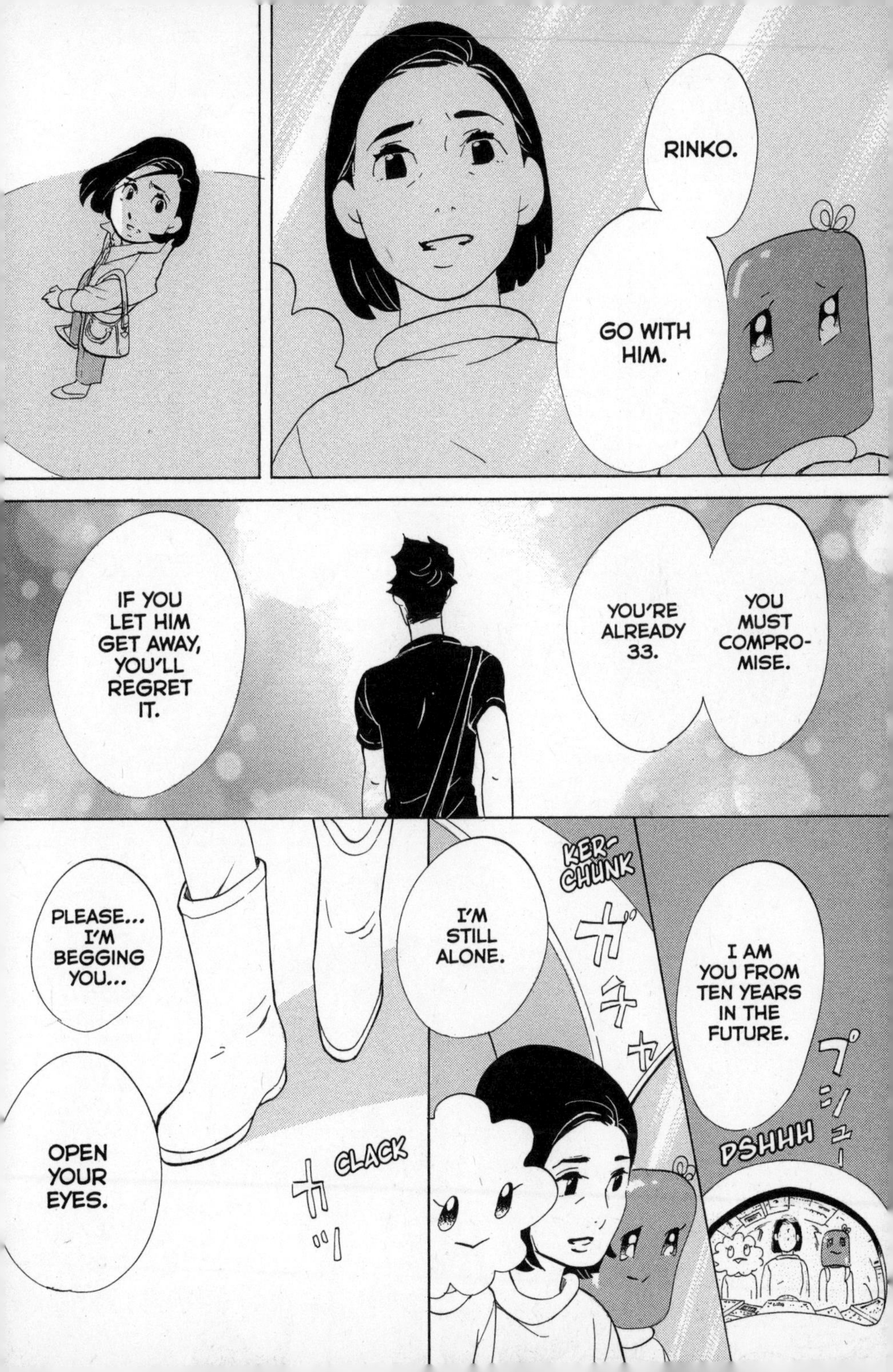
RINKO.
GO WITH HIM.
YOU MUST COMPROMISE.
YOU'RE ALREADY 33.
IF YOU LET HIM GET AWAY, YOU'LL REGRET IT.
KER-CHUNK
ガチャ
I AM YOU FROM TEN YEARS IN THE FUTURE.
プシューー
PSHHH
I'M STILL ALONE.
CLACK
カッ
PLEASE... I'M BEGGING YOU...
OPEN YOUR EYES.

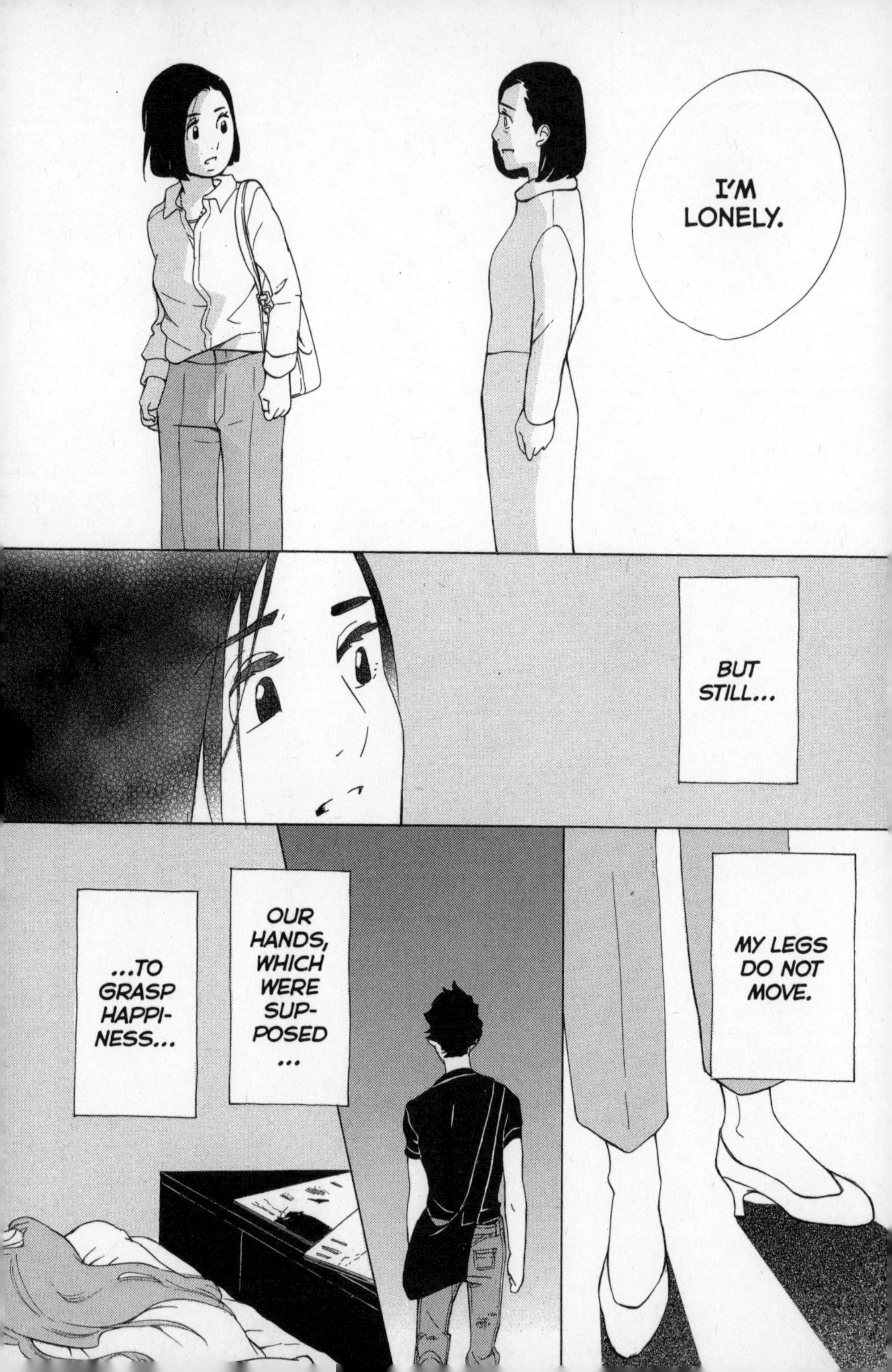
I'M LONELY.
BUT STILL...
MY LEGS DO NOT MOVE.
OUR HANDS, WHICH WERE SUP-POSED...
...TO GRASP HAPPI-NESS...

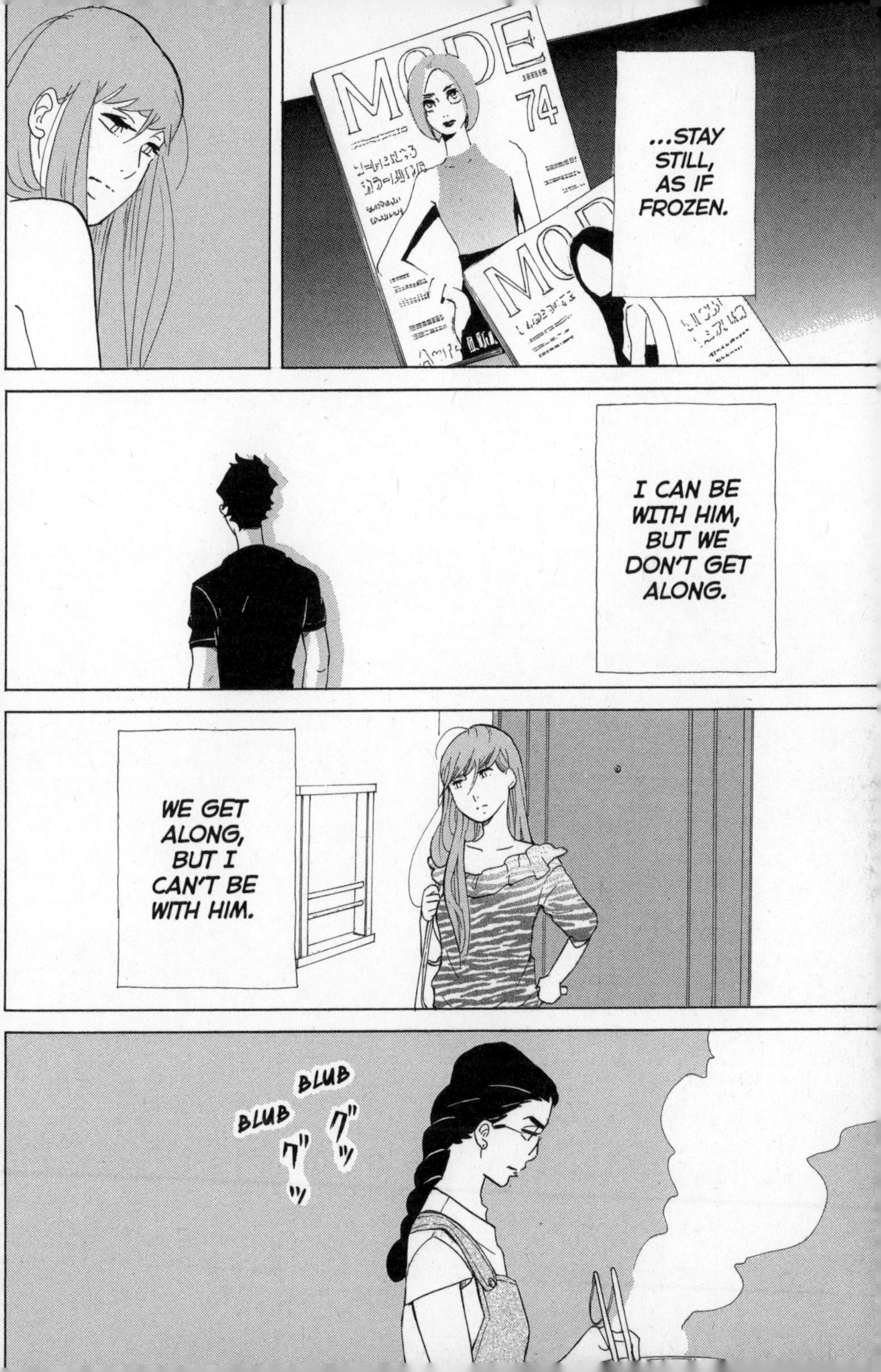
...STAY STILL, AS IF FROZEN.
MODE
74
MODE
I CAN BE WITH HIM, BUT WE DON'T GET ALONG.
WE GET ALONG, BUT I CAN'T BE WITH HIM.
BLUB
グツ
BLUB
グツ

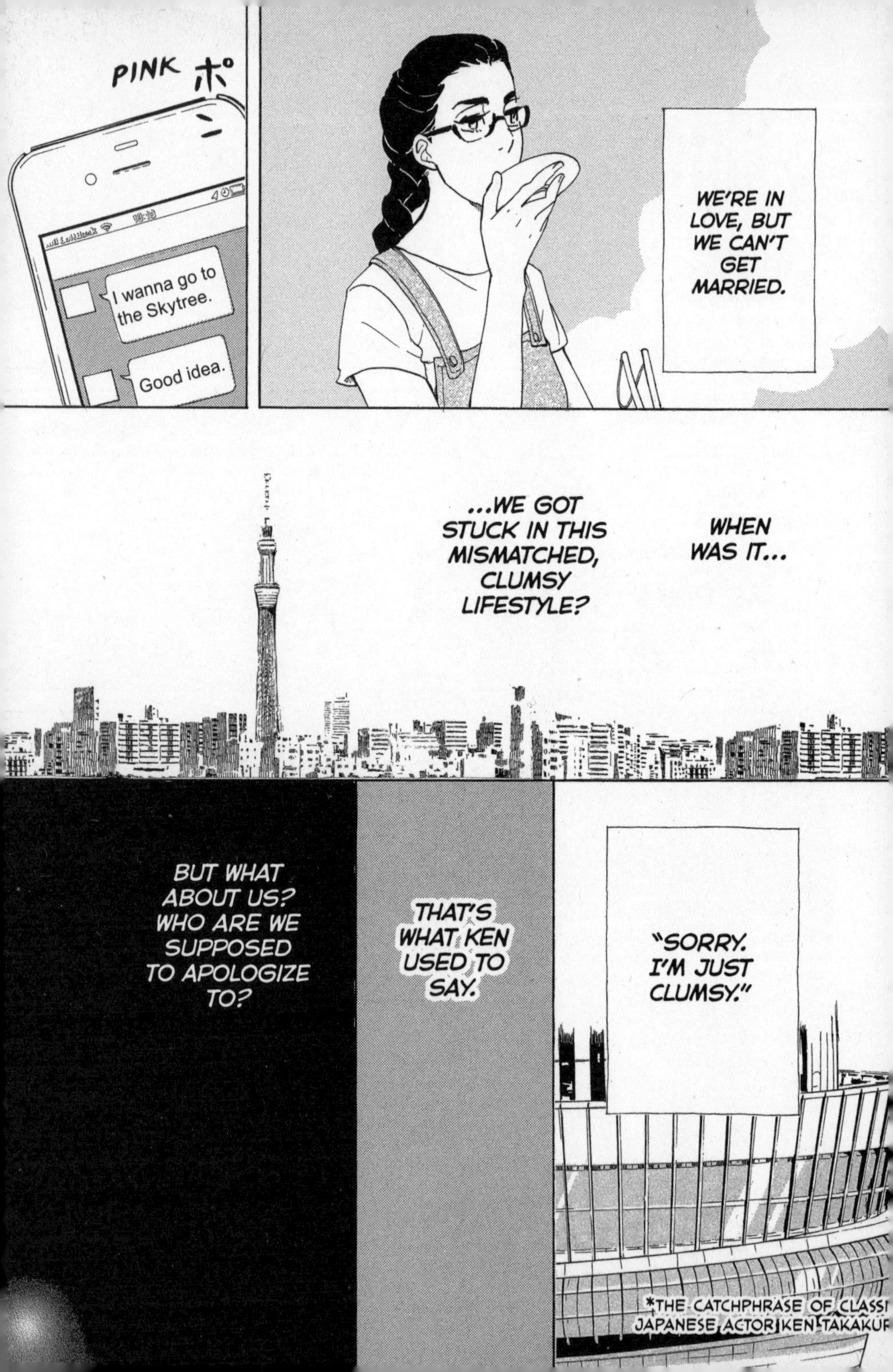
WE'RE IN LOVE, BUT WE CAN'T GET MARRIED.
PINK ポ
I wanna go to the Skytree.
Good idea.
WHEN WAS IT...
...WE GOT STUCK IN THIS MISMATCHED, CLUMSY LIFESTYLE?
"SORRY. I'M JUST CLUMSY."
*THE CATCHPHRASE OF CLASSI
JAPANESE ACTOR KEN TAKAKUR
THAT'S WHAT KEN USED TO SAY.
BUT WHAT ABOUT US? WHO ARE WE SUPPOSED TO APOLOGIZE TO?

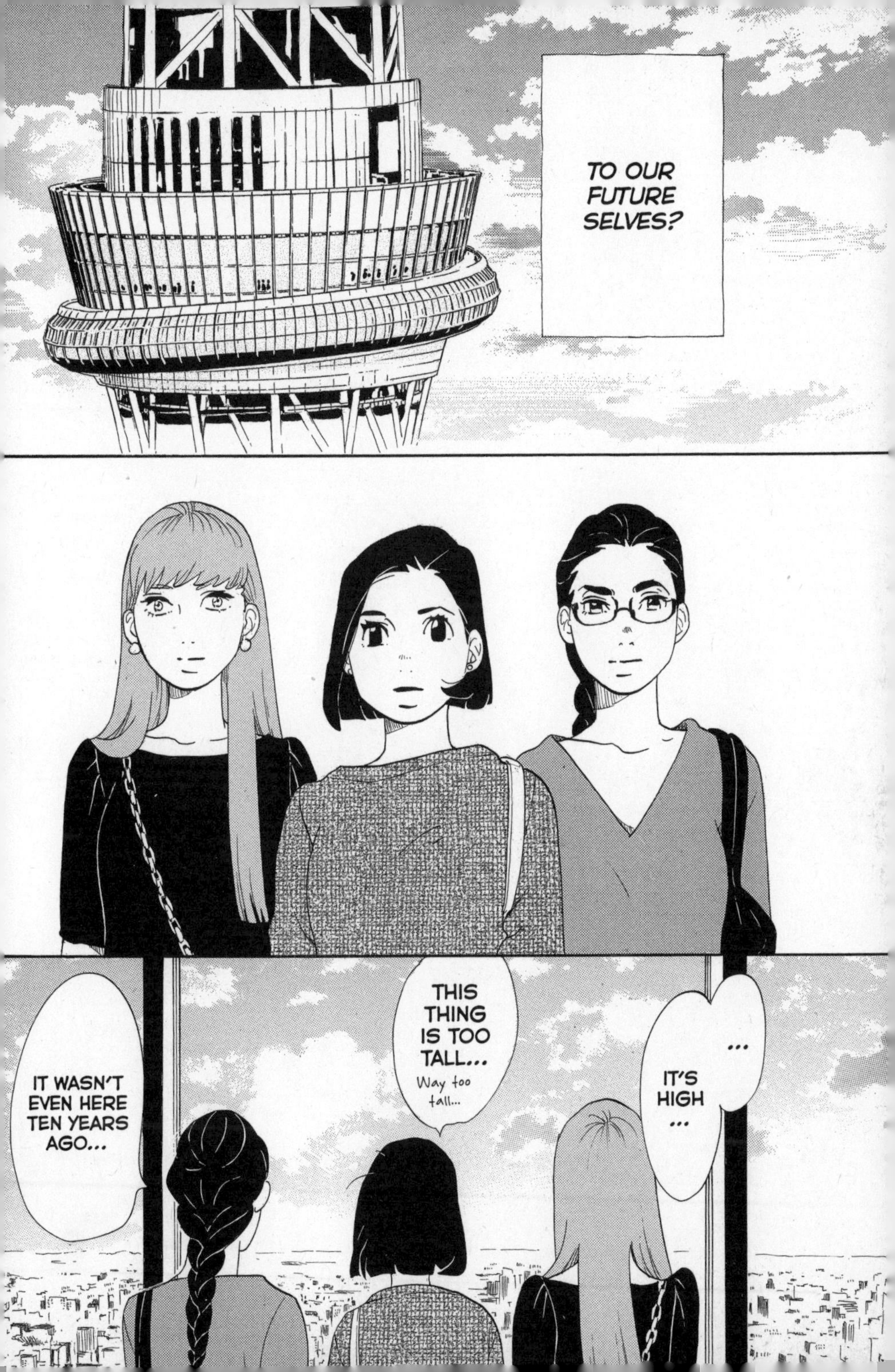
TO OUR FUTURE SELVES?
...
IT'S HIGH ...
THIS THING IS TOO TALL...
Way too tall...
IT WASN'T EVEN HERE TEN YEARS AGO...

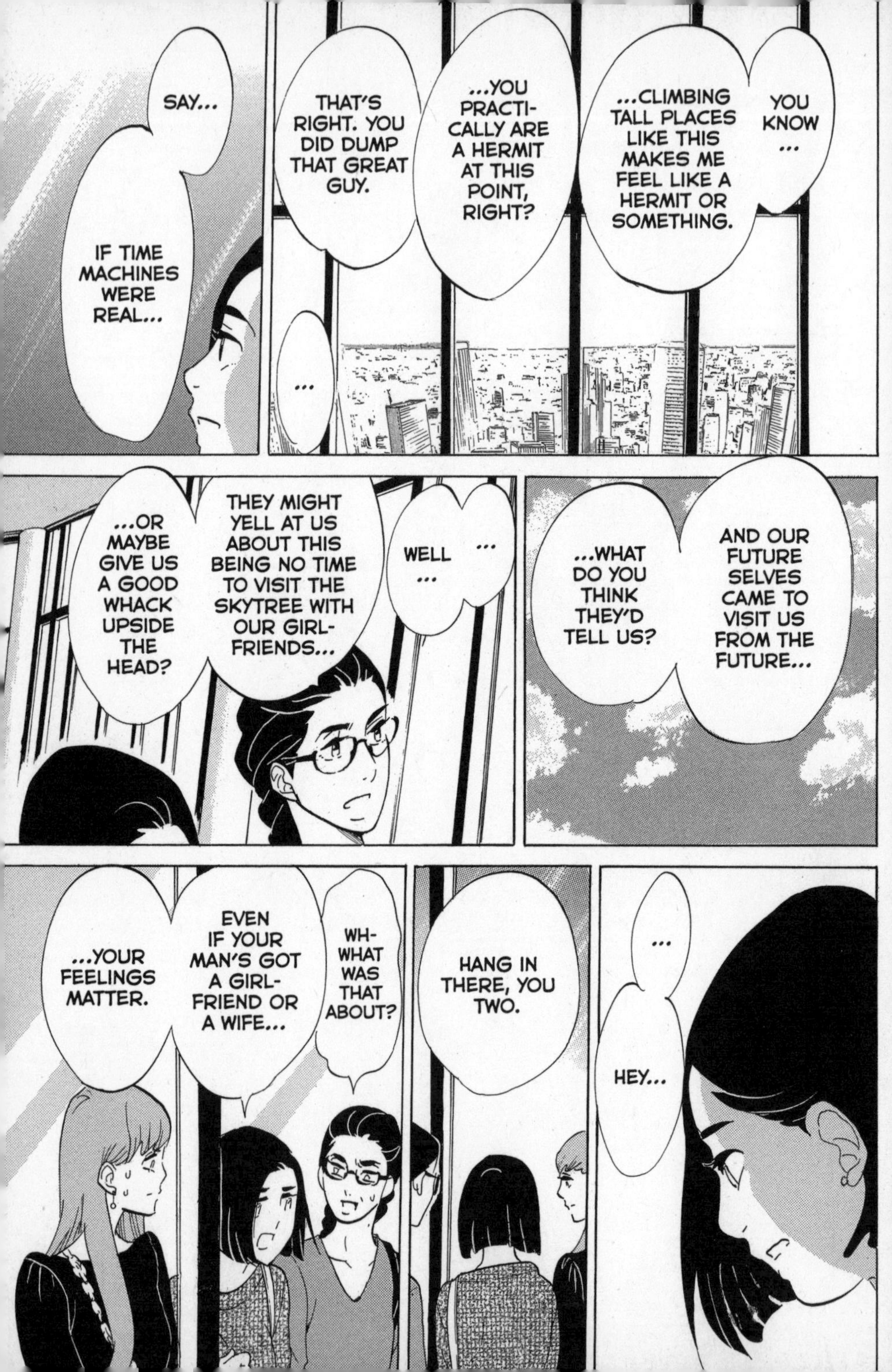
YOU KNOW...
...CLIMBING TALL PLACES LIKE THIS MAKES ME FEEL LIKE A HERMIT OR SOMETHING.
...YOU PRACTICALLY ARE A HERMIT AT THIS POINT, RIGHT?
THAT'S RIGHT. YOU DID DUMP THAT GREAT GUY.
...
SAY...
IF TIME MACHINES WERE REAL...
AND OUR FUTURE SELVES CAME TO VISIT US FROM THE FUTURE...
...WHAT DO YOU THINK THEY'D TELL US?
WELL... ...
THEY MIGHT YELL AT US ABOUT THIS BEING NO TIME TO VISIT THE SKYTREE WITH OUR GIRLFRIENDS...
...OR MAYBE GIVE US A GOOD WHACK UPSIDE THE HEAD?
...
HEY...
HANG IN THERE, YOU TWO.
WH-WHAT WAS THAT ABOUT?
EVEN IF YOUR MAN'S GOT A GIRLFRIEND OR A WIFE...
...YOUR FEELINGS MATTER.

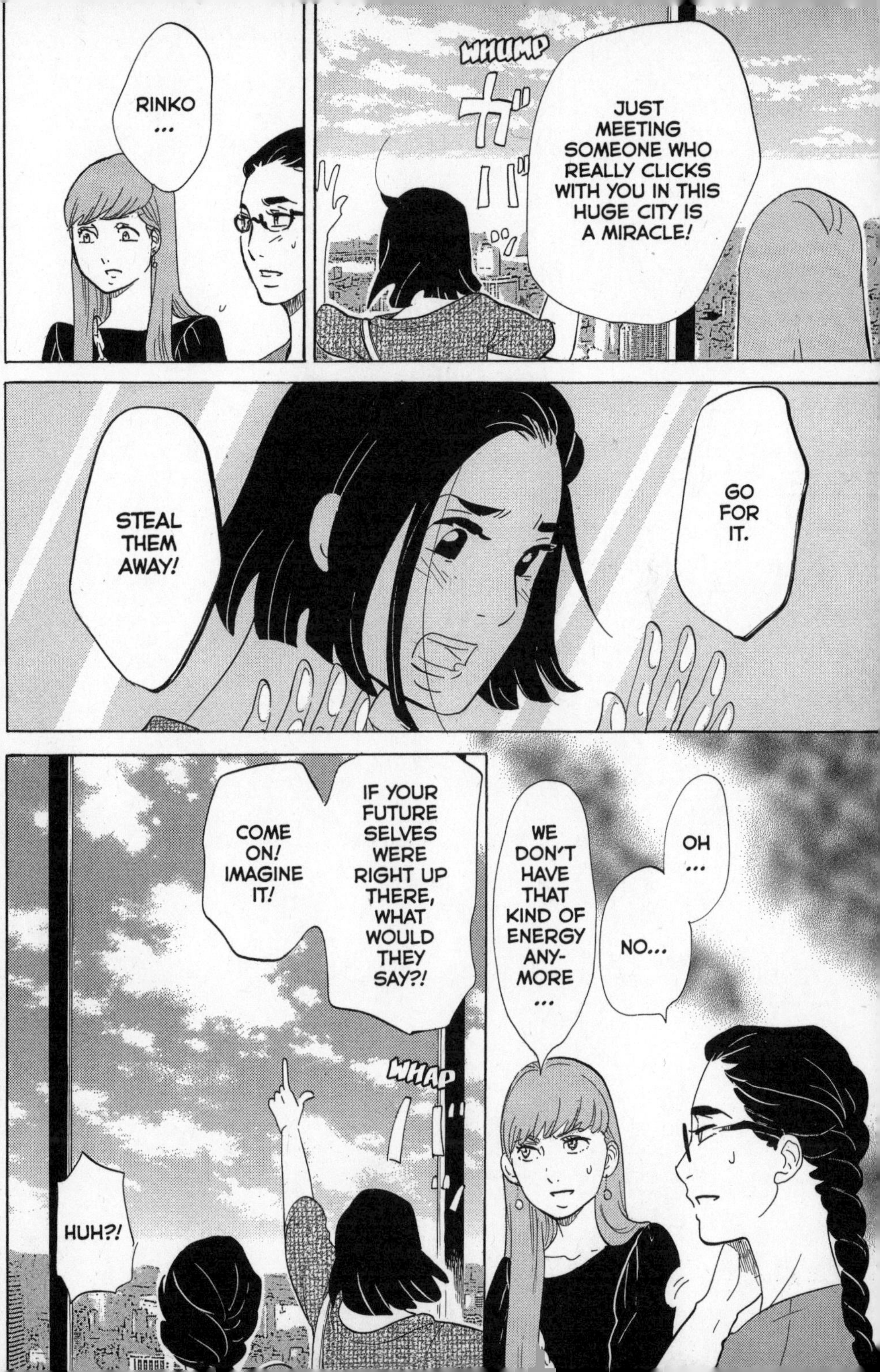
WHUMP
ガバ
JUST MEETING SOMEONE WHO REALLY CLICKS WITH YOU IN THIS HUGE CITY IS A MIRACLE!
RINKO ...
GO FOR IT.
STEAL THEM AWAY!
OH ...
NO...
WE DON'T HAVE THAT KIND OF ENERGY ANY-MORE ...
IF YOUR FUTURE SELVES WERE RIGHT UP THERE, WHAT WOULD THEY SAY?!
COME ON! IMAGINE IT!
WHAP
HUH?!

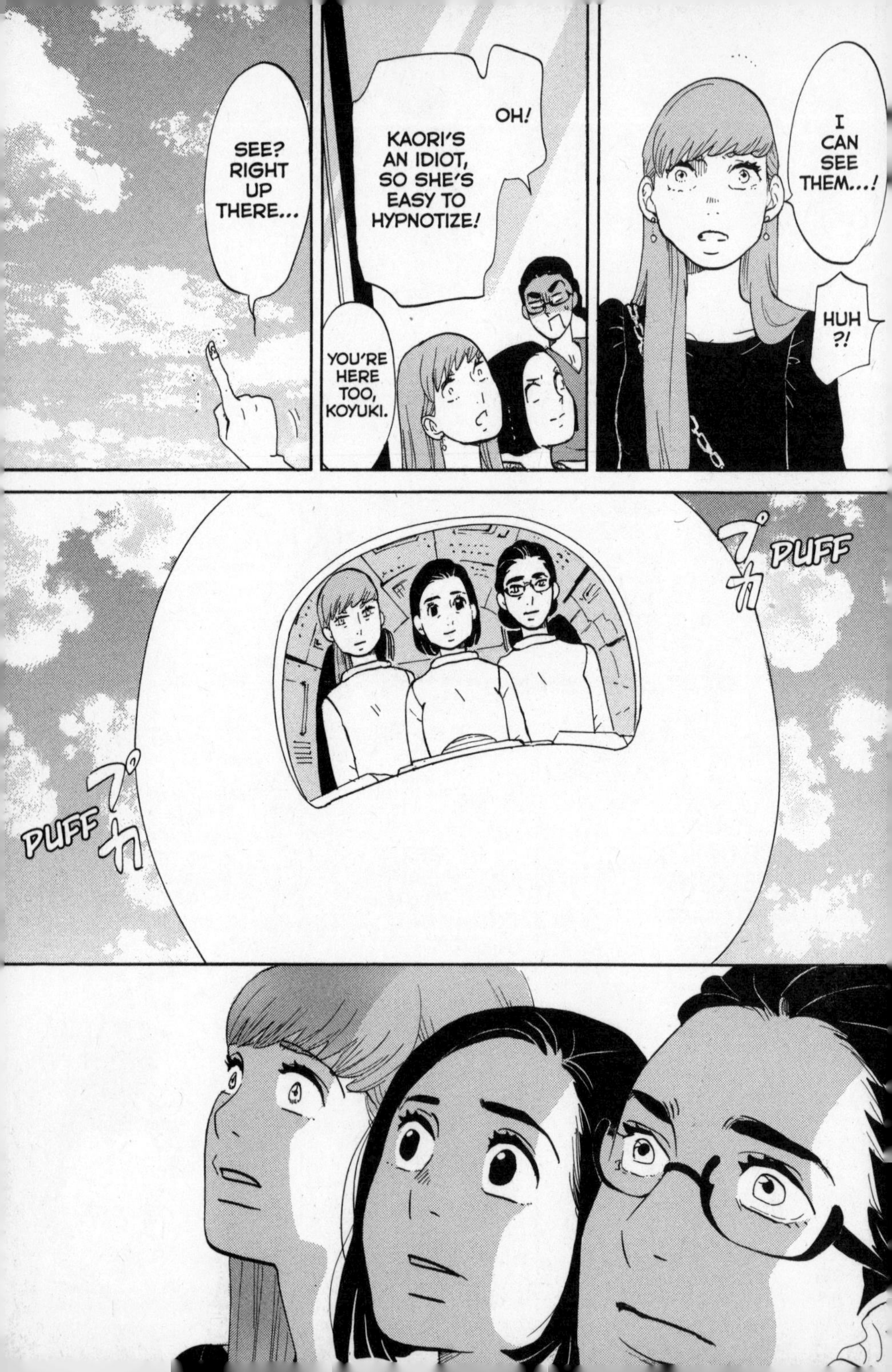
I CAN SEE THEM...!
HUH?!
OH!
KAORI'S AN IDIOT, SO SHE'S EASY TO HYPNOTIZE!
YOU'RE HERE TOO, KOYUKI.
SEE? RIGHT UP THERE...
プカ
PUFF
プカ
PUFF

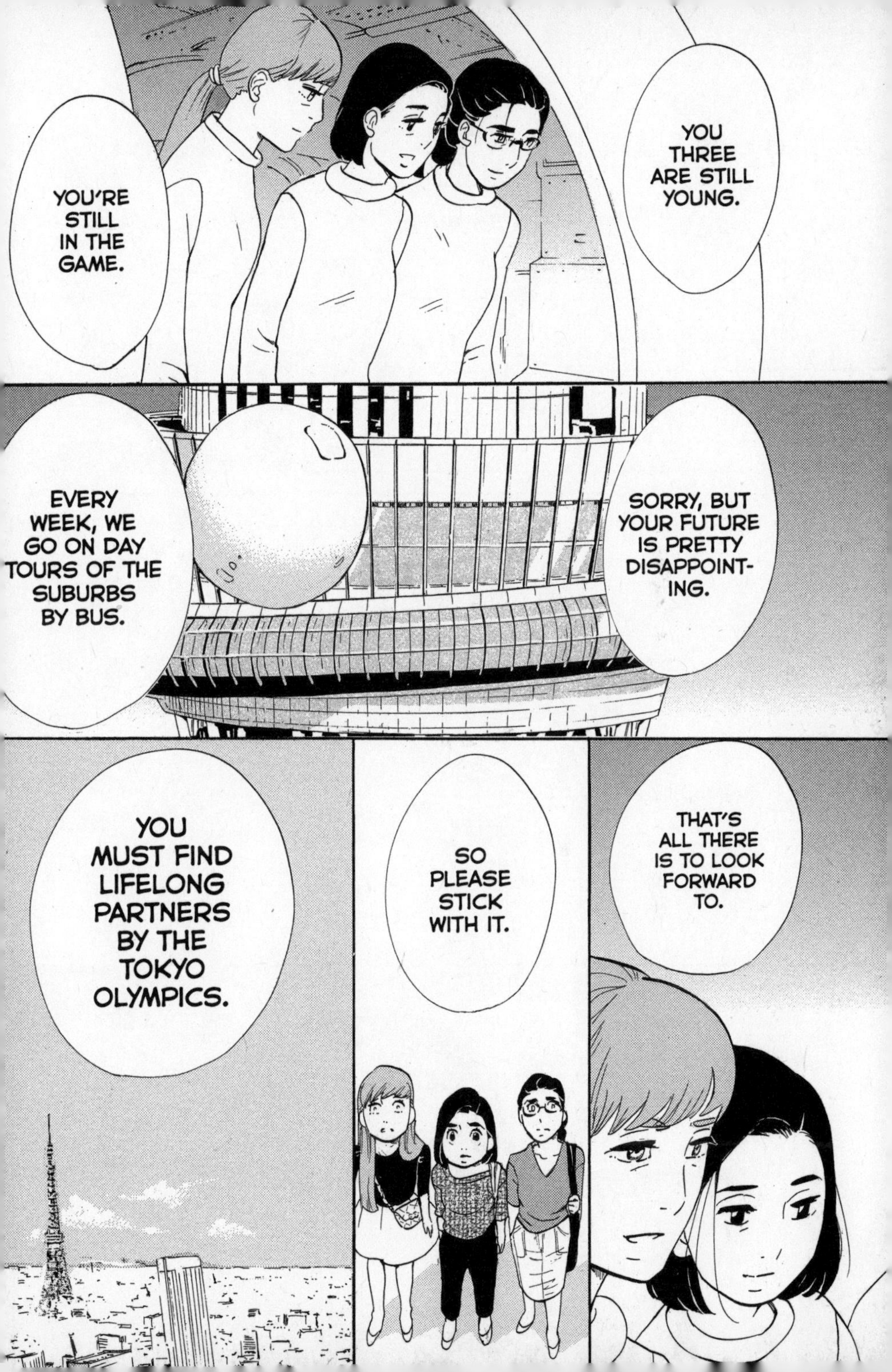
YOU THREE ARE STILL YOUNG.
YOU'RE STILL IN THE GAME.
SORRY, BUT YOUR FUTURE IS PRETTY DISAPPOINT-ING.
EVERY WEEK, WE GO ON DAY TOURS OF THE SUBURBS BY BUS.
THAT'S ALL THERE IS TO LOOK FORWARD TO.
SO PLEASE STICK WITH IT.
YOU MUST FIND LIFELONG PARTNERS BY THE TOKYO OLYMPICS.

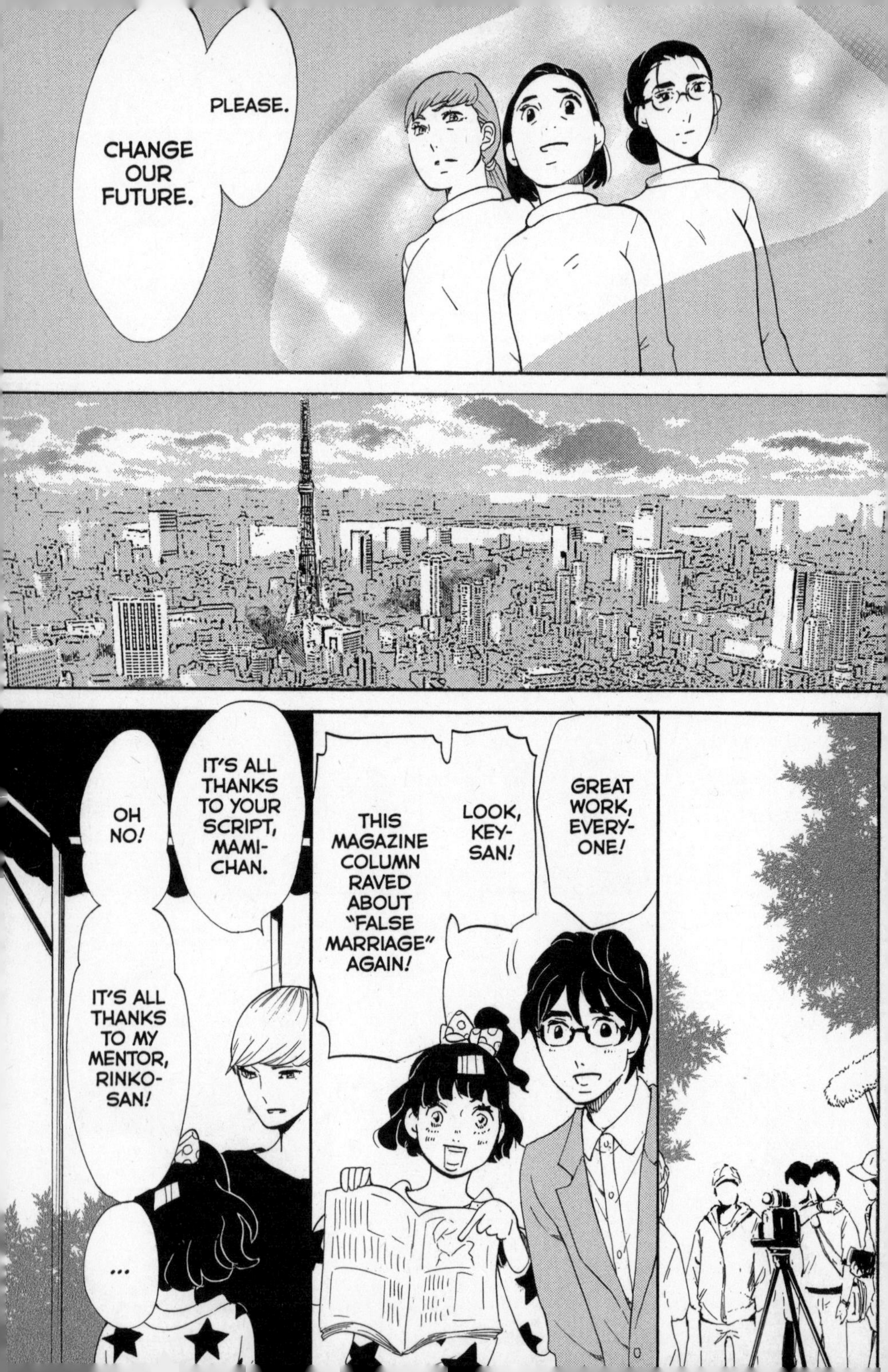
PLEASE.
CHANGE OUR FUTURE.
GREAT WORK, EVERYONE!
LOOK, KEY-SAN!
THIS MAGAZINE COLUMN RAVED ABOUT "FALSE MARRIAGE" AGAIN!
IT'S ALL THANKS TO YOUR SCRIPT, MAMI-CHAN.
OH NO!
IT'S ALL THANKS TO MY MENTOR, RINKO-SAN!
...

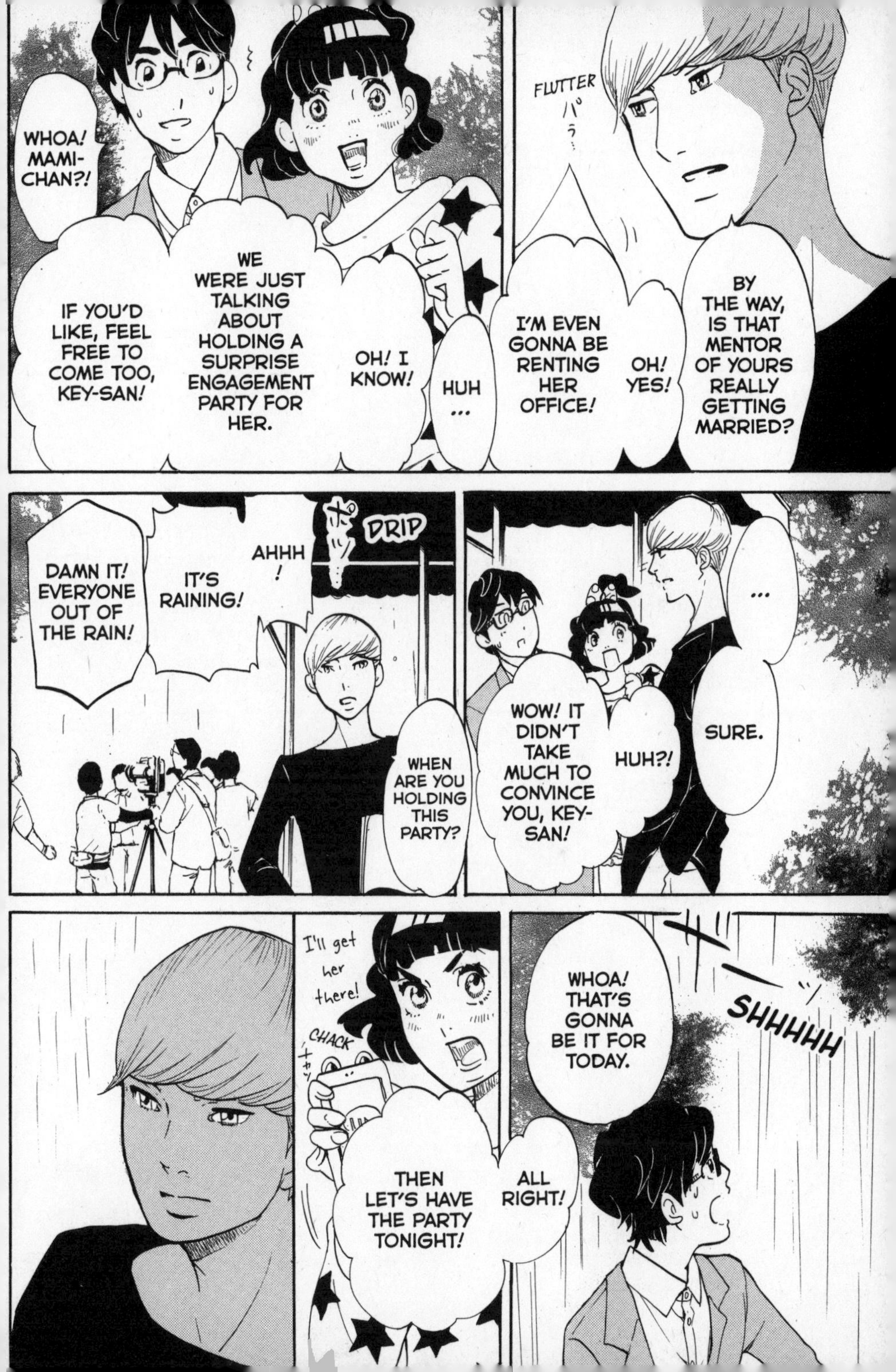
FLUTTER
BY THE WAY, IS THAT MENTOR OF YOURS REALLY GETTING MARRIED?
OH! YES!
I'M EVEN GONNA BE RENTING HER OFFICE!
HUH ...
OH! I KNOW!
WE WERE JUST TALKING ABOUT HOLDING A SURPRISE ENGAGEMENT PARTY FOR HER.
IF YOU'D LIKE, FEEL FREE TO COME TOO, KEY-SAN!
WHOA! MAMI-CHAN?!
...
SURE.
HUH?!
WOW! IT DIDN'T TAKE MUCH TO CONVINCE YOU, KEY-SAN!
DRIP
AHHH!
IT'S RAINING!
DAMN IT! EVERYONE OUT OF THE RAIN!
WHEN ARE YOU HOLDING THIS PARTY?
SHHHHH
WHOA! THAT'S GONNA BE IT FOR TODAY.
ALL RIGHT!
THEN LET'S HAVE THE PARTY TONIGHT!
I'll get her there!
CHACK

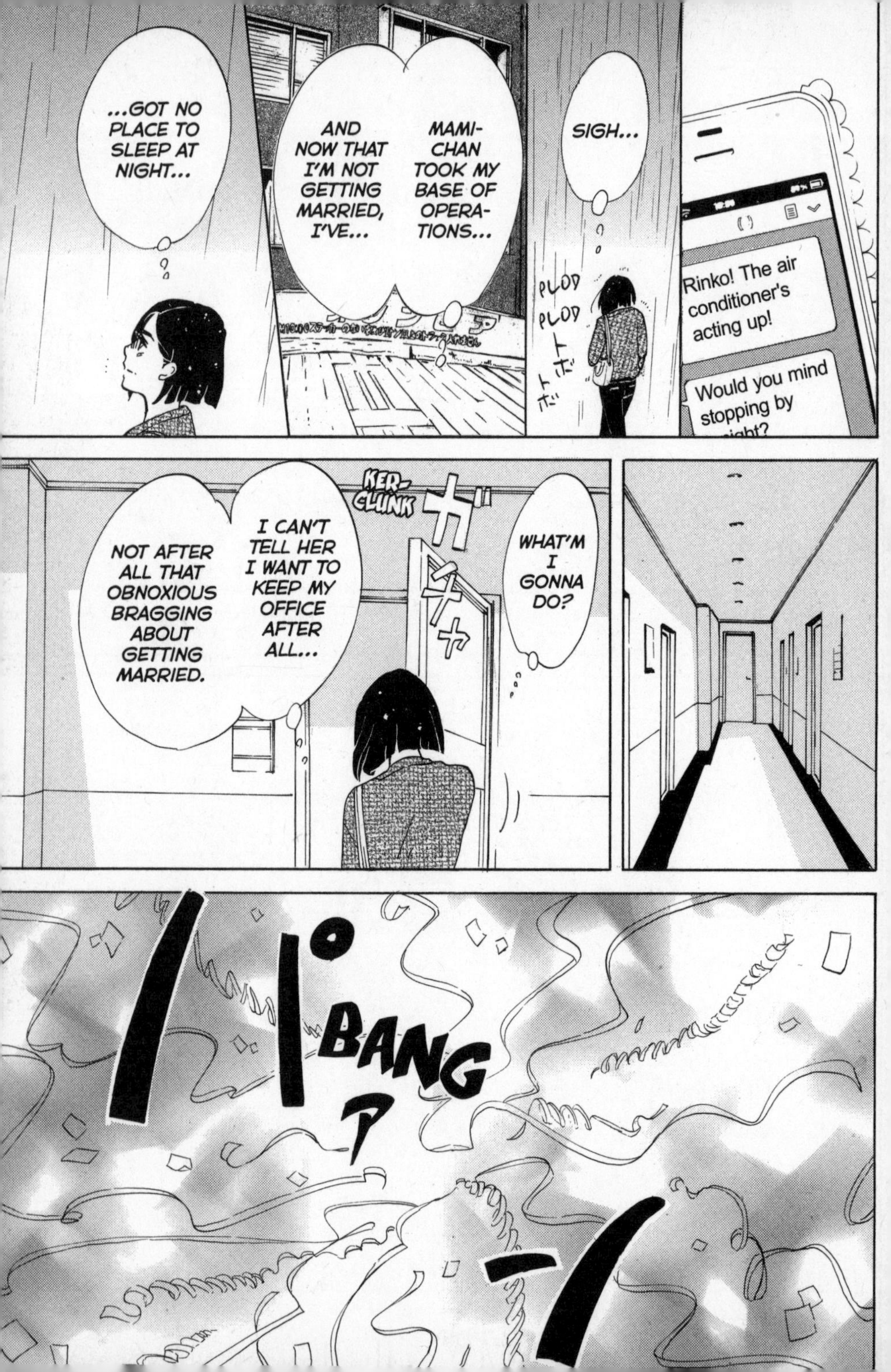
Rinko! The air conditioner's acting up!
Would you mind stopping by
SIGH...
PLOD PLOD
トボトボ
MAMI-CHAN TOOK MY BASE OF OPERA-TIONS...
AND NOW THAT I'M NOT GETTING MARRIED, I'VE...
...GOT NO PLACE TO SLEEP AT NIGHT...
WHAT'M I GONNA DO?
KER-CLUNK
ガチャ
I CAN'T TELL HER I WANT TO KEEP MY OFFICE AFTER ALL...
NOT AFTER ALL THAT OBNOXIOUS BRAGGING ABOUT GETTING MARRIED.
BANG
パーン

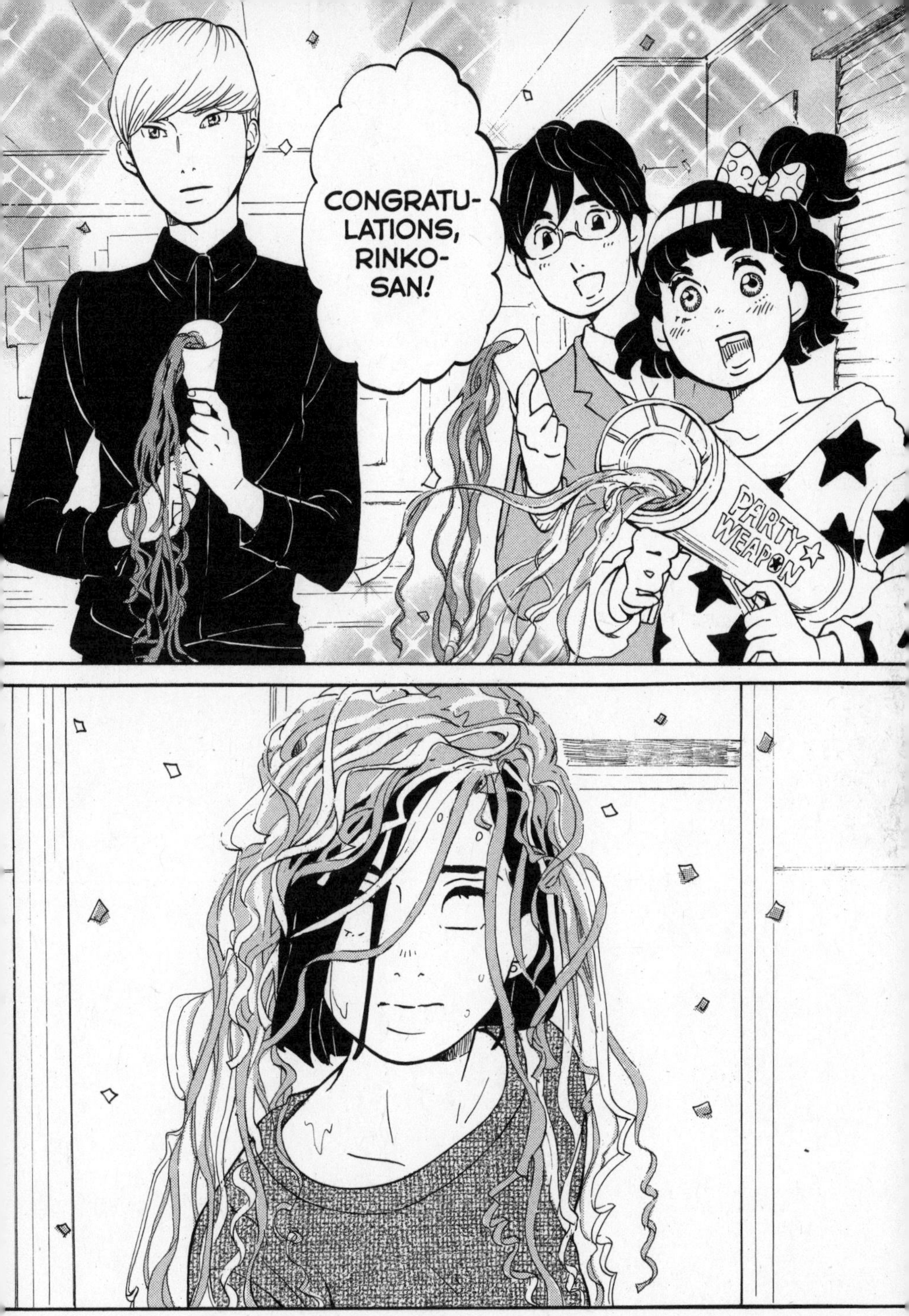
CONGRATU-LATIONS, RINKO-SAN!
PARTY☆WEAPON

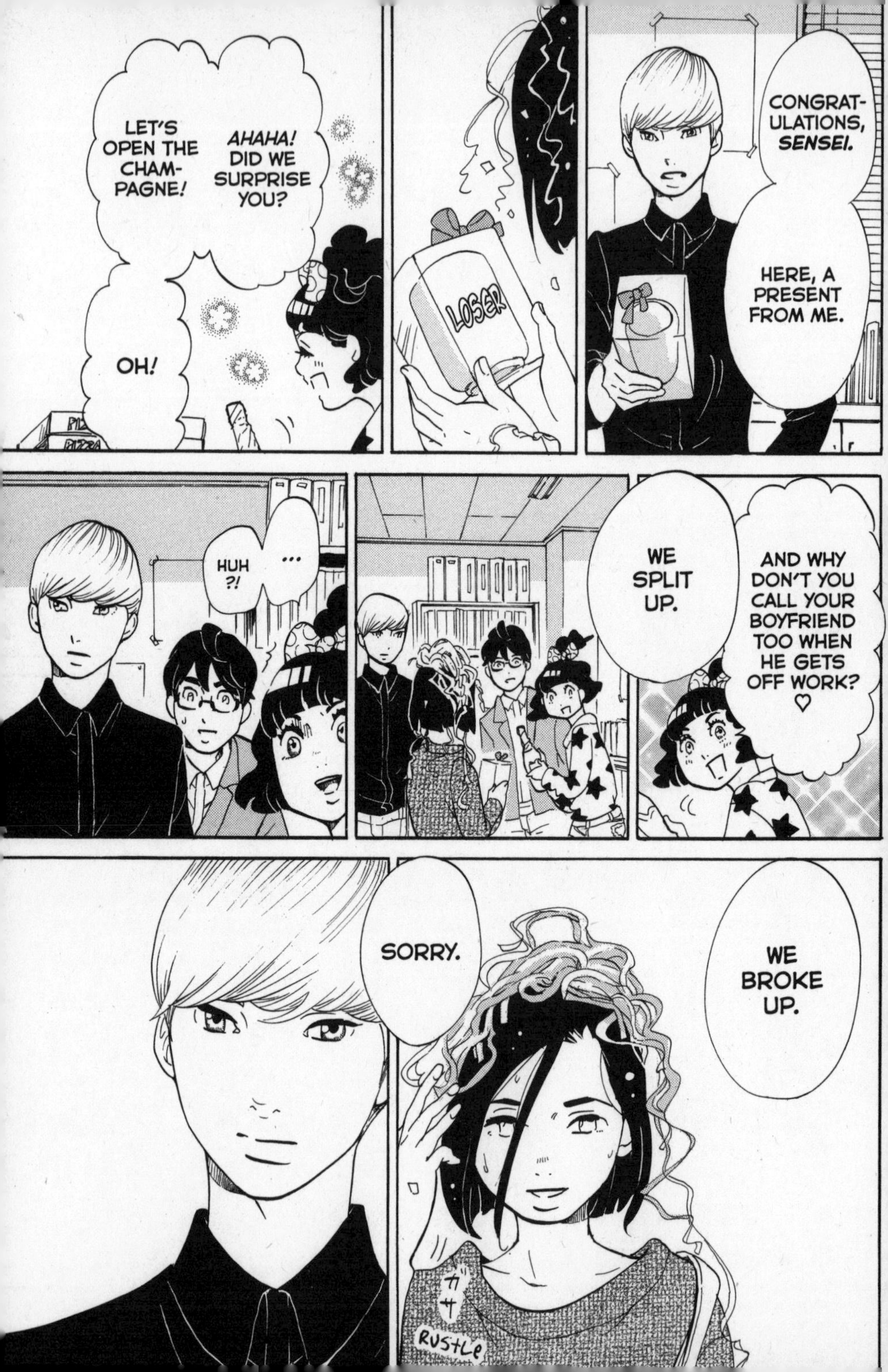
CONGRATULATIONS, *SENSEI.*
HERE, A PRESENT FROM ME.
LOSER
AHAHA! DID WE SURPRISE YOU?
LET'S OPEN THE CHAMPAGNE!
OH!
AND WHY DON'T YOU CALL YOUR BOYFRIEND TOO WHEN HE GETS OFF WORK? ♡
WE SPLIT UP.
...
HUH?!
WE BROKE UP.
SORRY.
ガサ
RUSTLE

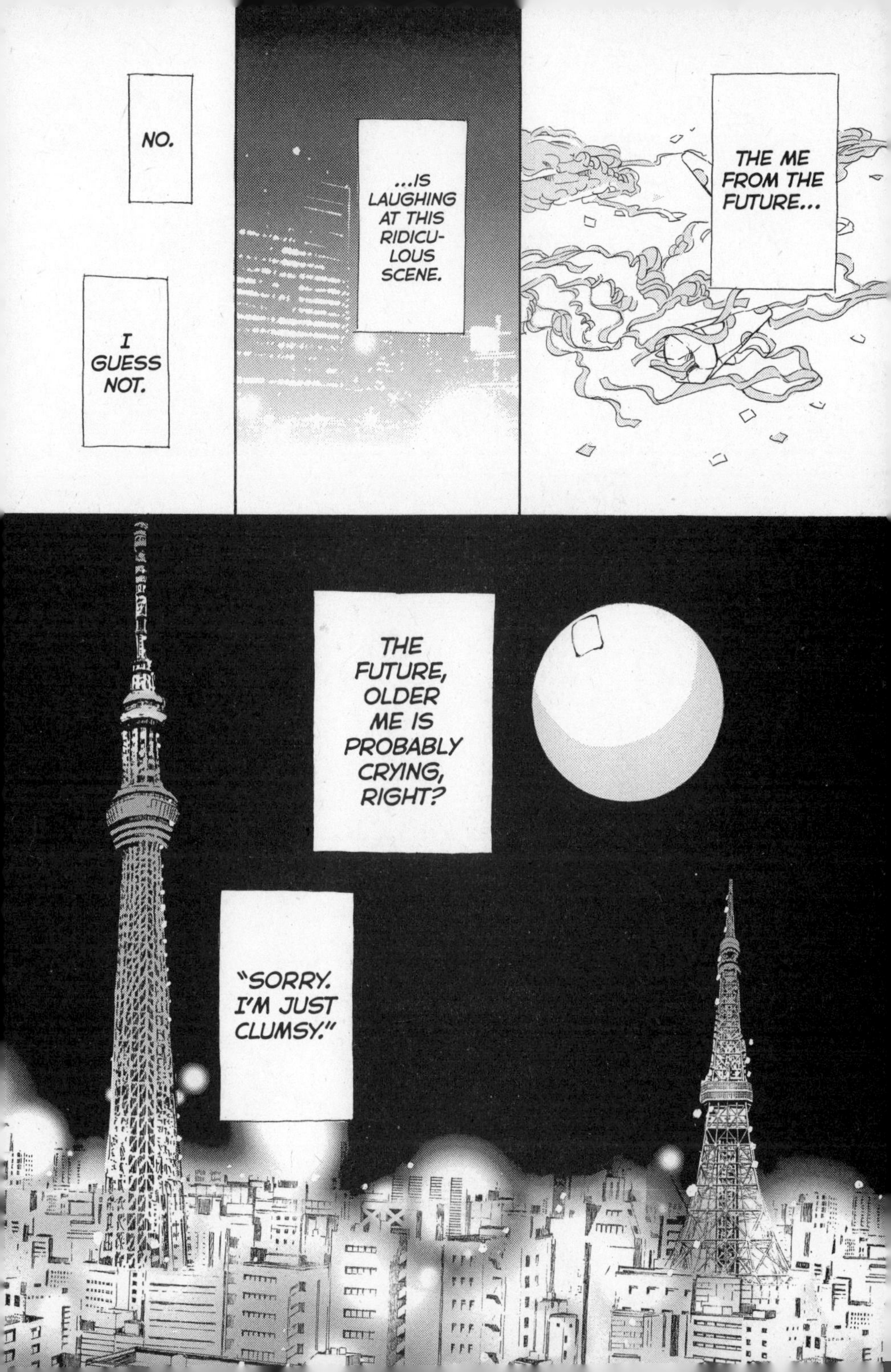
THE ME FROM THE FUTURE...
...IS LAUGHING AT THIS RIDICU-LOUS SCENE.
NO.
I GUESS NOT.
THE FUTURE, OLDER ME IS PROBABLY CRYING, RIGHT?
"SORRY. I'M JUST CLUMSY."

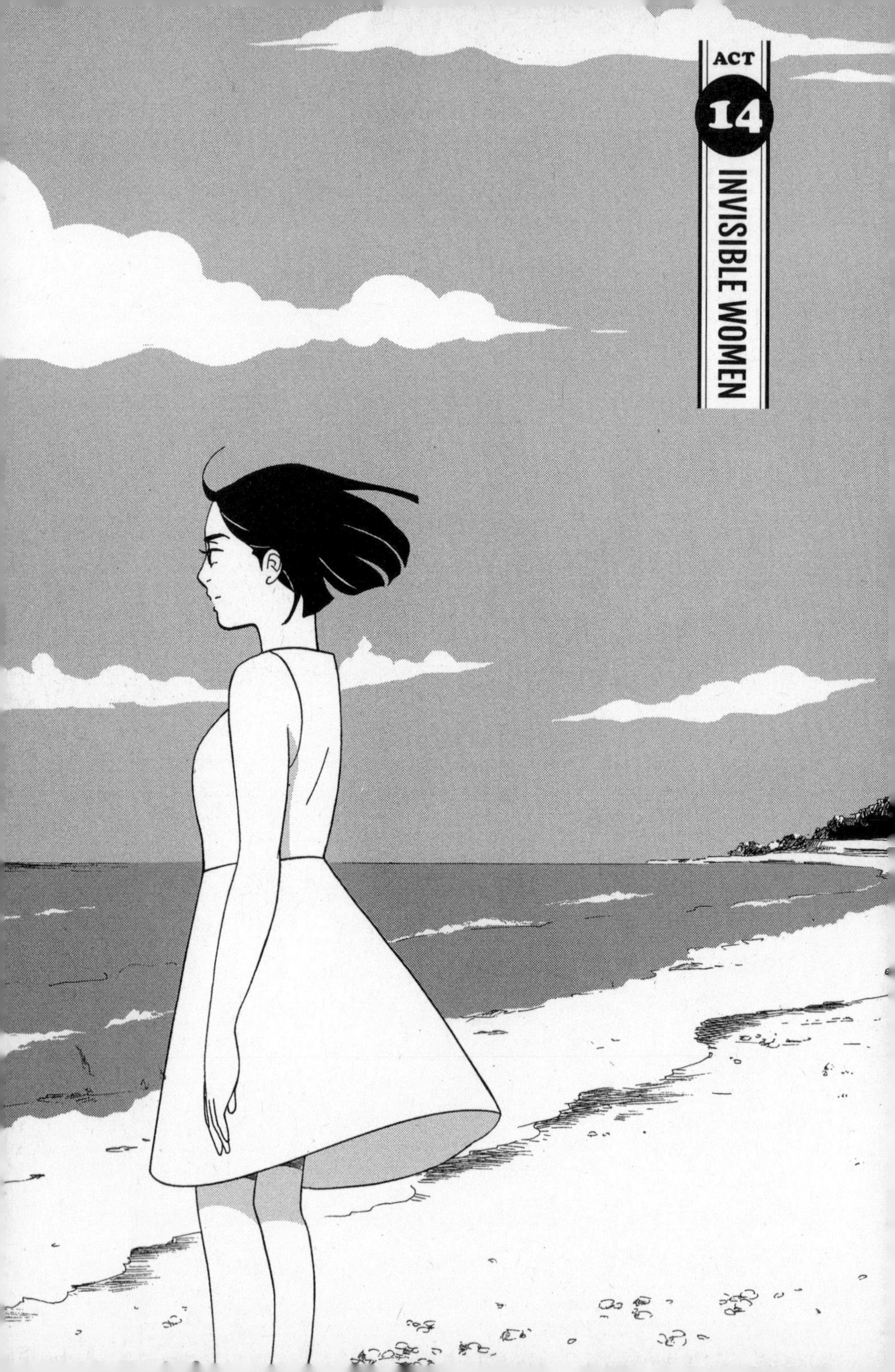
ACT
14
INVISIBLE WOMEN

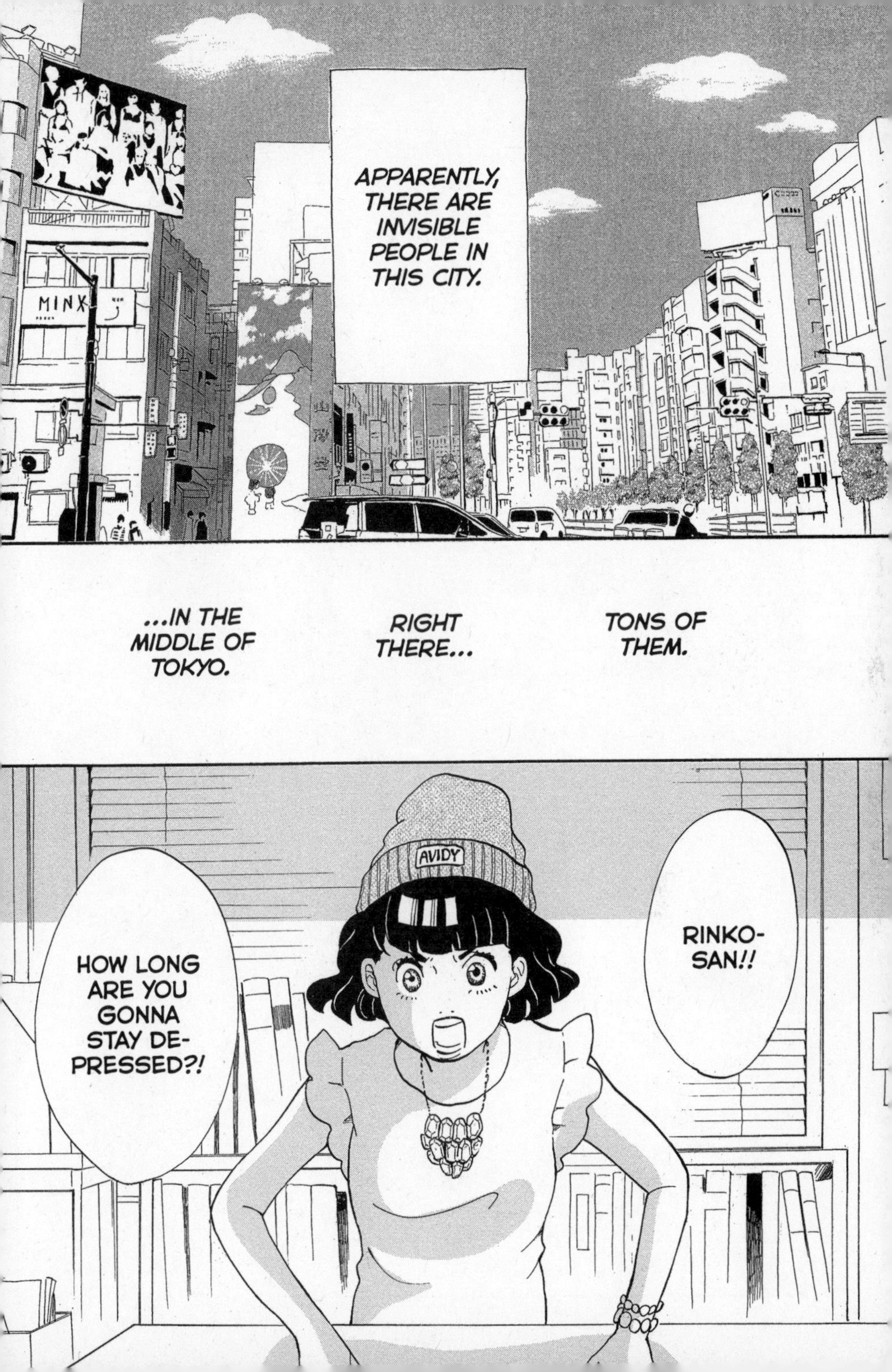
APPARENTLY, THERE ARE INVISIBLE PEOPLE IN THIS CITY.
MINX
TONS OF THEM.
RIGHT THERE...
...IN THE MIDDLE OF TOKYO.
AVIDY
RINKO-SAN!!
HOW LONG ARE YOU GONNA STAY DE-PRESSED?!

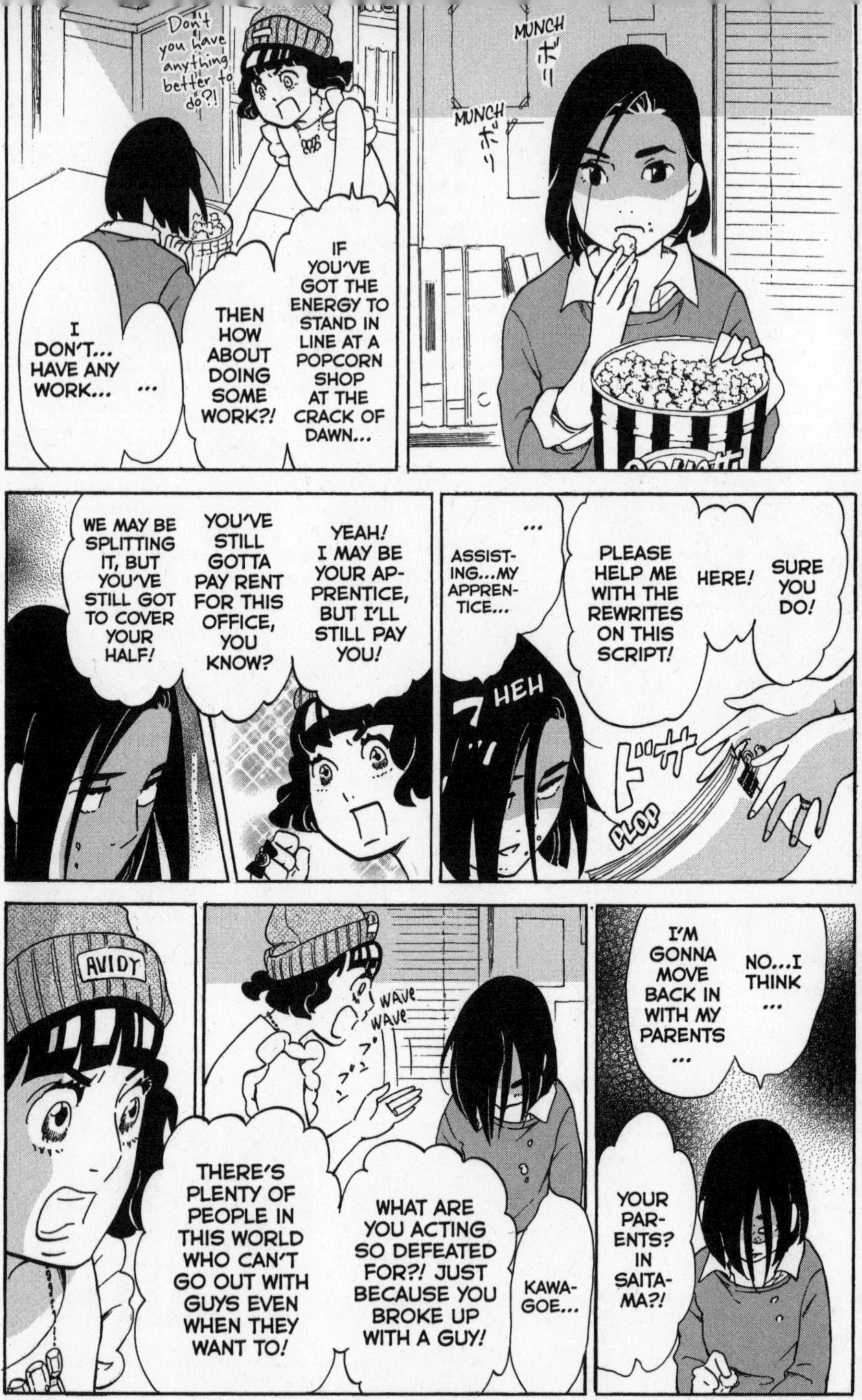

MUNCH
ボリ
MUNCH
ボリ
Don't you have anything better to do?!
IF YOU'VE GOT THE ENERGY TO STAND IN LINE AT A POPCORN SHOP AT THE CRACK OF DAWN...
THEN HOW ABOUT DOING SOME WORK?!
...
I DON'T... HAVE ANY WORK...
SURE YOU DO!
HERE!
PLEASE HELP ME WITH THE REWRITES ON THIS SCRIPT!
...
ASSISTING...MY APPRENTICE...
HEH
ドサ
PLOP
YEAH! I MAY BE YOUR APPRENTICE, BUT I'LL STILL PAY YOU!
YOU'VE STILL GOTTA PAY RENT FOR THIS OFFICE, YOU KNOW?
WE MAY BE SPLITTING IT, BUT YOU'VE STILL GOT TO COVER YOUR HALF!
NO...I THINK...
I'M GONNA MOVE BACK IN WITH MY PARENTS...
YOUR PARENTS? IN SAITAMA?!
WAVE
WAVE
KAWAGOE...
WHAT ARE YOU ACTING SO DEFEATED FOR?! JUST BECAUSE YOU BROKE UP WITH A GUY!
THERE'S PLENTY OF PEOPLE IN THIS WORLD WHO CAN'T GO OUT WITH GUYS EVEN WHEN THEY WANT TO!
AVIDY

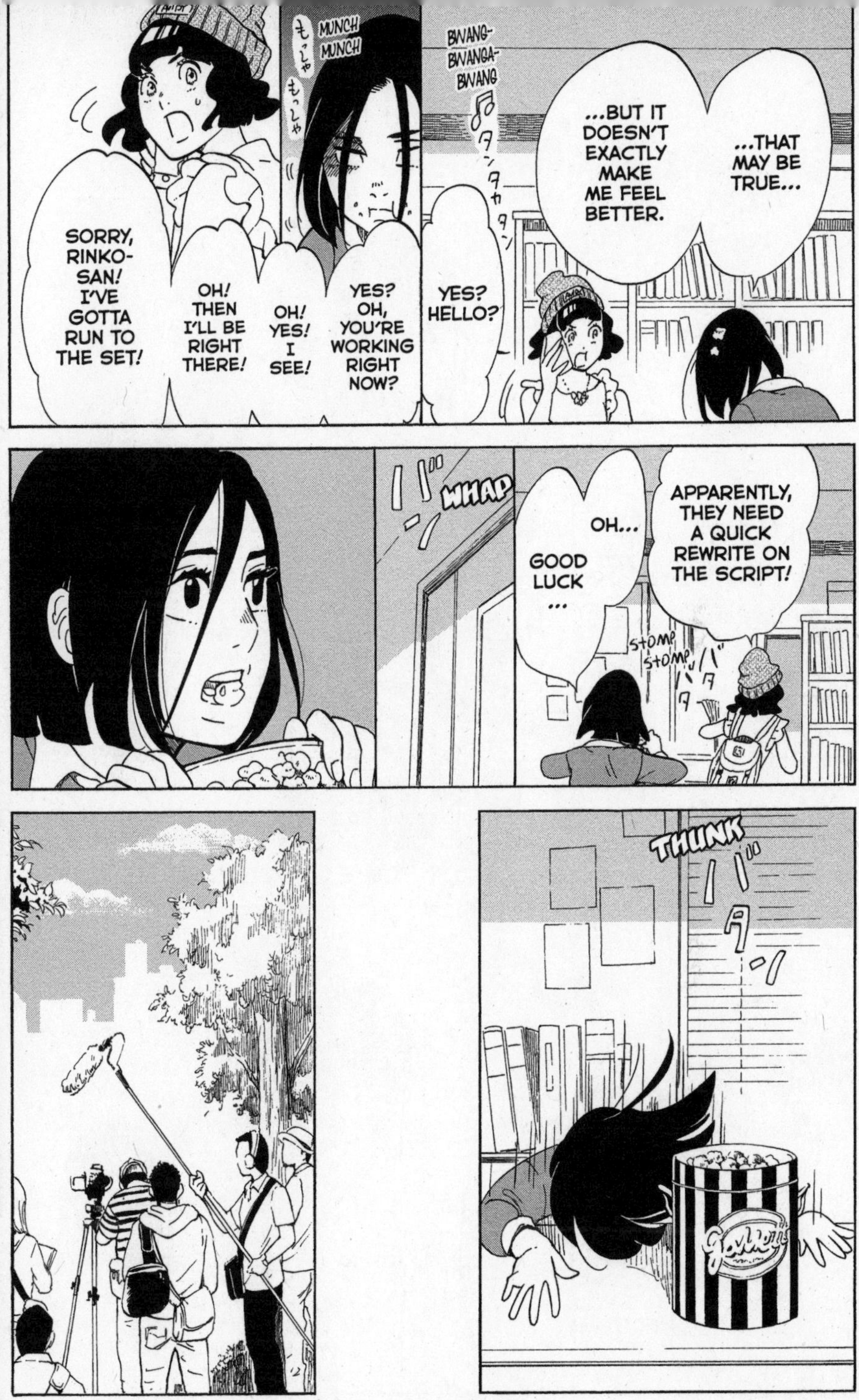
BWANG-BWANGA-BWANG
...THAT MAY BE TRUE...
...BUT IT DOESN'T EXACTLY MAKE ME FEEL BETTER.
YES? HELLO?
MUNCH MUNCH
もっしゃ もっしゃ
YES? OH, YOU'RE WORKING RIGHT NOW?
OH! YES! I SEE!
OH! THEN I'LL BE RIGHT THERE!
SORRY, RINKO-SAN! I'VE GOTTA RUN TO THE SET!
APPARENTLY, THEY NEED A QUICK REWRITE ON THE SCRIPT!
OH...
GOOD LUCK ...
STOMP STOMP
WHAP
THUNK

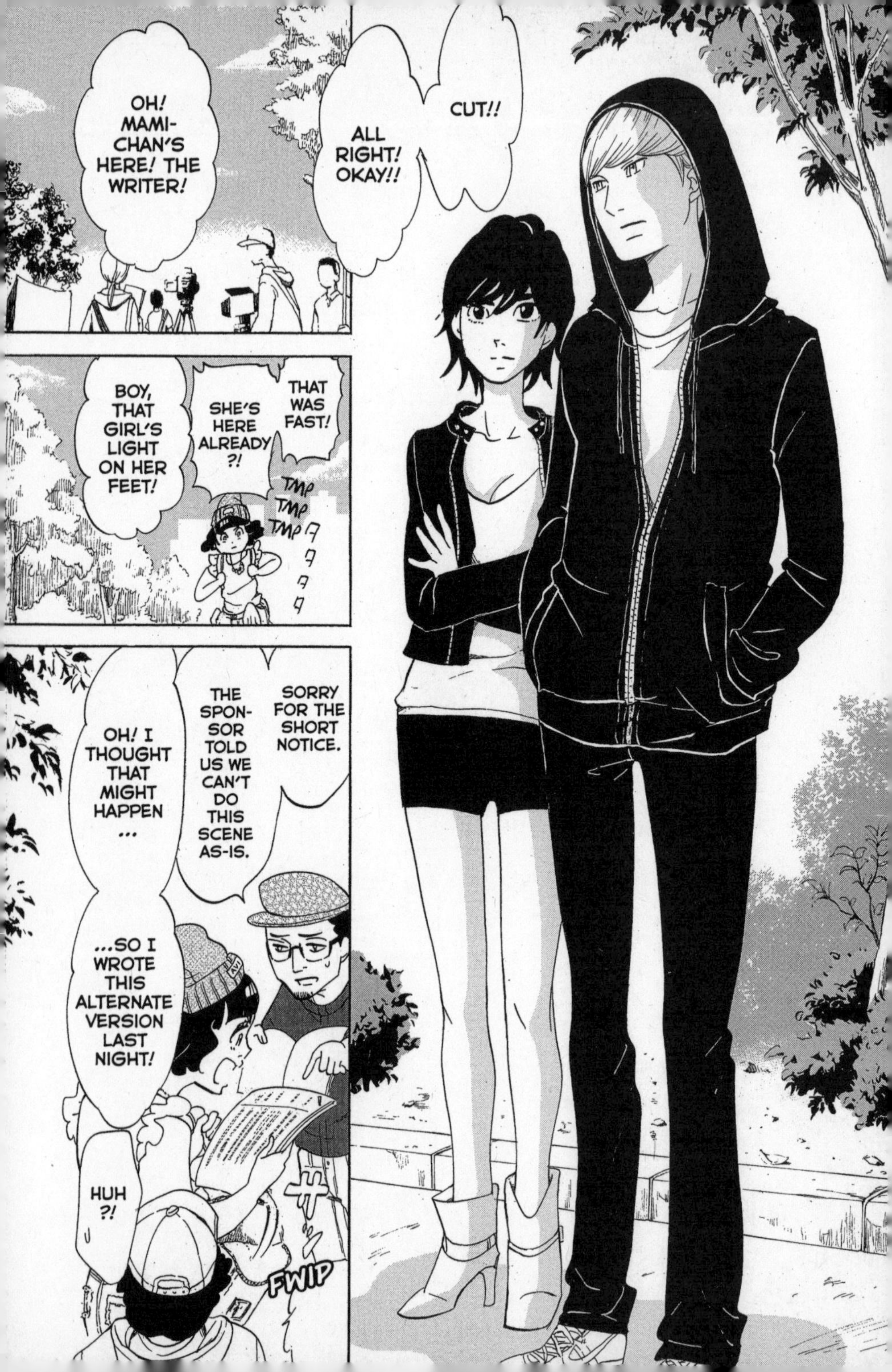
CUT!!
ALL RIGHT! OKAY!!
OH! MAMI-CHAN'S HERE! THE WRITER!
THAT WAS FAST!
SHE'S HERE ALREADY?!
BOY, THAT GIRL'S LIGHT ON HER FEET!
TMP TMP TMP
SORRY FOR THE SHORT NOTICE.
THE SPONSOR TOLD US WE CAN'T DO THIS SCENE AS-IS.
OH! I THOUGHT THAT MIGHT HAPPEN...
...SO I WROTE THIS ALTERNATE VERSION LAST NIGHT!
HUH?!
FWIP

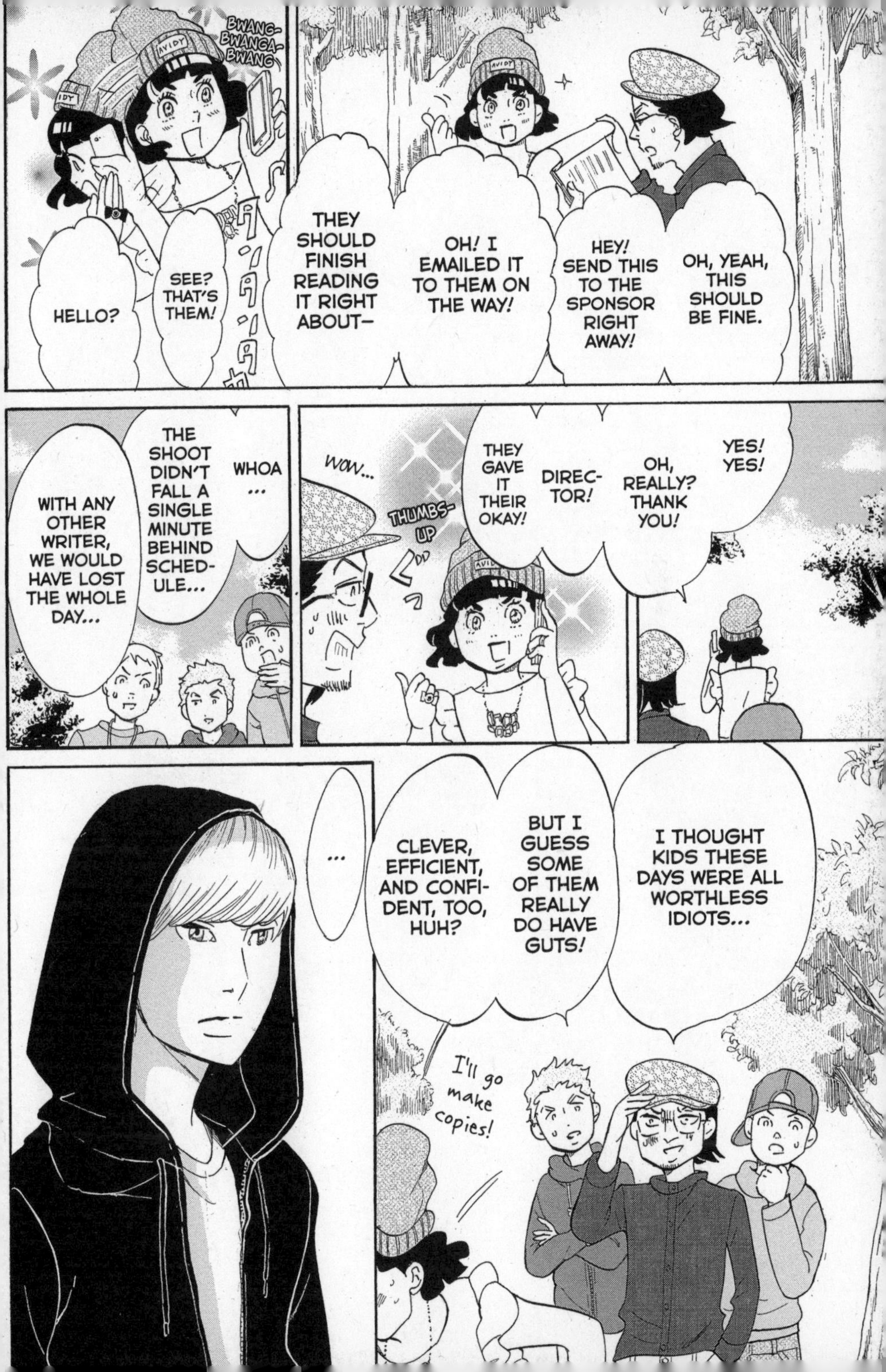
OH, YEAH, THIS SHOULD BE FINE.
HEY! SEND THIS TO THE SPONSOR RIGHT AWAY!
OH! I EMAILED IT TO THEM ON THE WAY!
THEY SHOULD FINISH READING IT RIGHT ABOUT—
BWANG-BWANGA-BWANG
SEE? THAT'S THEM!
HELLO?
YES! YES!
OH, REALLY? THANK YOU!
DIREC-TOR!
THEY GAVE IT THEIR OKAY!
WOW...
THUMBS-UP
WHOA ...
THE SHOOT DIDN'T FALL A SINGLE MINUTE BEHIND SCHED-ULE...
WITH ANY OTHER WRITER, WE WOULD HAVE LOST THE WHOLE DAY...
I THOUGHT KIDS THESE DAYS WERE ALL WORTHLESS IDIOTS...
BUT I GUESS SOME OF THEM REALLY DO HAVE GUTS!
CLEVER, EFFICIENT, AND CONFI-DENT, TOO, HUH?
I'll go make copies!
...

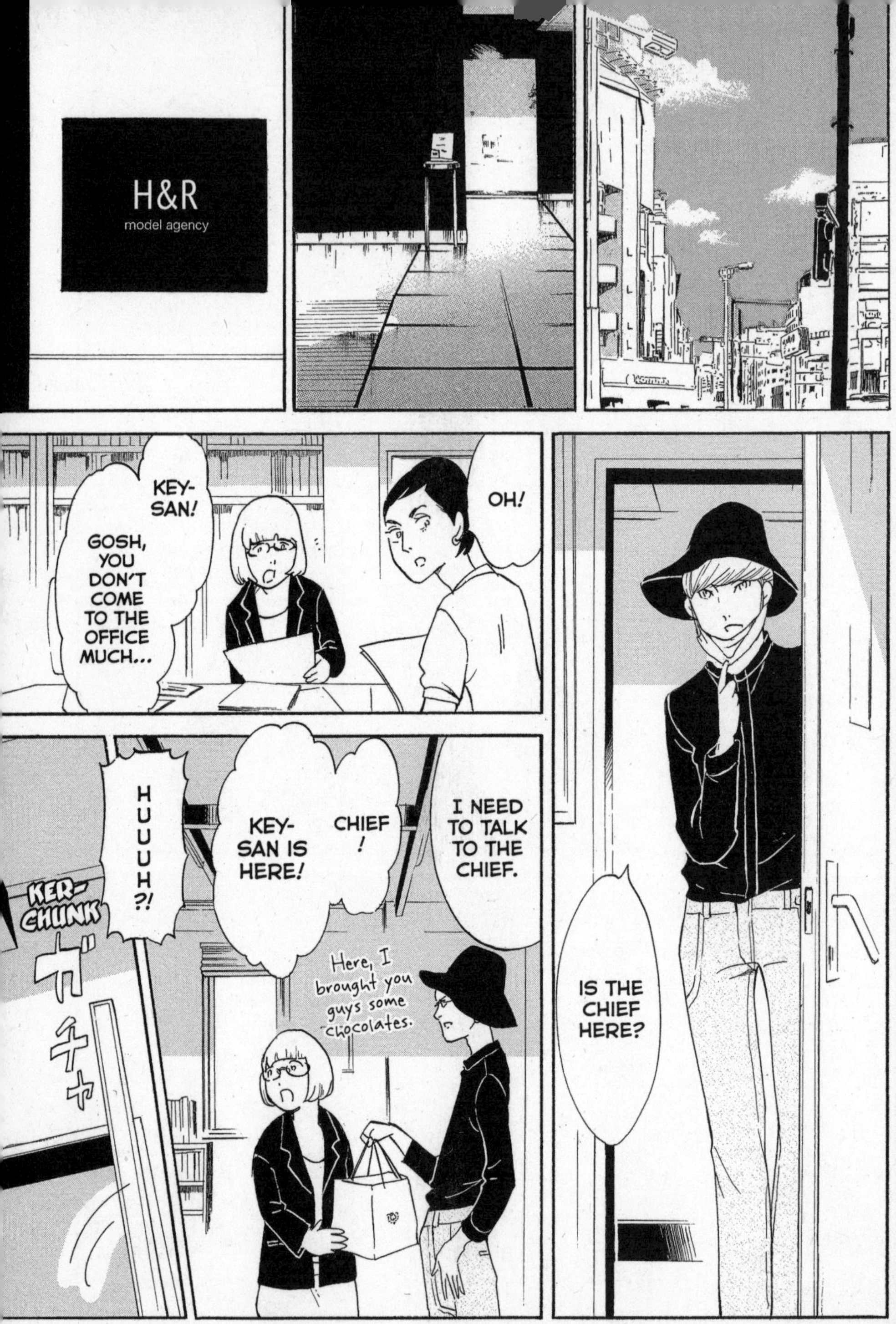
H&R
model agency
IS THE CHIEF HERE?
OH!
KEY-SAN!
GOSH, YOU DON'T COME TO THE OFFICE MUCH...
I NEED TO TALK TO THE CHIEF.
Here, I brought you guys some chocolates.
CHIEF!
KEY-SAN IS HERE!
HUUUUH?!
KER-CHUNK
ガチャ

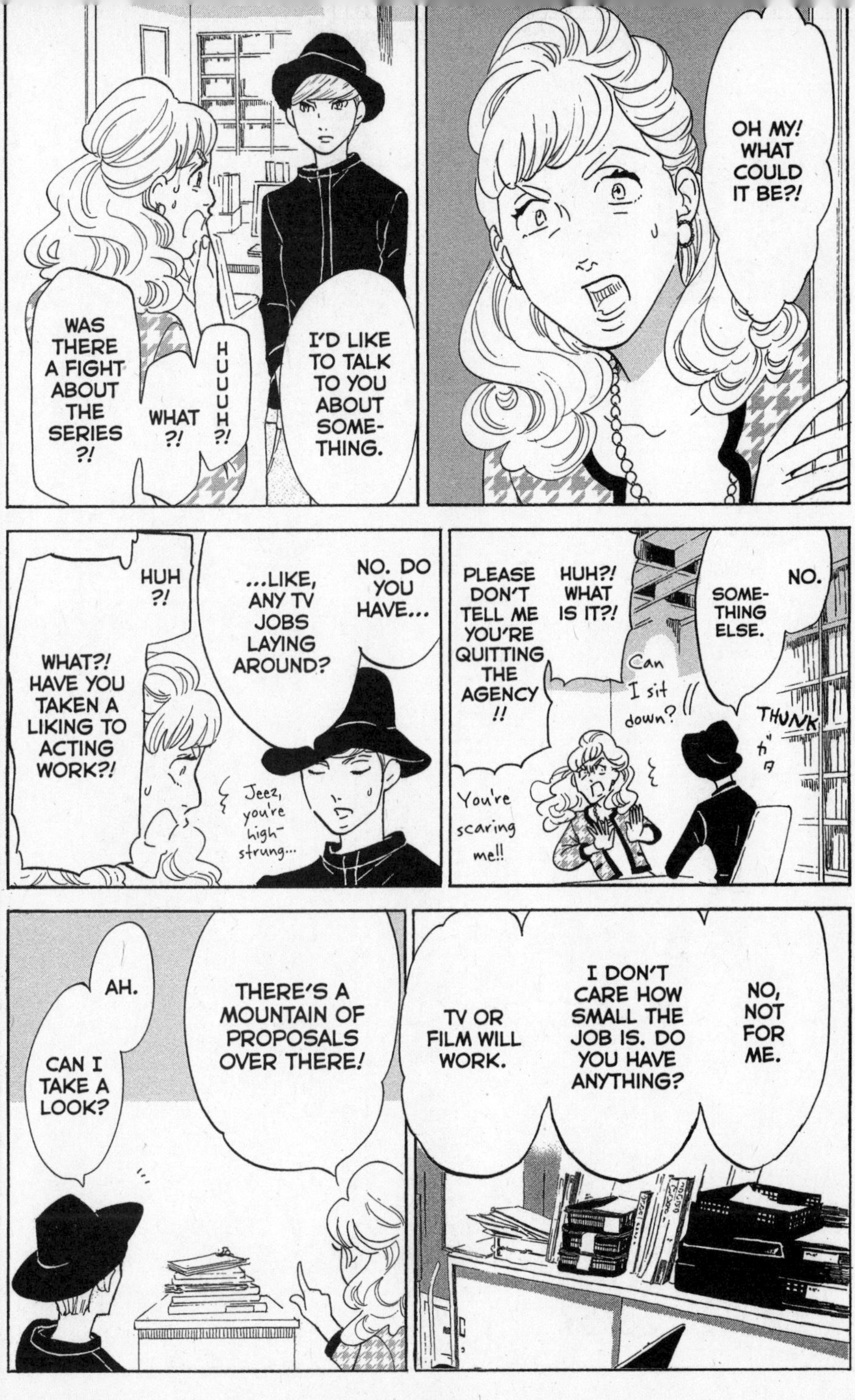
OH MY! WHAT COULD IT BE?!
I'D LIKE TO TALK TO YOU ABOUT SOME-THING.
HUUUUH?!
WHAT?!
WAS THERE A FIGHT ABOUT THE SERIES?!
NO.
SOME-THING ELSE.
HUH?! WHAT IS IT?!
PLEASE DON'T TELL ME YOU'RE QUITTING THE AGENCY!!
THUNK
Can I sit down?
You're scaring me!!
NO. DO YOU HAVE...
...LIKE, ANY TV JOBS LAYING AROUND?
HUH?!
WHAT?! HAVE YOU TAKEN A LIKING TO ACTING WORK?!
Jeez, you're high-strung...
NO, NOT FOR ME.
I DON'T CARE HOW SMALL THE JOB IS. DO YOU HAVE ANYTHING?
TV OR FILM WILL WORK.
THERE'S A MOUNTAIN OF PROPOSALS OVER THERE!
AH.
CAN I TAKE A LOOK?

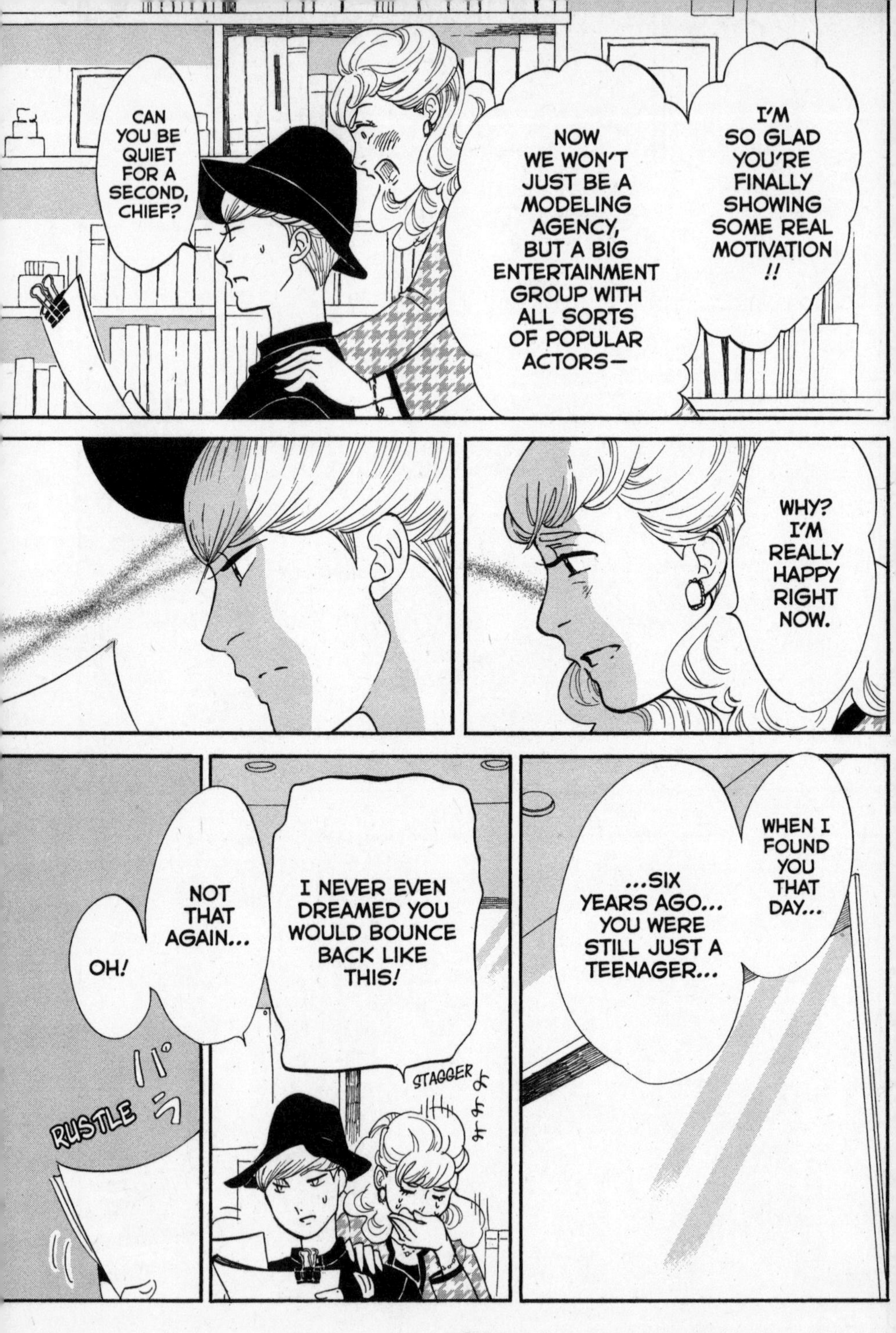
I'M SO GLAD YOU'RE FINALLY SHOWING SOME REAL MOTIVATION!!
NOW WE WON'T JUST BE A MODELING AGENCY, BUT A BIG ENTERTAINMENT GROUP WITH ALL SORTS OF POPULAR ACTORS—
CAN YOU BE QUIET FOR A SECOND, CHIEF?
WHY? I'M REALLY HAPPY RIGHT NOW.
WHEN I FOUND YOU THAT DAY...
...SIX YEARS AGO... YOU WERE STILL JUST A TEENAGER...
I NEVER EVEN DREAMED YOU WOULD BOUNCE BACK LIKE THIS!
STAGGER
NOT THAT AGAIN...
OH!
RUSTLE

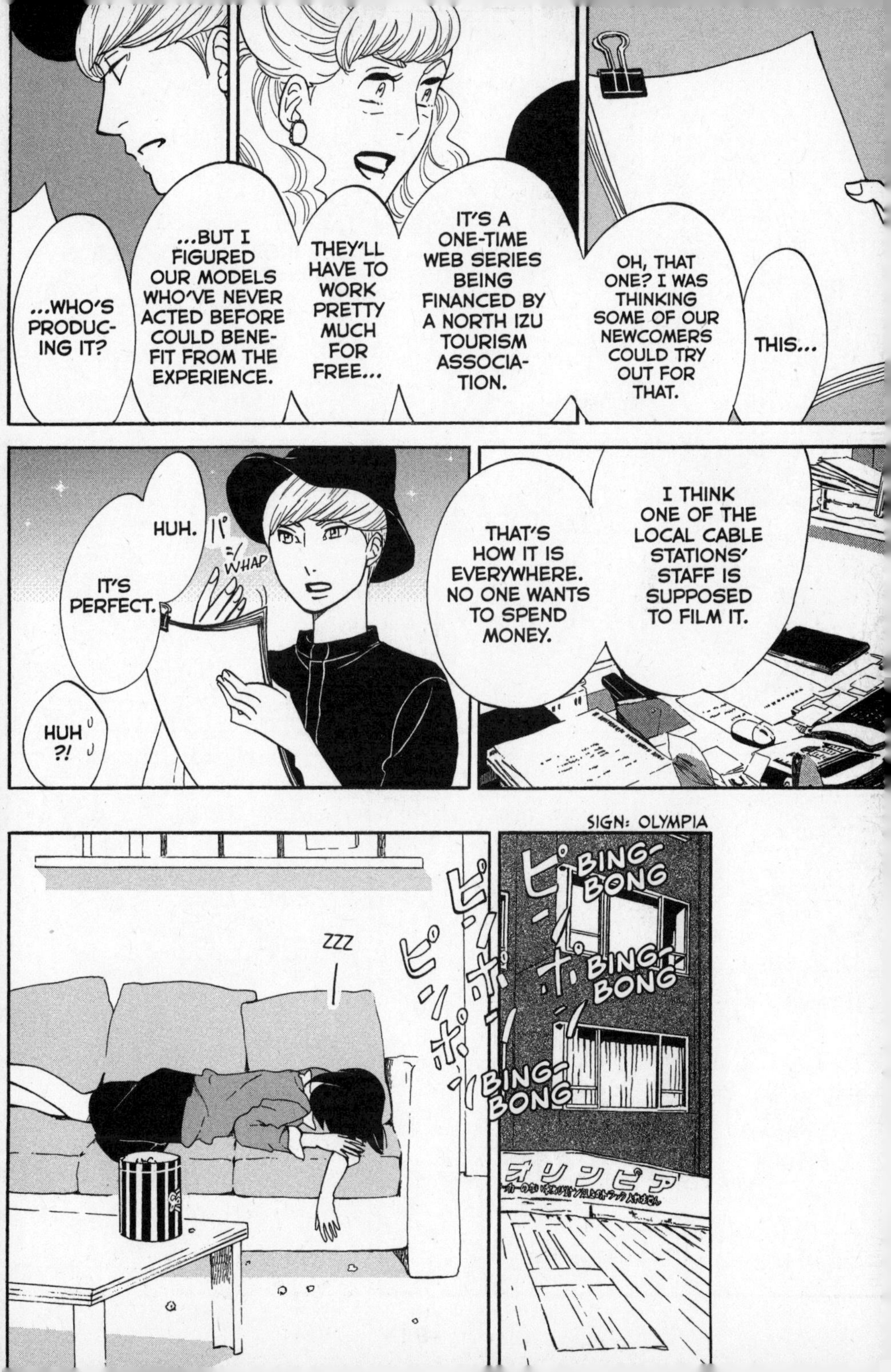
THIS...
OH, THAT ONE? I WAS THINKING SOME OF OUR NEWCOMERS COULD TRY OUT FOR THAT.
IT'S A ONE-TIME WEB SERIES BEING FINANCED BY A NORTH IZU TOURISM ASSOCIATION.
THEY'LL HAVE TO WORK PRETTY MUCH FOR FREE...
...BUT I FIGURED OUR MODELS WHO'VE NEVER ACTED BEFORE COULD BENEFIT FROM THE EXPERIENCE.
...WHO'S PRODUC-ING IT?
I THINK ONE OF THE LOCAL CABLE STATIONS' STAFF IS SUPPOSED TO FILM IT.
THAT'S HOW IT IS EVERYWHERE. NO ONE WANTS TO SPEND MONEY.
HUH.
パ
WHAP
IT'S PERFECT.
HUH ?!
SIGN: OLYMPIA
BING-BONG
BING-BONG
BING-BONG
オリンピア
ZZZ

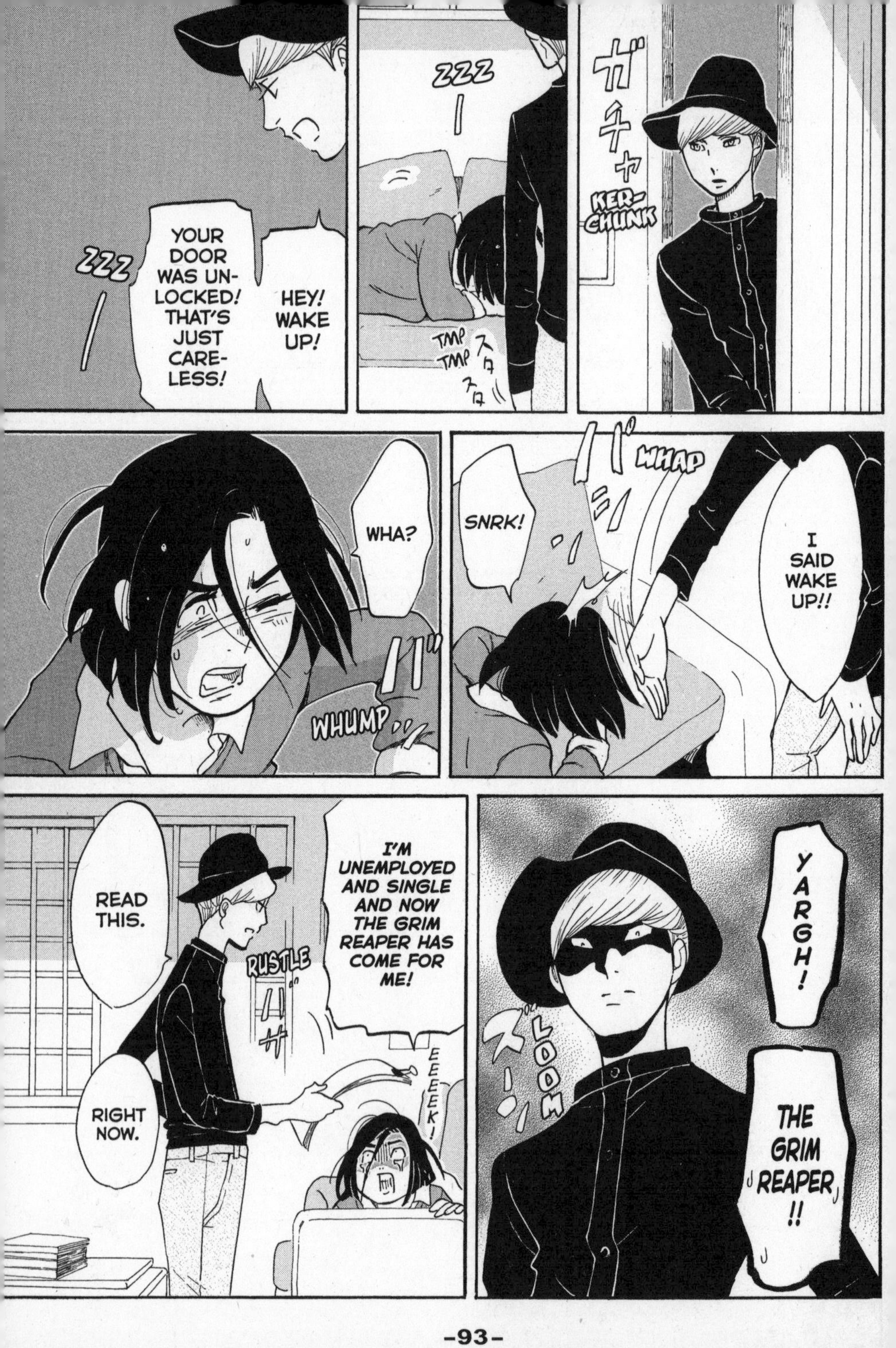
KER-CHUNK
ZZZ
TMP TMP
HEY! WAKE UP!
YOUR DOOR WAS UN-LOCKED! THAT'S JUST CARE-LESS!
ZZZ
WHAP
I SAID WAKE UP!!
SNRK!
WHA?
WHUMP
YARGH!
THE GRIM REAPER!!
LOOM
I'M UNEMPLOYED AND SINGLE AND NOW THE GRIM REAPER HAS COME FOR ME!
READ THIS.
RUSTLE
EEEEEK!
RIGHT NOW.

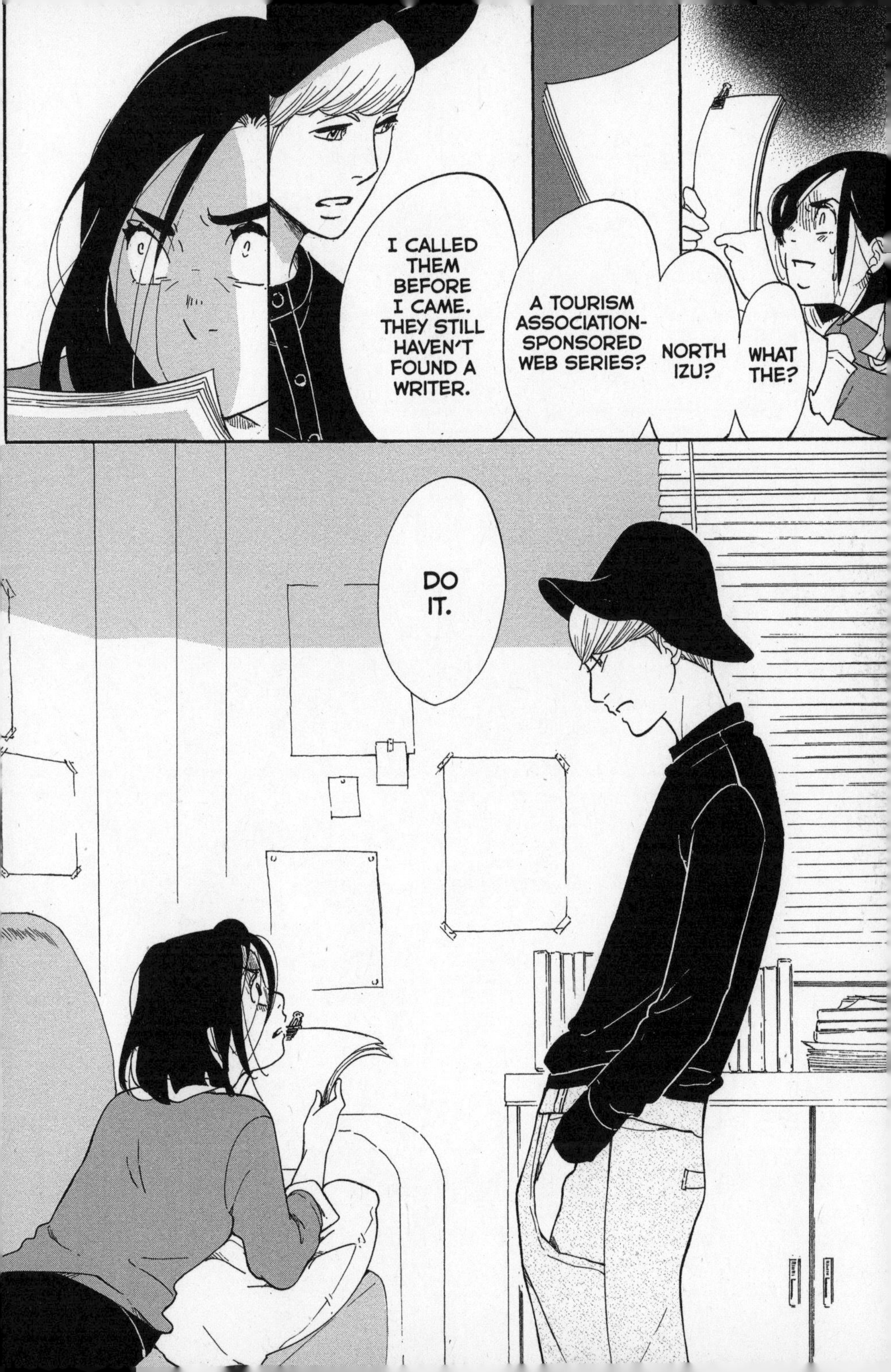
WHAT THE?
NORTH IZU?
A TOURISM ASSOCIATION-SPONSORED WEB SERIES?
I CALLED THEM BEFORE I CAME. THEY STILL HAVEN'T FOUND A WRITER.
DO IT.

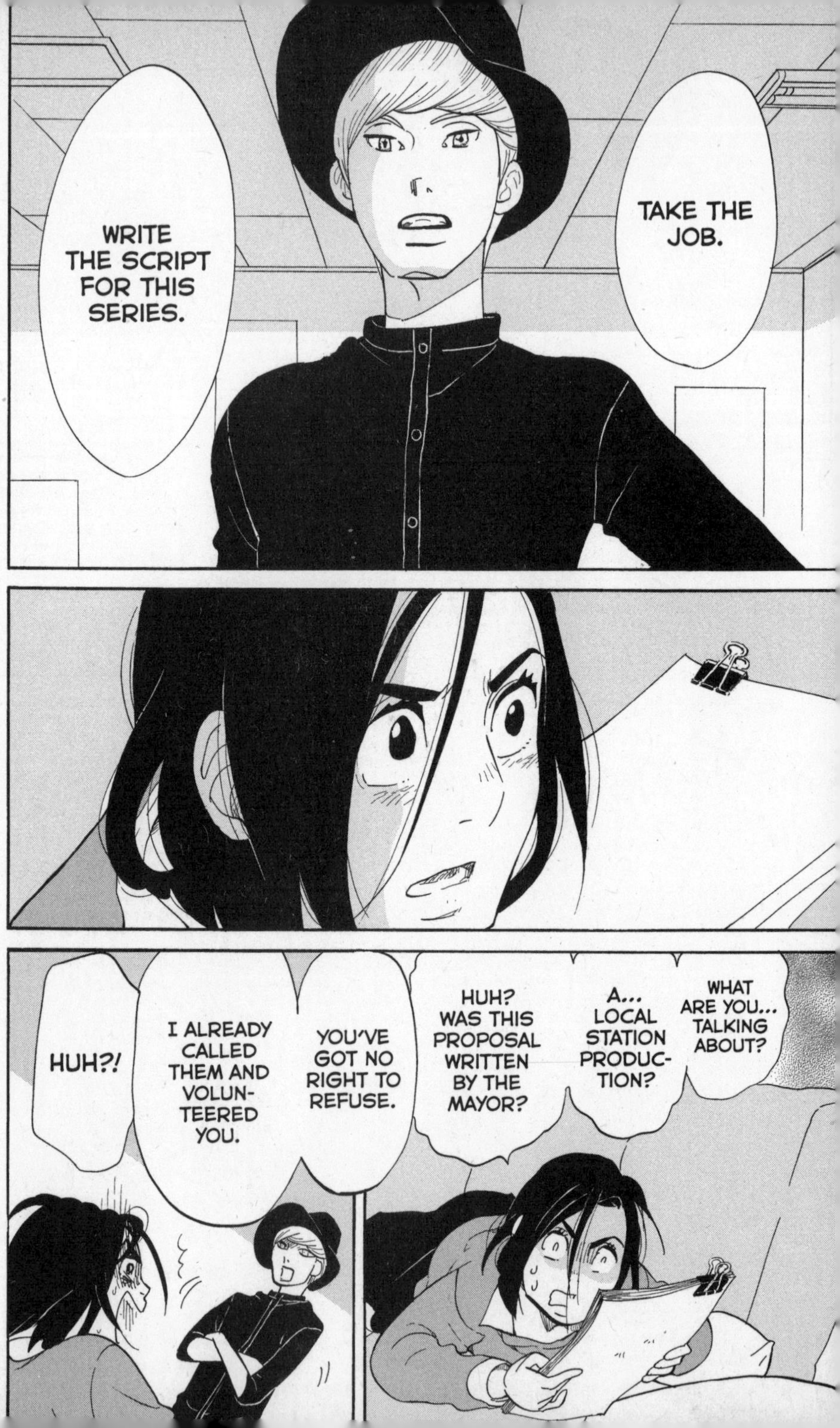
TAKE THE JOB.
WRITE THE SCRIPT FOR THIS SERIES.
WHAT ARE YOU... TALKING ABOUT?
A... LOCAL STATION PRODUCTION?
HUH? WAS THIS PROPOSAL WRITTEN BY THE MAYOR?
YOU'VE GOT NO RIGHT TO REFUSE.
I ALREADY CALLED THEM AND VOLUNTEERED YOU.
HUH?!

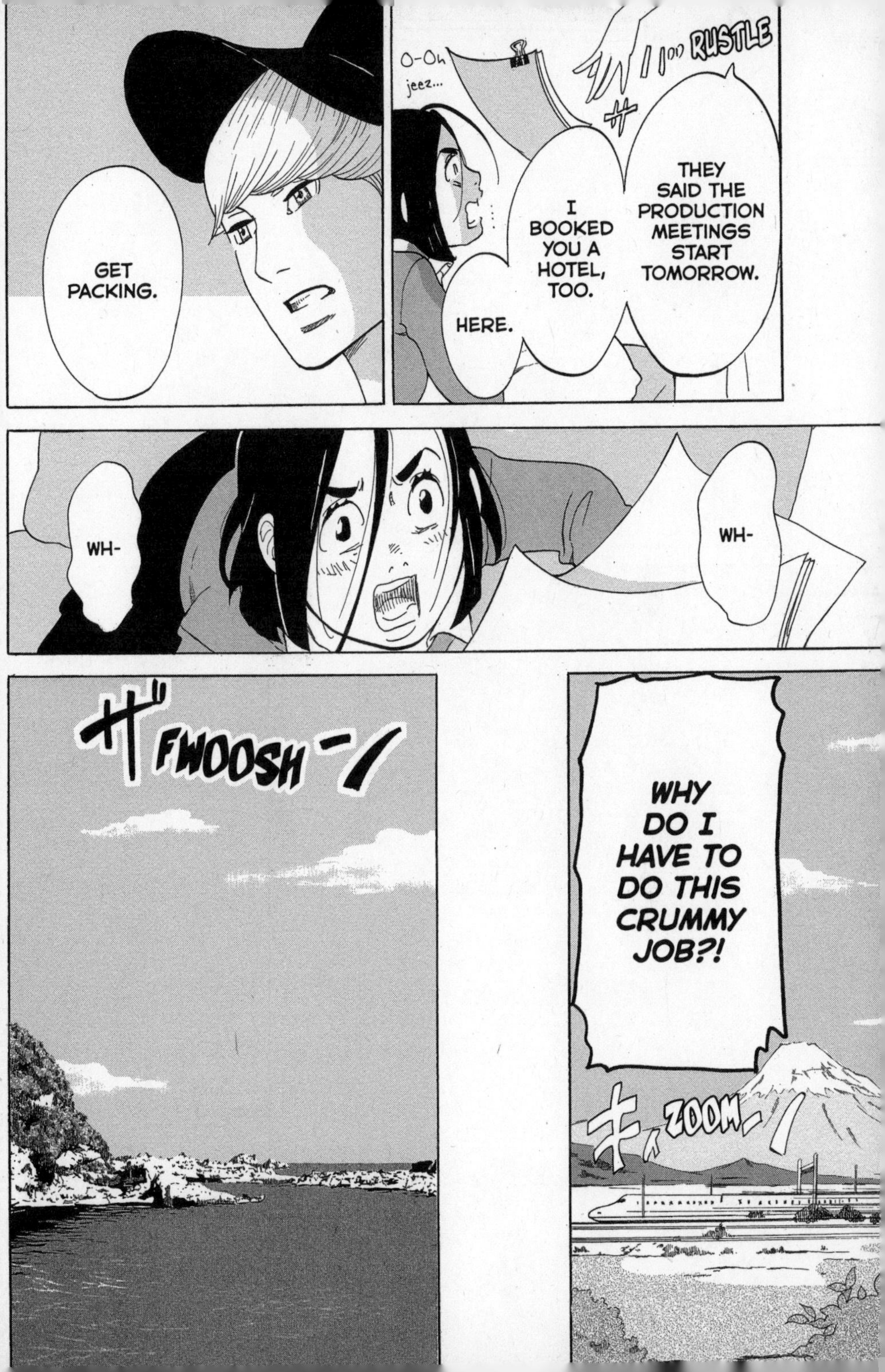
RUSTLE
O-Oh jeez...
THEY SAID THE PRODUCTION MEETINGS START TOMORROW.
I BOOKED YOU A HOTEL, TOO.
HERE.
GET PACKING.
WH-
WH-
WHY DO I HAVE TO DO THIS CRUMMY JOB?!
ZOOM
FWOOSH

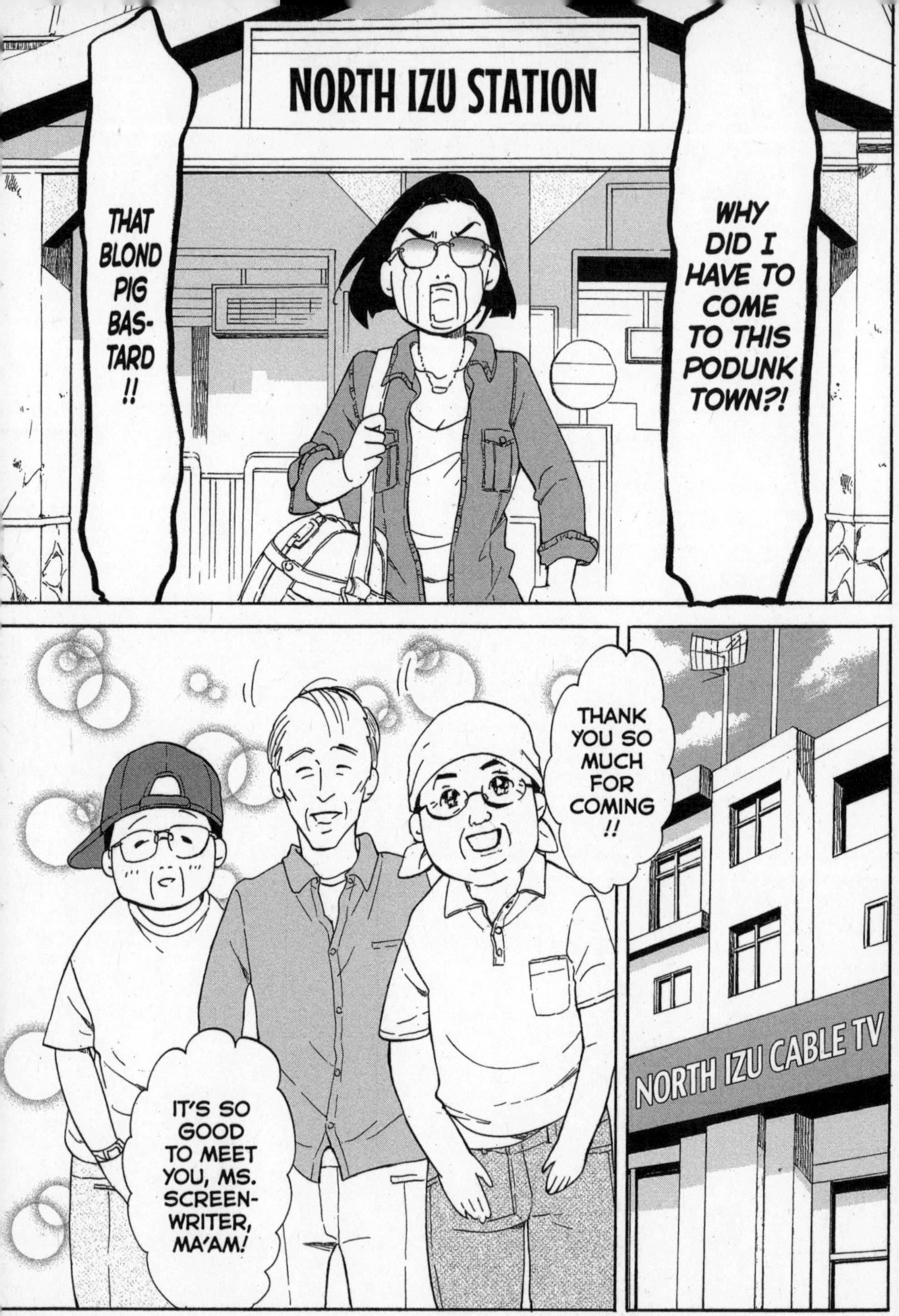
NORTH IZU STATION
WHY DID I HAVE TO COME TO THIS PODUNK TOWN?!
THAT BLOND PIG BAS-TARD !!
NORTH IZU CABLE TV
THANK YOU SO MUCH FOR COMING !!
IT'S SO GOOD TO MEET YOU, MS. SCREEN-WRITER, MA'AM!

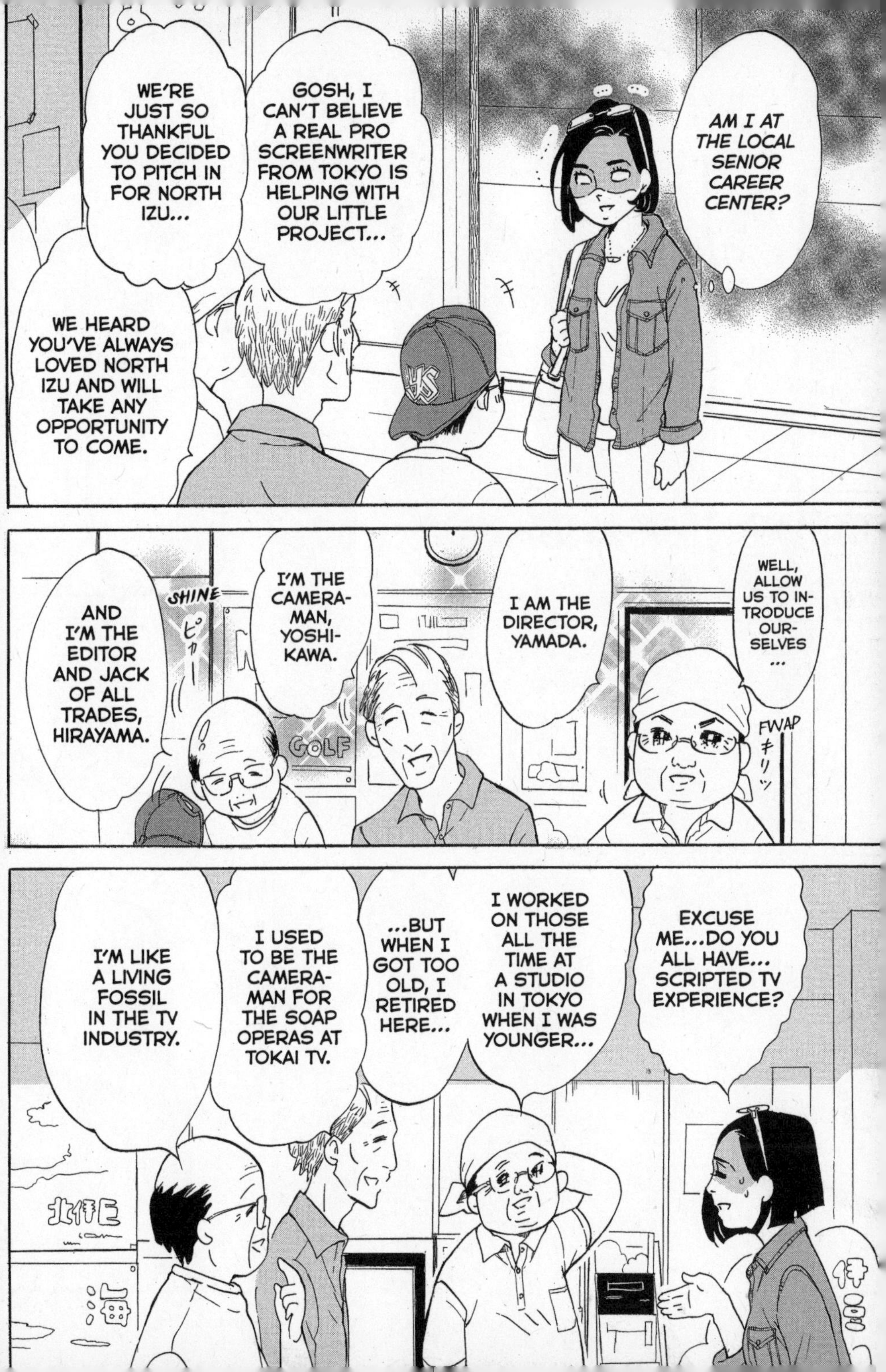
AM I AT THE LOCAL SENIOR CAREER CENTER?
... ...
GOSH, I CAN'T BELIEVE A REAL PRO SCREENWRITER FROM TOKYO IS HELPING WITH OUR LITTLE PROJECT...
WE'RE JUST SO THANKFUL YOU DECIDED TO PITCH IN FOR NORTH IZU...
WE HEARD YOU'VE ALWAYS LOVED NORTH IZU AND WILL TAKE ANY OPPORTUNITY TO COME.
WELL, ALLOW US TO INTRODUCE OURSELVES...
FWAP
キリッ
I AM THE DIRECTOR, YAMADA.
I'M THE CAMERAMAN, YOSHIKAWA.
GOLF
SHINE
ピカー
AND I'M THE EDITOR AND JACK OF ALL TRADES, HIRAYAMA.
EXCUSE ME...DO YOU ALL HAVE... SCRIPTED TV EXPERIENCE?
I WORKED ON THOSE ALL THE TIME AT A STUDIO IN TOKYO WHEN I WAS YOUNGER...
...BUT WHEN I GOT TOO OLD, I RETIRED HERE...
I USED TO BE THE CAMERAMAN FOR THE SOAP OPERAS AT TOKAI TV.
I'M LIKE A LIVING FOSSIL IN THE TV INDUSTRY.

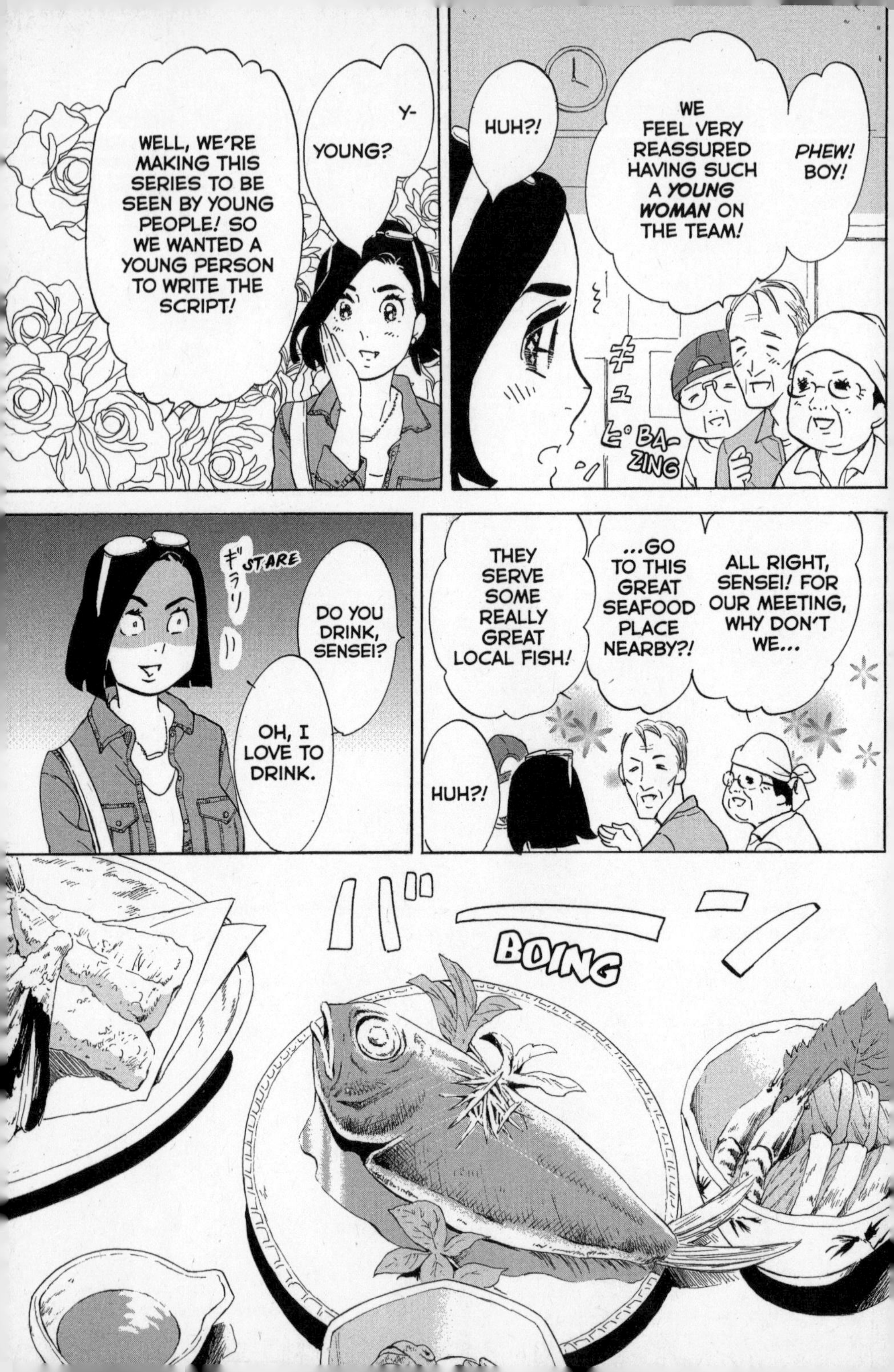
PHEW! BOY!
WE FEEL VERY REASSURED HAVING SUCH A *YOUNG WOMAN* ON THE TEAM!
HUH?!
キュピ
BA-ZING
Y- YOUNG?
WELL, WE'RE MAKING THIS SERIES TO BE SEEN BY YOUNG PEOPLE! SO WE WANTED A YOUNG PERSON TO WRITE THE SCRIPT!
ALL RIGHT, SENSEI! FOR OUR MEETING, WHY DON'T WE...
...GO TO THIS GREAT SEAFOOD PLACE NEARBY?!
THEY SERVE SOME REALLY GREAT LOCAL FISH!
HUH?!
ギラリ
STARE
DO YOU DRINK, SENSEI?
OH, I LOVE TO DRINK.
バーン
BOING

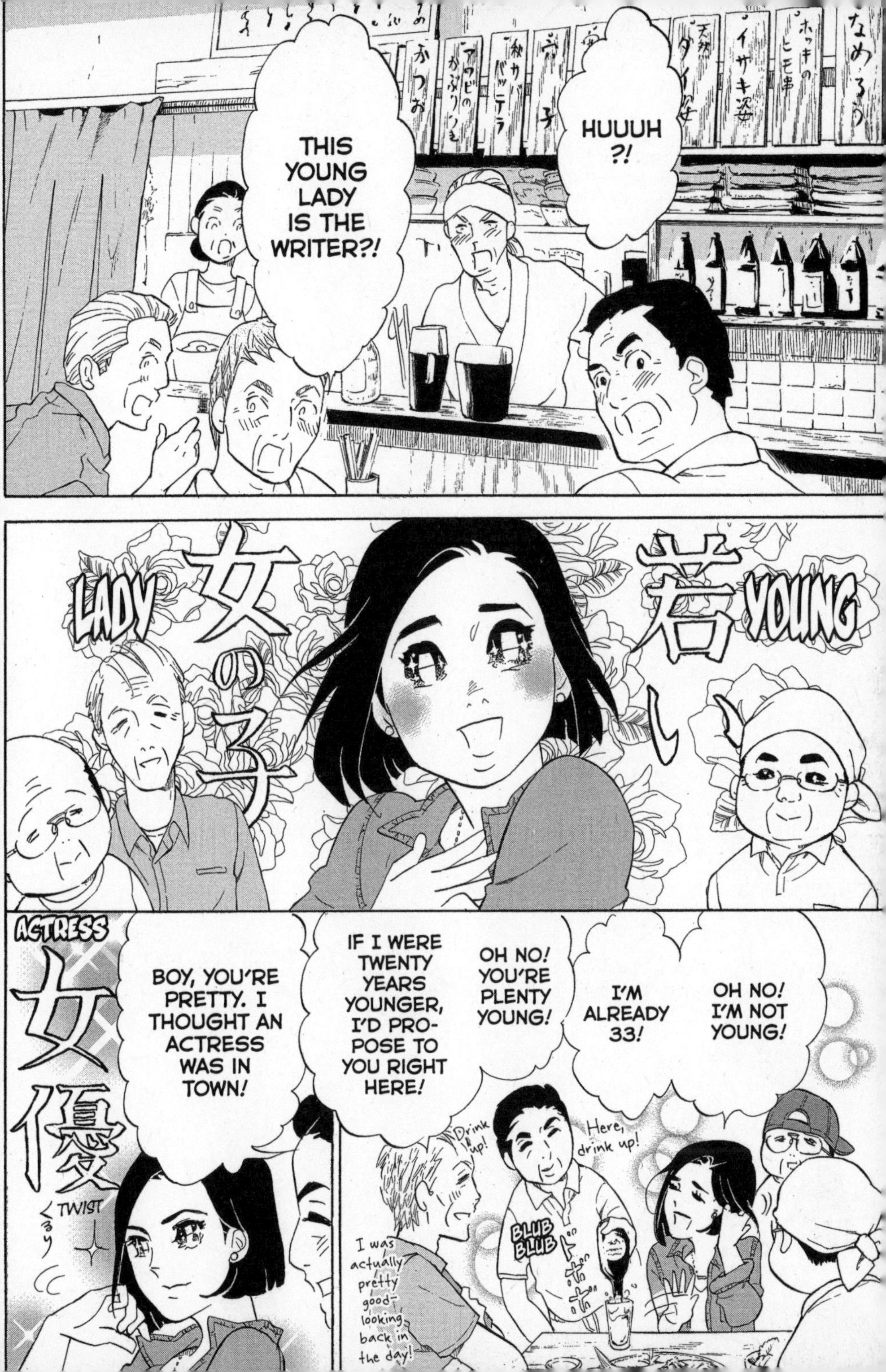

HUUUH ?!
THIS YOUNG LADY IS THE WRITER?!
若い YOUNG
女の子 LADY
OH NO! I'M NOT YOUNG!
I'M ALREADY 33!
OH NO! YOU'RE PLENTY YOUNG!
IF I WERE TWENTY YEARS YOUNGER, I'D PRO-POSE TO YOU RIGHT HERE!
Here, drink up!
Drink up!
BLUB BLUB ドボボ
I was actually pretty good-looking back in the day!
BOY, YOU'RE PRETTY. I THOUGHT AN ACTRESS WAS IN TOWN!
ACTRESS 女優
TWIST くるり

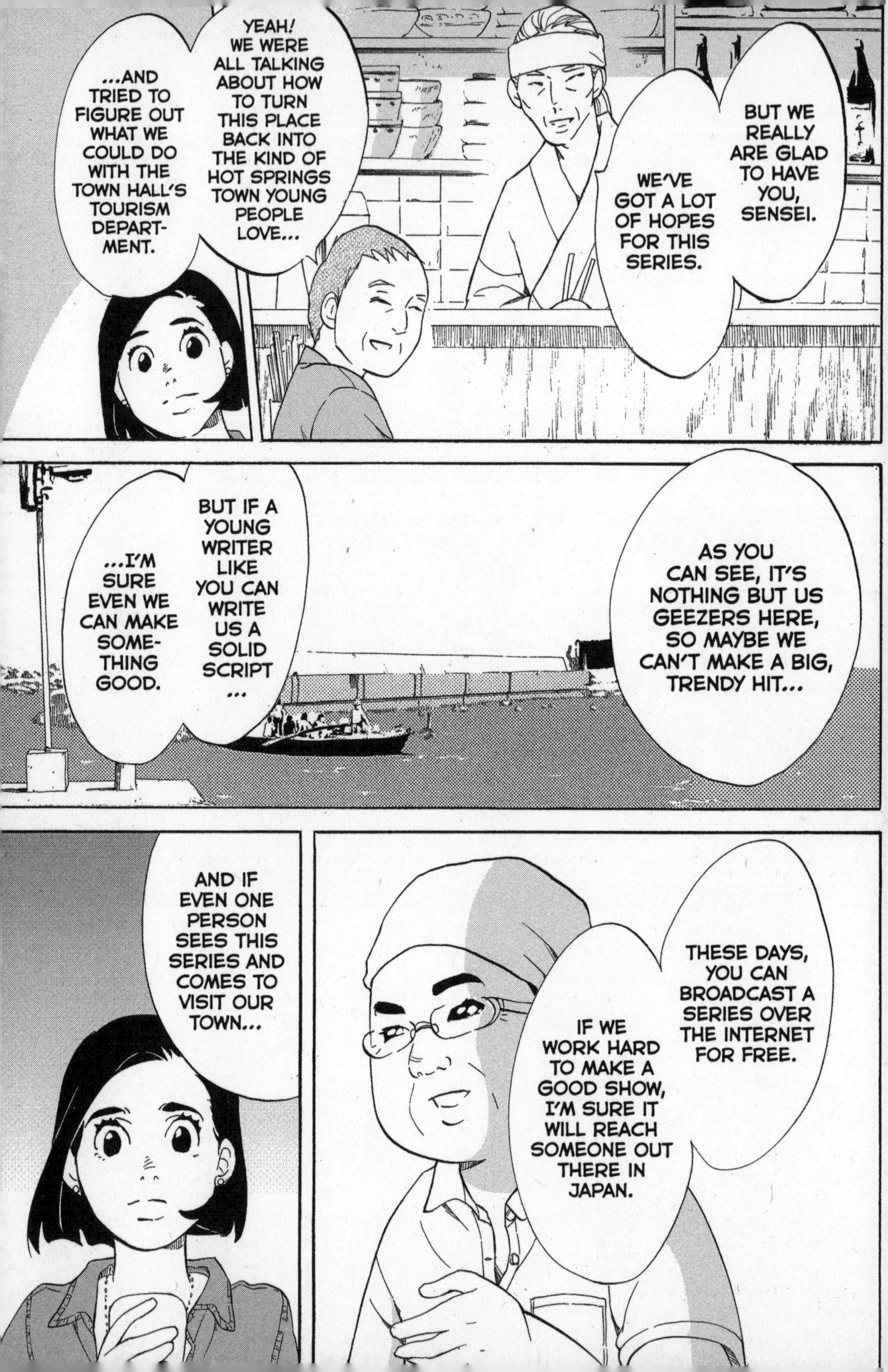
BUT WE REALLY ARE GLAD TO HAVE YOU, SENSEI.
WE'VE GOT A LOT OF HOPES FOR THIS SERIES.
YEAH! WE WERE ALL TALKING ABOUT HOW TO TURN THIS PLACE BACK INTO THE KIND OF HOT SPRINGS TOWN YOUNG PEOPLE LOVE...
...AND TRIED TO FIGURE OUT WHAT WE COULD DO WITH THE TOWN HALL'S TOURISM DEPART-MENT.
AS YOU CAN SEE, IT'S NOTHING BUT US GEEZERS HERE, SO MAYBE WE CAN'T MAKE A BIG, TRENDY HIT...
BUT IF A YOUNG WRITER LIKE YOU CAN WRITE US A SOLID SCRIPT...
...I'M SURE EVEN WE CAN MAKE SOME-THING GOOD.
THESE DAYS, YOU CAN BROADCAST A SERIES OVER THE INTERNET FOR FREE.
IF WE WORK HARD TO MAKE A GOOD SHOW, I'M SURE IT WILL REACH SOMEONE OUT THERE IN JAPAN.
AND IF EVEN ONE PERSON SEES THIS SERIES AND COMES TO VISIT OUR TOWN...

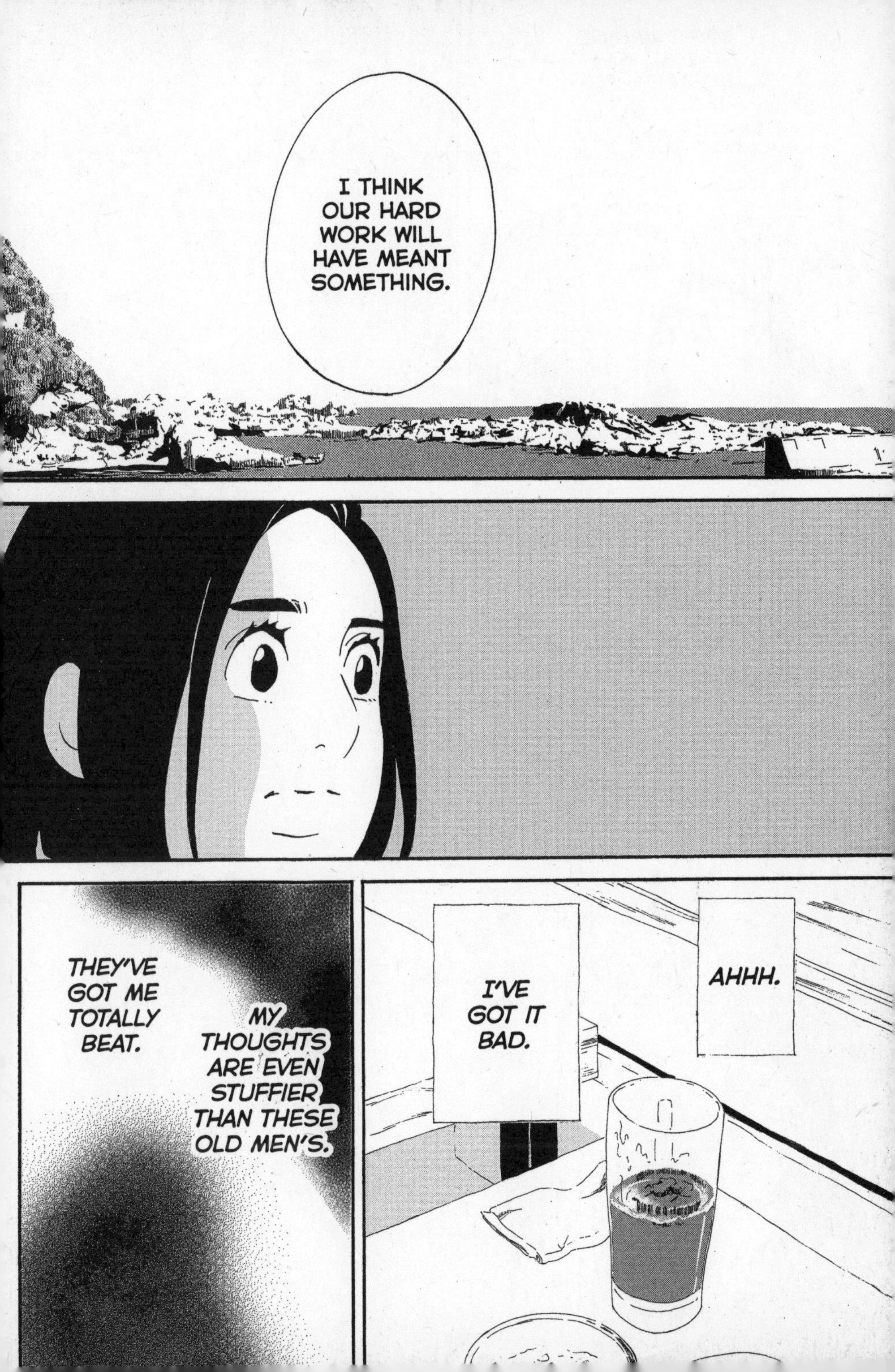
I THINK OUR HARD WORK WILL HAVE MEANT SOMETHING.
AHHH.
I'VE GOT IT BAD.
MY THOUGHTS ARE EVEN STUFFIER THAN THESE OLD MEN'S.
THEY'VE GOT ME TOTALLY BEAT.

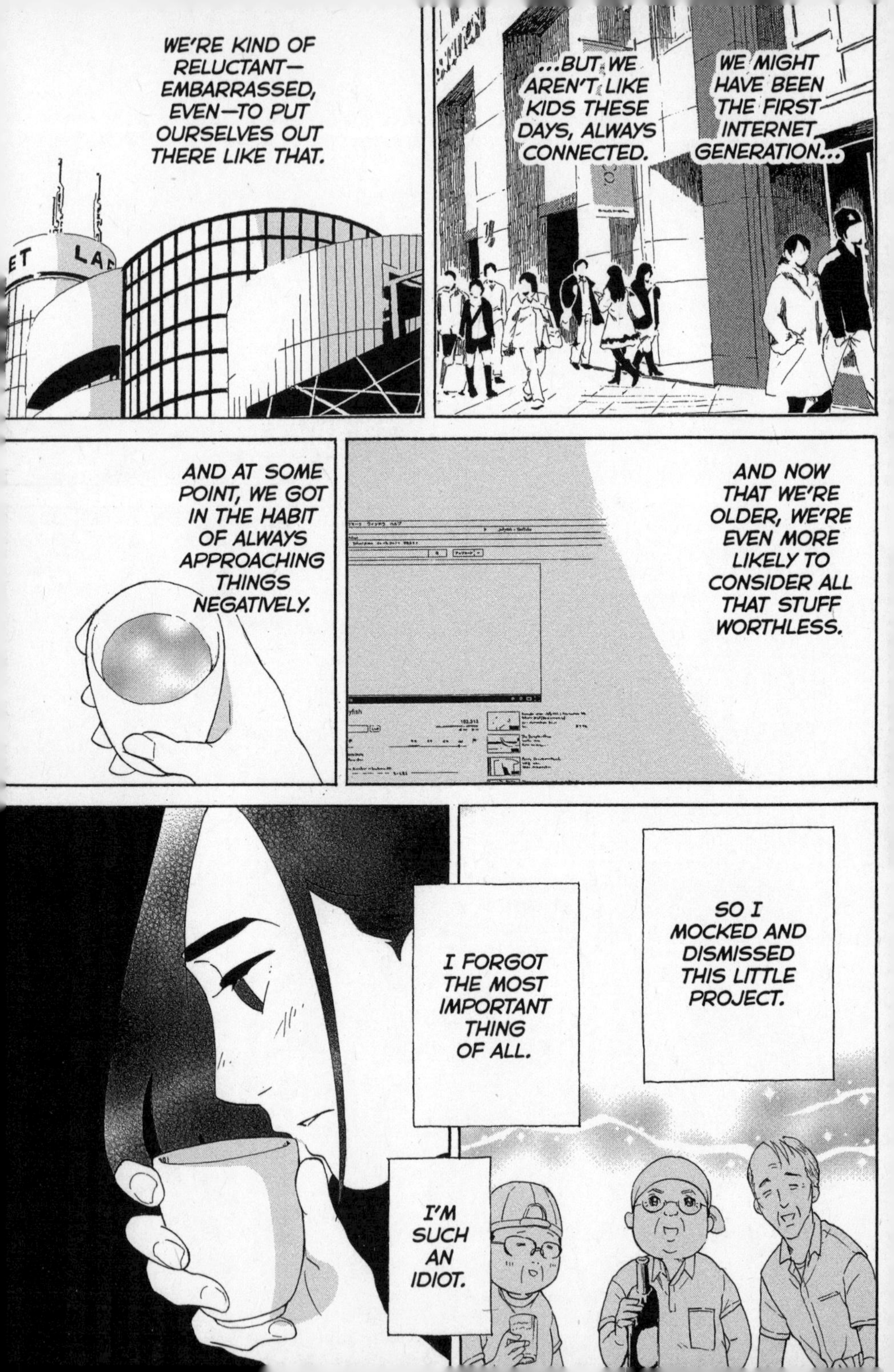
WE MIGHT HAVE BEEN THE FIRST INTERNET GENERATION...
...BUT WE AREN'T LIKE KIDS THESE DAYS, ALWAYS CONNECTED.
WE'RE KIND OF RELUCTANT—EMBARRASSED, EVEN—TO PUT OURSELVES OUT THERE LIKE THAT.
AND NOW THAT WE'RE OLDER, WE'RE EVEN MORE LIKELY TO CONSIDER ALL THAT STUFF WORTHLESS.
AND AT SOME POINT, WE GOT IN THE HABIT OF ALWAYS APPROACHING THINGS NEGATIVELY.
SO I MOCKED AND DISMISSED THIS LITTLE PROJECT.
I FORGOT THE MOST IMPORTANT THING OF ALL.
I'M SUCH AN IDIOT.

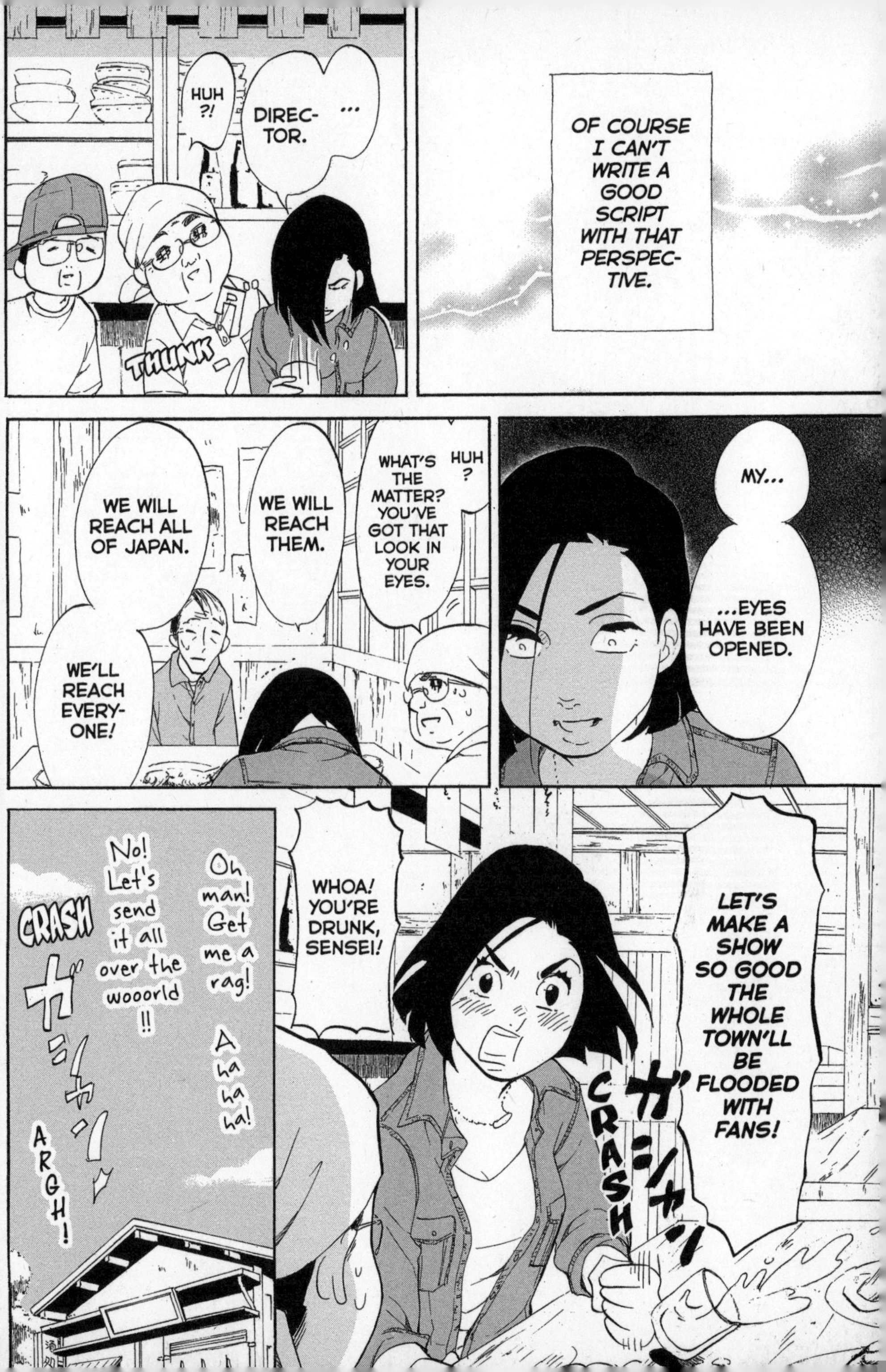
OF COURSE I CAN'T WRITE A GOOD SCRIPT WITH THAT PERSPECTIVE.
...
DIRECTOR.
HUH ?!
THUNK
MY...
...EYES HAVE BEEN OPENED.
HUH ?
WHAT'S THE MATTER? YOU'VE GOT THAT LOOK IN YOUR EYES.
WE WILL REACH THEM.
WE WILL REACH ALL OF JAPAN.
WE'LL REACH EVERYONE!
LET'S MAKE A SHOW SO GOOD THE WHOLE TOWN'LL BE FLOODED WITH FANS!
CRASH
WHOA! YOU'RE DRUNK, SENSEI!
Oh man! Get me a rag!
A ha ha ha!
No! Let's send it all over the wooorld !!
CRASH
ARGH!

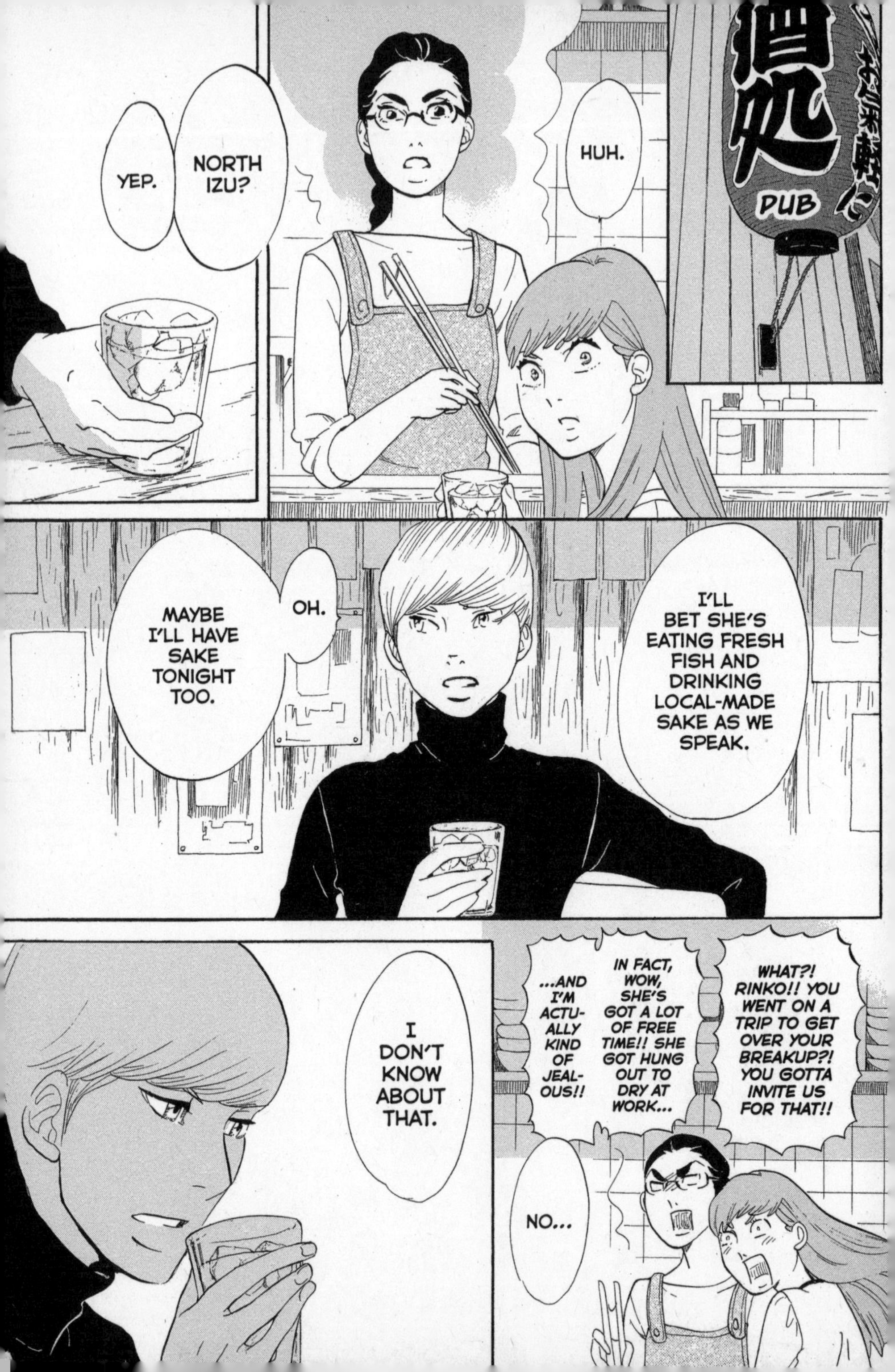
酒処
PUB
HUH.
NORTH IZU?
YEP.
I'LL BET SHE'S EATING FRESH FISH AND DRINKING LOCAL-MADE SAKE AS WE SPEAK.
OH.
MAYBE I'LL HAVE SAKE TONIGHT TOO.
WHAT?! RINKO!! YOU WENT ON A TRIP TO GET OVER YOUR BREAKUP?! YOU GOTTA INVITE US FOR THAT!!
IN FACT, WOW, SHE'S GOT A LOT OF FREE TIME!! SHE GOT HUNG OUT TO DRY AT WORK...
...AND I'M ACTU-ALLY KIND OF JEAL-OUS!!
NO...
I DON'T KNOW ABOUT THAT.

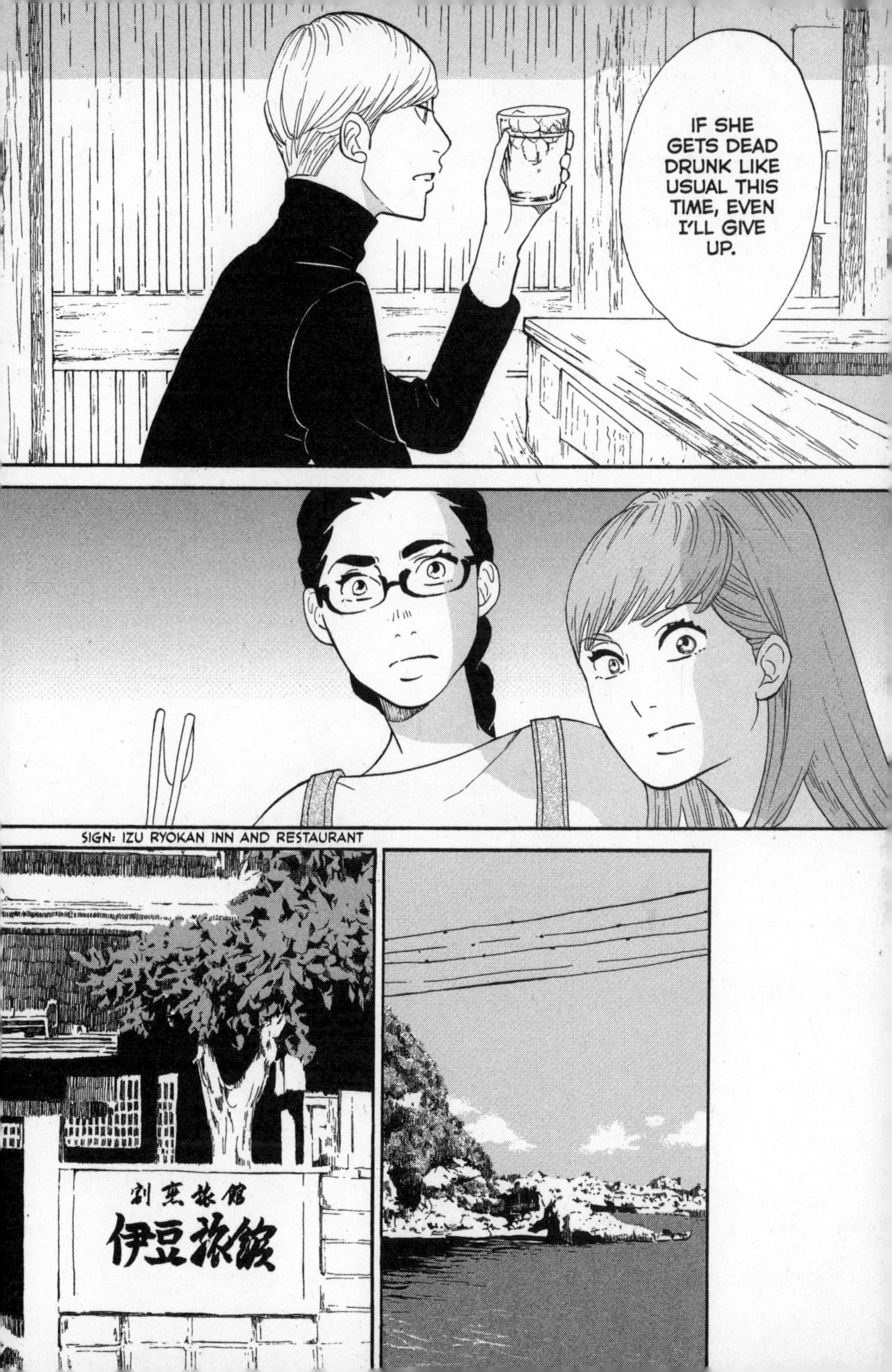
IF SHE GETS DEAD DRUNK LIKE USUAL THIS TIME, EVEN I'LL GIVE UP.
SIGN: IZU RYOKAN INN AND RESTAURANT
割烹旅館
伊豆旅館

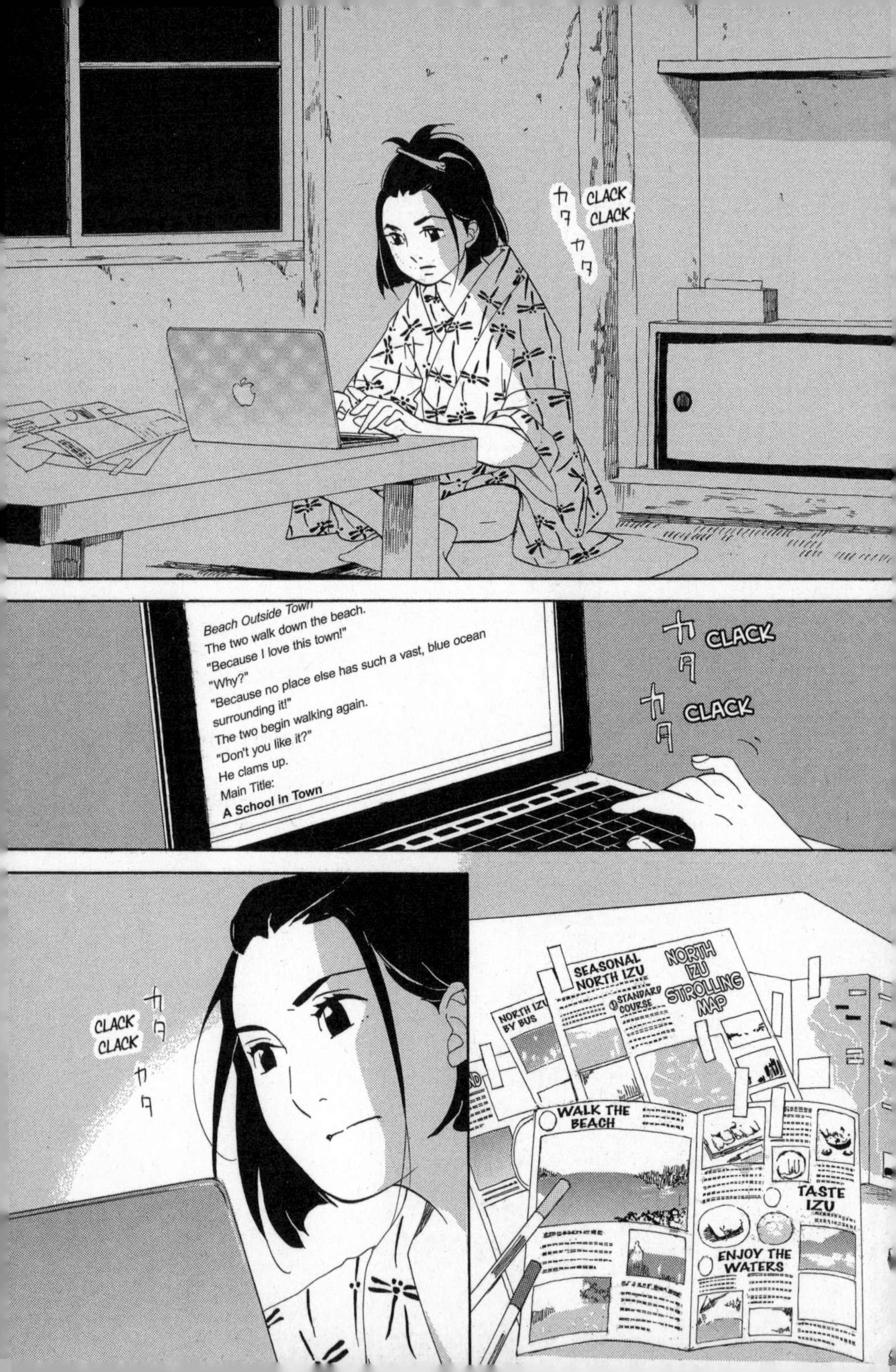
カタカタ
CLACK CLACK
Beach Outside Town
The two walk down the beach.
"Because I love this town!"
"Why?"
"Because no place else has such a vast, blue ocean surrounding it!"
The two begin walking again.
"Don't you like it?"
He clams up.
Main Title:
A School in Town
カタ
CLACK
カタ
CLACK
NORTH IZU STROLLING MAP
SEASONAL NORTH IZU
① STANDARD COURSE
NORTH IZU BY BUS
WALK THE BEACH
TASTE IZU
ENJOY THE WATERS
カタカタ
CLACK CLACK

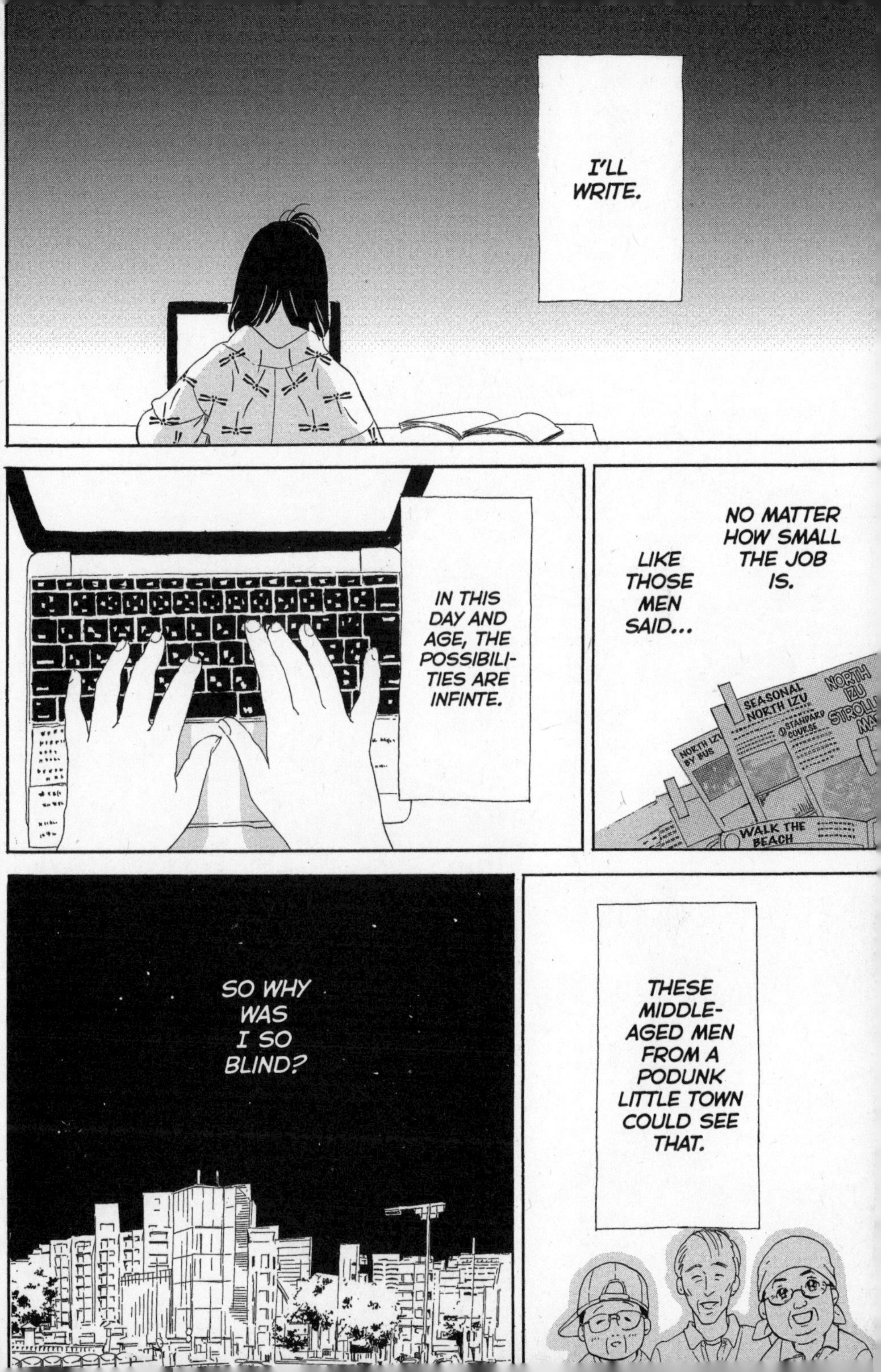
I'LL WRITE.
NO MATTER HOW SMALL THE JOB IS.
LIKE THOSE MEN SAID...
SEASONAL NORTH IZU
STANDARD COURSE
NORTH IZU BY BUS
WALK THE BEACH
IN THIS DAY AND AGE, THE POSSIBILITIES ARE INFINTE.
THESE MIDDLE-AGED MEN FROM A PODUNK LITTLE TOWN COULD SEE THAT.
SO WHY WAS I SO BLIND?

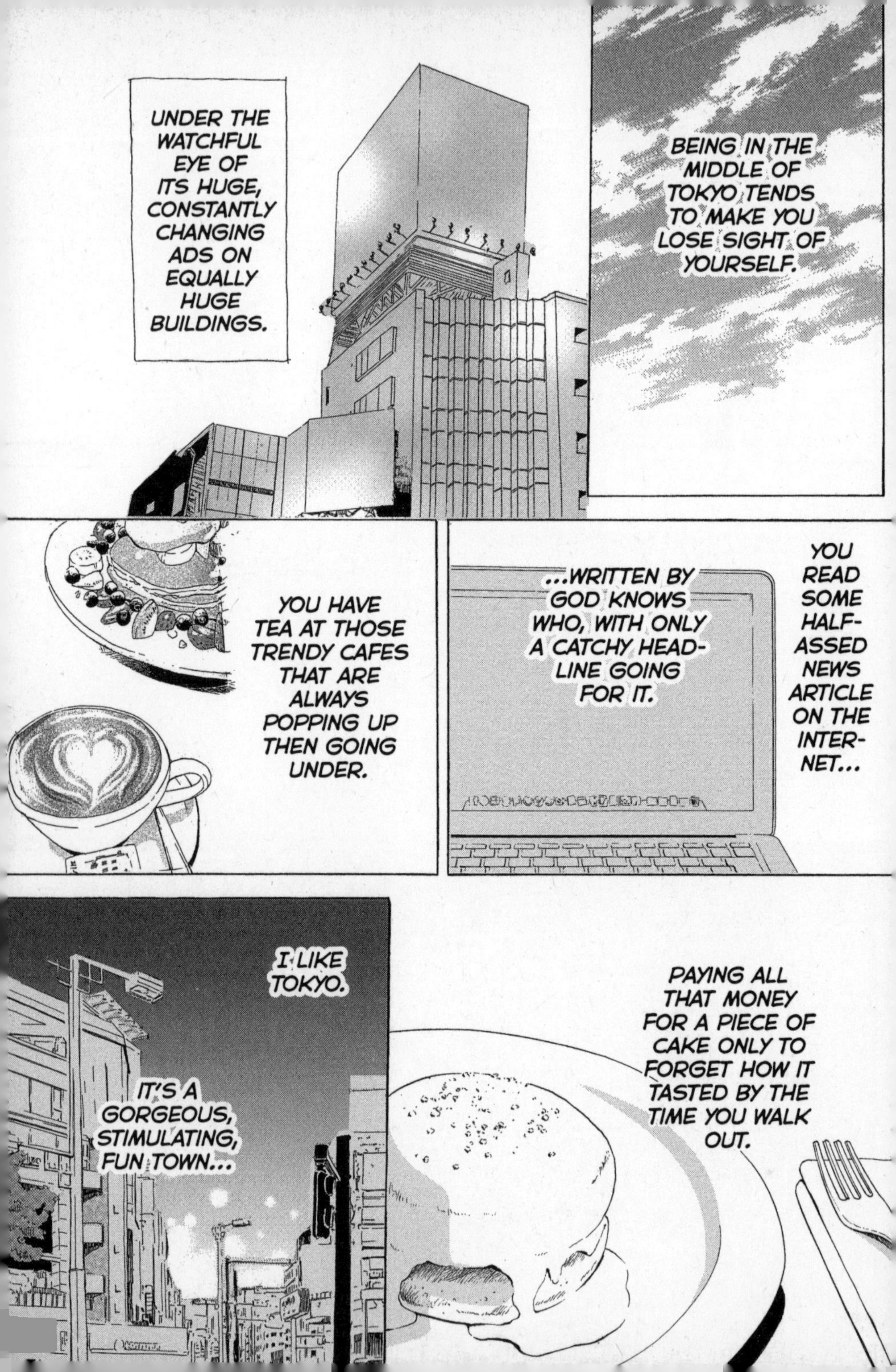
BEING IN THE MIDDLE OF TOKYO TENDS TO MAKE YOU LOSE SIGHT OF YOURSELF.
UNDER THE WATCHFUL EYE OF ITS HUGE, CONSTANTLY CHANGING ADS ON EQUALLY HUGE BUILDINGS.
YOU READ SOME HALF-ASSED NEWS ARTICLE ON THE INTER-NET...
...WRITTEN BY GOD KNOWS WHO, WITH ONLY A CATCHY HEAD-LINE GOING FOR IT.
YOU HAVE TEA AT THOSE TRENDY CAFES THAT ARE ALWAYS POPPING UP THEN GOING UNDER.
PAYING ALL THAT MONEY FOR A PIECE OF CAKE ONLY TO FORGET HOW IT TASTED BY THE TIME YOU WALK OUT.
I LIKE TOKYO.
IT'S A GORGEOUS, STIMULATING, FUN TOWN...

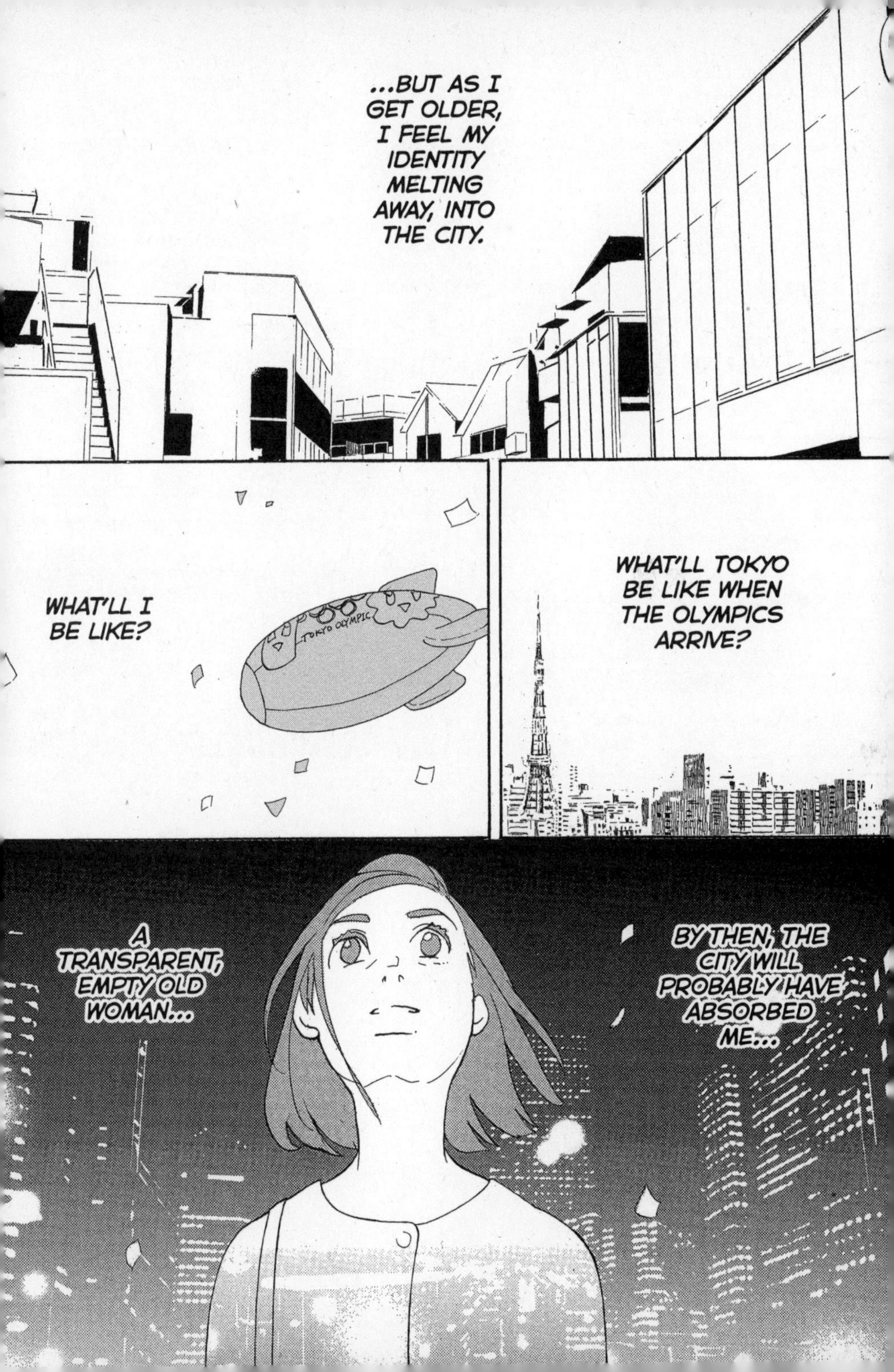
...BUT AS I GET OLDER, I FEEL MY IDENTITY MELTING AWAY, INTO THE CITY.
WHAT'LL TOKYO BE LIKE WHEN THE OLYMPICS ARRIVE?
TOKYO OLYMPIC
WHAT'LL I BE LIKE?
BY THEN, THE CITY WILL PROBABLY HAVE ABSORBED ME...
A TRANSPARENT, EMPTY OLD WOMAN...

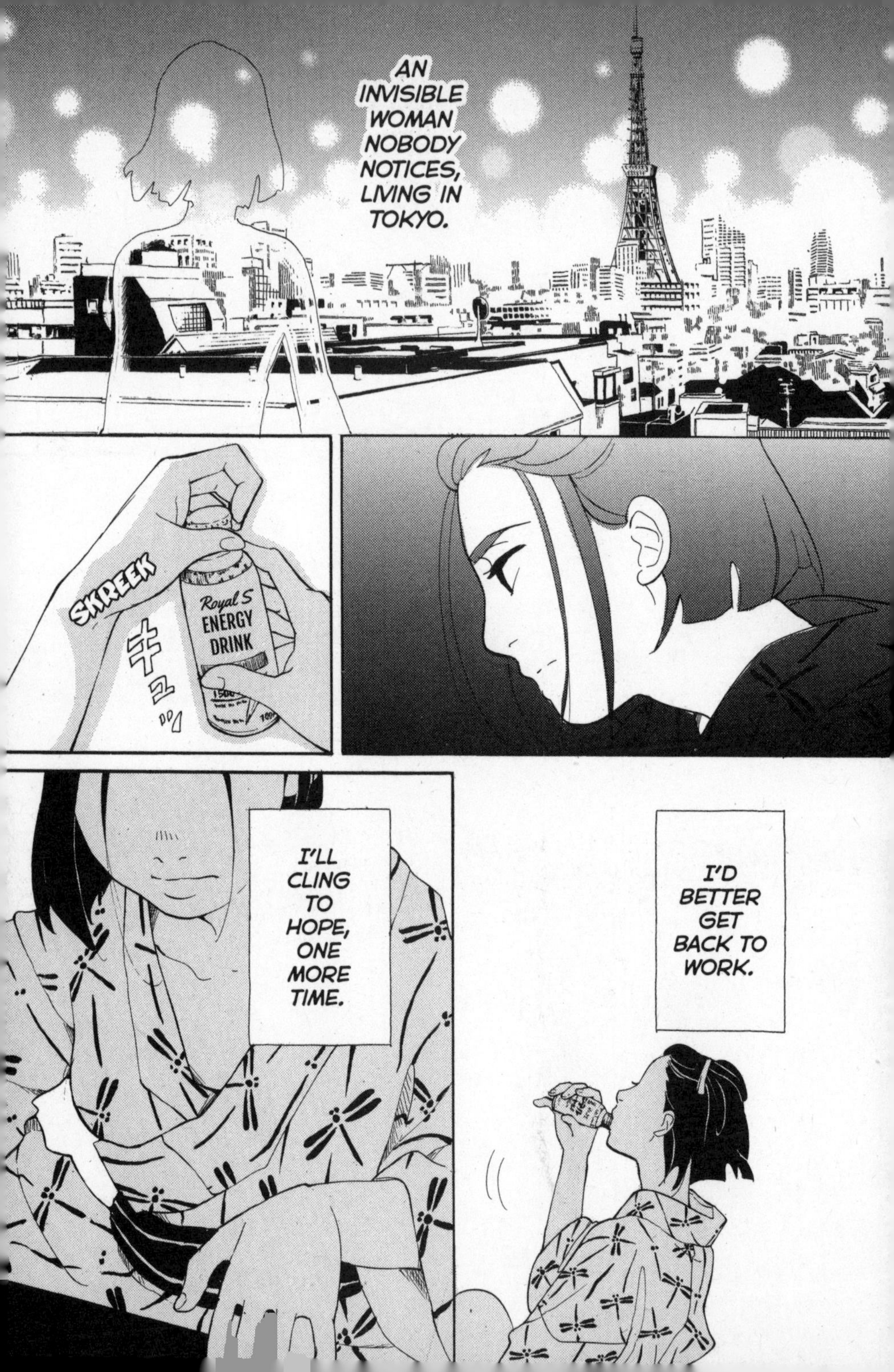
AN INVISIBLE WOMAN NOBODY NOTICES, LIVING IN TOKYO.
Royal S ENERGY DRINK
SKREEK
キュッ
I'D BETTER GET BACK TO WORK.
I'LL CLING TO HOPE, ONE MORE TIME.

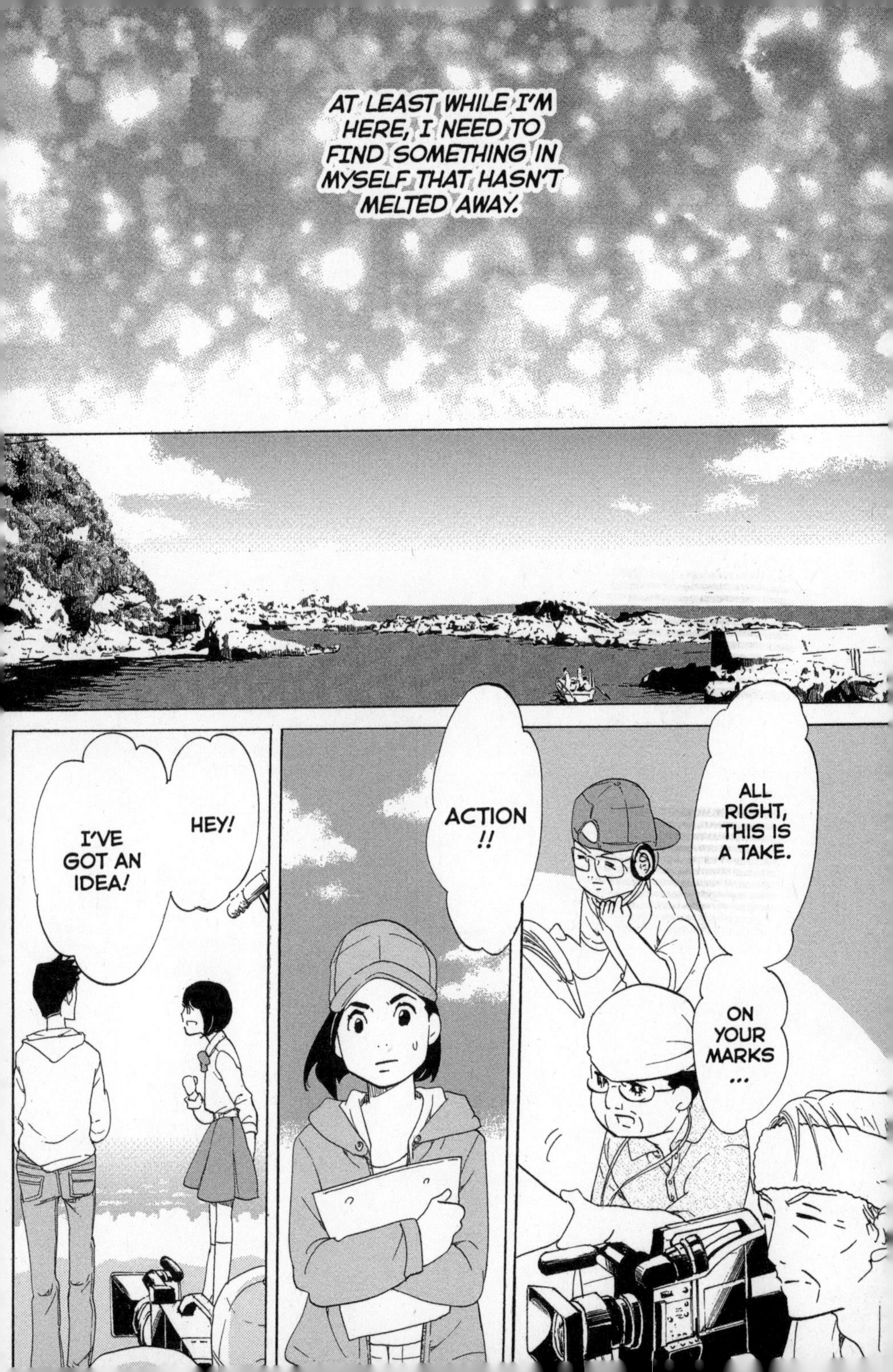
AT LEAST WHILE I'M HERE, I NEED TO FIND SOMETHING IN MYSELF THAT HASN'T MELTED AWAY.
ALL RIGHT, THIS IS A TAKE.
ON YOUR MARKS ...
ACTION !!
HEY!
I'VE GOT AN IDEA!

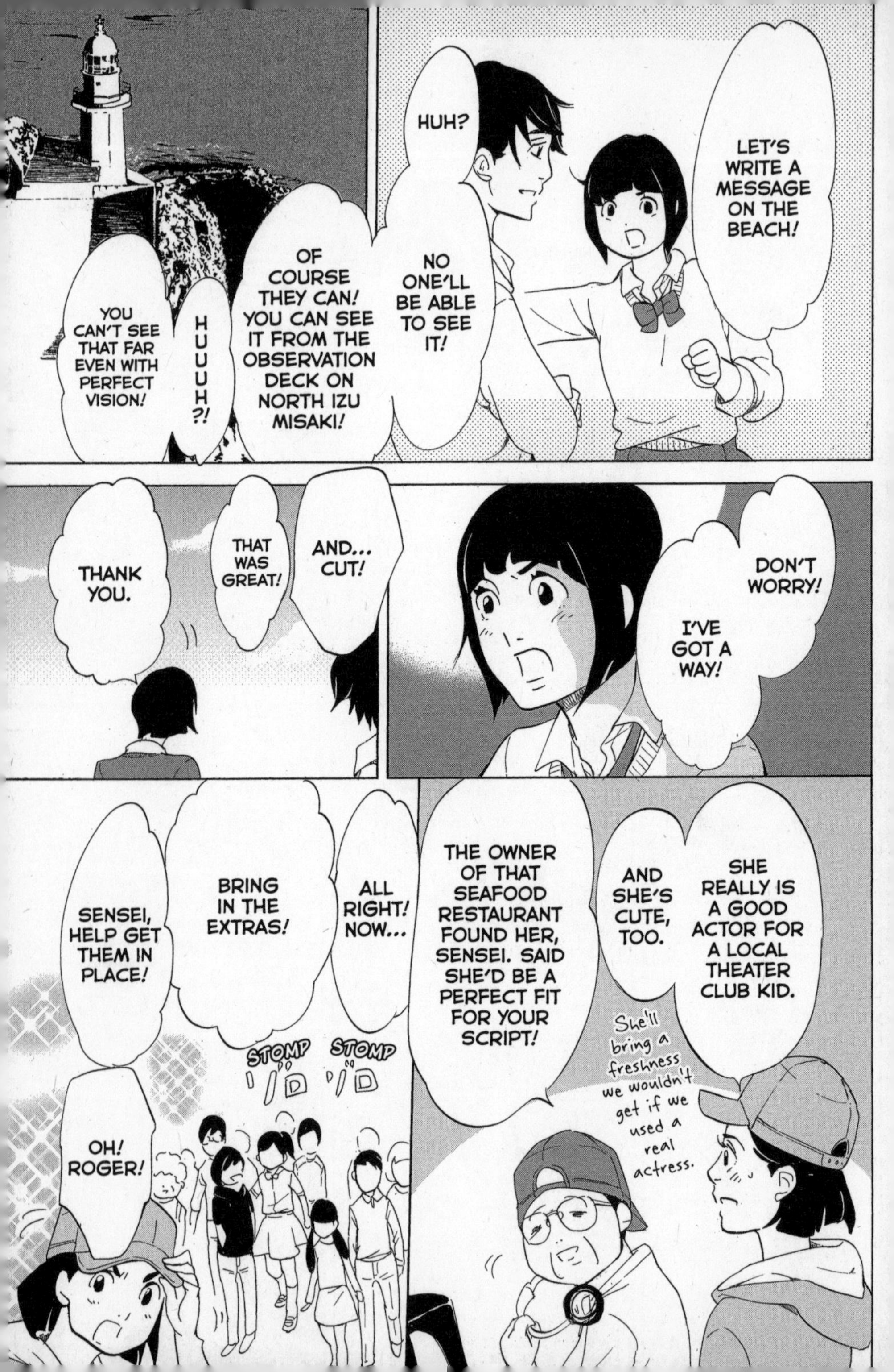
LET'S WRITE A MESSAGE ON THE BEACH!
HUH?
NO ONE'LL BE ABLE TO SEE IT!
OF COURSE THEY CAN! YOU CAN SEE IT FROM THE OBSERVATION DECK ON NORTH IZU MISAKI!
HUUUUH?!
YOU CAN'T SEE THAT FAR EVEN WITH PERFECT VISION!
DON'T WORRY!
I'VE GOT A WAY!
AND... CUT!
THAT WAS GREAT!
THANK YOU.
SHE REALLY IS A GOOD ACTOR FOR A LOCAL THEATER CLUB KID.
AND SHE'S CUTE, TOO.
She'll bring a freshness we wouldn't get if we used a real actress.
THE OWNER OF THAT SEAFOOD RESTAURANT FOUND HER, SENSEI. SAID SHE'D BE A PERFECT FIT FOR YOUR SCRIPT!
ALL RIGHT! NOW...
BRING IN THE EXTRAS!
SENSEI, HELP GET THEM IN PLACE!
STOMP STOMP
OH! ROGER!

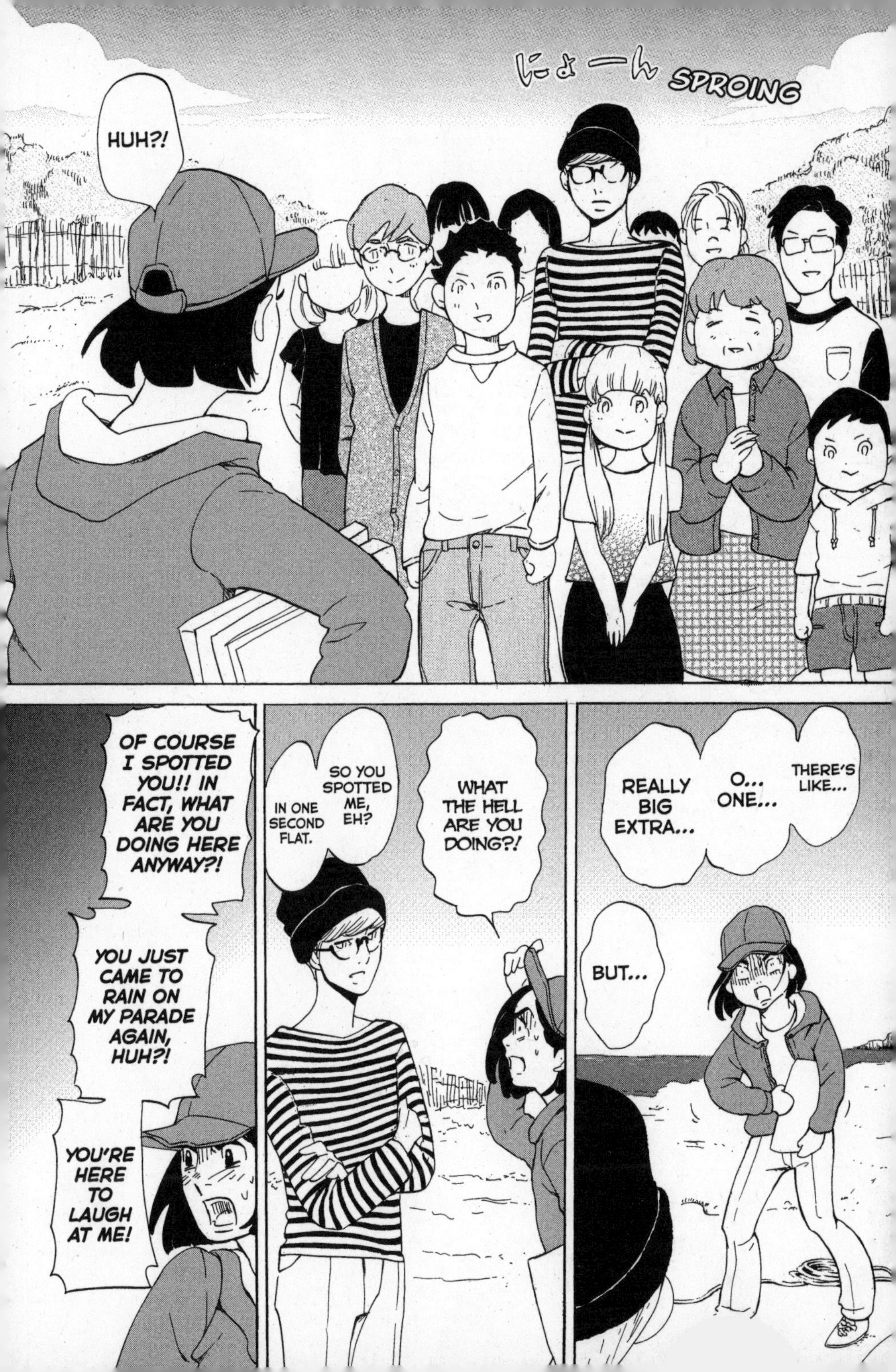
にょーん SPROING
HUH?!
THERE'S LIKE...
O... ONE...
REALLY BIG EXTRA...
BUT...
WHAT THE HELL ARE YOU DOING?!
SO YOU SPOTTED ME, EH?
IN ONE SECOND FLAT.
OF COURSE I SPOTTED YOU!! IN FACT, WHAT ARE YOU DOING HERE ANYWAY?!
YOU JUST CAME TO RAIN ON MY PARADE AGAIN, HUH?!
YOU'RE HERE TO LAUGH AT ME!

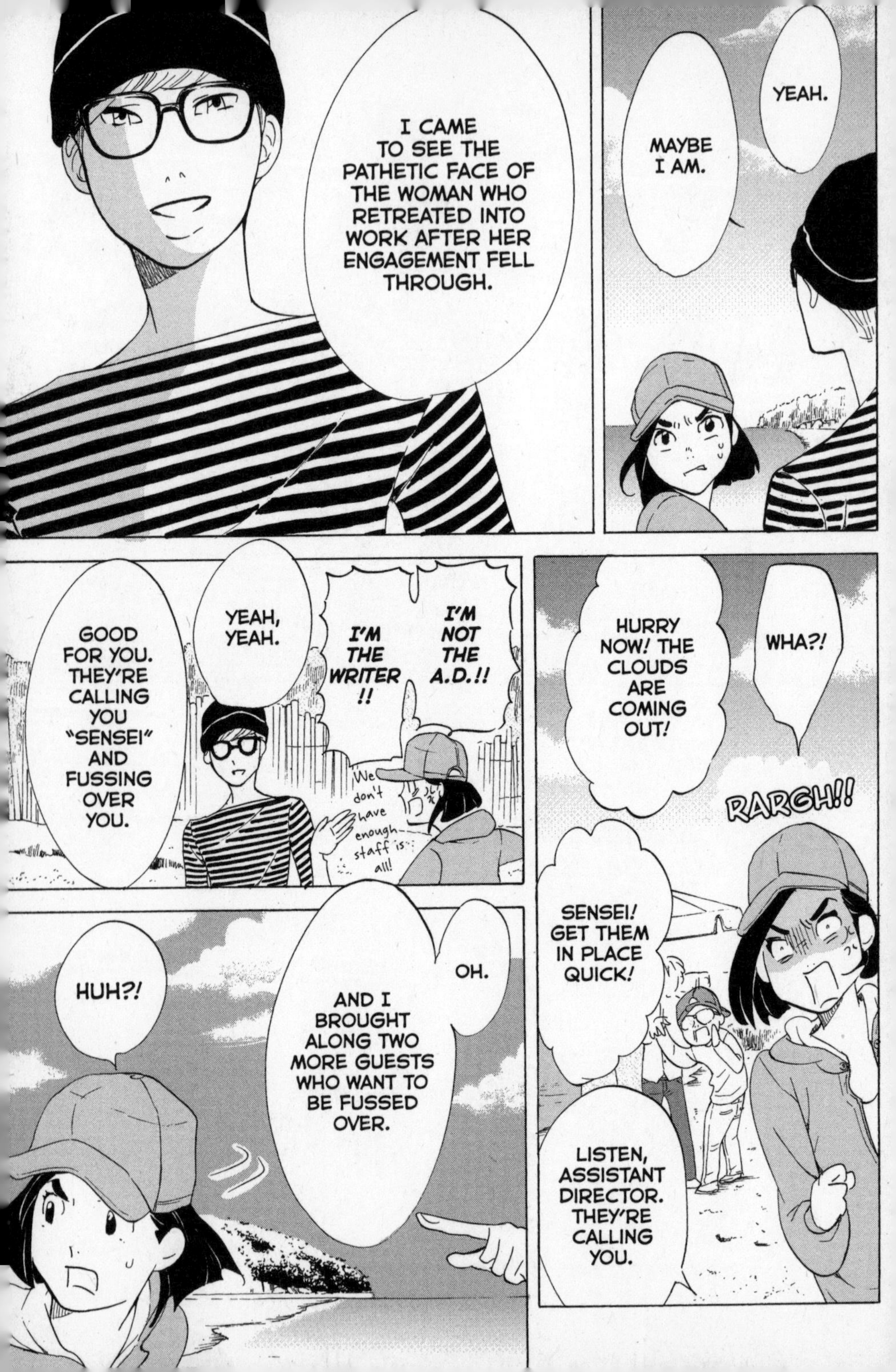
YEAH.
MAYBE I AM.
I CAME TO SEE THE PATHETIC FACE OF THE WOMAN WHO RETREATED INTO WORK AFTER HER ENGAGEMENT FELL THROUGH.
WHA?!
HURRY NOW! THE CLOUDS ARE COMING OUT!
RARGH!!
SENSEI! GET THEM IN PLACE QUICK!
LISTEN, ASSISTANT DIRECTOR. THEY'RE CALLING YOU.
I'M NOT THE A.D.!!
I'M THE WRITER!!
We don't have enough staff is all!
YEAH, YEAH.
GOOD FOR YOU. THEY'RE CALLING YOU "SENSEI" AND FUSSING OVER YOU.
OH.
AND I BROUGHT ALONG TWO MORE GUESTS WHO WANT TO BE FUSSED OVER.
HUH?!

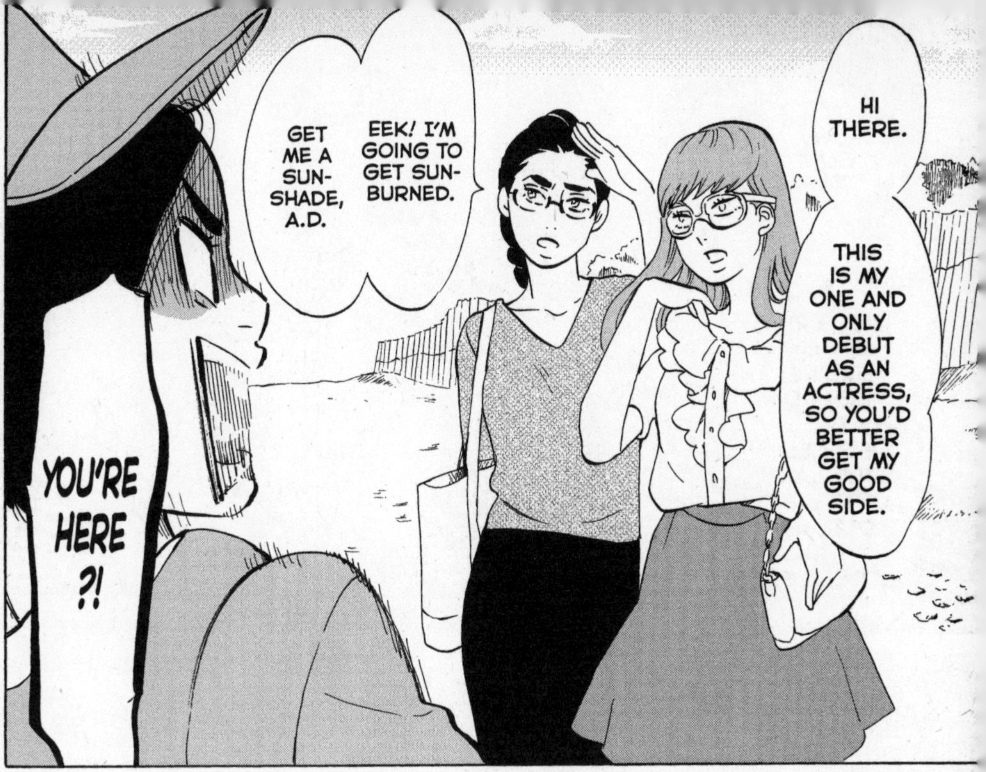
HI THERE.
THIS IS MY ONE AND ONLY DEBUT AS AN ACTRESS, SO YOU'D BETTER GET MY GOOD SIDE.
EEK! I'M GOING TO GET SUN-BURNED.
GET ME A SUN-SHADE, A.D.
YOU'RE HERE ?!

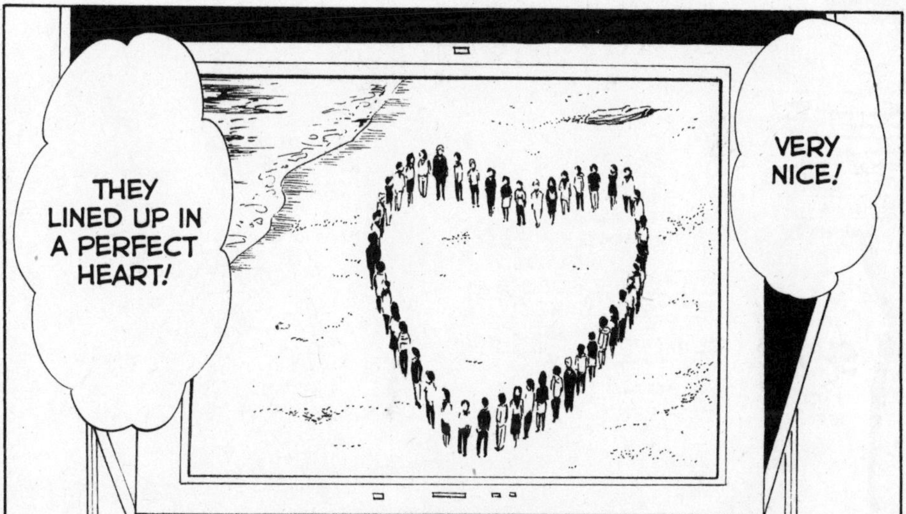
VERY NICE!
THEY LINED UP IN A PERFECT HEART!

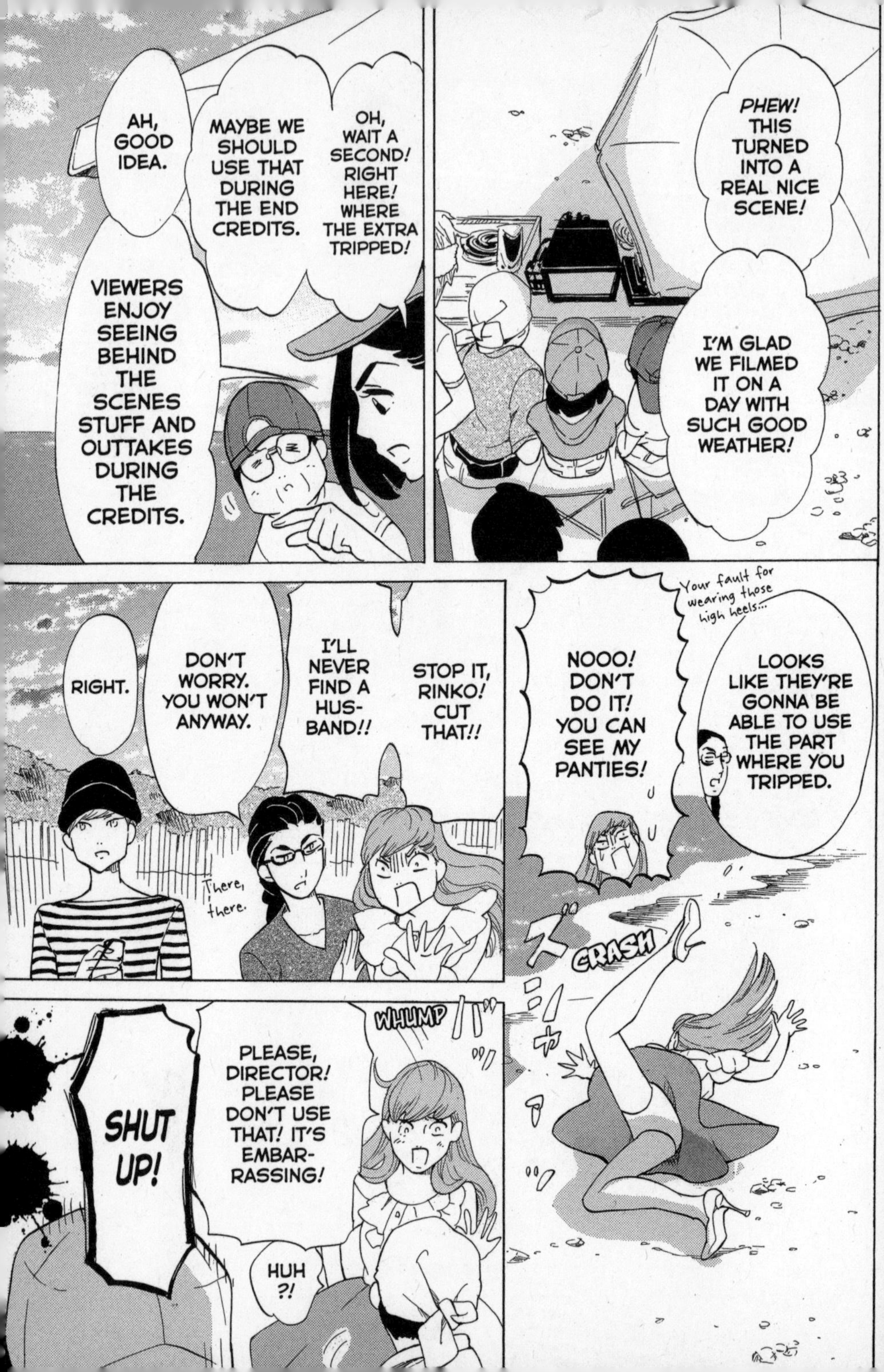
PHEW! THIS TURNED INTO A REAL NICE SCENE!
I'M GLAD WE FILMED IT ON A DAY WITH SUCH GOOD WEATHER!
OH, WAIT A SECOND! RIGHT HERE! WHERE THE EXTRA TRIPPED!
MAYBE WE SHOULD USE THAT DURING THE END CREDITS.
AH, GOOD IDEA.
VIEWERS ENJOY SEEING BEHIND THE SCENES STUFF AND OUTTAKES DURING THE CREDITS.
Your fault for wearing those high heels...
LOOKS LIKE THEY'RE GONNA BE ABLE TO USE THE PART WHERE YOU TRIPPED.
NOOO! DON'T DO IT! YOU CAN SEE MY PANTIES!
CRASH
STOP IT, RINKO! CUT THAT!!
I'LL NEVER FIND A HUS-BAND!!
DON'T WORRY. YOU WON'T ANYWAY.
There, there.
RIGHT.
WHUMP
PLEASE, DIRECTOR! PLEASE DON'T USE THAT! IT'S EMBAR-RASSING!
SHUT UP!
HUH ?!

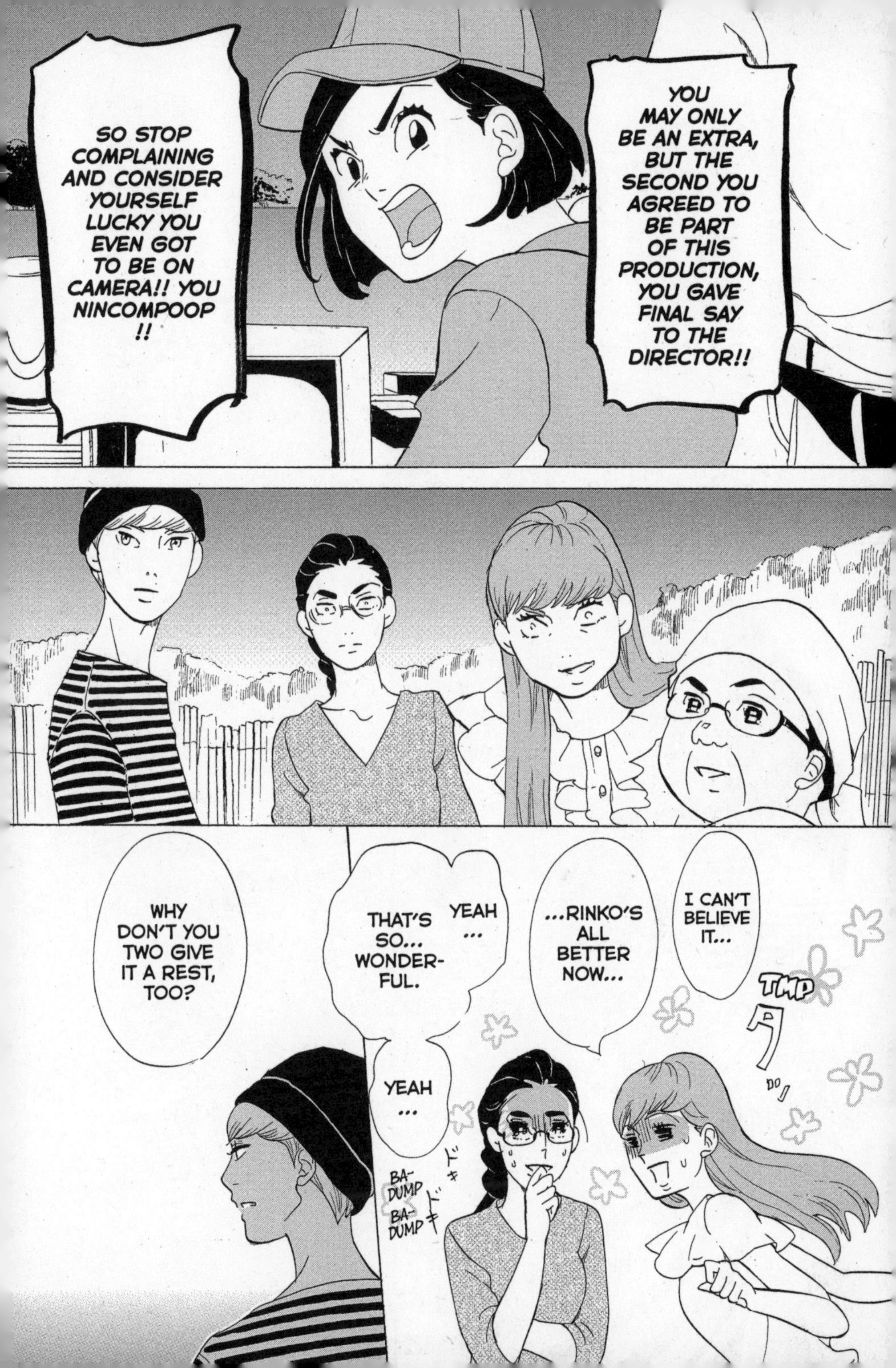
YOU MAY ONLY BE AN EXTRA, BUT THE SECOND YOU AGREED TO BE PART OF THIS PRODUCTION, YOU GAVE FINAL SAY TO THE DIRECTOR!!
SO STOP COMPLAINING AND CONSIDER YOURSELF LUCKY YOU EVEN GOT TO BE ON CAMERA!! YOU NINCOMPOOP!!
I CAN'T BELIEVE IT...
TMP
...RINKO'S ALL BETTER NOW...
YEAH ...
THAT'S SO... WONDERFUL.
YEAH ...
BA-DUMP
BA-DUMP
WHY DON'T YOU TWO GIVE IT A REST, TOO?

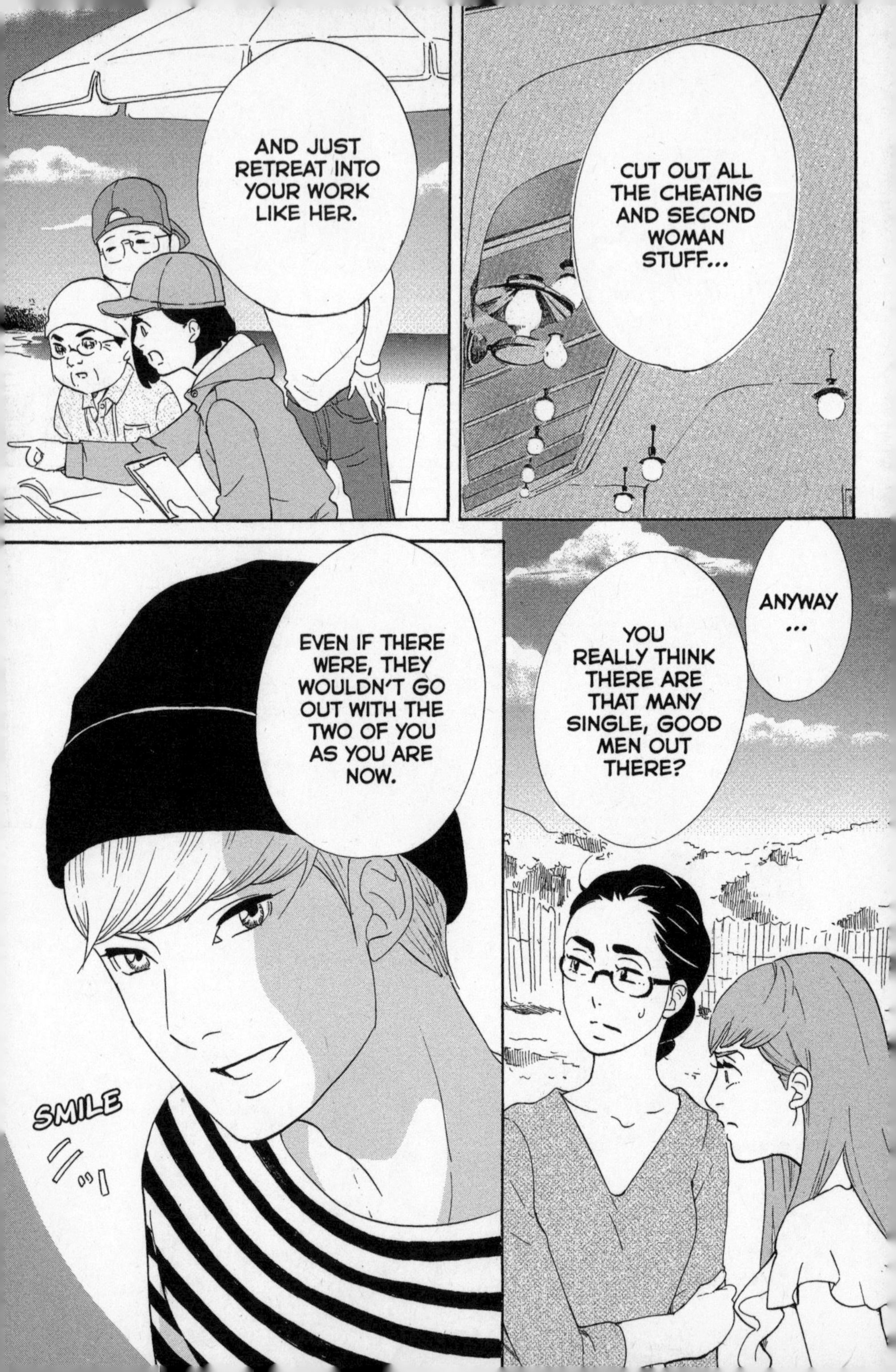
CUT OUT ALL THE CHEATING AND SECOND WOMAN STUFF...
AND JUST RETREAT INTO YOUR WORK LIKE HER.
ANYWAY...
YOU REALLY THINK THERE ARE THAT MANY SINGLE, GOOD MEN OUT THERE?
EVEN IF THERE WERE, THEY WOULDN'T GO OUT WITH THE TWO OF YOU AS YOU ARE NOW.
SMILE

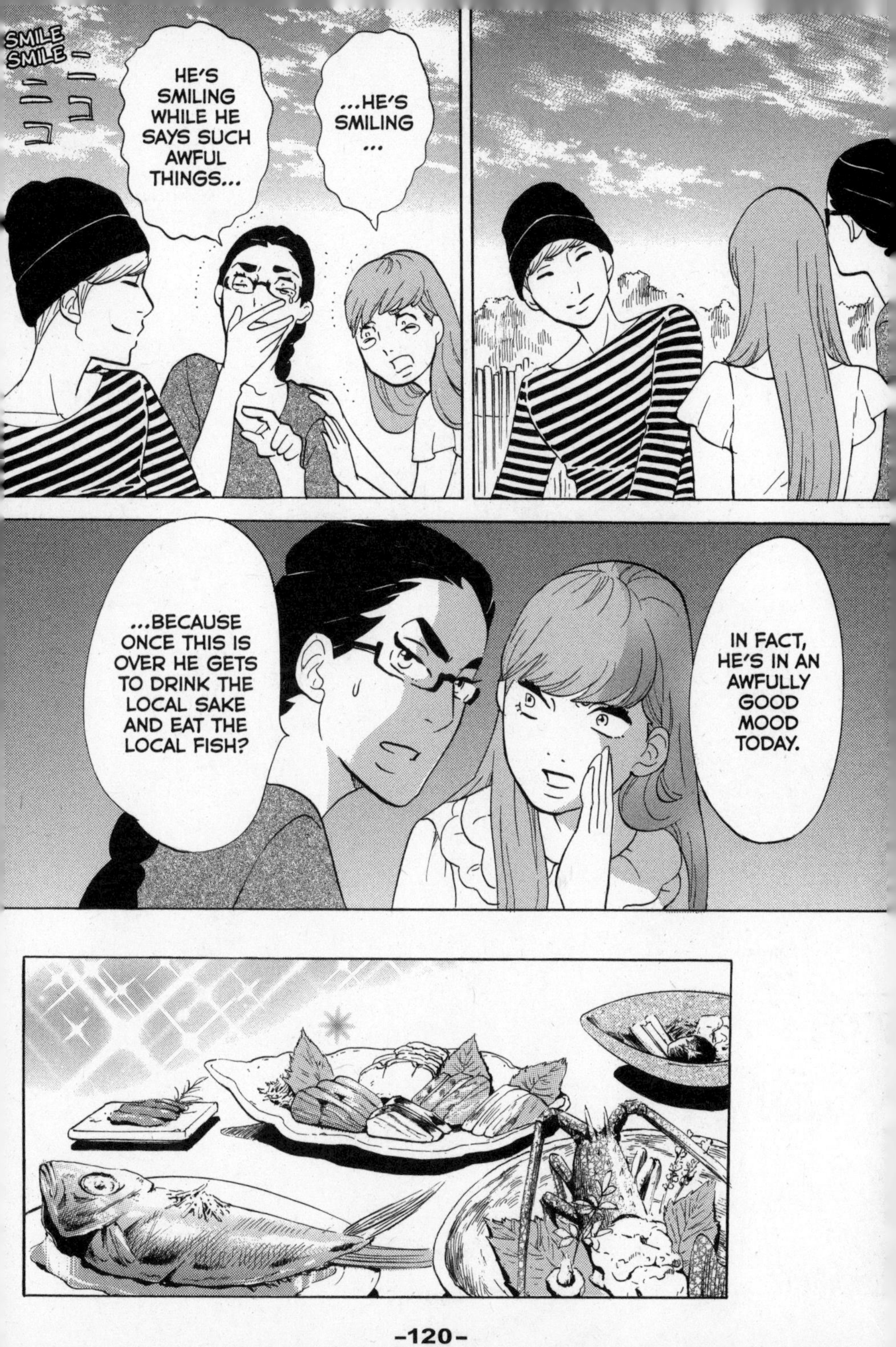
...HE'S SMILING ...
HE'S SMILING WHILE HE SAYS SUCH AWFUL THINGS...
SMILE SMILE
ニコニコ
IN FACT, HE'S IN AN AWFULLY GOOD MOOD TODAY.
...BECAUSE ONCE THIS IS OVER HE GETS TO DRINK THE LOCAL SAKE AND EAT THE LOCAL FISH?

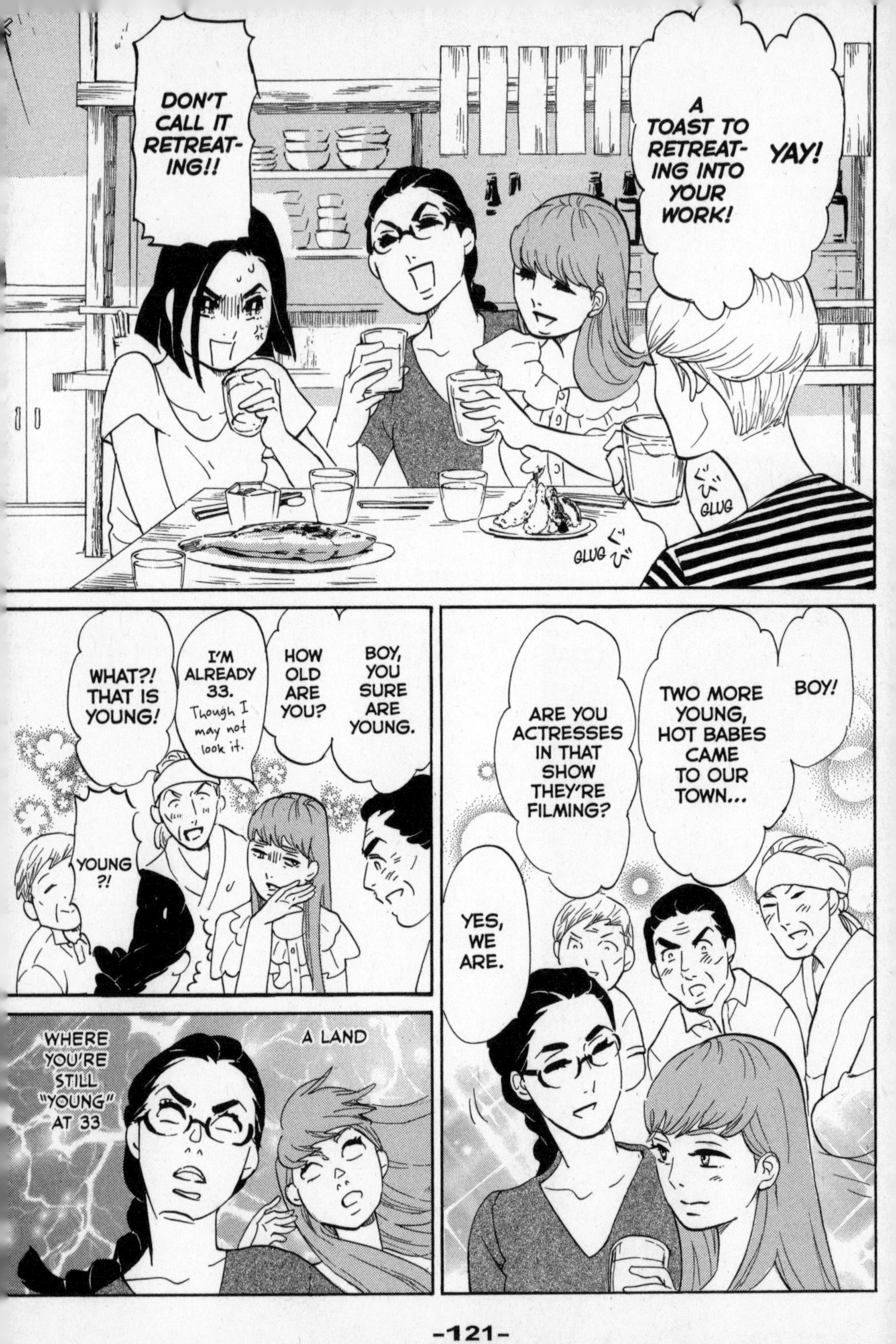

A TOAST TO RETREATING INTO YOUR WORK!
YAY!
DON'T CALL IT RETREATING!!
GLUG
GLUG
BOY!
TWO MORE YOUNG, HOT BABES CAME TO OUR TOWN...
ARE YOU ACTRESSES IN THAT SHOW THEY'RE FILMING?
YES, WE ARE.
BOY, YOU SURE ARE YOUNG.
HOW OLD ARE YOU?
I'M ALREADY 33. Though I may not look it.
WHAT?! THAT IS YOUNG!
YOUNG?!
A LAND
WHERE YOU'RE STILL "YOUNG" AT 33

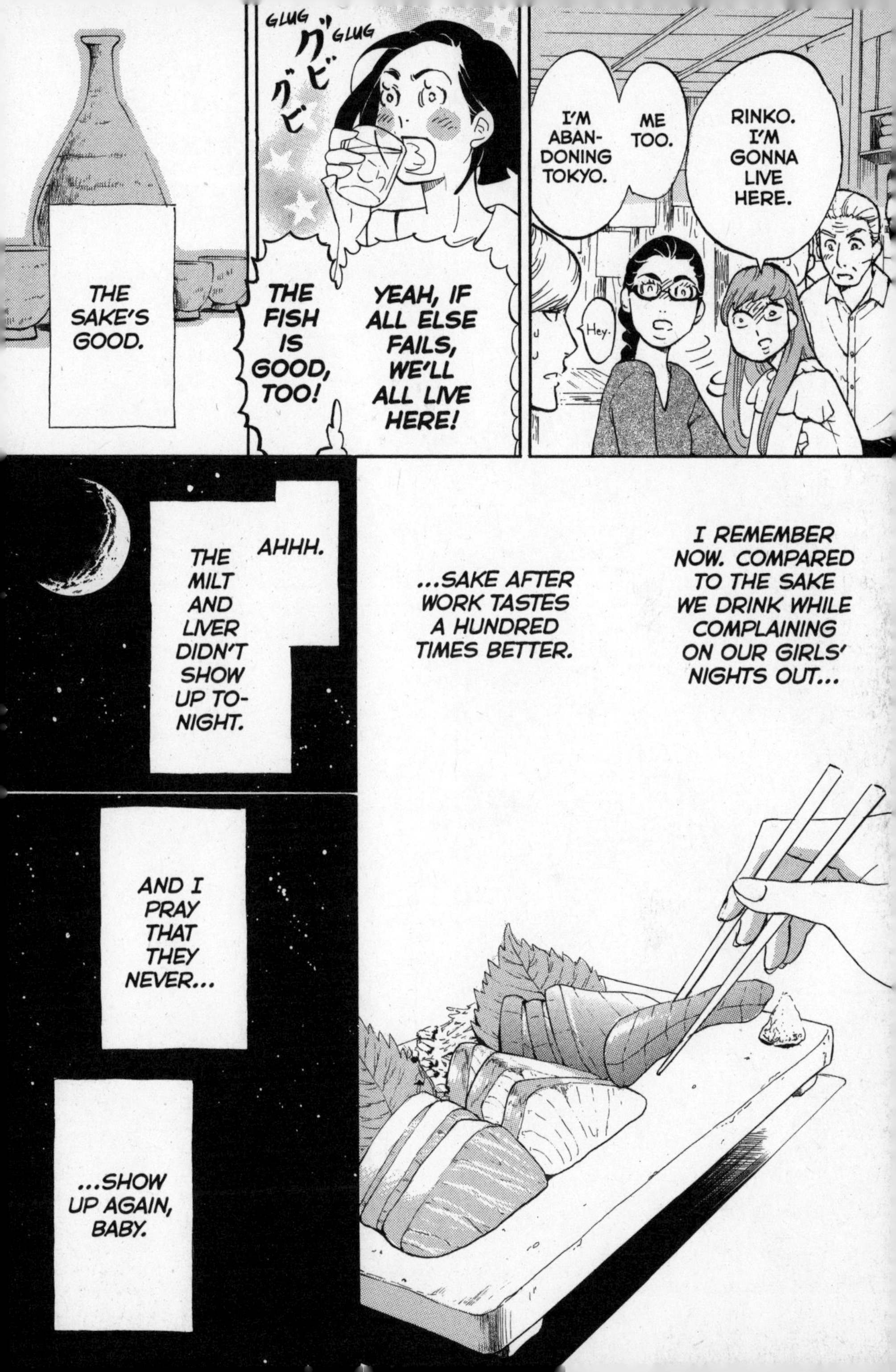
RINKO. I'M GONNA LIVE HERE.
ME TOO.
I'M ABAN-DONING TOKYO.
Hey.
GLUG GLUG
グビグビ
YEAH, IF ALL ELSE FAILS, WE'LL ALL LIVE HERE!
THE FISH IS GOOD, TOO!
THE SAKE'S GOOD.
I REMEMBER NOW. COMPARED TO THE SAKE WE DRINK WHILE COMPLAINING ON OUR GIRLS' NIGHTS OUT...
...SAKE AFTER WORK TASTES A HUNDRED TIMES BETTER.
AHHH.
THE MILT AND LIVER DIDN'T SHOW UP TO-NIGHT.
AND I PRAY THAT THEY NEVER...
...SHOW UP AGAIN, BABY.

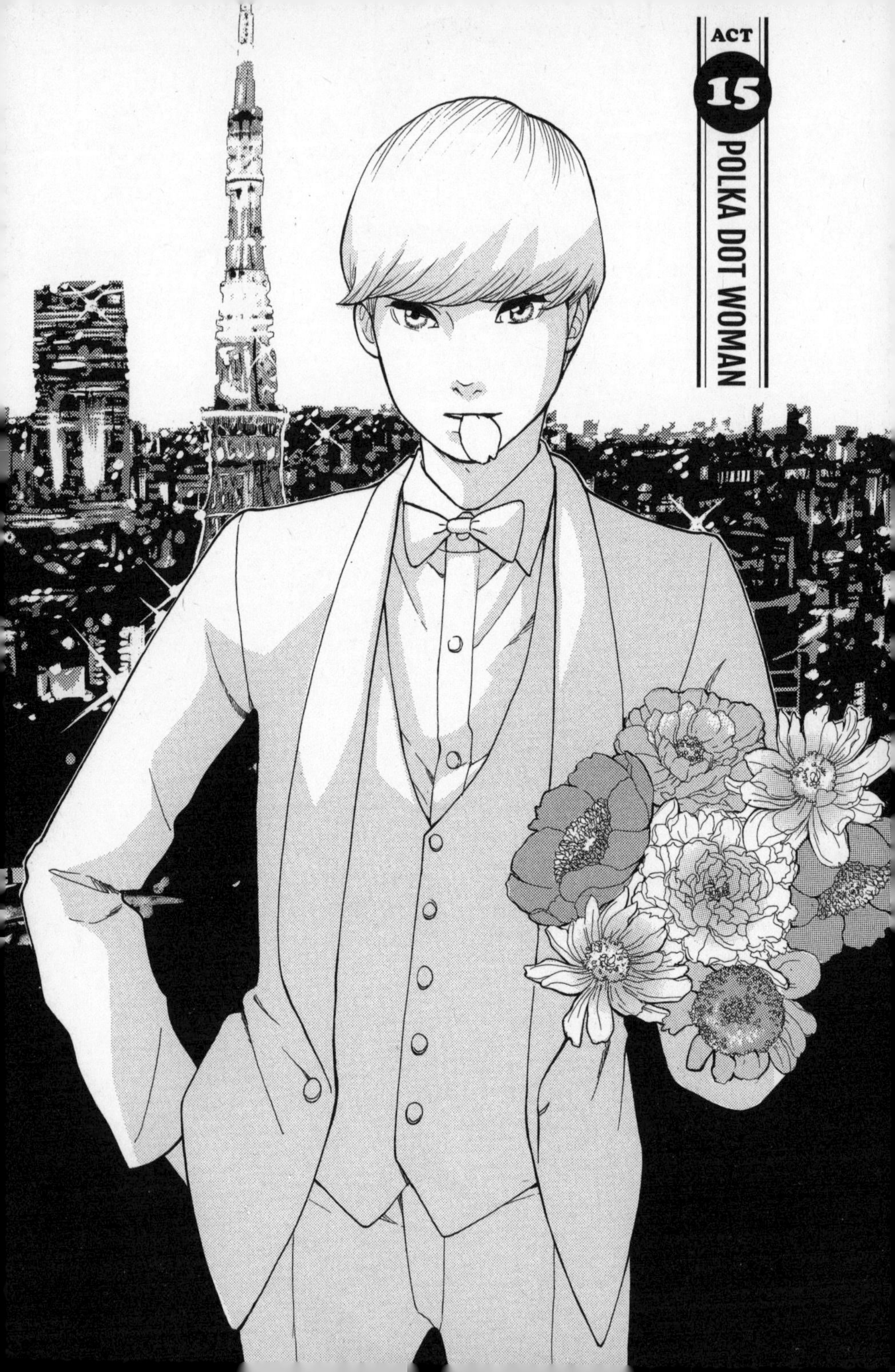
ACT
15
POLKA DOT WOMAN

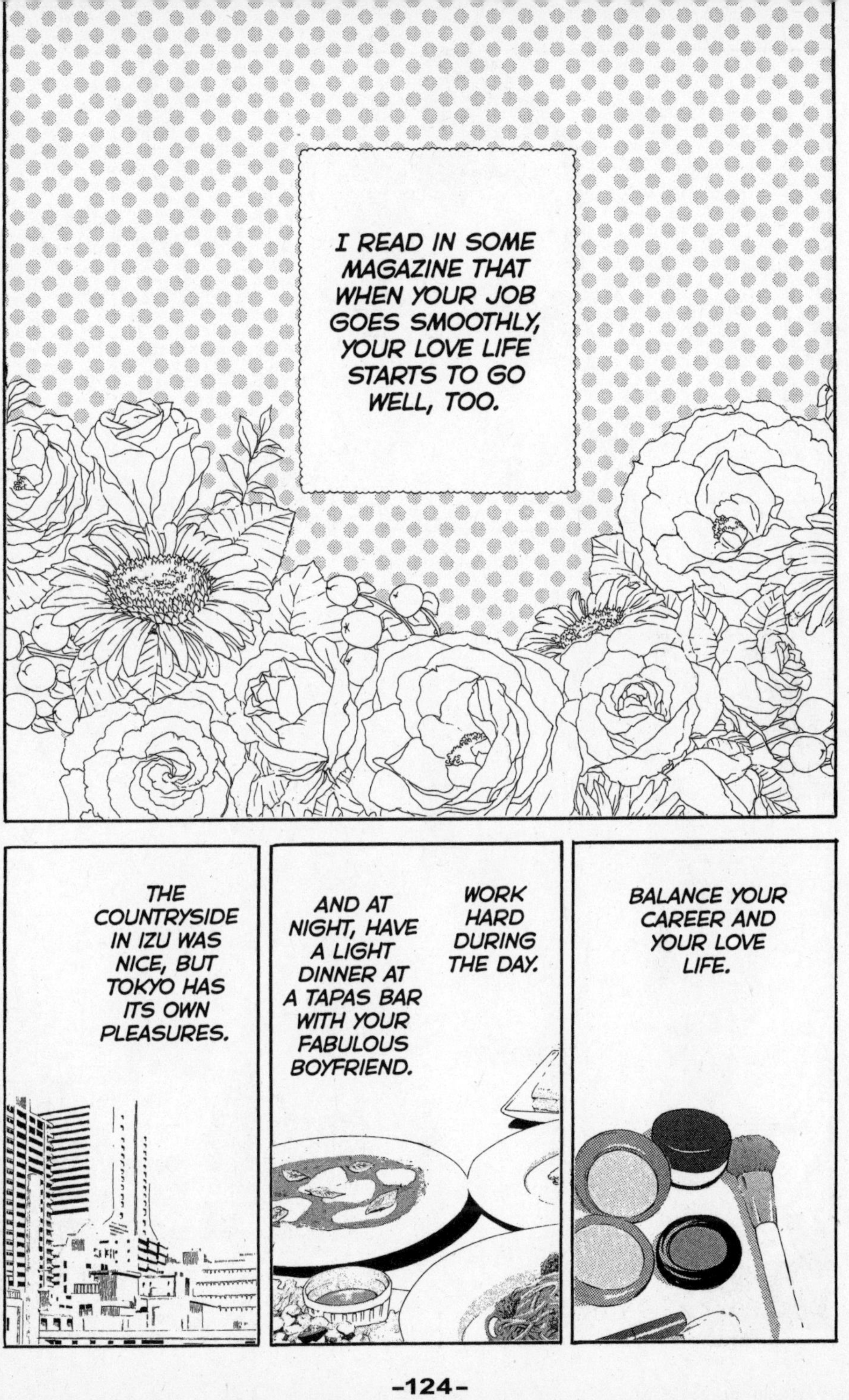
I READ IN SOME MAGAZINE THAT WHEN YOUR JOB GOES SMOOTHLY, YOUR LOVE LIFE STARTS TO GO WELL, TOO.
BALANCE YOUR CAREER AND YOUR LOVE LIFE.
WORK HARD DURING THE DAY.
AND AT NIGHT, HAVE A LIGHT DINNER AT A TAPAS BAR WITH YOUR FABULOUS BOYFRIEND.
THE COUNTRYSIDE IN IZU WAS NICE, BUT TOKYO HAS ITS OWN PLEASURES.

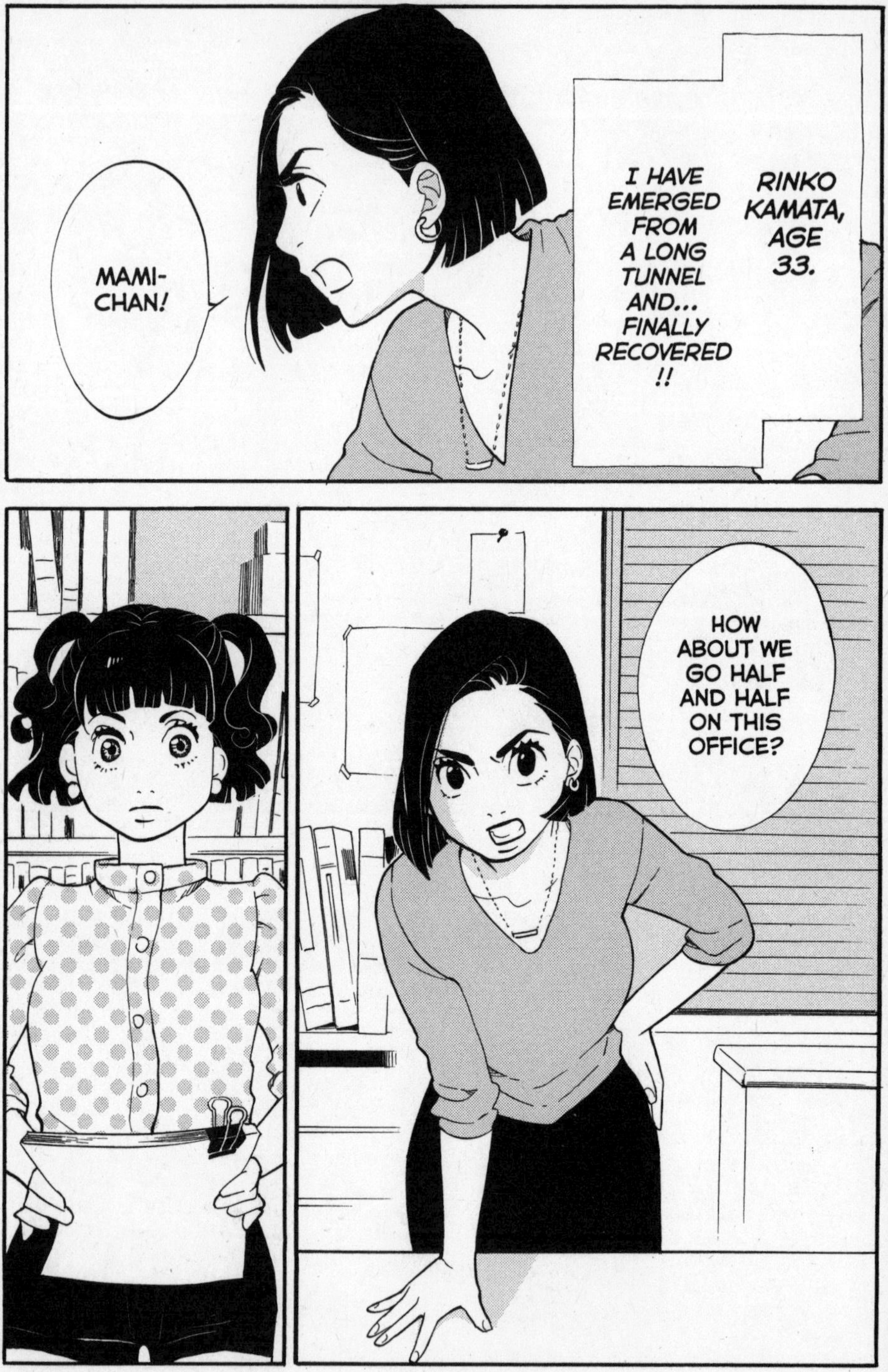
RINKO KAMATA, AGE 33.
I HAVE EMERGED FROM A LONG TUNNEL AND... FINALLY RECOVERED !!
MAMI-CHAN!
HOW ABOUT WE GO HALF AND HALF ON THIS OFFICE?

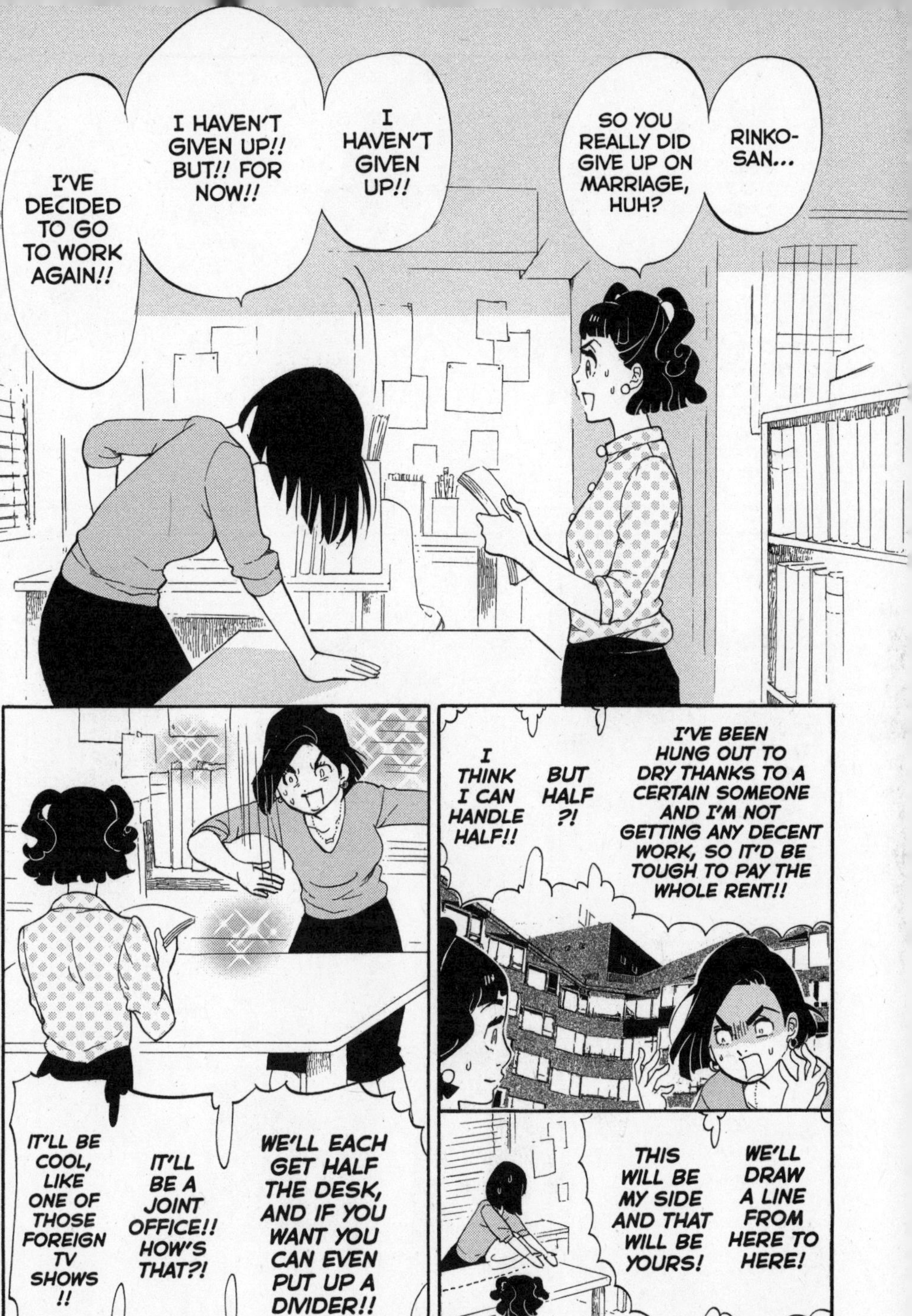

RINKO-SAN...
SO YOU REALLY DID GIVE UP ON MARRIAGE, HUH?
I HAVEN'T GIVEN UP!!
I HAVEN'T GIVEN UP!! BUT!! FOR NOW!!
I'VE DECIDED TO GO TO WORK AGAIN!!
I'VE BEEN HUNG OUT TO DRY THANKS TO A CERTAIN SOMEONE AND I'M NOT GETTING ANY DECENT WORK, SO IT'D BE TOUGH TO PAY THE WHOLE RENT!!
BUT HALF ?!
I THINK I CAN HANDLE HALF!!
WE'LL DRAW A LINE FROM HERE TO HERE!
THIS WILL BE MY SIDE AND THAT WILL BE YOURS!
WE'LL EACH GET HALF THE DESK, AND IF YOU WANT YOU CAN EVEN PUT UP A DIVIDER!!
IT'LL BE A JOINT OFFICE!! HOW'S THAT?!
IT'LL BE COOL, LIKE ONE OF THOSE FOREIGN TV SHOWS !!

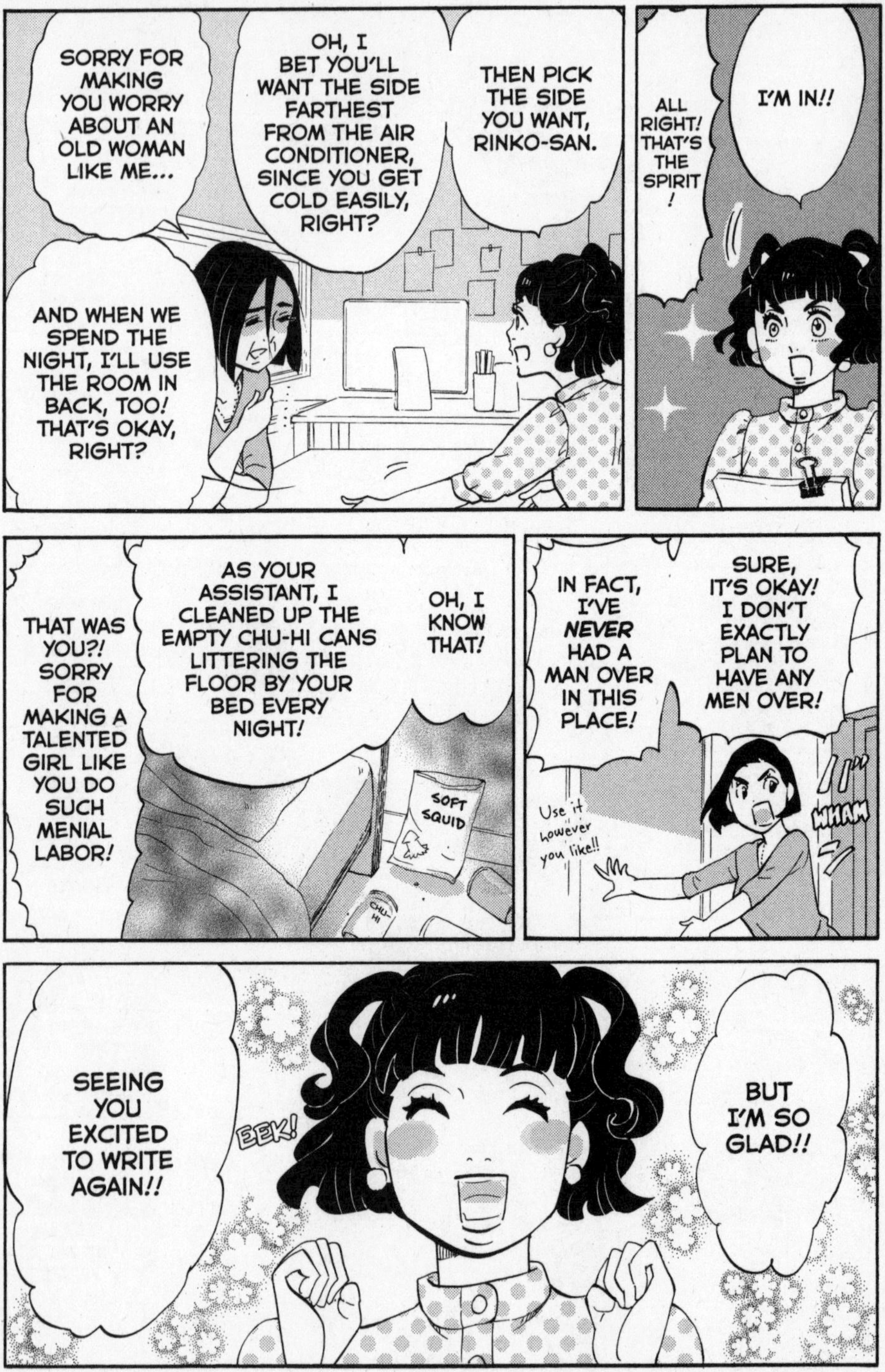
I'M IN!!
ALL RIGHT! THAT'S THE SPIRIT!
THEN PICK THE SIDE YOU WANT, RINKO-SAN.
OH, I BET YOU'LL WANT THE SIDE FARTHEST FROM THE AIR CONDITIONER, SINCE YOU GET COLD EASILY, RIGHT?
SORRY FOR MAKING YOU WORRY ABOUT AN OLD WOMAN LIKE ME...
AND WHEN WE SPEND THE NIGHT, I'LL USE THE ROOM IN BACK, TOO! THAT'S OKAY, RIGHT?
SURE, IT'S OKAY! I DON'T EXACTLY PLAN TO HAVE ANY MEN OVER!
IN FACT, I'VE *NEVER* HAD A MAN OVER IN THIS PLACE!
WHAM
Use it however you like!!
OH, I KNOW THAT!
AS YOUR ASSISTANT, I CLEANED UP THE EMPTY CHU-HI CANS LITTERING THE FLOOR BY YOUR BED EVERY NIGHT!
THAT WAS YOU?! SORRY FOR MAKING A TALENTED GIRL LIKE YOU DO SUCH MENIAL LABOR!
SOFT SQUID
CHU-HI
BUT I'M SO GLAD!!
SEEING YOU EXCITED TO WRITE AGAIN!!
EEK!

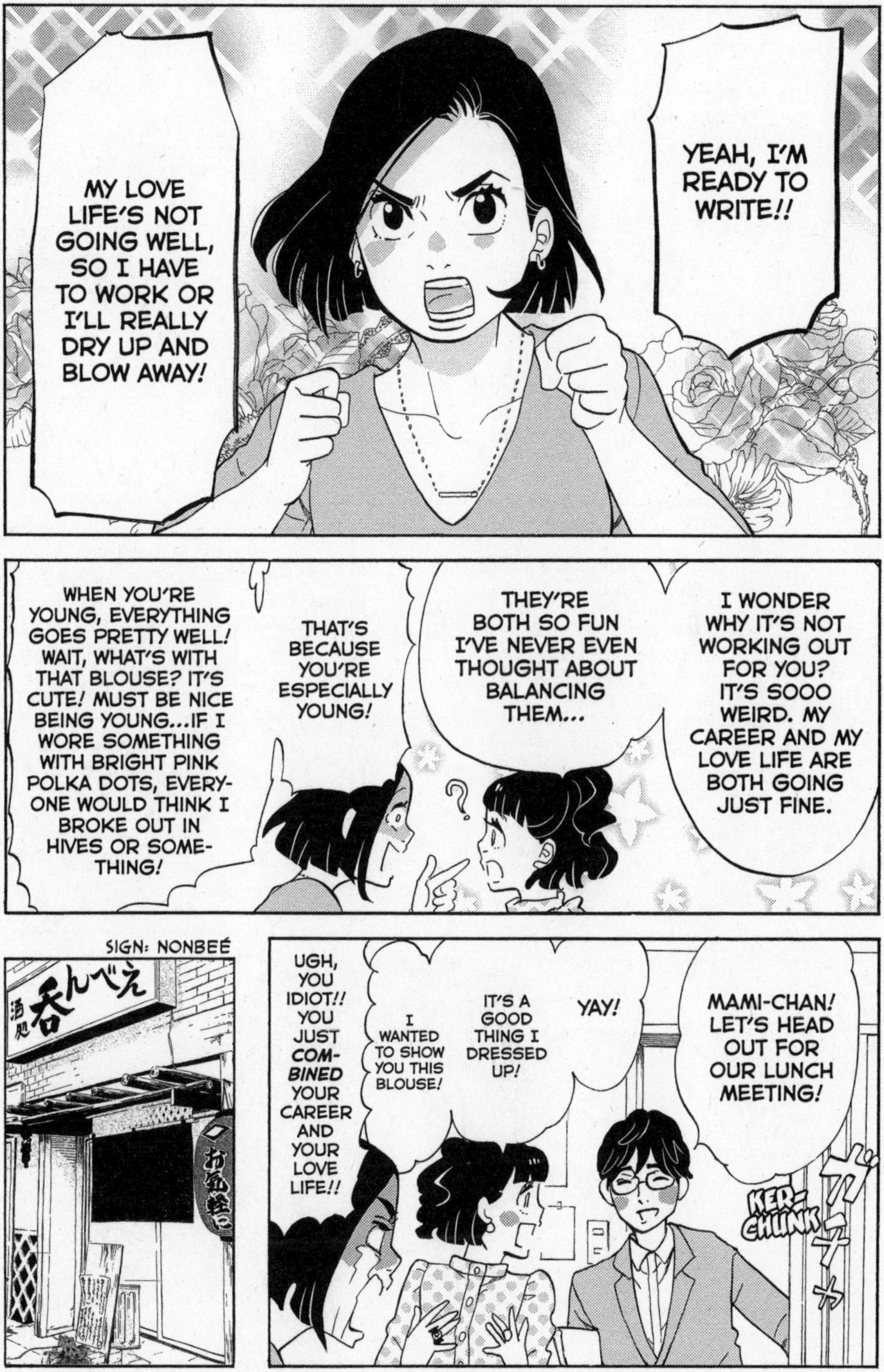

YEAH, I'M READY TO WRITE!!
MY LOVE LIFE'S NOT GOING WELL, SO I HAVE TO WORK OR I'LL REALLY DRY UP AND BLOW AWAY!
I WONDER WHY IT'S NOT WORKING OUT FOR YOU? IT'S SOOO WEIRD. MY CAREER AND MY LOVE LIFE ARE BOTH GOING JUST FINE.
THEY'RE BOTH SO FUN I'VE NEVER EVEN THOUGHT ABOUT BALANCING THEM...
THAT'S BECAUSE YOU'RE ESPECIALLY YOUNG!
WHEN YOU'RE YOUNG, EVERYTHING GOES PRETTY WELL! WAIT, WHAT'S WITH THAT BLOUSE? IT'S CUTE! MUST BE NICE BEING YOUNG...IF I WORE SOMETHING WITH BRIGHT PINK POLKA DOTS, EVERYONE WOULD THINK I BROKE OUT IN HIVES OR SOMETHING!
MAMI-CHAN! LET'S HEAD OUT FOR OUR LUNCH MEETING!
KER-CHUNK
YAY!
IT'S A GOOD THING I DRESSED UP!
I WANTED TO SHOW YOU THIS BLOUSE!
UGH, YOU IDIOT!! YOU JUST COMBINED YOUR CAREER AND YOUR LOVE LIFE!!
SIGN: NONBEÉ

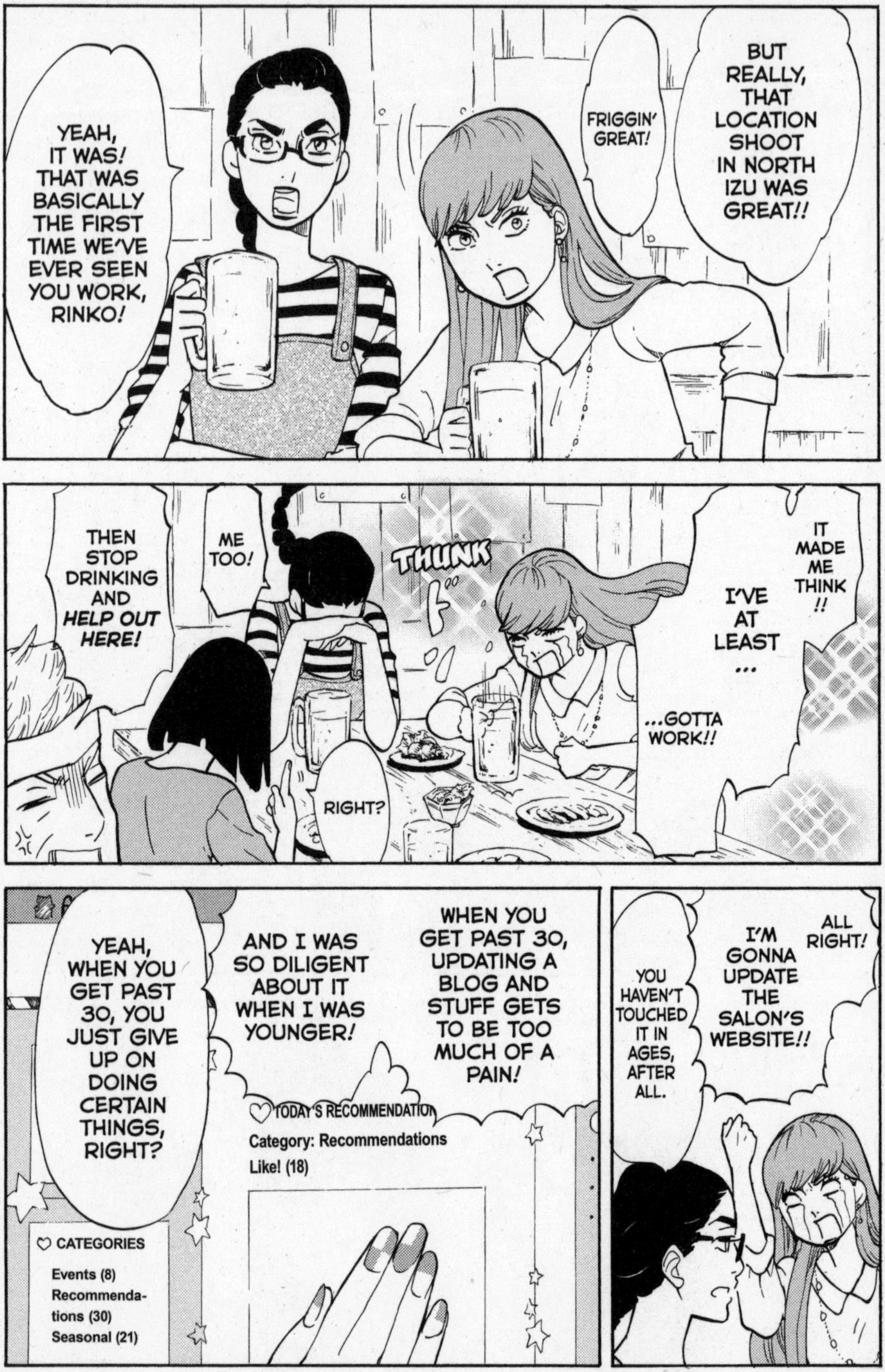
BUT REALLY, THAT LOCATION SHOOT IN NORTH IZU WAS GREAT!!
FRIGGIN' GREAT!
YEAH, IT WAS! THAT WAS BASICALLY THE FIRST TIME WE'VE EVER SEEN YOU WORK, RINKO!
IT MADE ME THINK!!
I'VE AT LEAST ...
...GOTTA WORK!!
THUNK
ME TOO!
THEN STOP DRINKING AND *HELP OUT HERE!*
RIGHT?
ALL RIGHT!
I'M GONNA UPDATE THE SALON'S WEBSITE!!
YOU HAVEN'T TOUCHED IT IN AGES, AFTER ALL.
WHEN YOU GET PAST 30, UPDATING A BLOG AND STUFF GETS TO BE TOO MUCH OF A PAIN!
AND I WAS SO DILIGENT ABOUT IT WHEN I WAS YOUNGER!
YEAH, WHEN YOU GET PAST 30, YOU JUST GIVE UP ON DOING CERTAIN THINGS, RIGHT?
TODAY'S RECOMMENDATIO
Category: Recommendations
Like! (18)
CATEGORIES
Events (8)
Recommendations (30)
Seasonal (21)

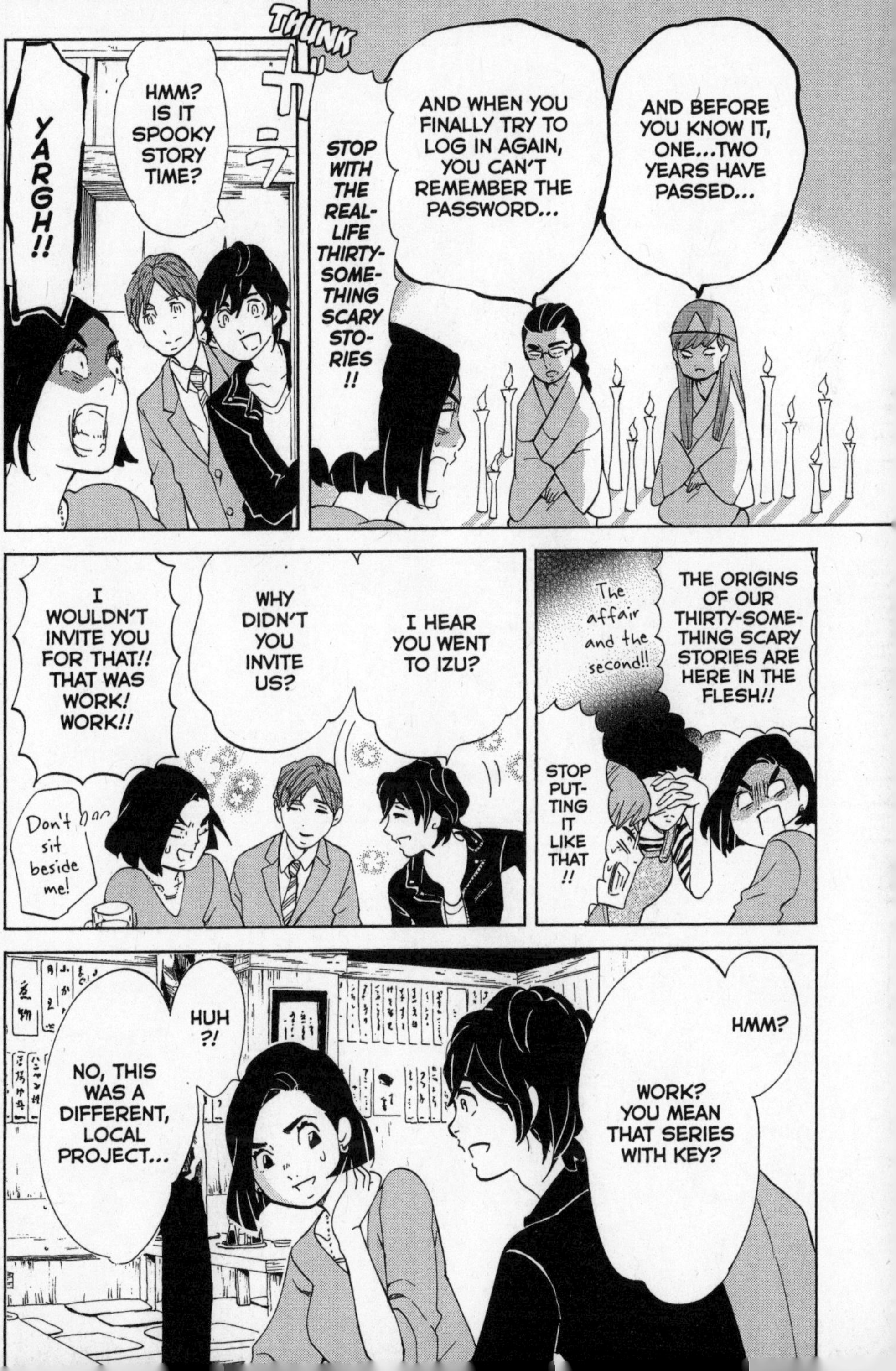
THUNK
AND BEFORE YOU KNOW IT, ONE...TWO YEARS HAVE PASSED...
AND WHEN YOU FINALLY TRY TO LOG IN AGAIN, YOU CAN'T REMEMBER THE PASSWORD...
STOP WITH THE REAL-LIFE THIRTY-SOMETHING SCARY STORIES!!
HMM? IS IT SPOOKY STORY TIME?
YARGH!!
THE ORIGINS OF OUR THIRTY-SOMETHING SCARY STORIES ARE HERE IN THE FLESH!!
The affair and the second!!
STOP PUTTING IT LIKE THAT!!
I HEAR YOU WENT TO IZU?
WHY DIDN'T YOU INVITE US?
I WOULDN'T INVITE YOU FOR THAT!! THAT WAS WORK! WORK!!
Don't sit beside me!
HMM?
WORK? YOU MEAN THAT SERIES WITH KEY?
HUH?!
NO, THIS WAS A DIFFERENT, LOCAL PROJECT...

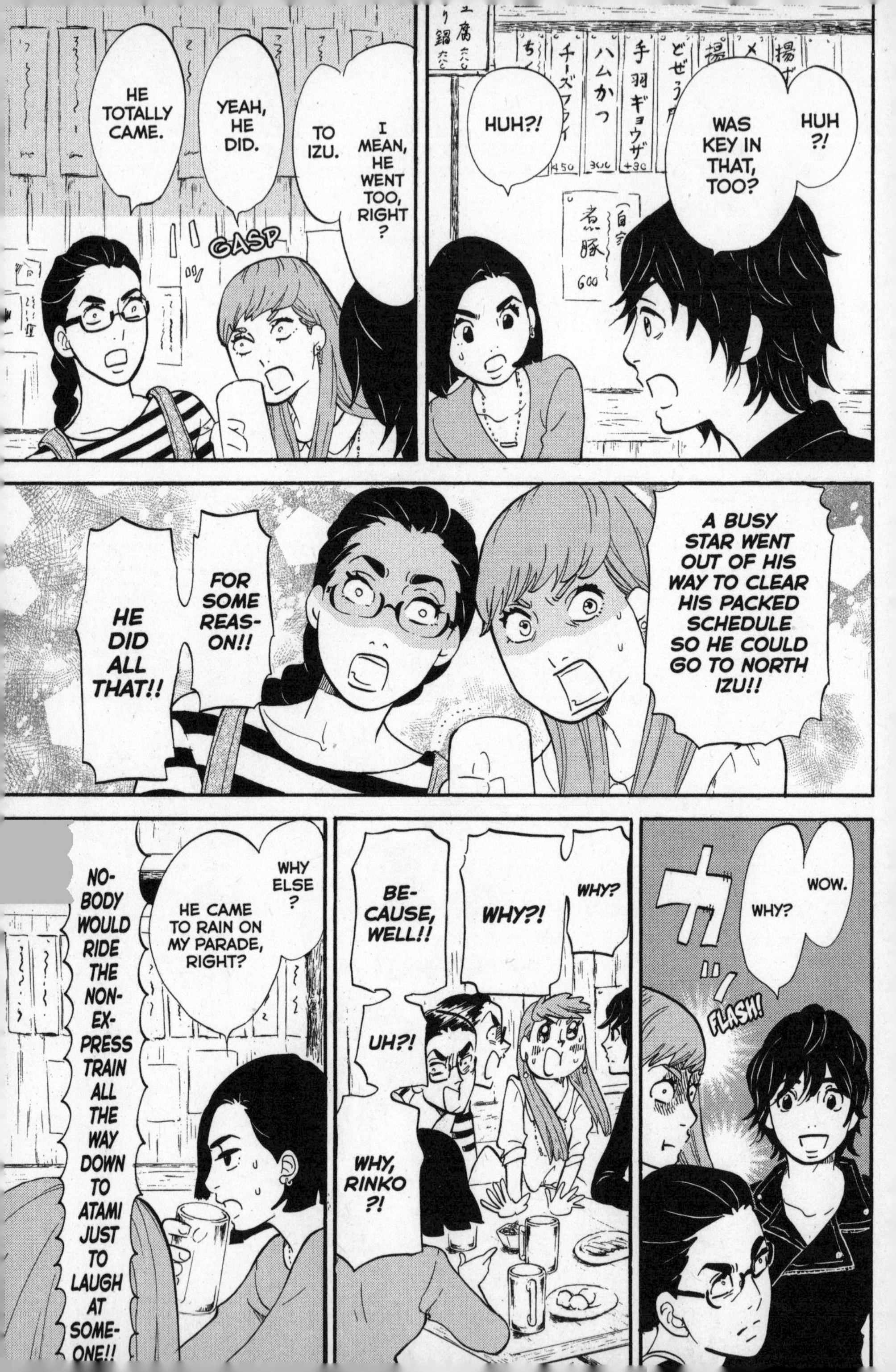
HUH?!
WAS KEY IN THAT, TOO?
HUH?!
手羽ギョウザ
ハムかつ
チーズフライ
煮豚
I MEAN, HE WENT TOO, RIGHT?
TO IZU.
YEAH, HE DID.
HE TOTALLY CAME.
GASP
A BUSY STAR WENT OUT OF HIS WAY TO CLEAR HIS PACKED SCHEDULE SO HE COULD GO TO NORTH IZU!!
FOR SOME REASON!!
HE DID ALL THAT!!
WOW.
WHY?
カッ
FLASH!
WHY?
WHY?!
BE-CAUSE, WELL!!
UH?!
WHY, RINKO?!
WHY ELSE?
HE CAME TO RAIN ON MY PARADE, RIGHT?
NO-BODY WOULD RIDE THE NON-EX-PRESS TRAIN ALL THE WAY DOWN TO ATAMI JUST TO LAUGH AT SOME-ONE!!

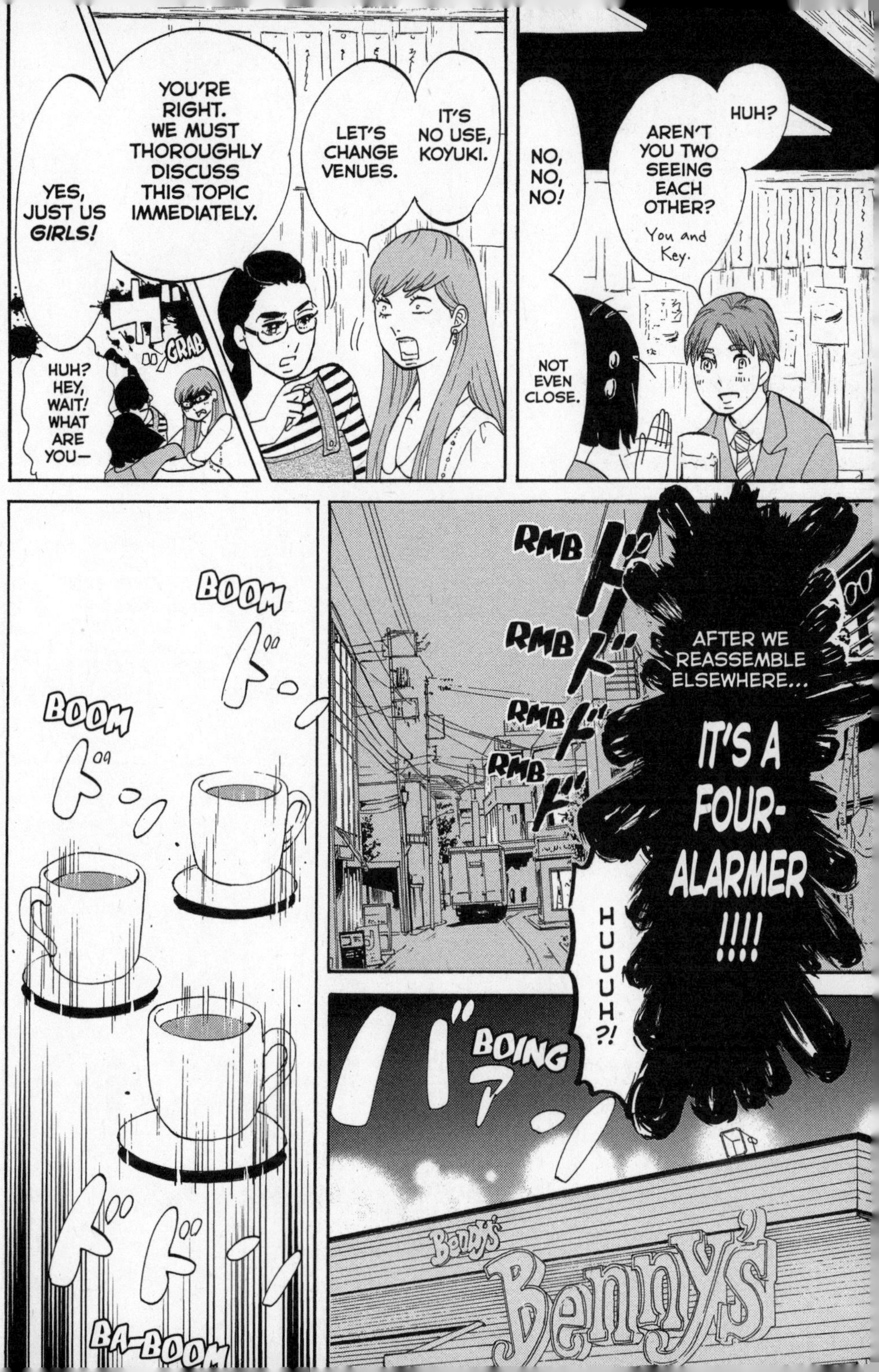
HUH?
AREN'T YOU TWO SEEING EACH OTHER?
You and Key.
NO, NO, NO!
NOT EVEN CLOSE.
IT'S NO USE, KOYUKI.
LET'S CHANGE VENUES.
YOU'RE RIGHT. WE MUST THOROUGHLY DISCUSS THIS TOPIC IMMEDIATELY.
YES, JUST US GIRLS!
GRAB
HUH? HEY, WAIT! WHAT ARE YOU—
RMB
RMB
RMB
RMB
HUUUUH?!
AFTER WE REASSEMBLE ELSEWHERE...
IT'S A FOUR-ALARMER!!!!
BOING
Benny's
Benny's
BOOM
BOOM
BA-BOOM

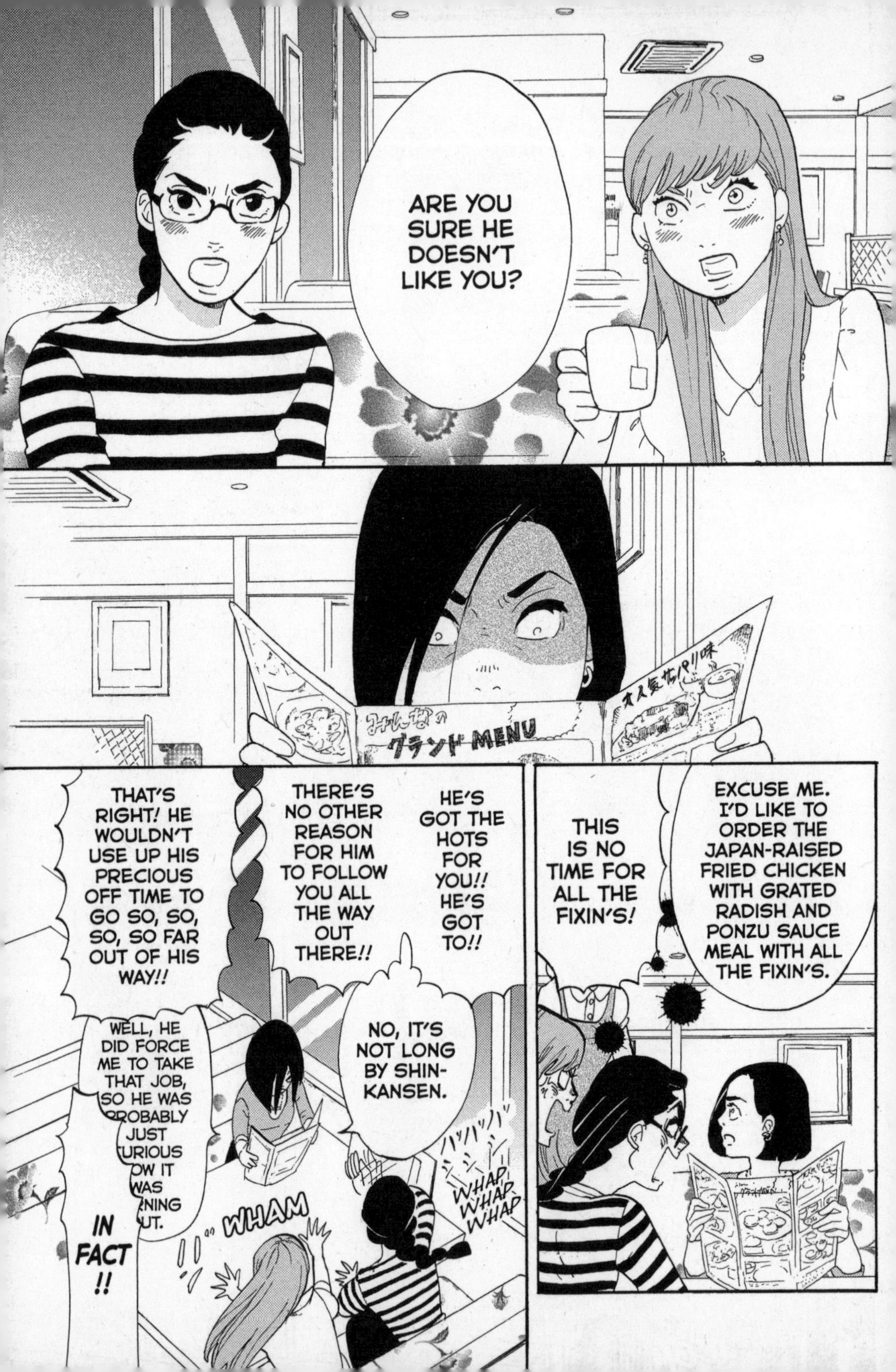
ARE YOU SURE HE DOESN'T LIKE YOU?
みんなの
グランド MENU
EXCUSE ME. I'D LIKE TO ORDER THE JAPAN-RAISED FRIED CHICKEN WITH GRATED RADISH AND PONZU SAUCE MEAL WITH ALL THE FIXIN'S.
THIS IS NO TIME FOR ALL THE FIXIN'S!
HE'S GOT THE HOTS FOR YOU!! HE'S GOT TO!!
THERE'S NO OTHER REASON FOR HIM TO FOLLOW YOU ALL THE WAY OUT THERE!!
THAT'S RIGHT! HE WOULDN'T USE UP HIS PRECIOUS OFF TIME TO GO SO, SO, SO, SO FAR OUT OF HIS WAY!!
WHAP WHAP WHAP
NO, IT'S NOT LONG BY SHIN-KANSEN.
WHAM
WELL, HE DID FORCE ME TO TAKE THAT JOB, SO HE WAS ROBABLY JUST URIOUS OW IT WAS NING UT.
IN FACT!!

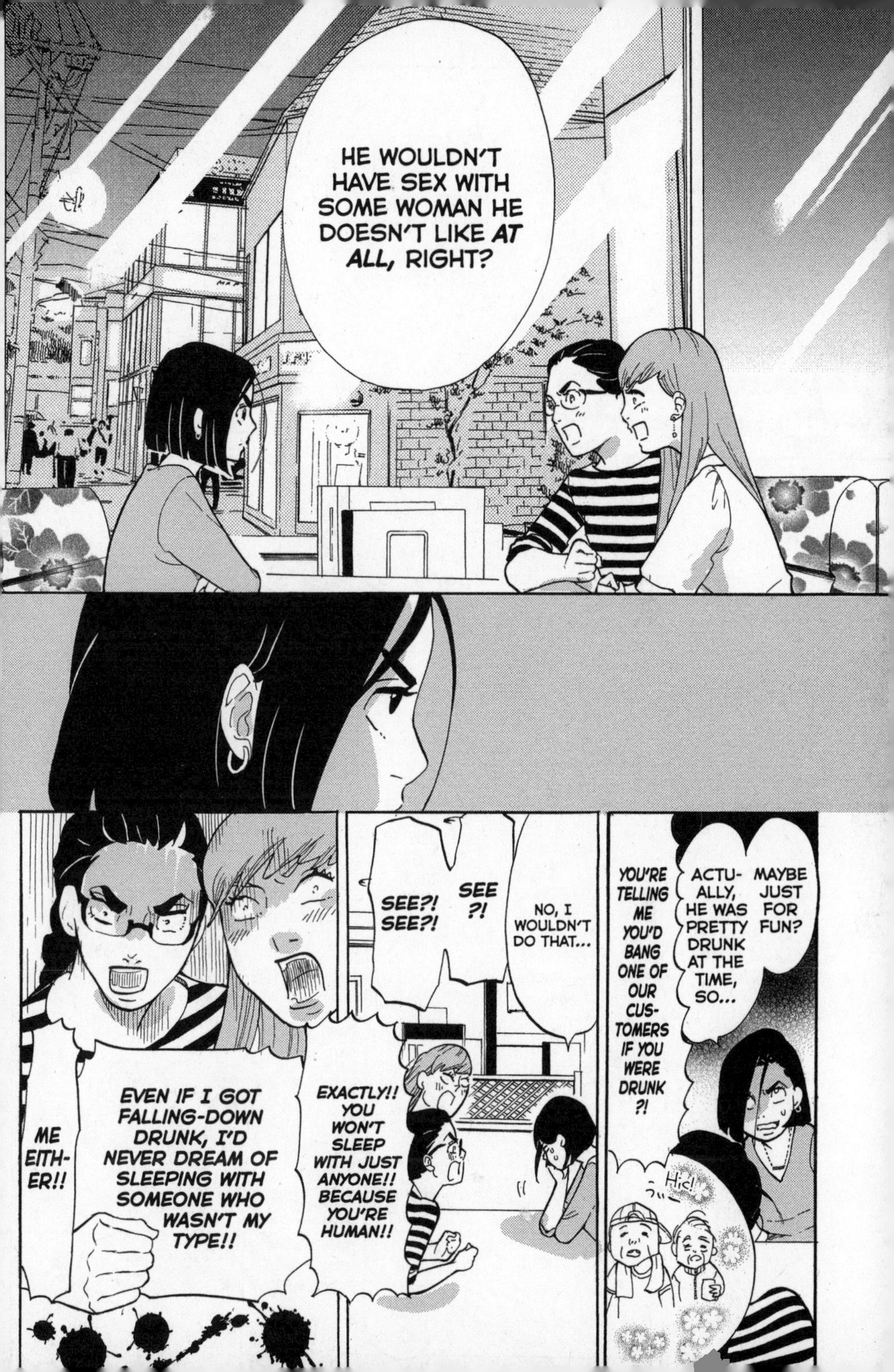
HE WOULDN'T HAVE SEX WITH SOME WOMAN HE DOESN'T LIKE *AT ALL*, RIGHT?
MAYBE JUST FOR FUN?
ACTU-ALLY, HE WAS PRETTY DRUNK AT THE TIME, SO...
YOU'RE TELLING ME YOU'D BANG ONE OF OUR CUS-TOMERS IF YOU WERE DRUNK ?!
Hic!
NO, I WOULDN'T DO THAT...
SEE ?!
SEE?! SEE?!
EXACTLY!! YOU WON'T SLEEP WITH JUST ANYONE!! BECAUSE YOU'RE HUMAN!!
EVEN IF I GOT FALLING-DOWN DRUNK, I'D NEVER DREAM OF SLEEPING WITH SOMEONE WHO WASN'T MY TYPE!!
ME EITH-ER!!

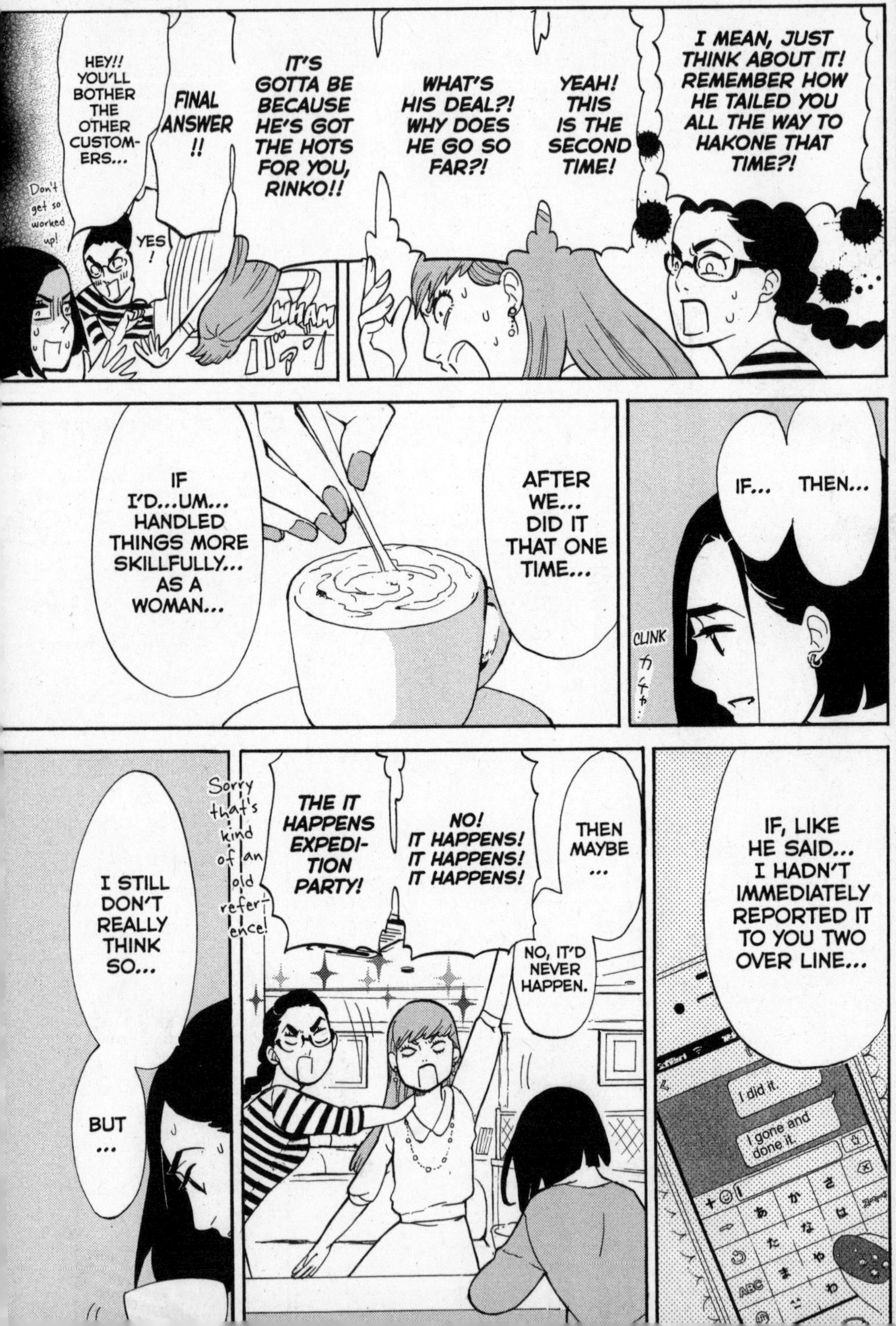
I MEAN, JUST THINK ABOUT IT! REMEMBER HOW HE TAILED YOU ALL THE WAY TO HAKONE THAT TIME?!
YEAH! THIS IS THE SECOND TIME!
WHAT'S HIS DEAL?! WHY DOES HE GO SO FAR?!
IT'S GOTTA BE BECAUSE HE'S GOT THE HOTS FOR YOU, RINKO!!
FINAL ANSWER !!
WHAM
HEY!! YOU'LL BOTHER THE OTHER CUSTOMERS...
YES!
Don't get so worked up!
IF... THEN...
CLINK
AFTER WE... DID IT THAT ONE TIME...
IF I'D...UM... HANDLED THINGS MORE SKILLFULLY... AS A WOMAN...
IF, LIKE HE SAID... I HADN'T IMMEDIATELY REPORTED IT TO YOU TWO OVER LINE...
I did it.
I gone and done it.
THEN MAYBE ...
NO! IT HAPPENS! IT HAPPENS! IT HAPPENS!
THE IT HAPPENS EXPEDITION PARTY!
Sorry that's kind of an old reference!
NO, IT'D NEVER HAPPEN.
I STILL DON'T REALLY THINK SO...
BUT ...

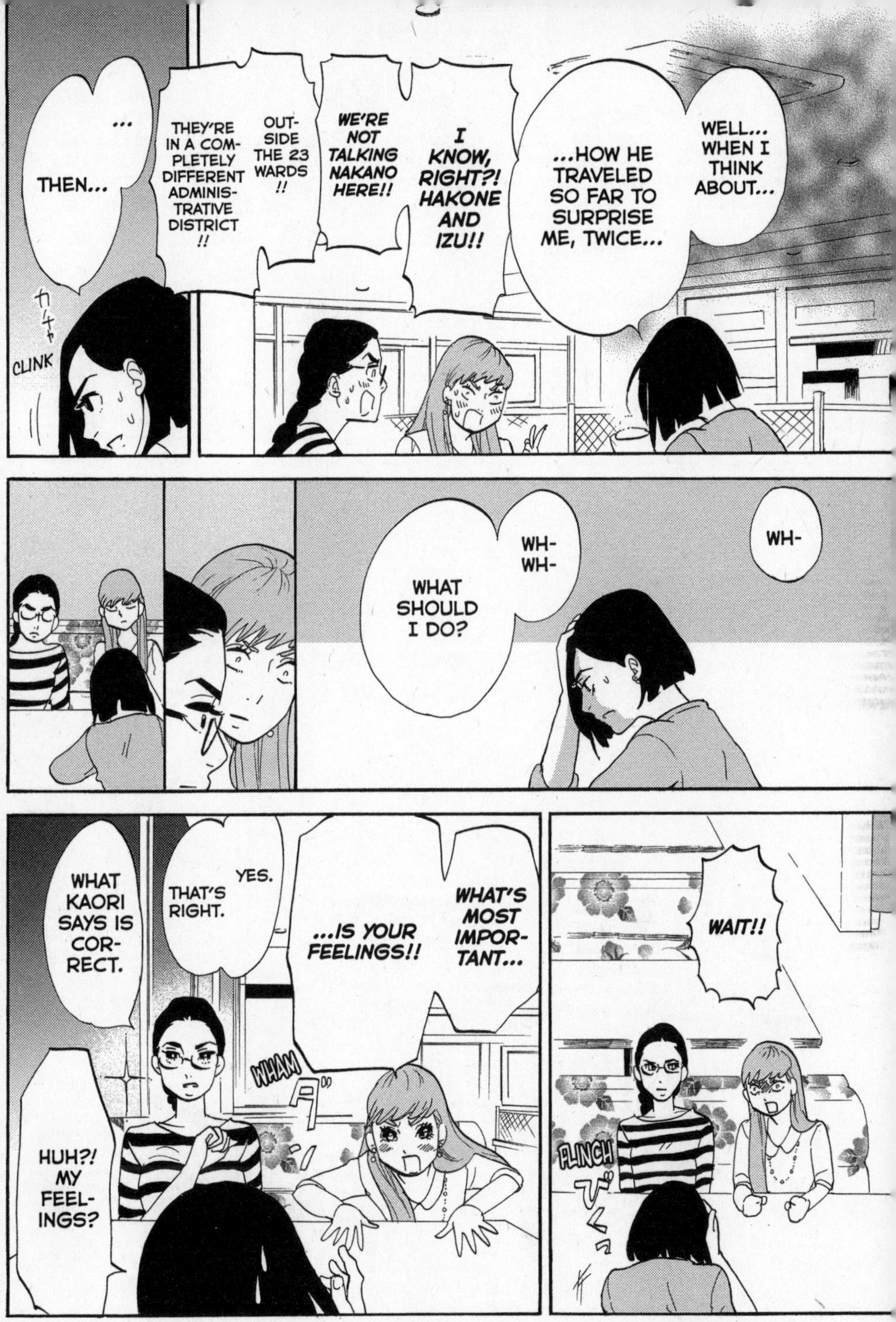
WELL... WHEN I THINK ABOUT...
...HOW HE TRAVELED SO FAR TO SURPRISE ME, TWICE...
I KNOW, RIGHT?! HAKONE AND IZU!!
WE'RE NOT TALKING NAKANO HERE!!
OUTSIDE THE 23 WARDS !!
THEY'RE IN A COMPLETELY DIFFERENT ADMINISTRATIVE DISTRICT !!
...
THEN...
CLINK
WH-
WH- WH-
WHAT SHOULD I DO?
WAIT!!
FLINCH
WHAT'S MOST IMPORTANT...
...IS YOUR FEELINGS!!
WHAM
YES. THAT'S RIGHT.
WHAT KAORI SAYS IS CORRECT.
HUH?! MY FEELINGS?

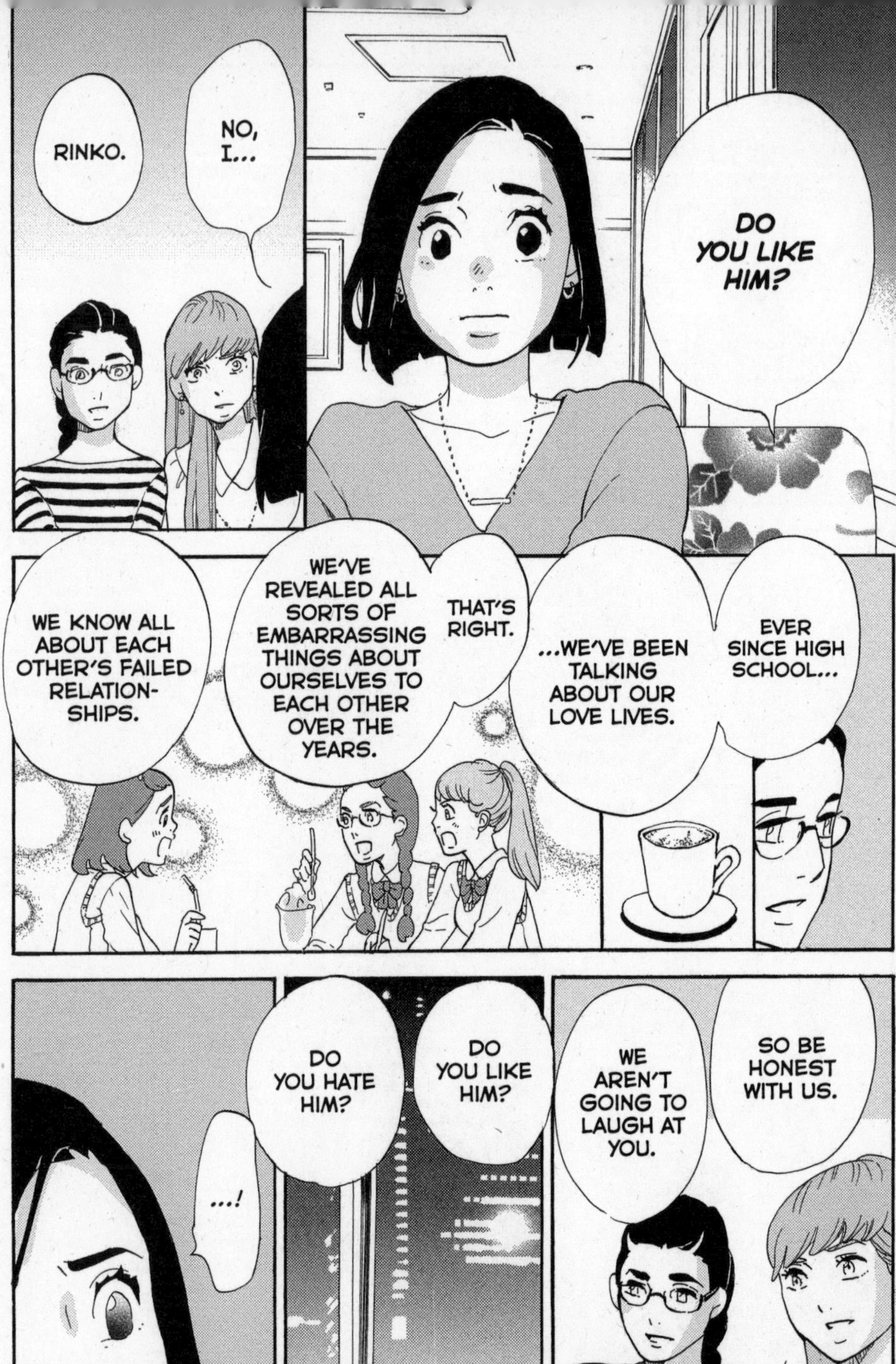
DO YOU LIKE HIM?
NO, I...
RINKO.
EVER SINCE HIGH SCHOOL...
...WE'VE BEEN TALKING ABOUT OUR LOVE LIVES.
THAT'S RIGHT.
WE'VE REVEALED ALL SORTS OF EMBARRASSING THINGS ABOUT OURSELVES TO EACH OTHER OVER THE YEARS.
WE KNOW ALL ABOUT EACH OTHER'S FAILED RELATION-SHIPS.
SO BE HONEST WITH US.
WE AREN'T GOING TO LAUGH AT YOU.
DO YOU LIKE HIM?
DO YOU HATE HIM?
...!

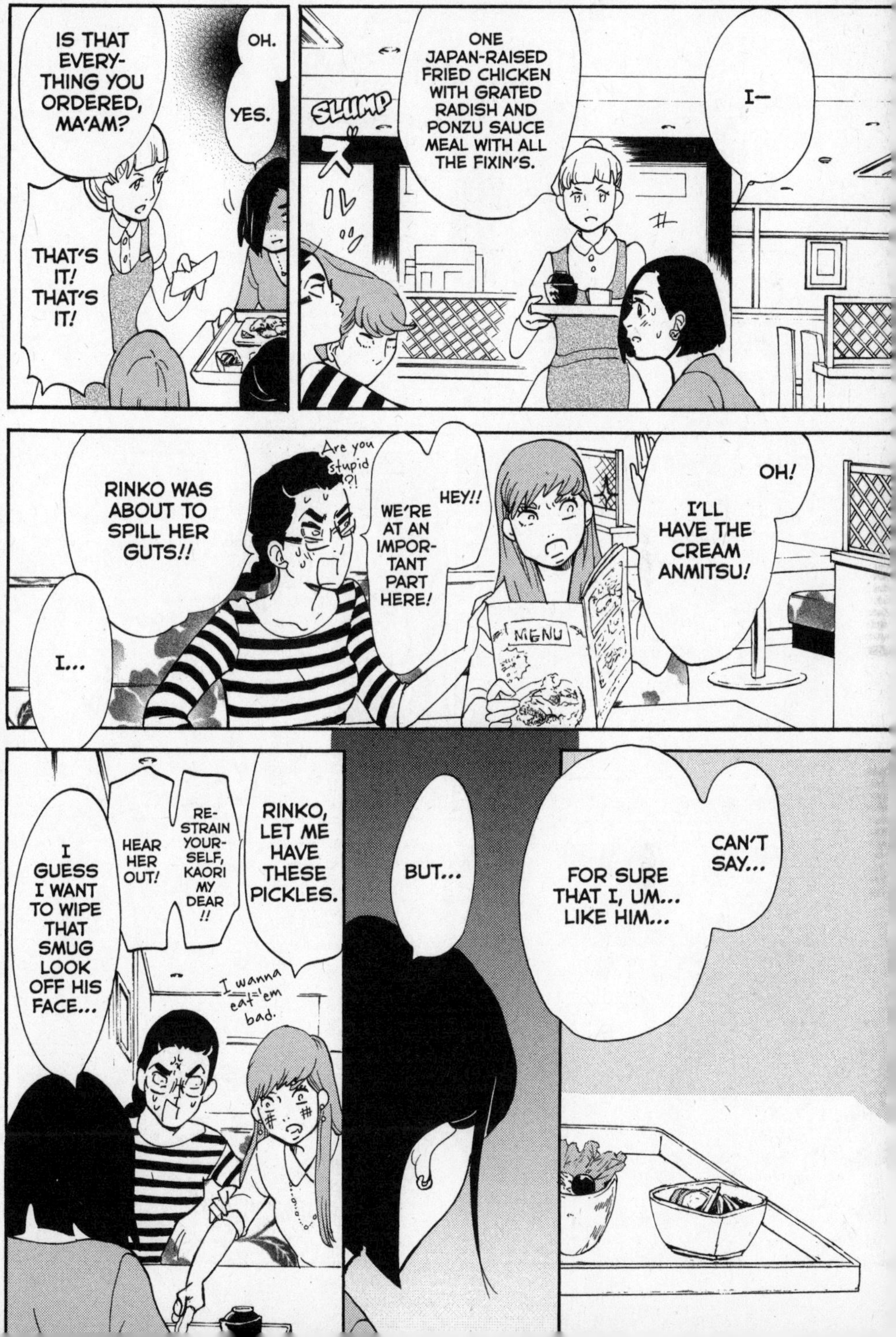
I—
ONE JAPAN-RAISED FRIED CHICKEN WITH GRATED RADISH AND PONZU SAUCE MEAL WITH ALL THE FIXIN'S.
SLUMP
ズル
OH.
YES.
IS THAT EVERY-THING YOU ORDERED, MA'AM?
THAT'S IT! THAT'S IT!
OH!
I'LL HAVE THE CREAM ANMITSU!
HEY!!
WE'RE AT AN IMPOR-TANT PART HERE!
Are you stupid?!
RINKO WAS ABOUT TO SPILL HER GUTS!!
I...
CAN'T SAY...
FOR SURE THAT I, UM... LIKE HIM...
BUT...
RINKO, LET ME HAVE THESE PICKLES.
RE-STRAIN YOUR-SELF, KAORI MY DEAR!!
HEAR HER OUT!
I wanna eat'em bad.
I GUESS I WANT TO WIPE THAT SMUG LOOK OFF HIS FACE...

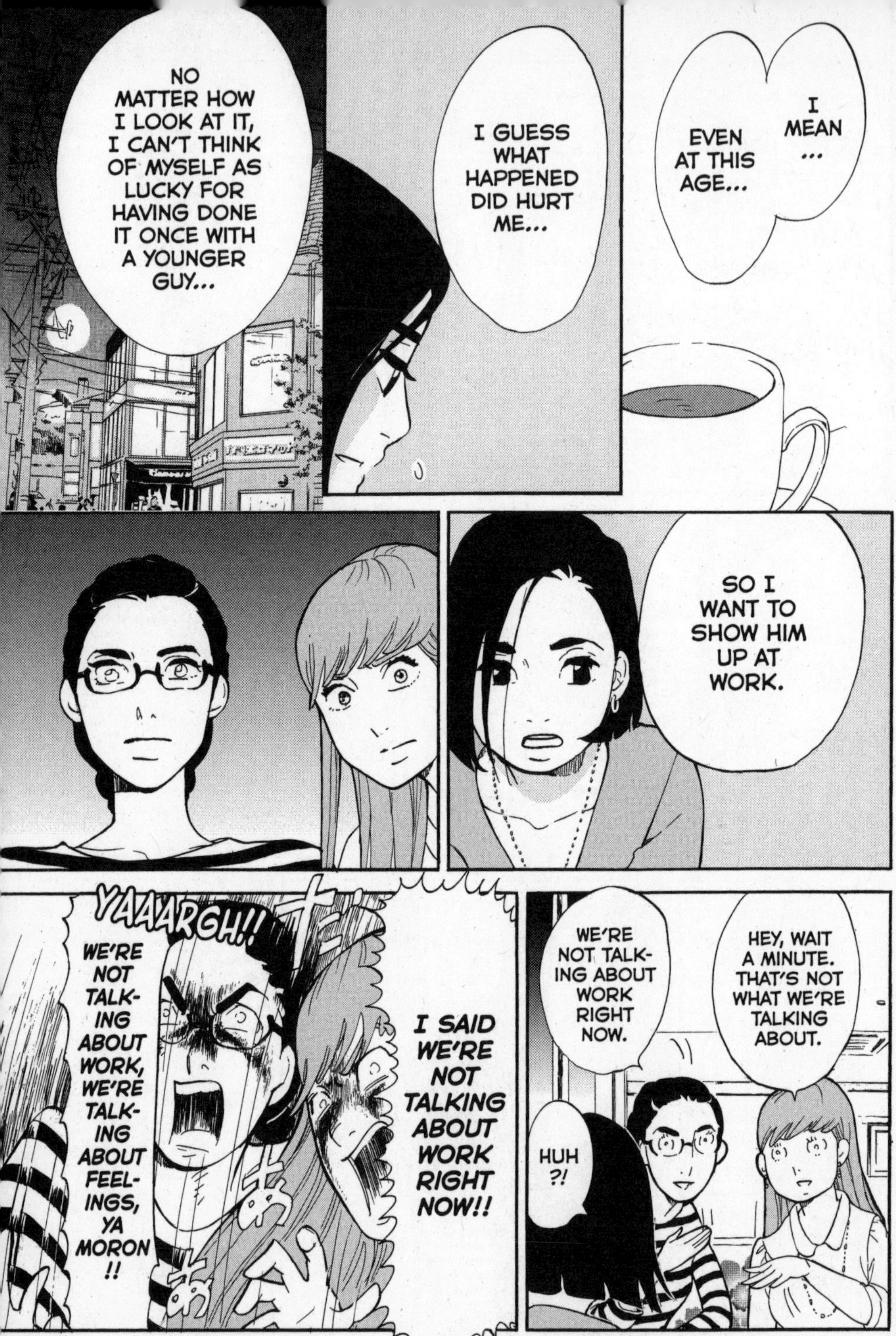
I MEAN ...
EVEN AT THIS AGE...
I GUESS WHAT HAPPENED DID HURT ME...
NO MATTER HOW I LOOK AT IT, I CAN'T THINK OF MYSELF AS LUCKY FOR HAVING DONE IT ONCE WITH A YOUNGER GUY...
SO I WANT TO SHOW HIM UP AT WORK.
HEY, WAIT A MINUTE. THAT'S NOT WHAT WE'RE TALKING ABOUT.
WE'RE NOT TALKING ABOUT WORK RIGHT NOW.
HUH?!
YAAARGH!!
I SAID WE'RE NOT TALKING ABOUT WORK RIGHT NOW!!
WE'RE NOT TALKING ABOUT WORK, WE'RE TALKING ABOUT FEELINGS, YA MORON!!

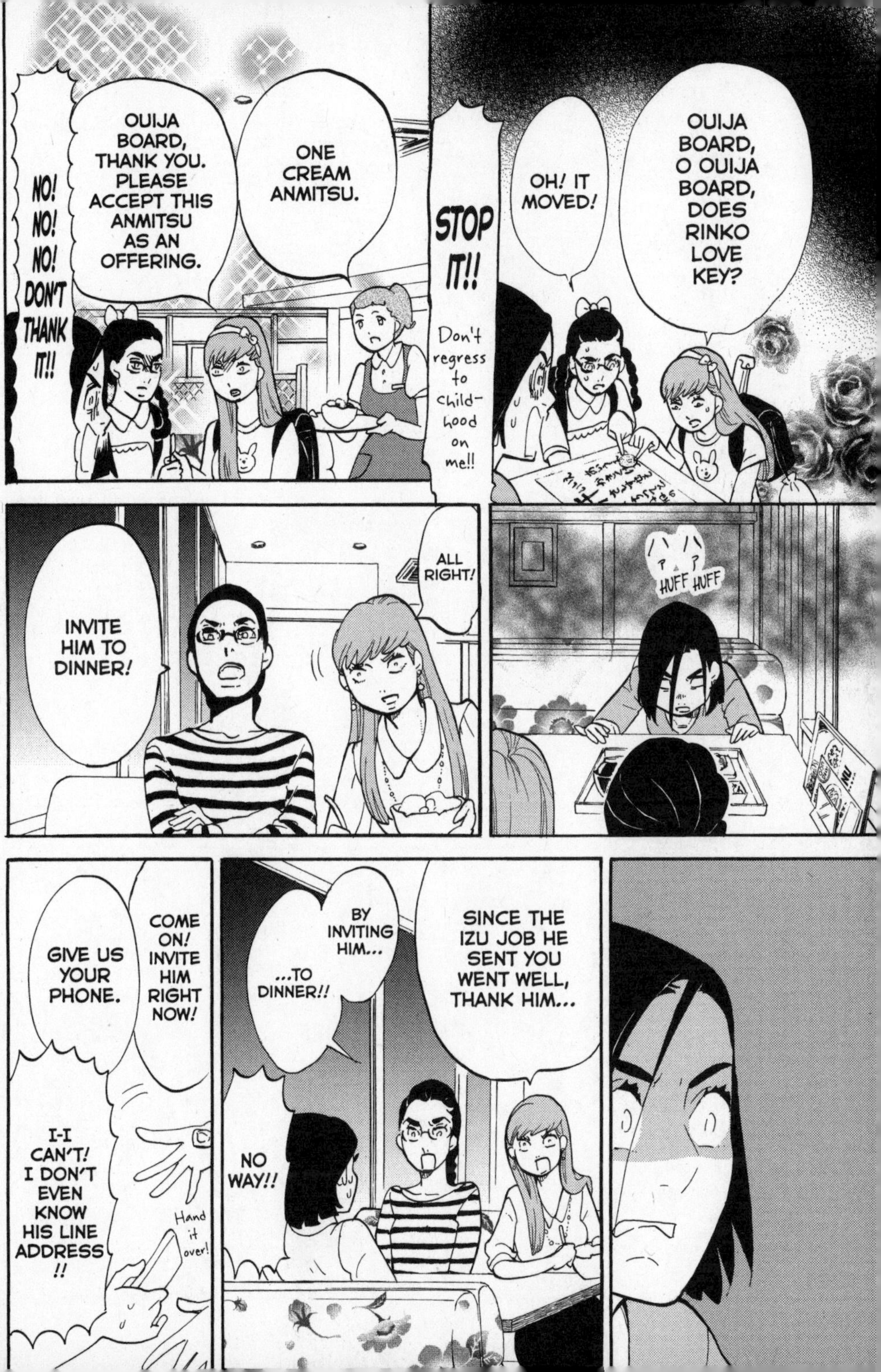
OUIJA BOARD, O OUIJA BOARD, DOES RINKO LOVE KEY?
OH! IT MOVED!
STOP IT!!
Don't regress to child-hood on me!!
ONE CREAM ANMITSU.
OUIJA BOARD, THANK YOU. PLEASE ACCEPT THIS ANMITSU AS AN OFFERING.
NO! NO! NO! DON'T THANK IT!!
HUFF HUFF
ALL RIGHT!
INVITE HIM TO DINNER!
SINCE THE IZU JOB HE SENT YOU WENT WELL, THANK HIM...
BY INVITING HIM...
...TO DINNER!!
NO WAY!!
COME ON! INVITE HIM RIGHT NOW!
GIVE US YOUR PHONE.
I-I CAN'T! I DON'T EVEN KNOW HIS LINE ADDRESS!!
Hand it over!

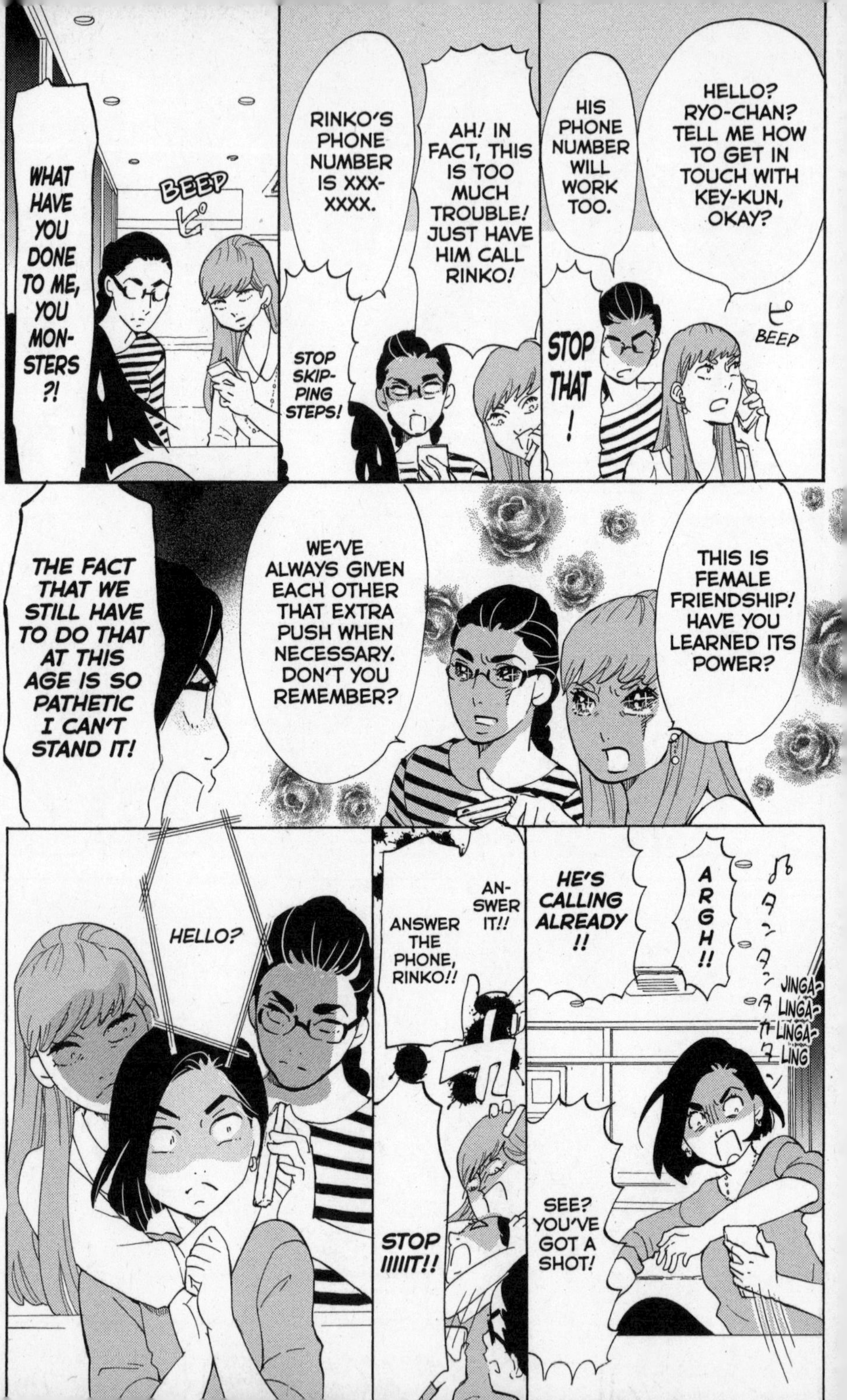
HELLO? RYO-CHAN? TELL ME HOW TO GET IN TOUCH WITH KEY-KUN, OKAY?
ピ
BEEP
HIS PHONE NUMBER WILL WORK TOO.
STOP THAT!
AH! IN FACT, THIS IS TOO MUCH TROUBLE! JUST HAVE HIM CALL RINKO!
RINKO'S PHONE NUMBER IS XXX-XXXX.
STOP SKIPPING STEPS!
BEEP
ピ
WHAT HAVE YOU DONE TO ME, YOU MONSTERS?!
THIS IS FEMALE FRIENDSHIP! HAVE YOU LEARNED ITS POWER?
WE'VE ALWAYS GIVEN EACH OTHER THAT EXTRA PUSH WHEN NECESSARY. DON'T YOU REMEMBER?
THE FACT THAT WE STILL HAVE TO DO THAT AT THIS AGE IS SO PATHETIC I CAN'T STAND IT!
JINGA-LINGA-LINGA-LING
ARGH!!
HE'S CALLING ALREADY!!
SEE? YOU'VE GOT A SHOT!
AN-SWER IT!!
ANSWER THE PHONE, RINKO!!
STOP IIIIIT!!
HELLO?

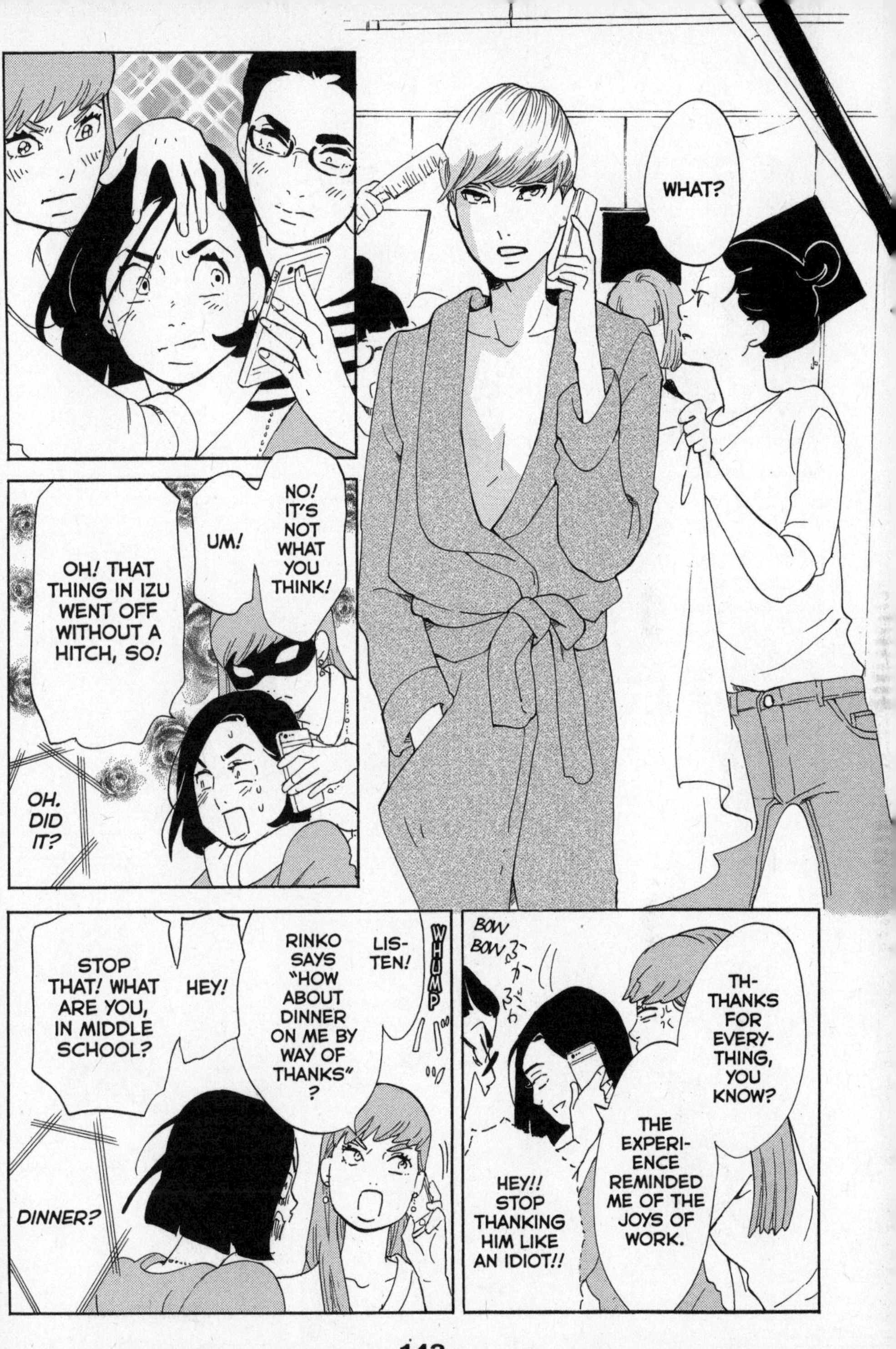
WHAT?
NO! IT'S NOT WHAT YOU THINK!
UM!
OH! THAT THING IN IZU WENT OFF WITHOUT A HITCH, SO!
OH. DID IT?
BOW BOW
TH-THANKS FOR EVERYTHING, YOU KNOW?
THE EXPERIENCE REMINDED ME OF THE JOYS OF WORK.
HEY!! STOP THANKING HIM LIKE AN IDIOT!!
WHUMP
LIS-TEN!
RINKO SAYS "HOW ABOUT DINNER ON ME BY WAY OF THANKS"?
HEY!
STOP THAT! WHAT ARE YOU, IN MIDDLE SCHOOL?
DINNER?

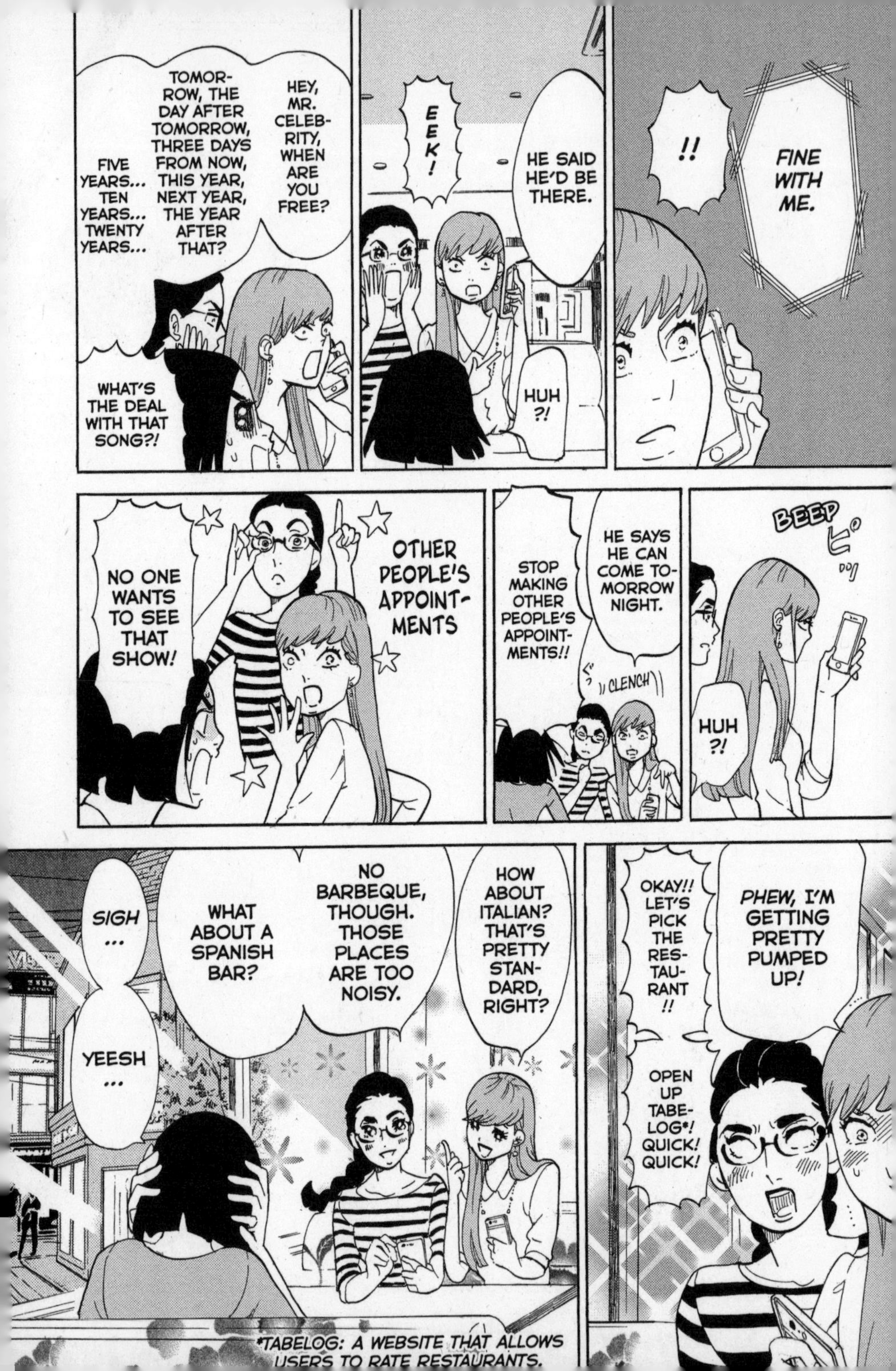
FINE WITH ME.
!!
HE SAID HE'D BE THERE.
EEK!
HUH?!
HEY, MR. CELEBRITY, WHEN ARE YOU FREE?
TOMORROW, THE DAY AFTER TOMORROW, THREE DAYS FROM NOW, THIS YEAR, NEXT YEAR, THE YEAR AFTER THAT?
FIVE YEARS... TEN YEARS... TWENTY YEARS...
WHAT'S THE DEAL WITH THAT SONG?!
BEEP
ピ
HUH?!
HE SAYS HE CAN COME TOMORROW NIGHT.
STOP MAKING OTHER PEOPLE'S APPOINTMENTS!!
ぐっ CLENCH
OTHER PEOPLE'S APPOINTMENTS
NO ONE WANTS TO SEE THAT SHOW!
PHEW, I'M GETTING PRETTY PUMPED UP!
OKAY!! LET'S PICK THE RESTAURANT!!
OPEN UP TABELOG*! QUICK! QUICK!
HOW ABOUT ITALIAN? THAT'S PRETTY STANDARD, RIGHT?
NO BARBEQUE, THOUGH. THOSE PLACES ARE TOO NOISY.
WHAT ABOUT A SPANISH BAR?
SIGH...
YEESH...
*TABELOG: A WEBSITE THAT ALLOWS USERS TO RATE RESTAURANTS.

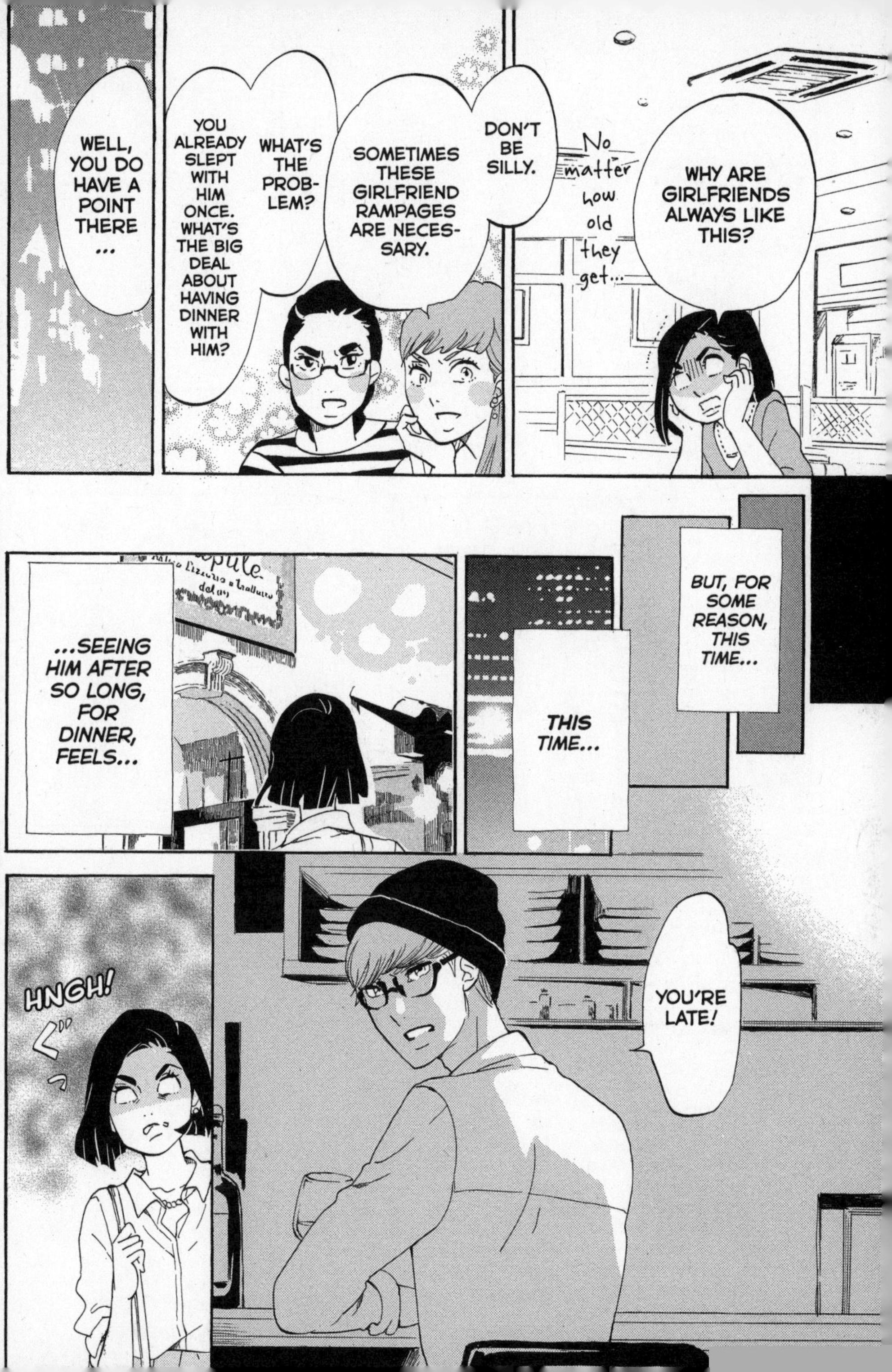
WHY ARE GIRLFRIENDS ALWAYS LIKE THIS?
No matter how old they get...
DON'T BE SILLY.
SOMETIMES THESE GIRLFRIEND RAMPAGES ARE NECESSARY.
WHAT'S THE PROBLEM?
YOU ALREADY SLEPT WITH HIM ONCE. WHAT'S THE BIG DEAL ABOUT HAVING DINNER WITH HIM?
WELL, YOU DO HAVE A POINT THERE...
BUT, FOR SOME REASON, THIS TIME...
THIS TIME...
...SEEING HIM AFTER SO LONG, FOR DINNER, FEELS...
YOU'RE LATE!
HNGH!

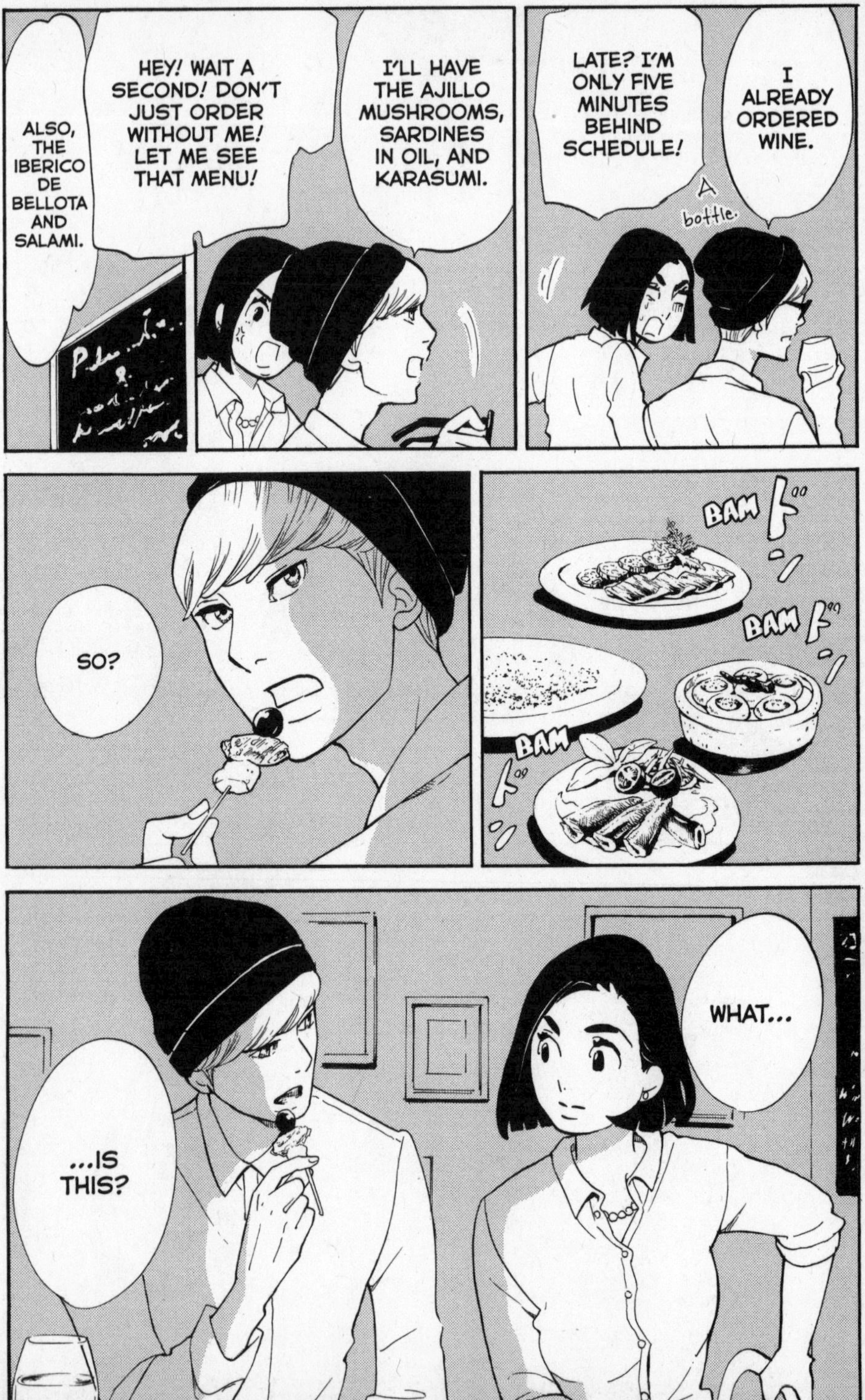
I ALREADY ORDERED WINE.
A bottle.
LATE? I'M ONLY FIVE MINUTES BEHIND SCHEDULE!
I'LL HAVE THE AJILLO MUSHROOMS, SARDINES IN OIL, AND KARASUMI.
HEY! WAIT A SECOND! DON'T JUST ORDER WITHOUT ME! LET ME SEE THAT MENU!
ALSO, THE IBERICO DE BELLOTA AND SALAMI.
BAM
BAM
BAM
SO?
WHAT...
...IS THIS?

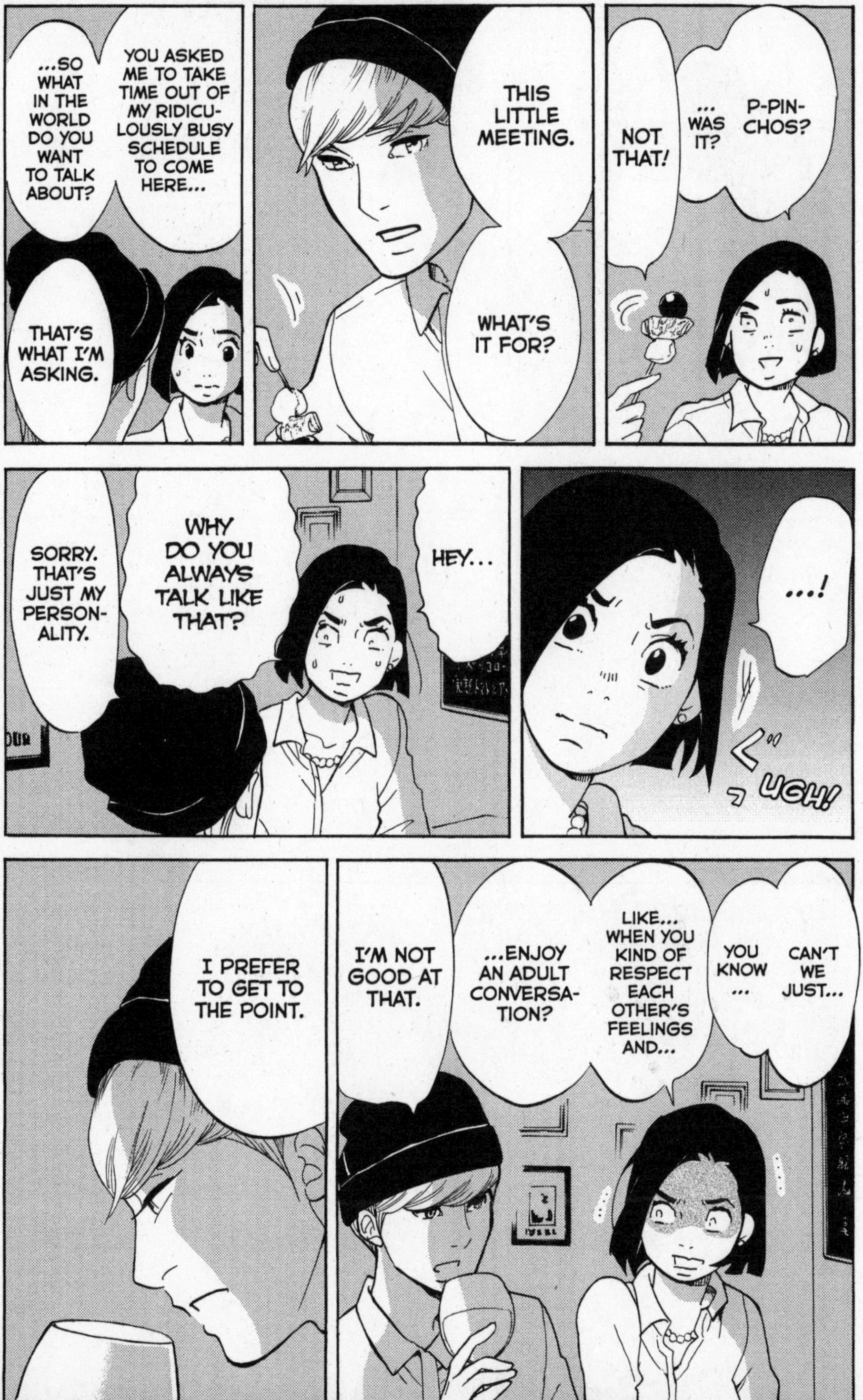
P-PIN-CHOS?
...WAS IT?
NOT THAT!
THIS LITTLE MEETING.
WHAT'S IT FOR?
YOU ASKED ME TO TAKE TIME OUT OF MY RIDICULOUSLY BUSY SCHEDULE TO COME HERE...
...SO WHAT IN THE WORLD DO YOU WANT TO TALK ABOUT?
THAT'S WHAT I'M ASKING.
...!
UGH!
HEY...
WHY DO YOU ALWAYS TALK LIKE THAT?
SORRY. THAT'S JUST MY PERSONALITY.
CAN'T WE JUST...
YOU KNOW...
LIKE... WHEN YOU KIND OF RESPECT EACH OTHER'S FEELINGS AND...
...ENJOY AN ADULT CONVERSATION?
I'M NOT GOOD AT THAT.
I PREFER TO GET TO THE POINT.

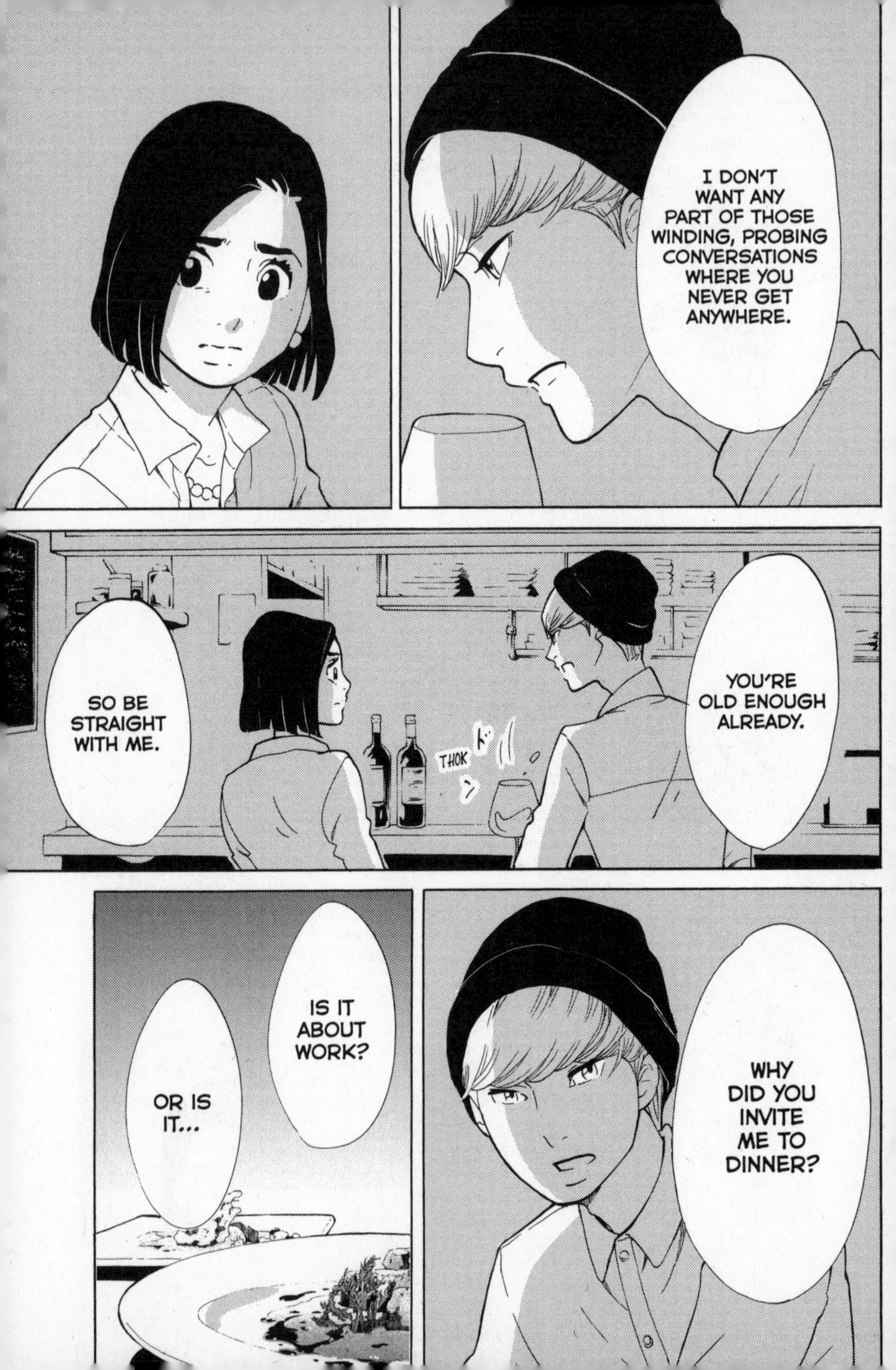
I DON'T WANT ANY PART OF THOSE WINDING, PROBING CONVERSATIONS WHERE YOU NEVER GET ANYWHERE.
YOU'RE OLD ENOUGH ALREADY.
THOK
SO BE STRAIGHT WITH ME.
WHY DID YOU INVITE ME TO DINNER?
IS IT ABOUT WORK?
OR IS IT...

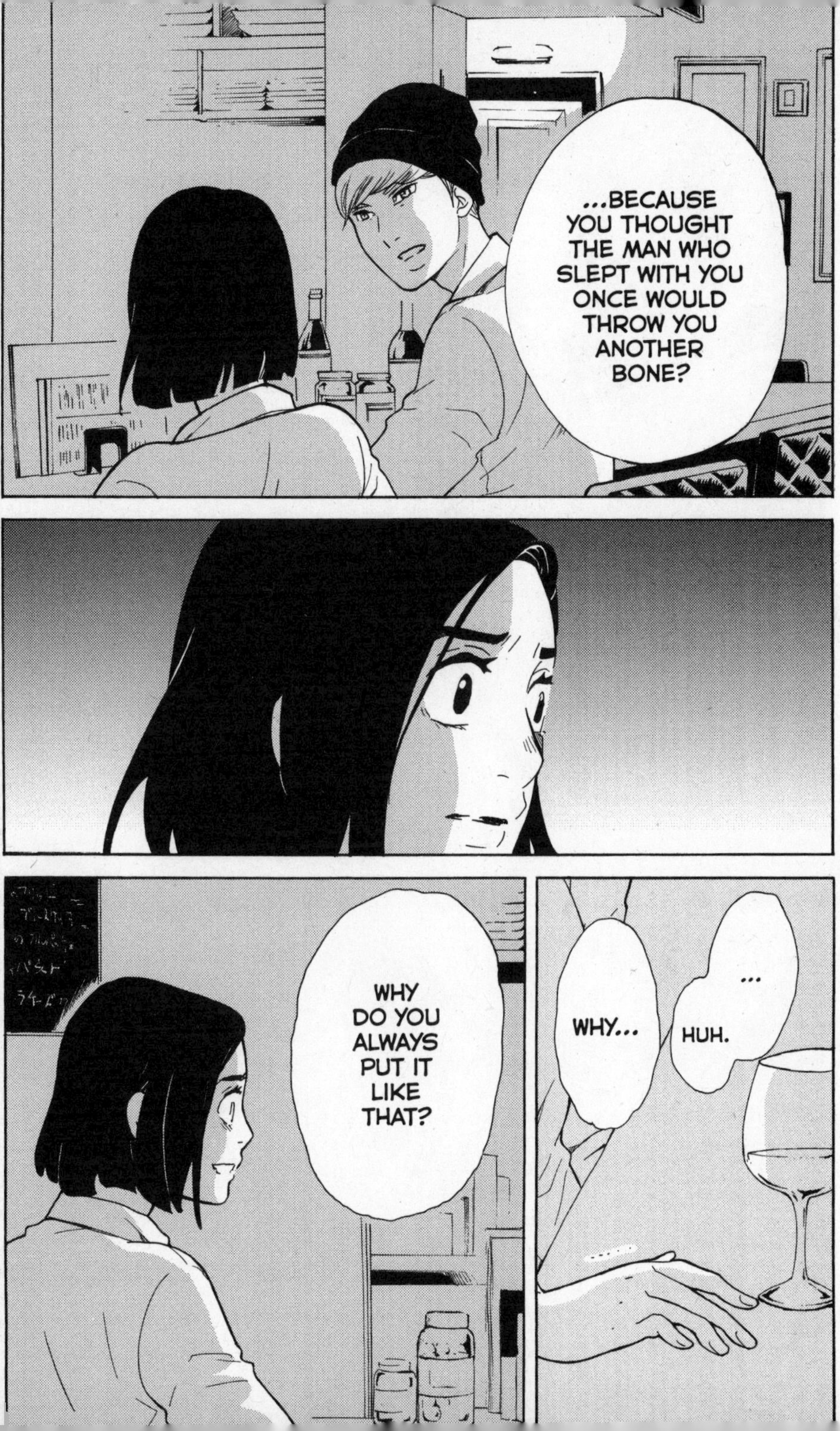
...BECAUSE YOU THOUGHT THE MAN WHO SLEPT WITH YOU ONCE WOULD THROW YOU ANOTHER BONE?
...
HUH.
WHY...
WHY DO YOU ALWAYS PUT IT LIKE THAT?

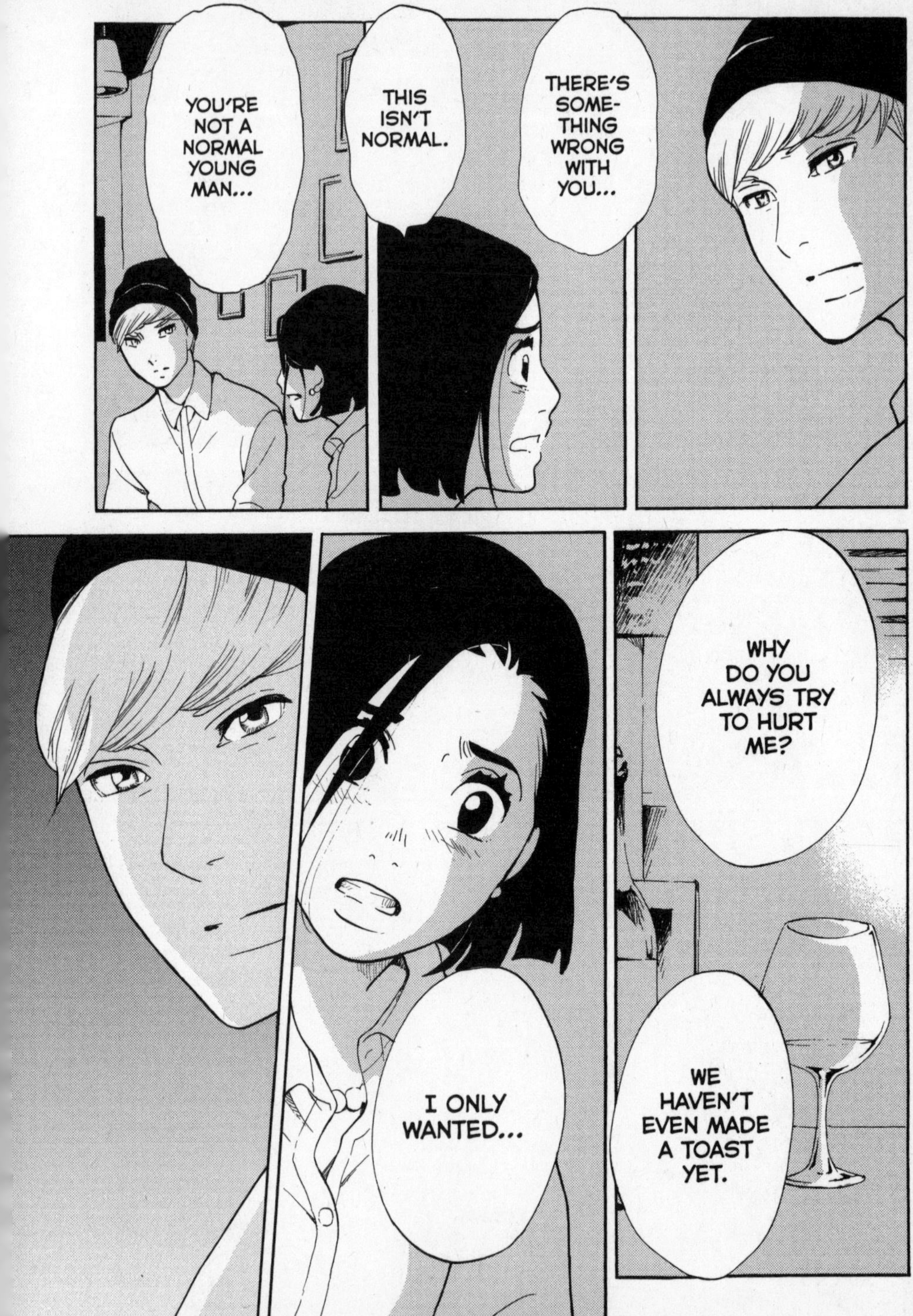
THERE'S SOMETHING WRONG WITH YOU...
THIS ISN'T NORMAL.
YOU'RE NOT A NORMAL YOUNG MAN...
WHY DO YOU ALWAYS TRY TO HURT ME?
WE HAVEN'T EVEN MADE A TOAST YET.
I ONLY WANTED...

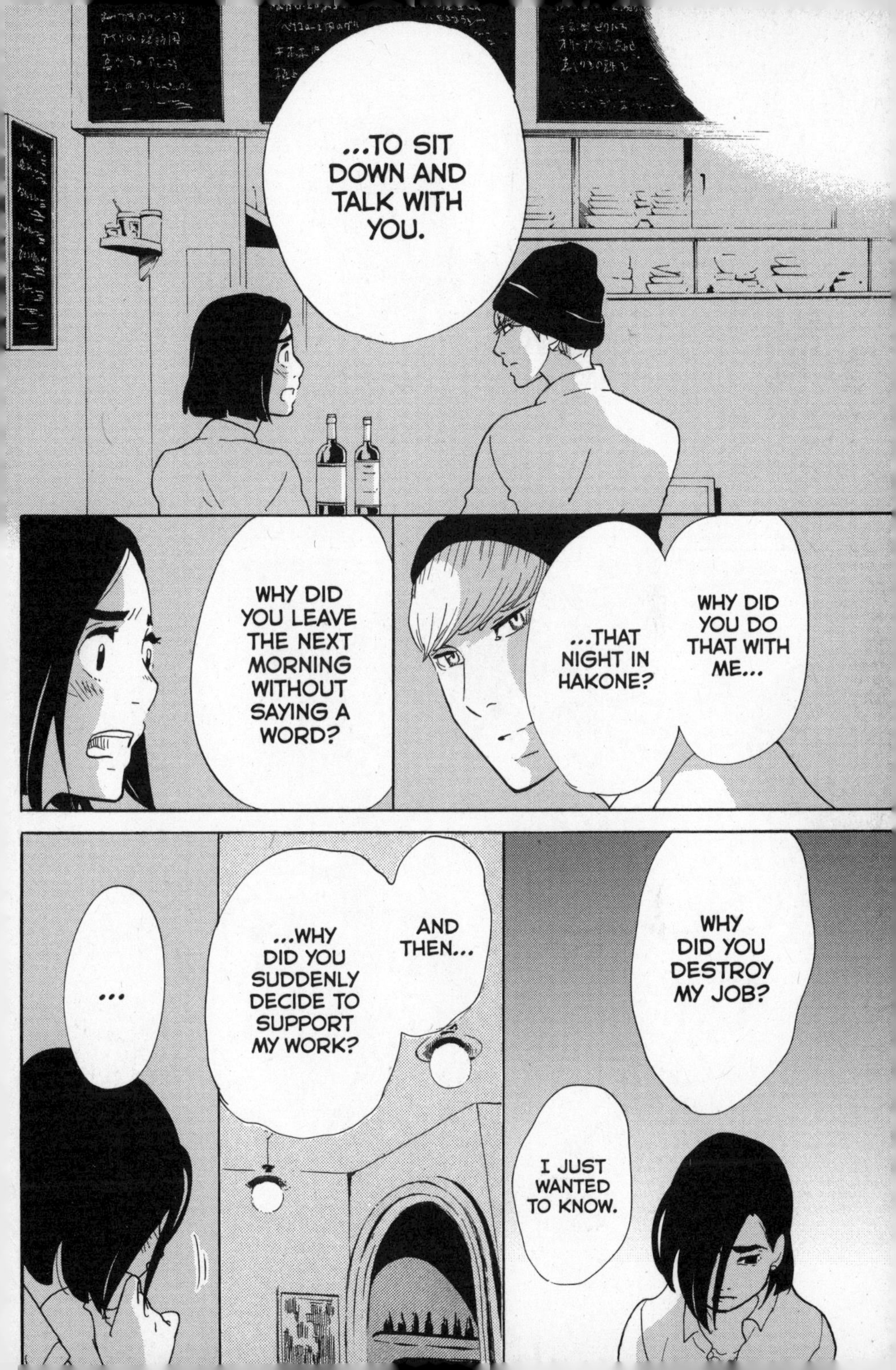
...TO SIT DOWN AND TALK WITH YOU.
WHY DID YOU DO THAT WITH ME...
...THAT NIGHT IN HAKONE?
WHY DID YOU LEAVE THE NEXT MORNING WITHOUT SAYING A WORD?
WHY DID YOU DESTROY MY JOB?
I JUST WANTED TO KNOW.
AND THEN...
...WHY DID YOU SUDDENLY DECIDE TO SUPPORT MY WORK?
...

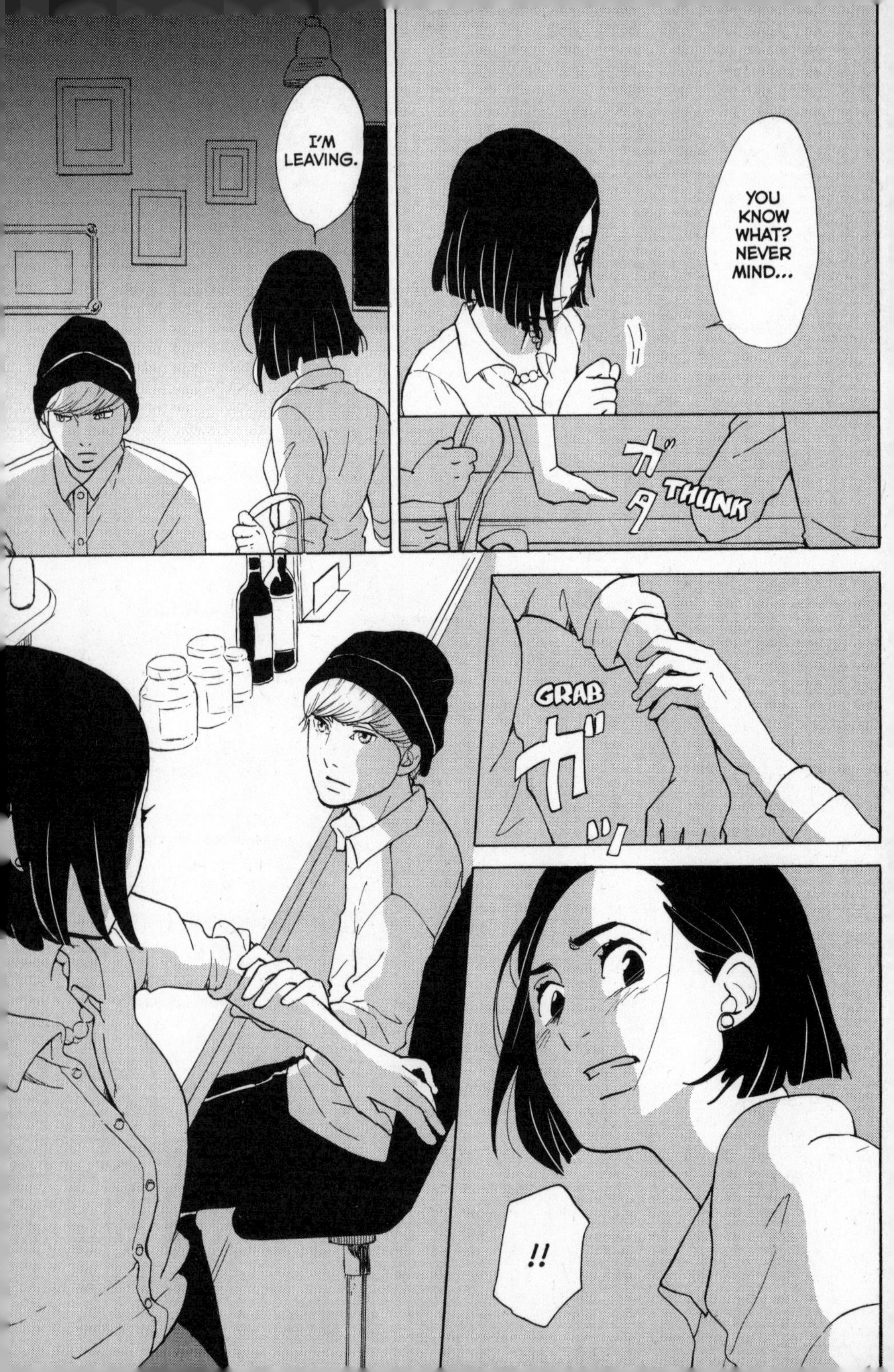
YOU KNOW WHAT? NEVER MIND...
ガタ
THUNK
I'M LEAVING.
GRAB
ガッ
!!

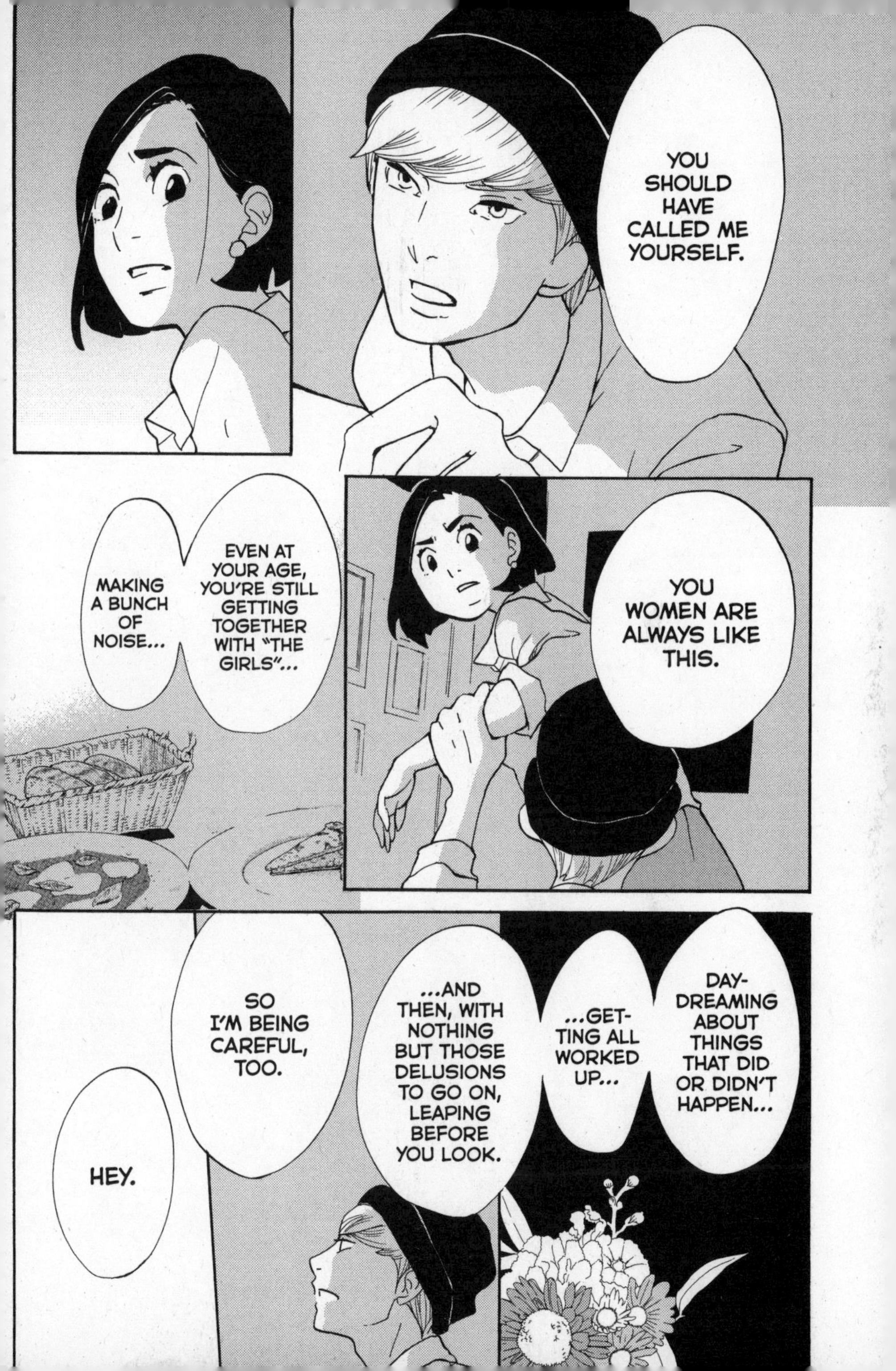
YOU SHOULD HAVE CALLED ME YOURSELF.
YOU WOMEN ARE ALWAYS LIKE THIS.
EVEN AT YOUR AGE, YOU'RE STILL GETTING TOGETHER WITH "THE GIRLS"...
MAKING A BUNCH OF NOISE...
DAY-DREAMING ABOUT THINGS THAT DID OR DIDN'T HAPPEN...
...GETTING ALL WORKED UP...
...AND THEN, WITH NOTHING BUT THOSE DELUSIONS TO GO ON, LEAPING BEFORE YOU LOOK.
SO I'M BEING CAREFUL, TOO.
HEY.

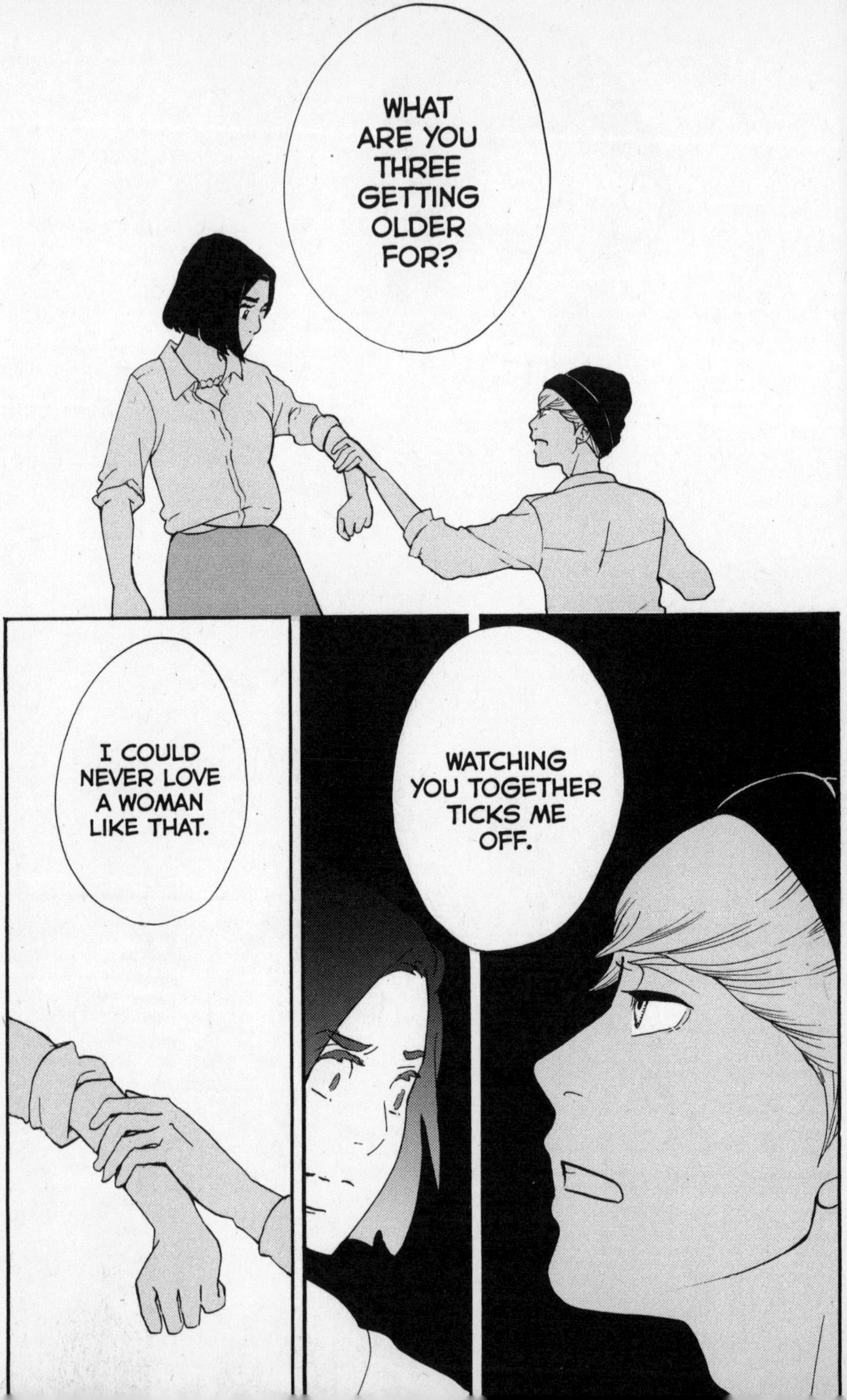
WHAT ARE YOU THREE GETTING OLDER FOR?
WATCHING YOU TOGETHER TICKS ME OFF.
I COULD NEVER LOVE A WOMAN LIKE THAT.

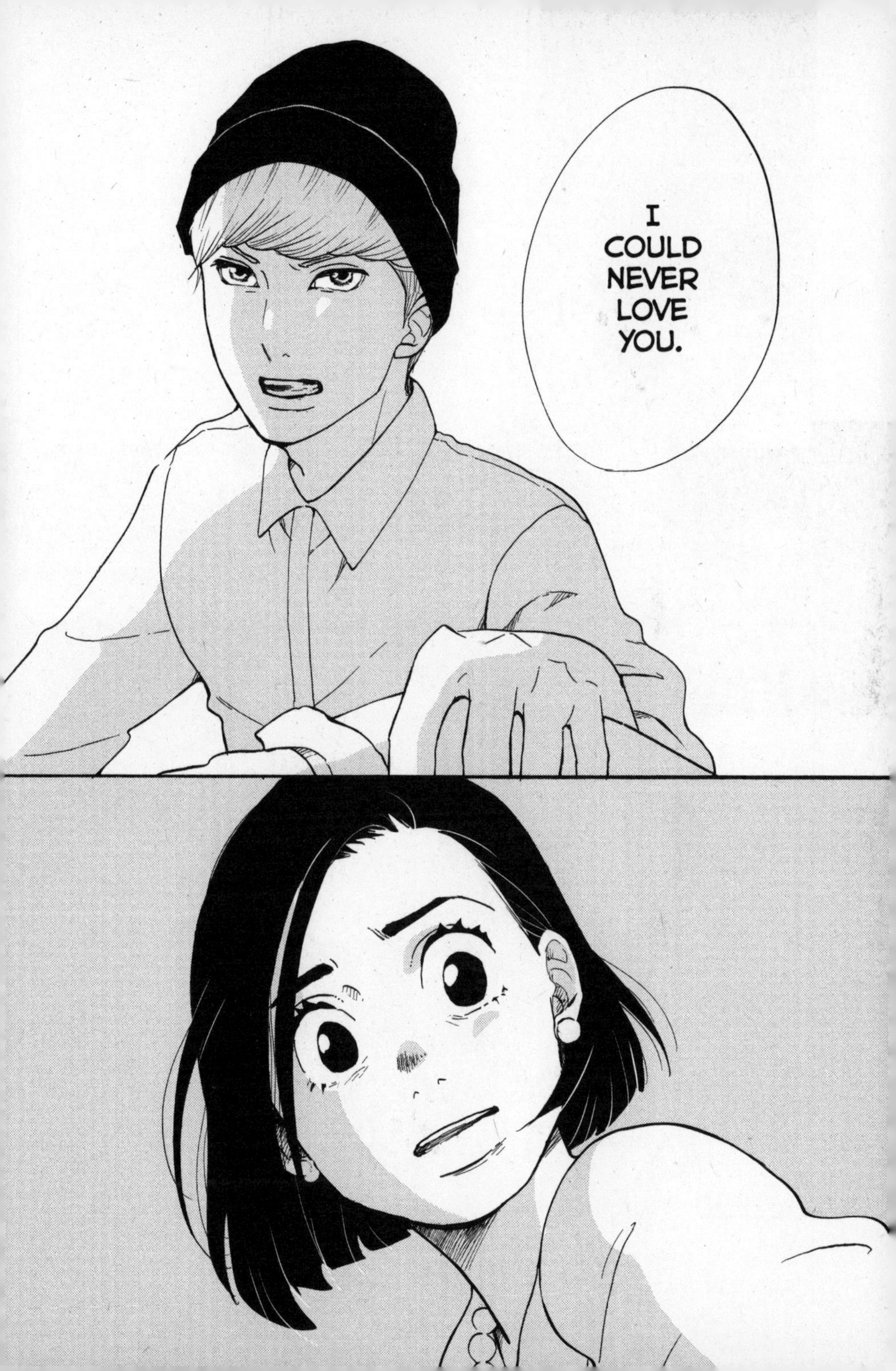
I COULD NEVER LOVE YOU.

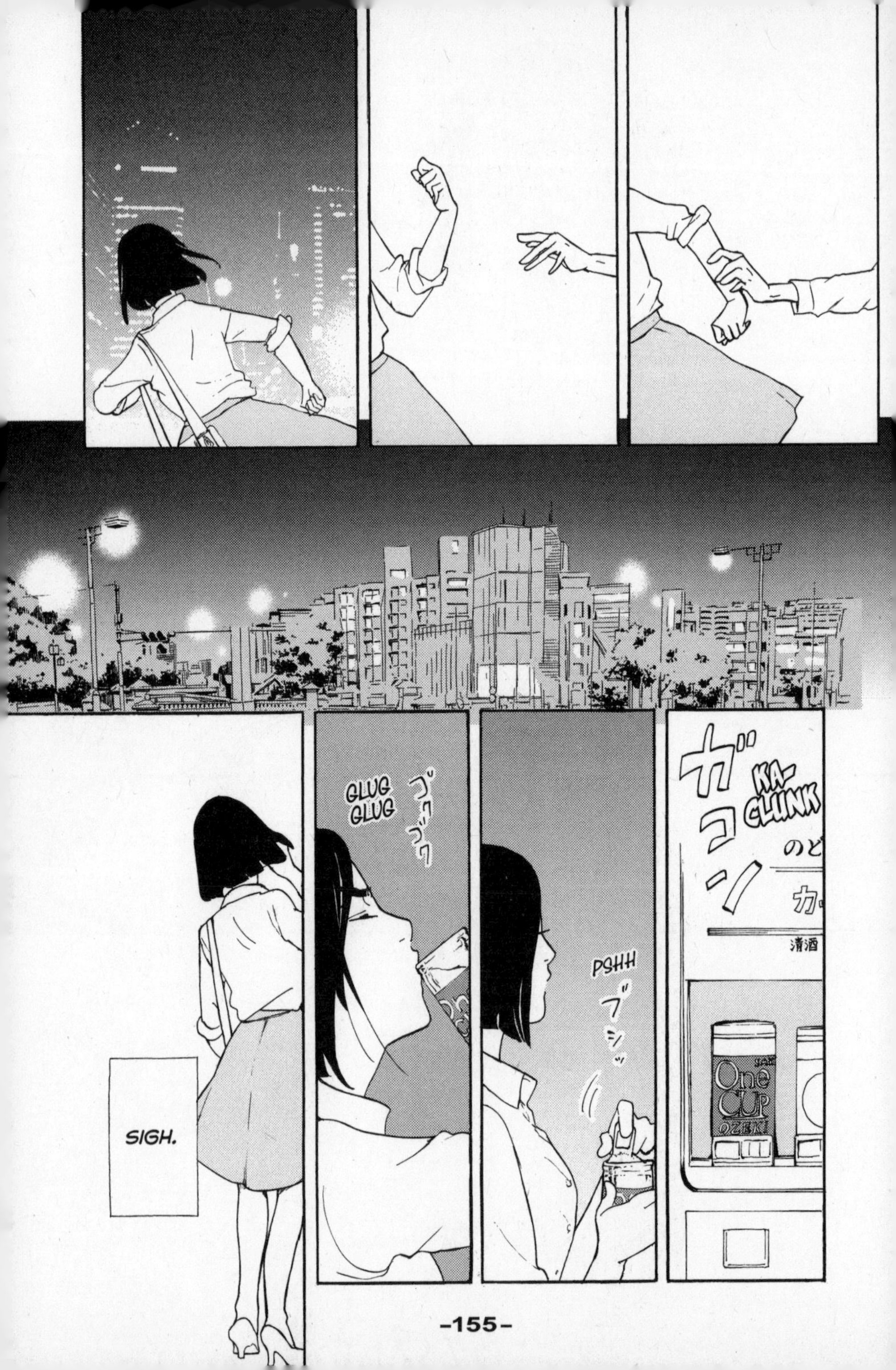
ガコン
KA-CLUNK
のど
清酒
One CUP
OZEKI
PSHH
プシッ
GLUG GLUG
ゴクゴク
SIGH.

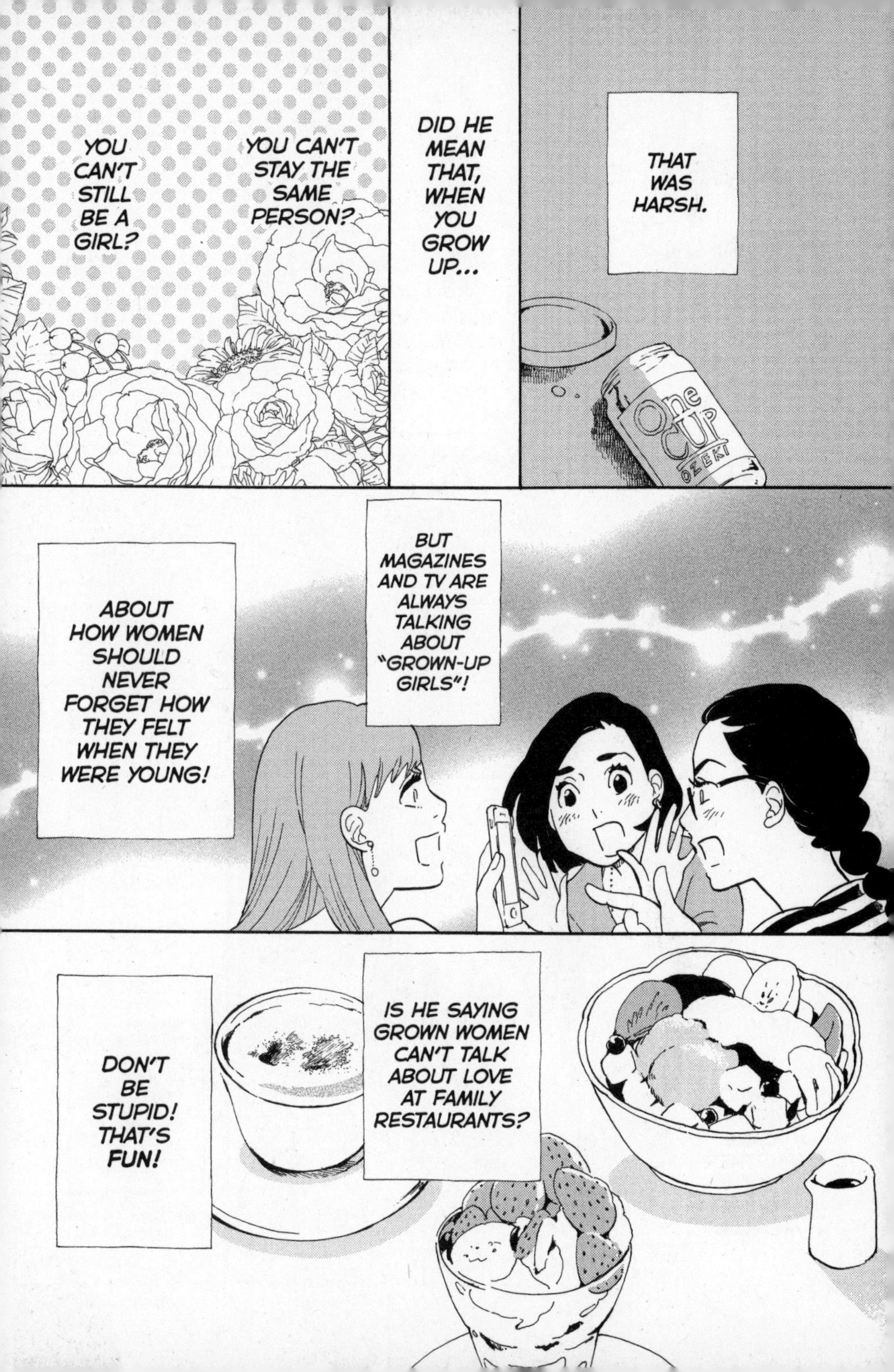
THAT WAS HARSH.
One CUP OZEKI
DID HE MEAN THAT, WHEN YOU GROW UP...
YOU CAN'T STAY THE SAME PERSON?
YOU CAN'T STILL BE A GIRL?
BUT MAGAZINES AND TV ARE ALWAYS TALKING ABOUT "GROWN-UP GIRLS"!
ABOUT HOW WOMEN SHOULD NEVER FORGET HOW THEY FELT WHEN THEY WERE YOUNG!
IS HE SAYING GROWN WOMEN CAN'T TALK ABOUT LOVE AT FAMILY RESTAURANTS?
DON'T BE STUPID! THAT'S FUN!

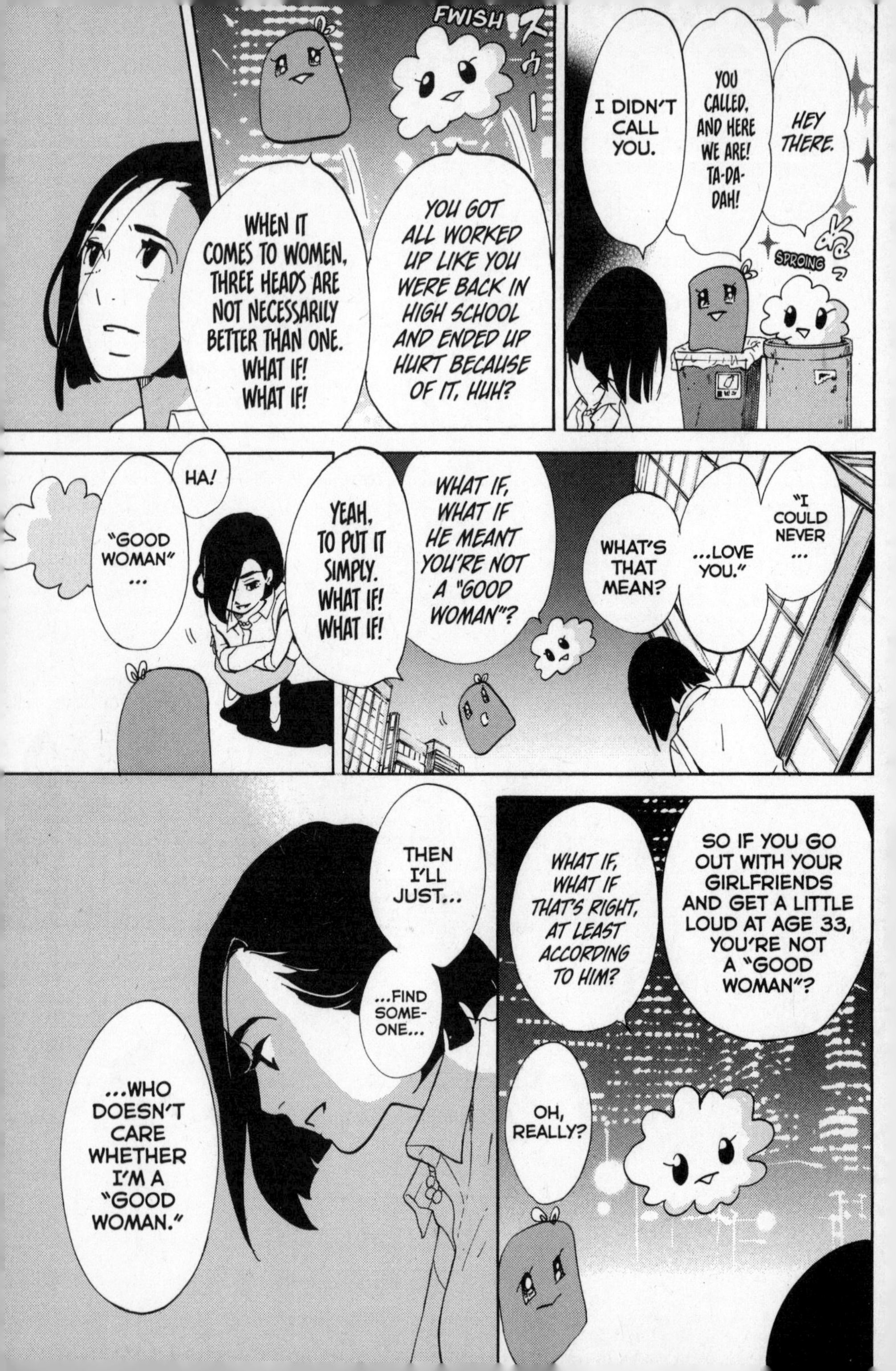
HEY THERE.
YOU CALLED, AND HERE WE ARE! TA-DA-DAH!
I DIDN'T CALL YOU.
SPROING
FWISH
YOU GOT ALL WORKED UP LIKE YOU WERE BACK IN HIGH SCHOOL AND ENDED UP HURT BECAUSE OF IT, HUH?
WHEN IT COMES TO WOMEN, THREE HEADS ARE NOT NECESSARILY BETTER THAN ONE. WHAT IF! WHAT IF!
"I COULD NEVER...
...LOVE YOU."
WHAT'S THAT MEAN?
WHAT IF, WHAT IF HE MEANT YOU'RE NOT A "GOOD WOMAN"?
YEAH, TO PUT IT SIMPLY. WHAT IF! WHAT IF!
HA!
"GOOD WOMAN"...
SO IF YOU GO OUT WITH YOUR GIRLFRIENDS AND GET A LITTLE LOUD AT AGE 33, YOU'RE NOT A "GOOD WOMAN"?
WHAT IF, WHAT IF THAT'S RIGHT, AT LEAST ACCORDING TO HIM?
OH, REALLY?
THEN I'LL JUST...
...FIND SOMEONE...
...WHO DOESN'T CARE WHETHER I'M A "GOOD WOMAN."

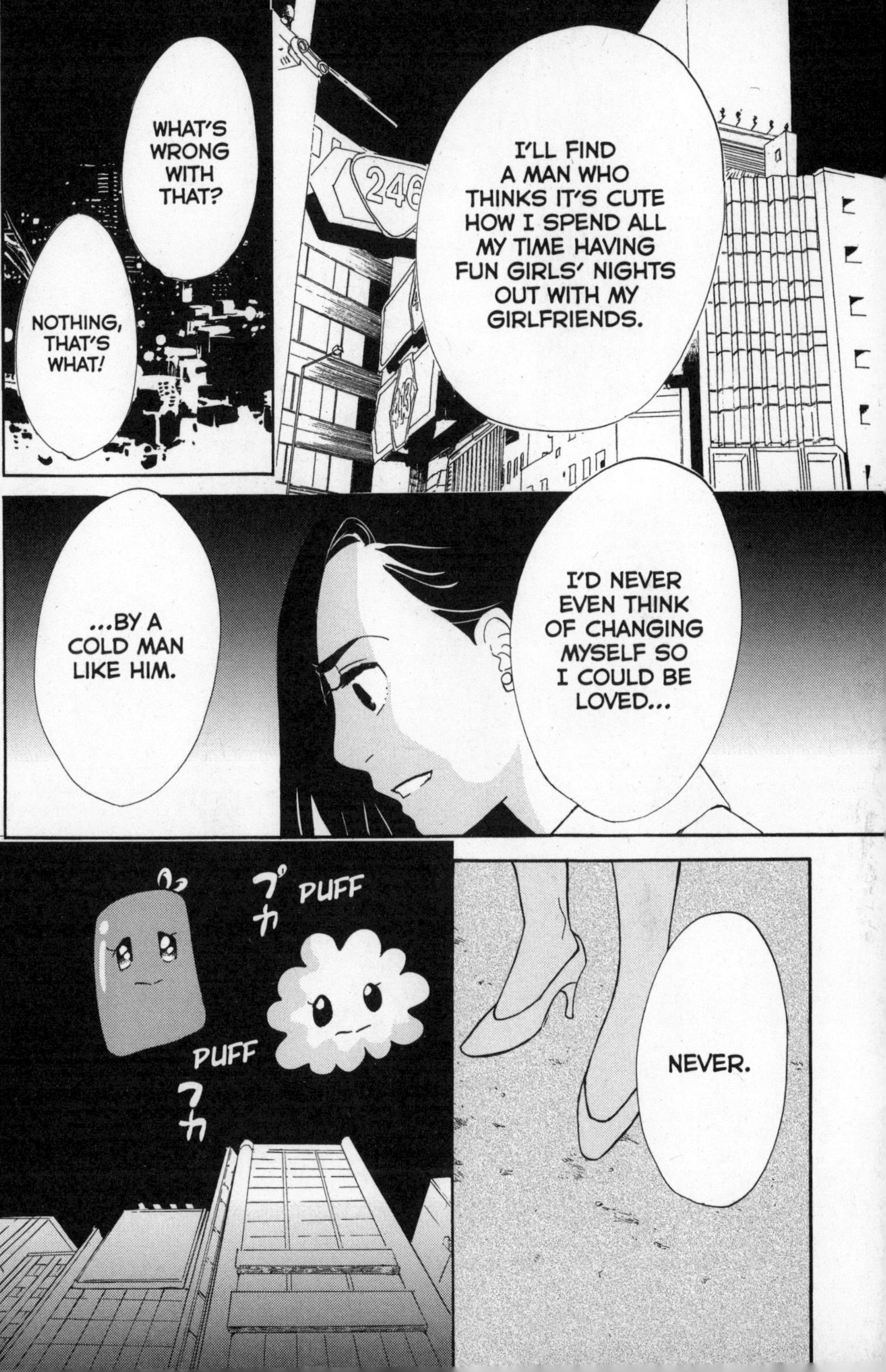
I'LL FIND A MAN WHO THINKS IT'S CUTE HOW I SPEND ALL MY TIME HAVING FUN GIRLS' NIGHTS OUT WITH MY GIRLFRIENDS.
WHAT'S WRONG WITH THAT?
NOTHING, THAT'S WHAT!
I'D NEVER EVEN THINK OF CHANGING MYSELF SO I COULD BE LOVED...
...BY A COLD MAN LIKE HIM.
NEVER.
プカ PUFF
PUFF プカ

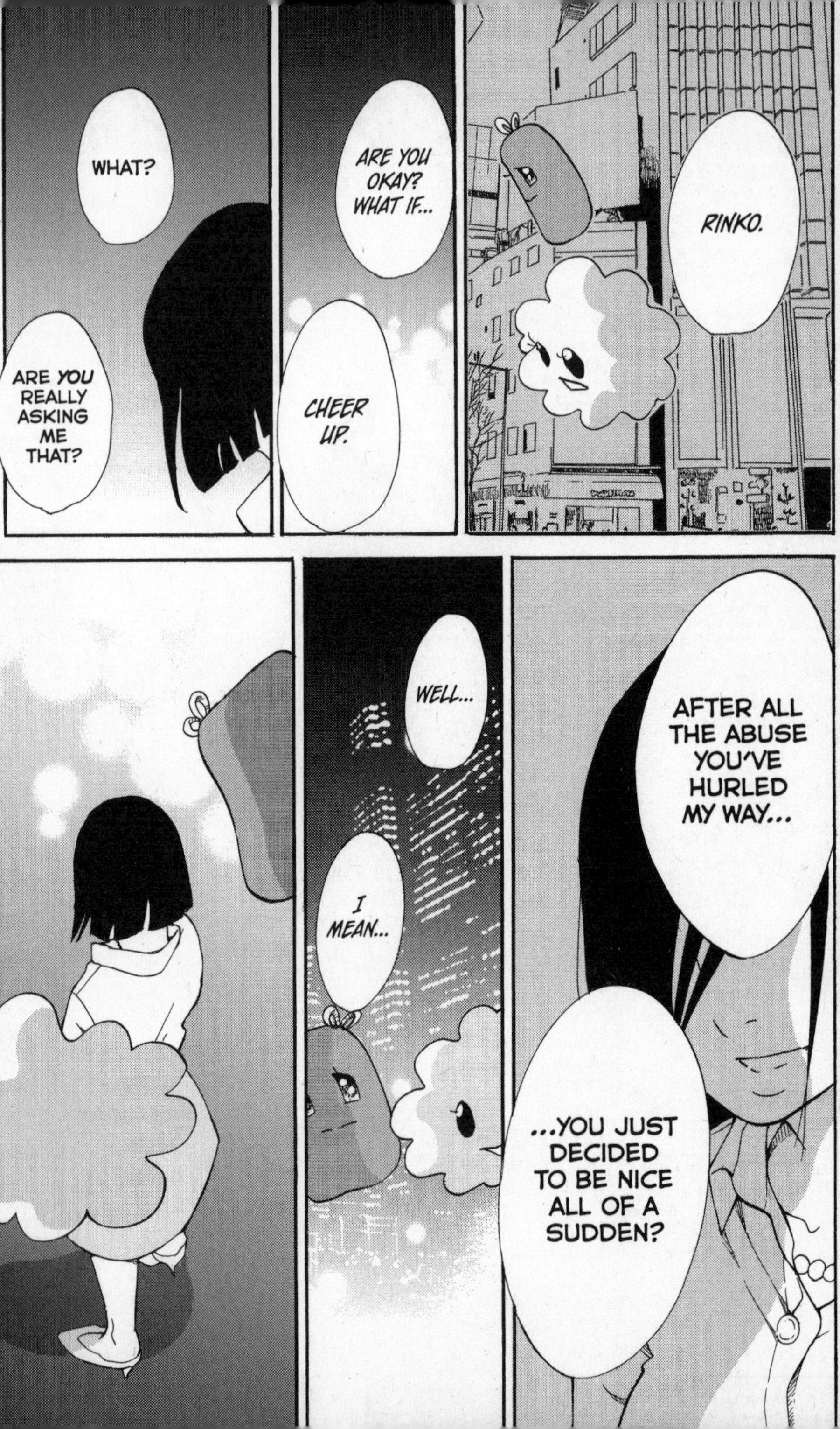
RINKO.
ARE YOU OKAY? WHAT IF...
CHEER UP.
WHAT?
ARE YOU REALLY ASKING ME THAT?
AFTER ALL THE ABUSE YOU'VE HURLED MY WAY...
...YOU JUST DECIDED TO BE NICE ALL OF A SUDDEN?
WELL...
I MEAN...

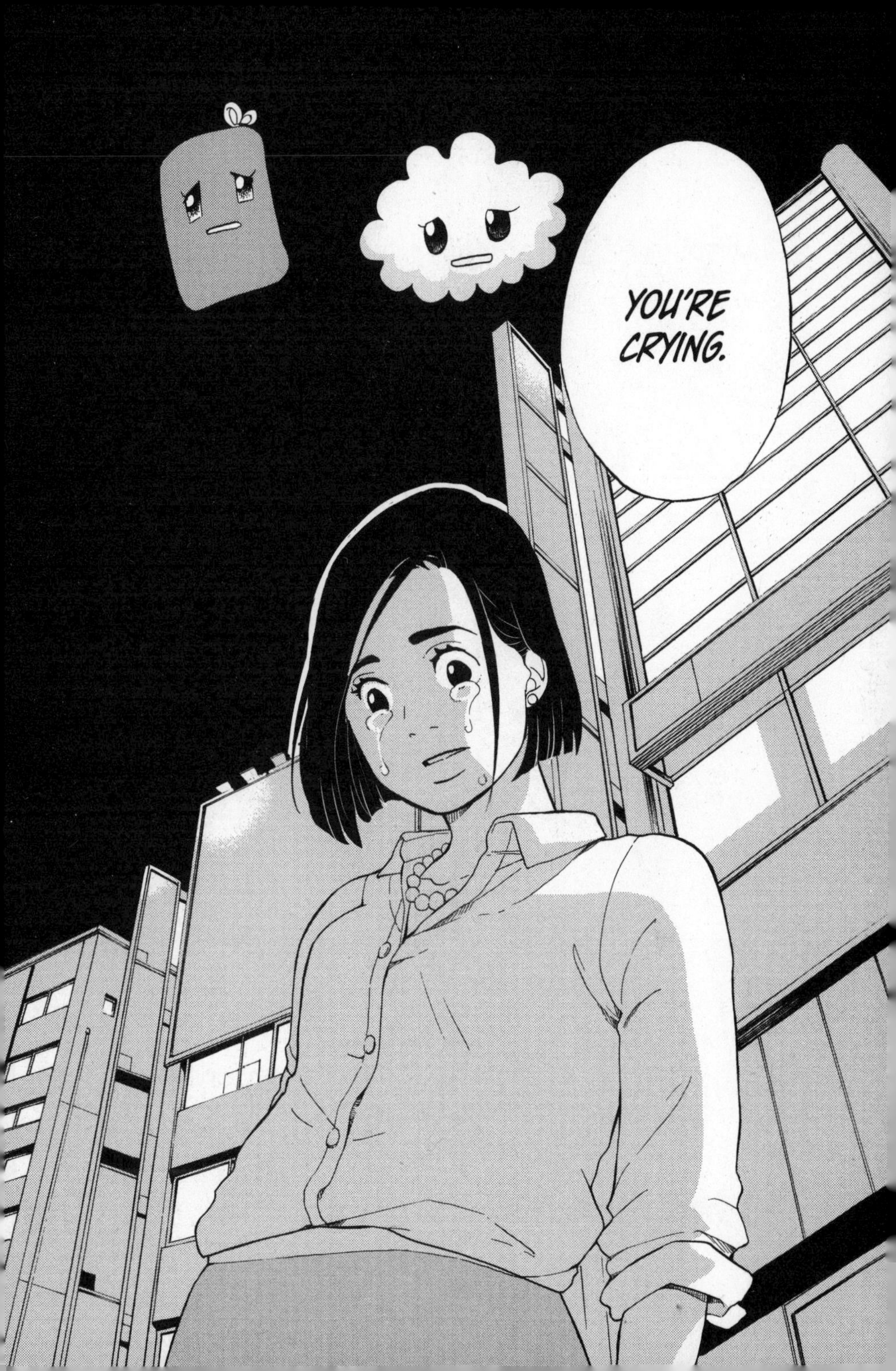
YOU'RE CRYING.

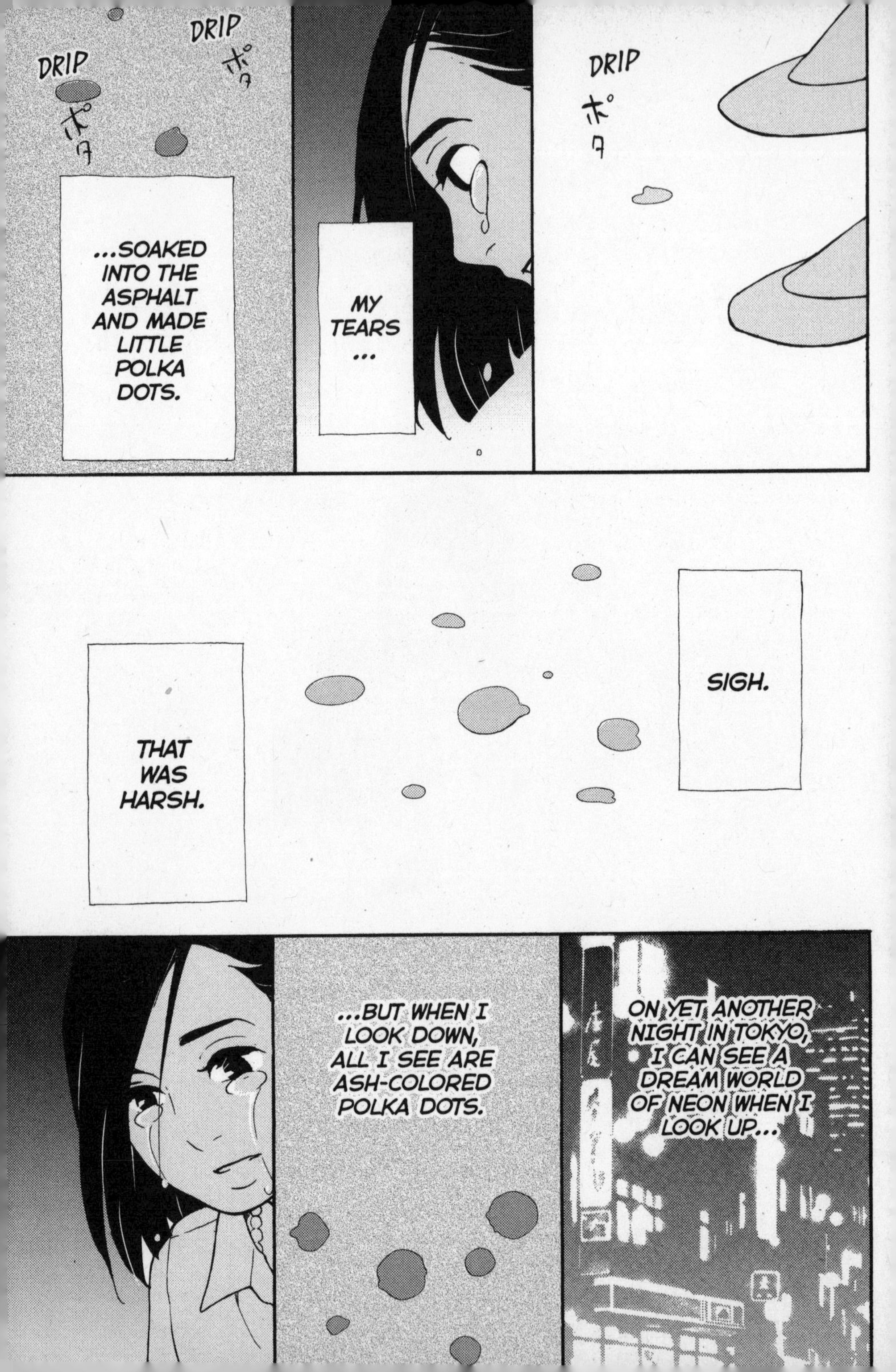
DRIP
ポタ
MY TEARS ...
DRIP
ポタ
DRIP
ポタ
...SOAKED INTO THE ASPHALT AND MADE LITTLE POLKA DOTS.
SIGH.
THAT WAS HARSH.
ON YET ANOTHER NIGHT IN TOKYO, I CAN SEE A DREAM WORLD OF NEON WHEN I LOOK UP...
...BUT WHEN I LOOK DOWN, ALL I SEE ARE ASH-COLORED POLKA DOTS.

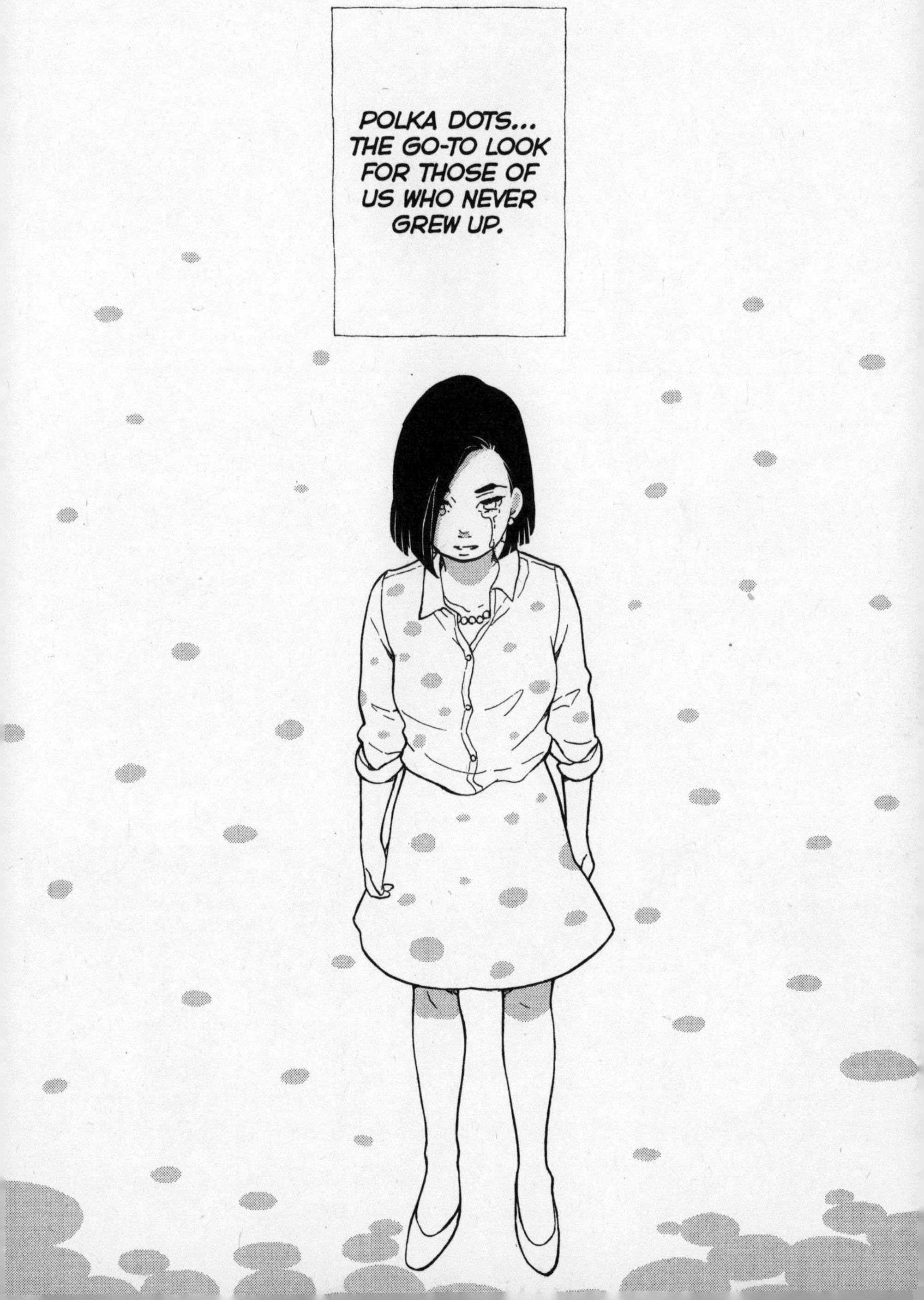
POLKA DOTS... THE GO-TO LOOK FOR THOSE OF US WHO NEVER GREW UP.

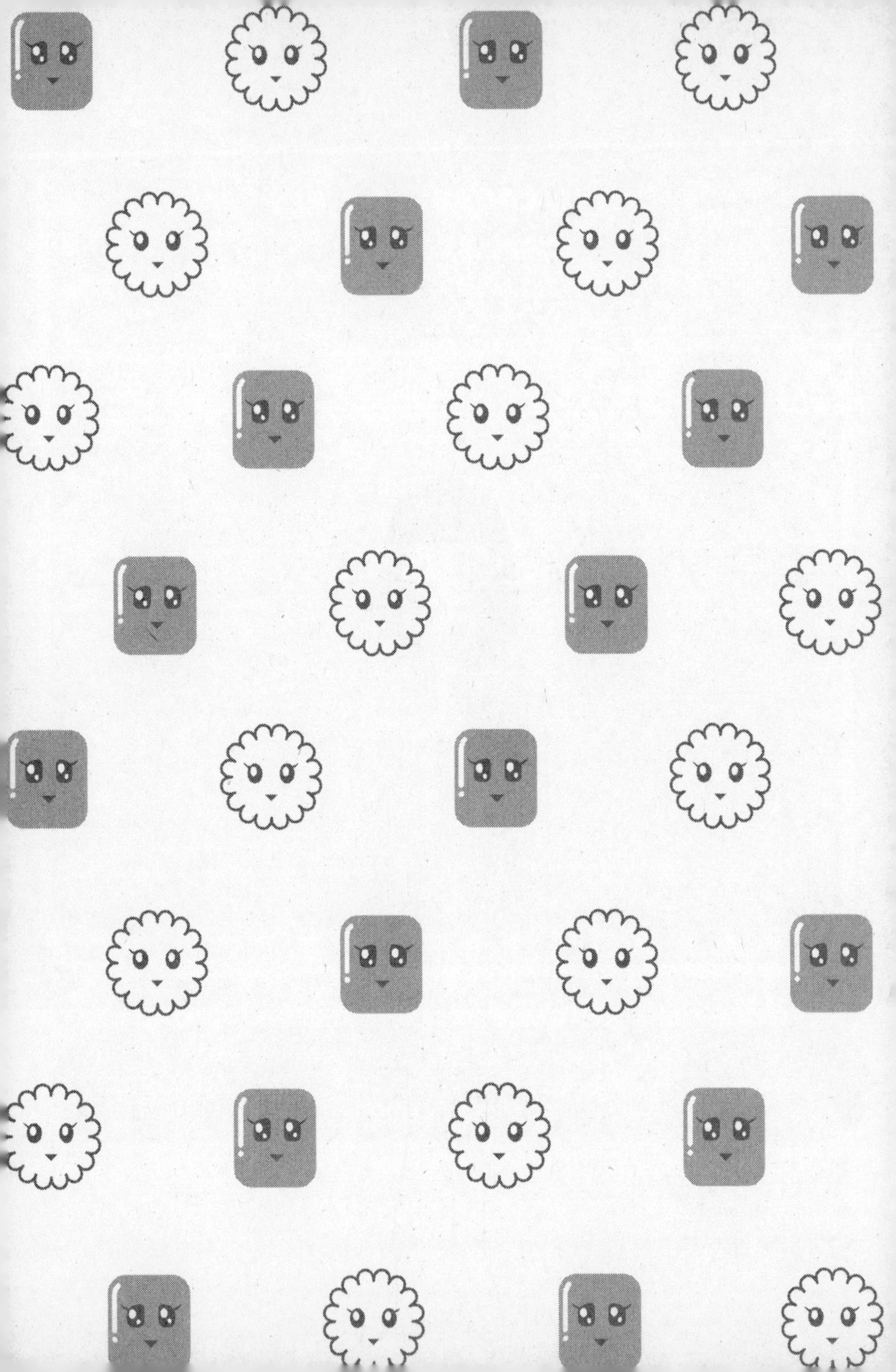

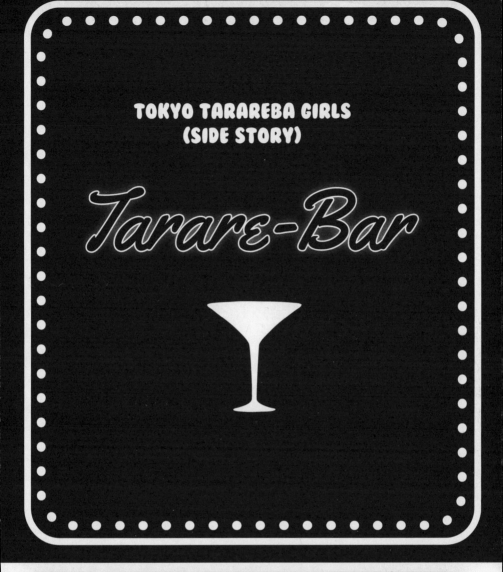

TOKYO TARAREBA GIRLS (SIDE STORY)

Tarare-Bar

IN THE FOLLOWING SIDE STORY, "TARARE-BAR," WE EXAMINE THE PROBLEMS OF WHAT-IF GIRLS AROUND THE COUNTRY!

PLEASE SEND YOUR PROBLEM, PSEUDONYM, CONTACT DETAILS (POSTAL CODE, ADDRESS, PHONE NUMBER, AND REAL NAME), AGE, AND A PHOTOGRAPH (FOR DRAWING REFERENCE ONLY) TO:

KODANSHA KISS EDITING DEPARTMENT "TARARE-BAR"
112-8001 OTOWA, BUNKYO, TOKYO 2-12-21

*WARNING: THERE IS THE POSSIBILITY IT WILL ONLY REND YOUR HEART FURTHER, SO PLEASE BE AWARE OF THAT BEFORE WRITING IN.
ANY PERSONAL INFORMATION WILL BE USED ONLY FOR THE PURPOSES OF THIS COMIC; ONCE IT HAS BEEN COMPLETED, ALL INFORMATION WILL BE PROMPTLY DISPOSED OF.

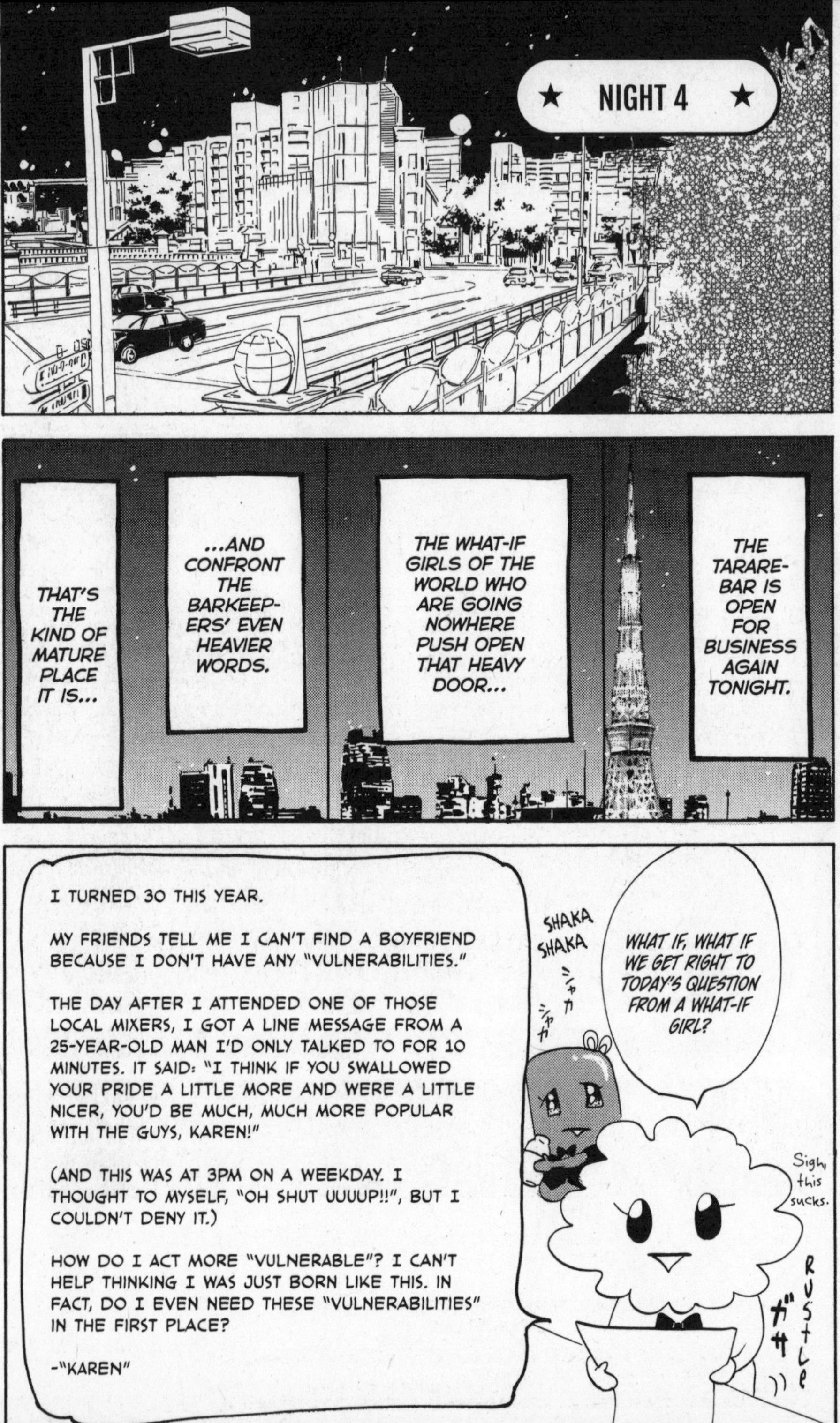
NIGHT 4
THE TARARE-BAR IS OPEN FOR BUSINESS AGAIN TONIGHT.
THE WHAT-IF GIRLS OF THE WORLD WHO ARE GOING NOWHERE PUSH OPEN THAT HEAVY DOOR...
...AND CONFRONT THE BARKEEPERS' EVEN HEAVIER WORDS.
THAT'S THE KIND OF MATURE PLACE IT IS...
WHAT IF, WHAT IF WE GET RIGHT TO TODAY'S QUESTION FROM A WHAT-IF GIRL?
SHAKA SHAKA
Sigh, this sucks.
RUSTLE
I TURNED 30 THIS YEAR.
MY FRIENDS TELL ME I CAN'T FIND A BOYFRIEND BECAUSE I DON'T HAVE ANY "VULNERABILITIES."
THE DAY AFTER I ATTENDED ONE OF THOSE LOCAL MIXERS, I GOT A LINE MESSAGE FROM A 25-YEAR-OLD MAN I'D ONLY TALKED TO FOR 10 MINUTES. IT SAID: "I THINK IF YOU SWALLOWED YOUR PRIDE A LITTLE MORE AND WERE A LITTLE NICER, YOU'D BE MUCH, MUCH MORE POPULAR WITH THE GUYS, KAREN!"
(AND THIS WAS AT 3PM ON A WEEKDAY. I THOUGHT TO MYSELF, "OH SHUT UUUUP!!", BUT I COULDN'T DENY IT.)
HOW DO I ACT MORE "VULNERABLE"? I CAN'T HELP THINKING I WAS JUST BORN LIKE THIS. IN FACT, DO I EVEN NEED THESE "VULNERABILITIES" IN THE FIRST PLACE?
-"KAREN"

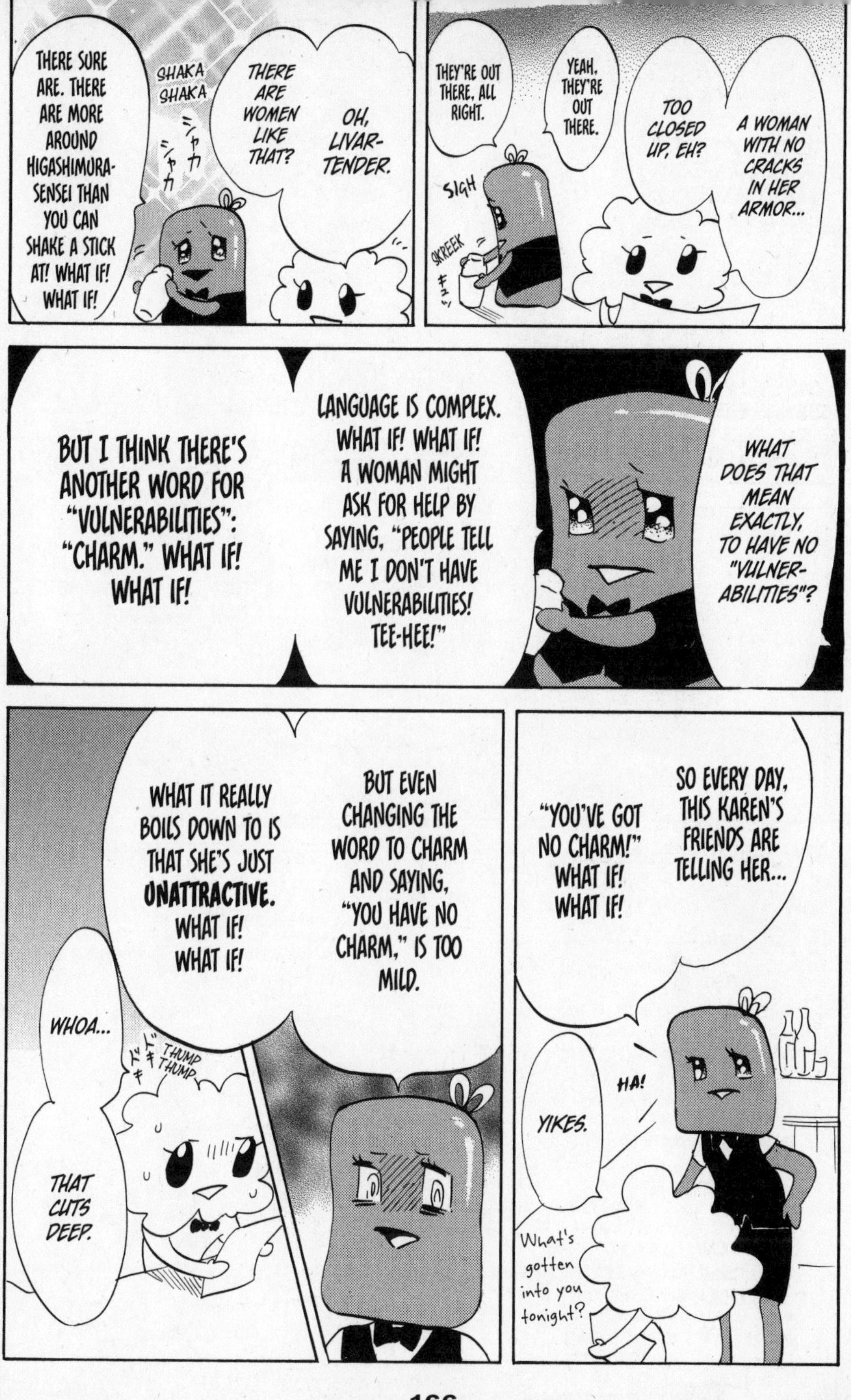
A WOMAN WITH NO CRACKS IN HER ARMOR...
TOO CLOSED UP, EH?
YEAH, THEY'RE OUT THERE.
SIGH
SKREEK
THEY'RE OUT THERE, ALL RIGHT.
OH, LIVAR-TENDER.
THERE ARE WOMEN LIKE THAT?
SHAKA SHAKA
シャカ シャカ
THERE SURE ARE. THERE ARE MORE AROUND HIGASHIMURA-SENSEI THAN YOU CAN SHAKE A STICK AT! WHAT IF! WHAT IF!
WHAT DOES THAT MEAN EXACTLY, TO HAVE NO "VULNER-ABILITIES"?
LANGUAGE IS COMPLEX. WHAT IF! WHAT IF! A WOMAN MIGHT ASK FOR HELP BY SAYING, "PEOPLE TELL ME I DON'T HAVE VULNERABILITIES! TEE-HEE!"
BUT I THINK THERE'S ANOTHER WORD FOR "VULNERABILITIES": "CHARM." WHAT IF! WHAT IF!
SO EVERY DAY, THIS KAREN'S FRIENDS ARE TELLING HER...
"YOU'VE GOT NO CHARM!" WHAT IF! WHAT IF!
HA!
YIKES.
What's gotten into you tonight?
BUT EVEN CHANGING THE WORD TO CHARM AND SAYING, "YOU HAVE NO CHARM," IS TOO MILD.
WHAT IT REALLY BOILS DOWN TO IS THAT SHE'S JUST **UNATTRACTIVE.** WHAT IF! WHAT IF!
ドキ ドキ
THUMP THUMP
WHOA...
THAT CUTS DEEP.

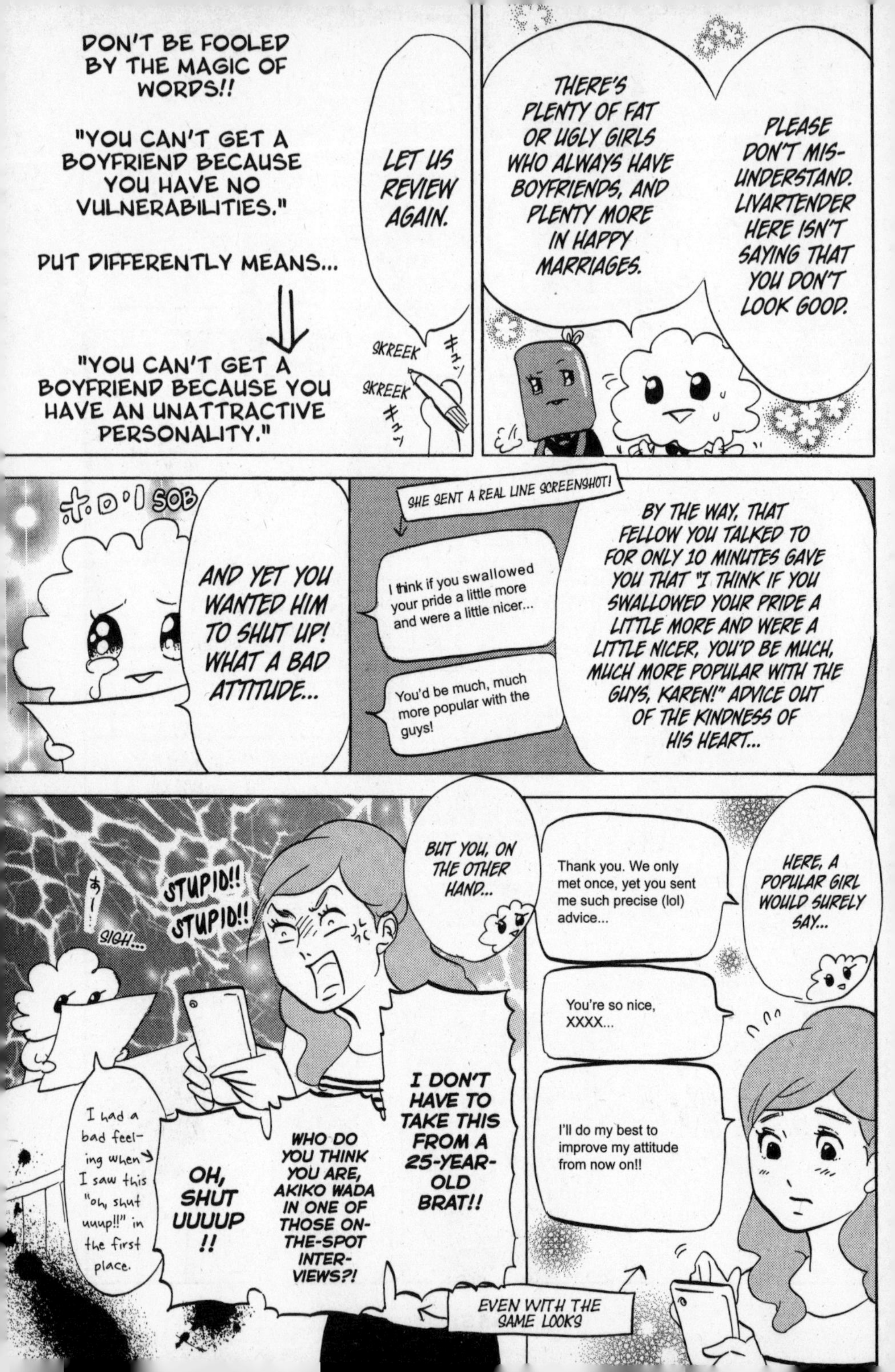
PLEASE DON'T MIS-UNDERSTAND. LIVARTENDER HERE ISN'T SAYING THAT YOU DON'T LOOK GOOD.
THERE'S PLENTY OF FAT OR UGLY GIRLS WHO ALWAYS HAVE BOYFRIENDS, AND PLENTY MORE IN HAPPY MARRIAGES.
LET US REVIEW AGAIN.
SKREEK キュッ
SKREEK キュッ
DON'T BE FOOLED BY THE MAGIC OF WORDS!!
"YOU CAN'T GET A BOYFRIEND BECAUSE YOU HAVE NO VULNERABILITIES."
PUT DIFFERENTLY MEANS...
"YOU CAN'T GET A BOYFRIEND BECAUSE YOU HAVE AN UNATTRACTIVE PERSONALITY."
BY THE WAY, THAT FELLOW YOU TALKED TO FOR ONLY 10 MINUTES GAVE YOU THAT "I THINK IF YOU SWALLOWED YOUR PRIDE A LITTLE MORE AND WERE A LITTLE NICER, YOU'D BE MUCH, MUCH MORE POPULAR WITH THE GUYS, KAREN!" ADVICE OUT OF THE KINDNESS OF HIS HEART...
SHE SENT A REAL LINE SCREENSHOT!
I think if you swallowed your pride a little more and were a little nicer...
You'd be much, much more popular with the guys!
SOB
AND YET YOU WANTED HIM TO SHUT UP! WHAT A BAD ATTITUDE...
HERE, A POPULAR GIRL WOULD SURELY SAY...
Thank you. We only met once, yet you sent me such precise (lol) advice...
You're so nice, XXXX...
I'll do my best to improve my attitude from now on!!
BUT YOU, ON THE OTHER HAND...
STUPID!! STUPID!!
SIGH...
I DON'T HAVE TO TAKE THIS FROM A 25-YEAR-OLD BRAT!!
WHO DO YOU THINK YOU ARE, AKIKO WADA IN ONE OF THOSE ON-THE-SPOT INTERVIEWS?!
OH, SHUT UUUUP!!
I had a bad feeling when I saw this "oh, shut uuup!!" in the first place.
EVEN WITH THE SAME LOOKS

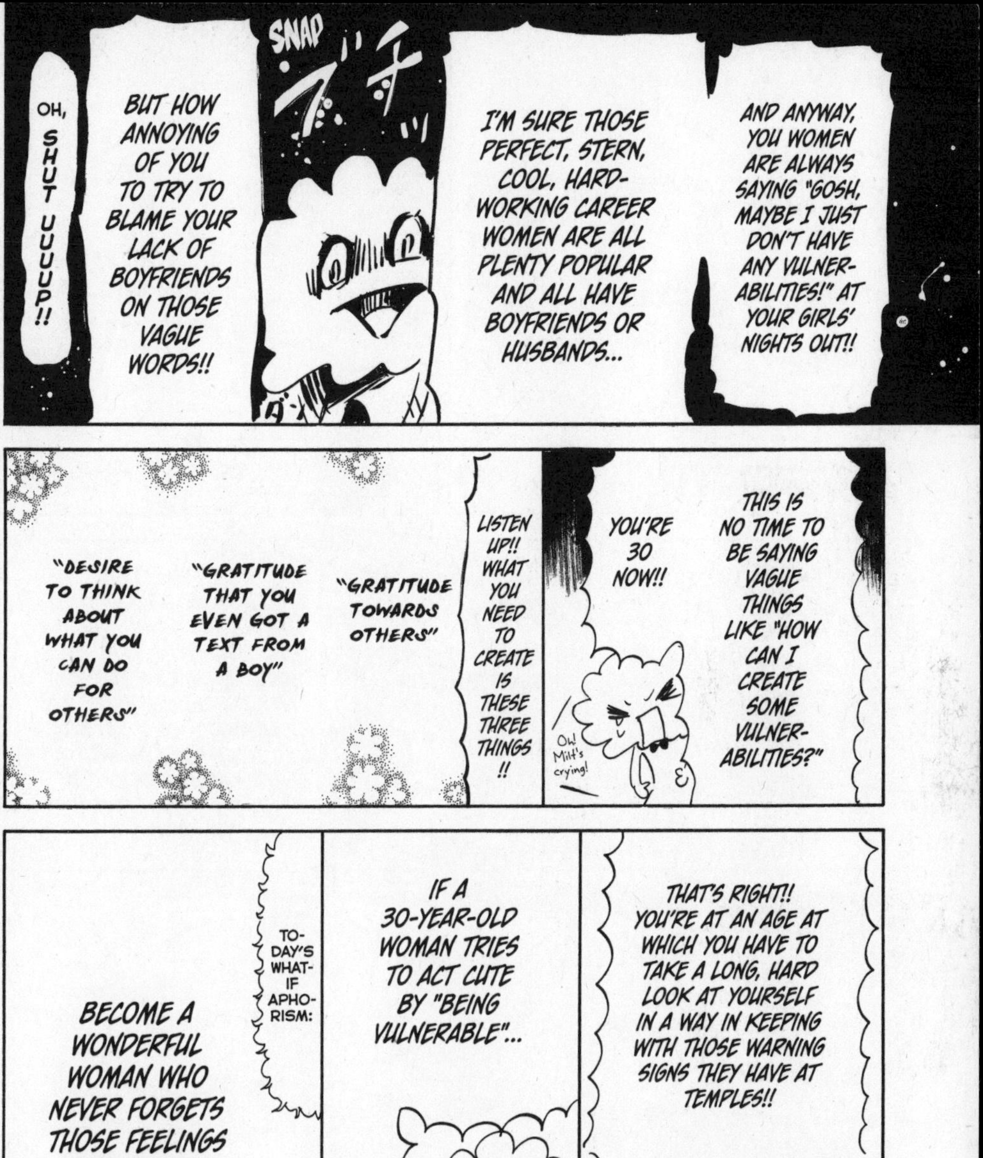
AND ANYWAY, YOU WOMEN ARE ALWAYS SAYING "GOSH, MAYBE I JUST DON'T HAVE ANY VULNER-ABILITIES!" AT YOUR GIRLS' NIGHTS OUT!!
I'M SURE THOSE PERFECT, STERN, COOL, HARD-WORKING CAREER WOMEN ARE ALL PLENTY POPULAR AND ALL HAVE BOYFRIENDS OR HUSBANDS...
SNAP
BUT HOW ANNOYING OF YOU TO TRY TO BLAME YOUR LACK OF BOYFRIENDS ON THOSE VAGUE WORDS!!
OH, SHUT UUUUP!!
THIS IS NO TIME TO BE SAYING VAGUE THINGS LIKE "HOW CAN I CREATE SOME VULNER-ABILITIES?"
YOU'RE 30 NOW!!
Oh! Milt's crying!
LISTEN UP!! WHAT YOU NEED TO CREATE IS THESE THREE THINGS!!
"GRATITUDE TOWARDS OTHERS"
"GRATITUDE THAT YOU EVEN GOT A TEXT FROM A BOY"
"DESIRE TO THINK ABOUT WHAT YOU CAN DO FOR OTHERS"
THAT'S RIGHT!! YOU'RE AT AN AGE AT WHICH YOU HAVE TO TAKE A LONG, HARD LOOK AT YOURSELF IN A WAY IN KEEPING WITH THOSE WARNING SIGNS THEY HAVE AT TEMPLES!!
DON'T SCOLD CHILDREN, FOR THEIR JOURNEY IS JUST BEGINNING. DON'T LAUGH AT SENIORS, FOR THEIR JOURNEY IS AT ITS END.
IF A 30-YEAR-OLD WOMAN TRIES TO ACT CUTE BY "BEING VULNERABLE"...
BOOM
...SHE'LL COME OFF AS A DESPERATE OLD WOMAN!!
TODAY'S WHAT-IF APHORISM:
BECOME A WONDERFUL WOMAN WHO NEVER FORGETS THOSE FEELINGS OF GRATITUDE AND IS KIND TO OTHERS, YOU DUMB IDIOT.

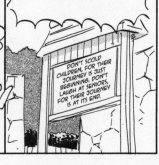

★ NIGHT 5 ★

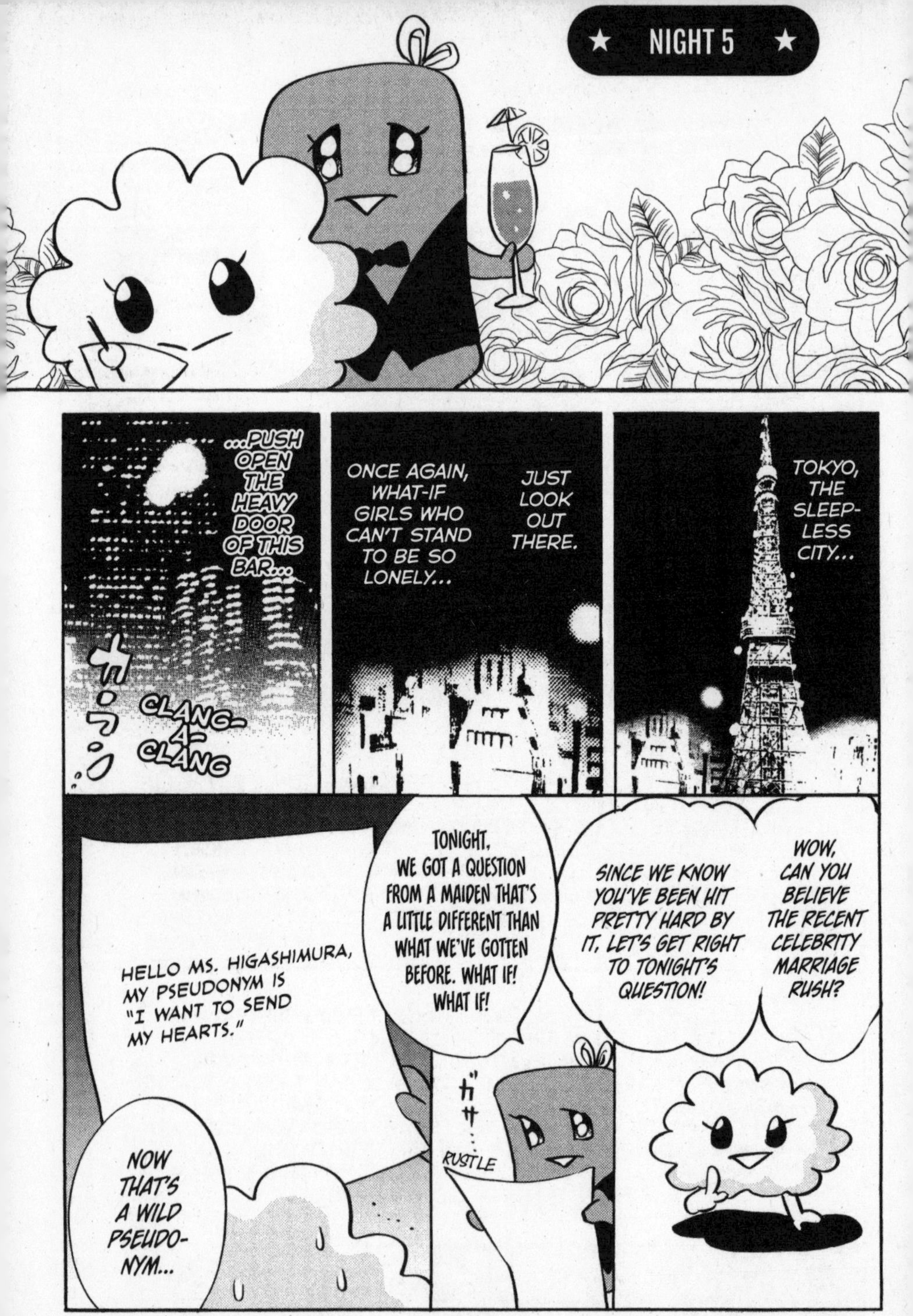
TOKYO, THE SLEEPLESS CITY...
JUST LOOK OUT THERE.
ONCE AGAIN, WHAT-IF GIRLS WHO CAN'T STAND TO BE SO LONELY...
...PUSH OPEN THE HEAVY DOOR OF THIS BAR...
CLANG-A-CLANG
WOW, CAN YOU BELIEVE THE RECENT CELEBRITY MARRIAGE RUSH?
SINCE WE KNOW YOU'VE BEEN HIT PRETTY HARD BY IT, LET'S GET RIGHT TO TONIGHT'S QUESTION!
TONIGHT, WE GOT A QUESTION FROM A MAIDEN THAT'S A LITTLE DIFFERENT THAN WHAT WE'VE GOTTEN BEFORE. WHAT IF! WHAT IF!
RUSTLE
HELLO MS. HIGASHIMURA, MY PSEUDONYM IS "I WANT TO SEND MY HEARTS."
NOW THAT'S A WILD PSEUDONYM...

I TURNED 28 THIS YEAR, BUT FOR ABOUT TWO YEARS, I'VE BEEN FOLLOWING VISUAL-KEI BANDS, BECOMING ONE OF THOSE "BAND GALS."

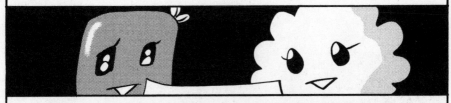

I DON'T HAVE MUCH MONEY OR STAMINA, SO I CAN ONLY GO TO CONCERTS ABOUT TWICE A MONTH, BUT WHEN I DO MAKE IT TO THE SHOWS, I WATCH MY FAVORITE BAND MEMBERS AND CRY WHILE SCREAMING THINGS LIKE, "LOOK AT HOW AGGRESSIVELY YOU'RE PLAYING THAT BASS WITH THAT THIN BODY! I'LL FEED YOU ANYTHING YOU WANT!" OR "XXXX ACTUALLY EXISTS IN THIS WORLD!!"

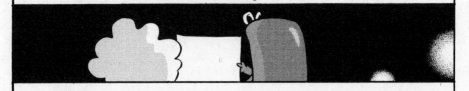

MY FRIENDS SAY, "SO WHAT? YOU'RE HAVING FUN!" BUT WHEN I LOOK AT ALL THE CDS AND MERCHANDISE IN MY ROOM, IT JUST MAKES ME DEPRESSED. I THINK, "WHAT AM I DOING?" IF I GOT SICK OR LOST MY JOB, IT'S NOT LIKE THESE MUSICIANS WOULD SUPPORT ME, AND AT THIS RATE I'M GOING TO DIE ALONE SURROUNDED BY THESE CDS AND MERCHANDISE.

I WANT TO MARRY A NORMAL, KIND OFFICE WORKER WHO LOVES ME. BUT WHEN I GO TO CONCERTS, I FEEL LIKE "THIS MOMENT IS EVERYTHING!!" WHEN MY FRIENDS ARRANGE MIXER-TYPE THINGS FOR ME, I CAN'T GET EVEN THE MEN I LIKE TO BE INTERESTED IN ME. AFTERWARDS, I'LL GO TO CONCERTS AND DREAM ABOUT THE BAND MEMBERS AND DOWNGRADE THE REAL-LIFE GUY I'M INTERESTED IN TO THE RANK OF "MAYBE." BUT SINCE HE ISN'T INTERESTED IN ME EITHER, IT NEVER GOES ANYWHERE.

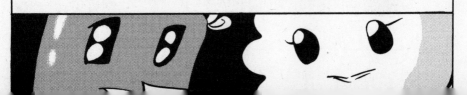

I DON'T WANT TO DIE ALONE. I'M SCARED. I REALLY DO WANT TO GET MARRIED.

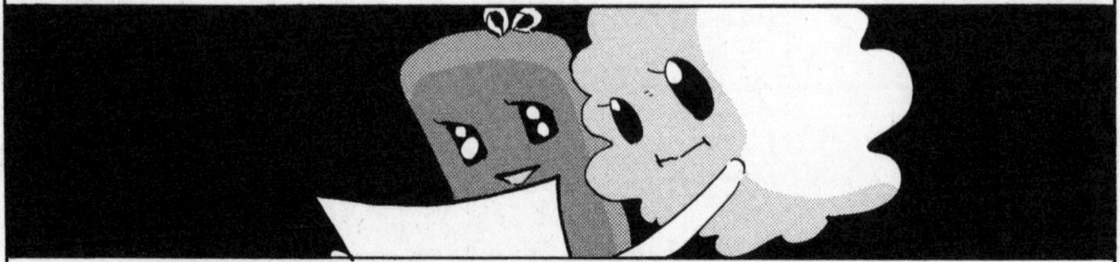

BUT BEFORE I KNOW IT, I'VE BOUGHT MORE CONCERT TICKETS, I WATCH NOTHING BUT MOVIES WITH THESE BAND MEMBERS ON MY DAYS OFF, AND IF I DIDN'T HAVE TO WORK, I'D PROBABLY GRAB MY PASSBOOK AND GO ALL AROUND THE COUNTRY WITH MY FAVORITE MUSICIANS. THAT'S HOW BAD IT IS. (VISUAL-KEI BANDS DO A LOT OF SHOWS. THE MOST PROLIFIC ONES CAN HAVE OVER 100 CONCERTS A YEAR.)

I DON'T KNOW WHAT TO DO. SERIOUSLY.

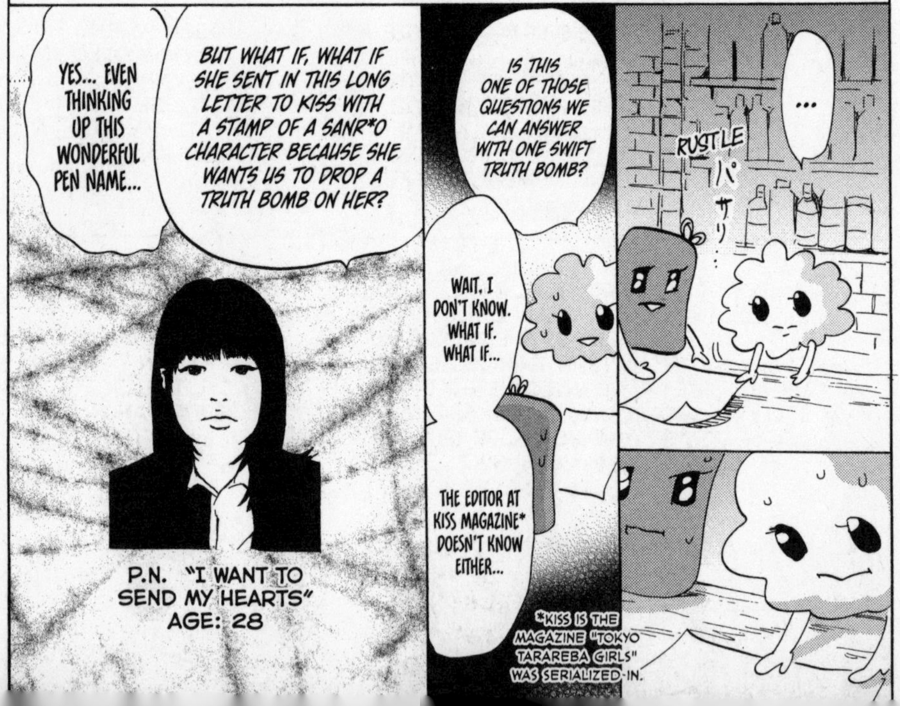
...
RUSTLE
パサリ…
IS THIS ONE OF THOSE QUESTIONS WE CAN ANSWER WITH ONE SWIFT TRUTH BOMB?
WAIT, I DON'T KNOW. WHAT IF. WHAT IF...
THE EDITOR AT KISS MAGAZINE* DOESN'T KNOW EITHER...
*KISS IS THE MAGAZINE "TOKYO TARAREBA GIRLS" WAS SERIALIZED IN.
BUT WHAT IF, WHAT IF SHE SENT IN THIS LONG LETTER TO KISS WITH A STAMP OF A SANR*O CHARACTER BECAUSE SHE WANTS US TO DROP A TRUTH BOMB ON HER?
YES... EVEN THINKING UP THIS WONDERFUL PEN NAME...
P.N. "I WANT TO SEND MY HEARTS" AGE: 28

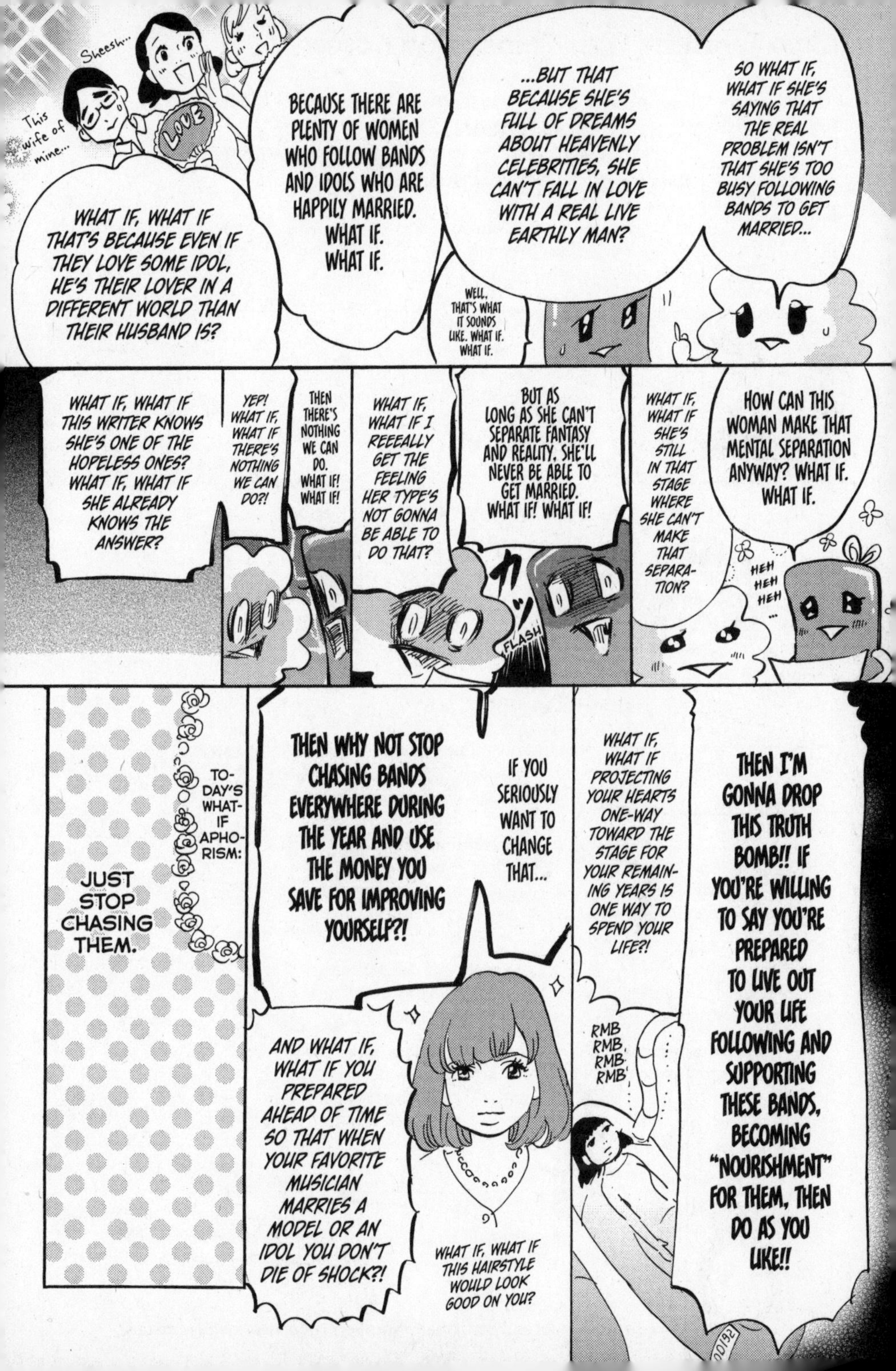
SO WHAT IF, WHAT IF SHE'S SAYING THAT THE REAL PROBLEM ISN'T THAT SHE'S TOO BUSY FOLLOWING BANDS TO GET MARRIED...
...BUT THAT BECAUSE SHE'S FULL OF DREAMS ABOUT HEAVENLY CELEBRITIES, SHE CAN'T FALL IN LOVE WITH A REAL LIVE EARTHLY MAN?
WELL, THAT'S WHAT IT SOUNDS LIKE. WHAT IF. WHAT IF.
BECAUSE THERE ARE PLENTY OF WOMEN WHO FOLLOW BANDS AND IDOLS WHO ARE HAPPILY MARRIED. WHAT IF. WHAT IF.
Sheesh...
LOVE
This wife of mine...
WHAT IF, WHAT IF THAT'S BECAUSE EVEN IF THEY LOVE SOME IDOL, HE'S THEIR LOVER IN A DIFFERENT WORLD THAN THEIR HUSBAND IS?
HOW CAN THIS WOMAN MAKE THAT MENTAL SEPARATION ANYWAY? WHAT IF. WHAT IF.
HEH HEH HEH...
WHAT IF, WHAT IF SHE'S STILL IN THAT STAGE WHERE SHE CAN'T MAKE THAT SEPARATION?
BUT AS LONG AS SHE CAN'T SEPARATE FANTASY AND REALITY, SHE'LL NEVER BE ABLE TO GET MARRIED. WHAT IF! WHAT IF!
FLASH
WHAT IF, WHAT IF I REEEALLY GET THE FEELING HER TYPE'S NOT GONNA BE ABLE TO DO THAT?
THEN THERE'S NOTHING WE CAN DO. WHAT IF! WHAT IF!
YEP! WHAT IF, WHAT IF THERE'S NOTHING WE CAN DO?!
WHAT IF, WHAT IF THIS WRITER KNOWS SHE'S ONE OF THE HOPELESS ONES? WHAT IF, WHAT IF SHE ALREADY KNOWS THE ANSWER?
THEN I'M GONNA DROP THIS TRUTH BOMB!! IF YOU'RE WILLING TO SAY YOU'RE PREPARED TO LIVE OUT YOUR LIFE FOLLOWING AND SUPPORTING THESE BANDS, BECOMING "NOURISHMENT" FOR THEM, THEN DO AS YOU LIKE!!
WHAT IF, WHAT IF PROJECTING YOUR HEARTS ONE-WAY TOWARD THE STAGE FOR YOUR REMAINING YEARS IS ONE WAY TO SPEND YOUR LIFE?!
RMB RMB RMB RMB
IF YOU SERIOUSLY WANT TO CHANGE THAT...
THEN WHY NOT STOP CHASING BANDS EVERYWHERE DURING THE YEAR AND USE THE MONEY YOU SAVE FOR IMPROVING YOURSELF?!
AND WHAT IF, WHAT IF YOU PREPARED AHEAD OF TIME SO THAT WHEN YOUR FAVORITE MUSICIAN MARRIES A MODEL OR AN IDOL YOU DON'T DIE OF SHOCK?!
WHAT IF, WHAT IF THIS HAIRSTYLE WOULD LOOK GOOD ON YOU?
TODAY'S WHAT-IF APHORISM:
JUST STOP CHASING THEM.

Tokyo Tarareba Girls Translation notes

About the name: "Tarareba" means "What-if," like the "What-if" stories you tell yourself about what could be or could have been.

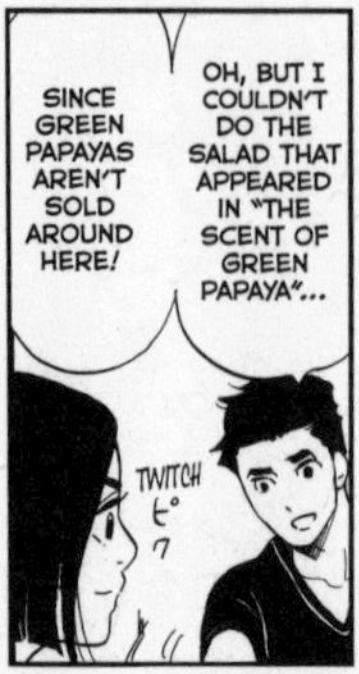
OH, BUT I COULDN'T DO THE SALAD THAT APPEARED IN "THE SCENT OF GREEN PAPAYA"...
SINCE GREEN PAPAYAS AREN'T SOLD AROUND HERE!
TWITCH ピ

The Scent of Green Papaya, page 21
A French-made, Vietnamese-language film from 1993 about the life of a girl who becomes the servant of a wealthy family when she is young.

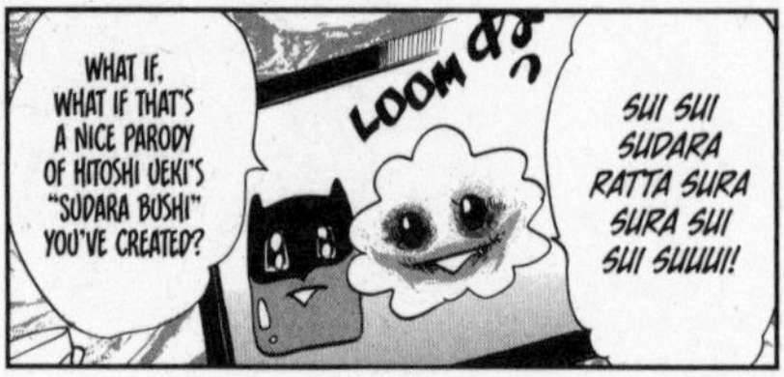
SUI SUI SUDARA RATTA SURA SURA SUI SUI SUUUU!
LOOM ぬっ
WHAT IF, WHAT IF THAT'S A NICE PARODY OF HITOSHI UEKI'S "SUDARA BUSHI" YOU'VE CREATED?

Sudara Bushi, page 37
A Showa-era pop song about a man who keeps doing things he knows are bad for him but he can't stop doing, like over-drinking and gambling away his bonus money. Each verse ends with the phrase "I know (I shouldn't), but I just can't stop," which Rinko twists into her "I know that, but I just can't bear it." The "Sui Sui Sudara Ratta" bit is from the nonsense chorus of the song.

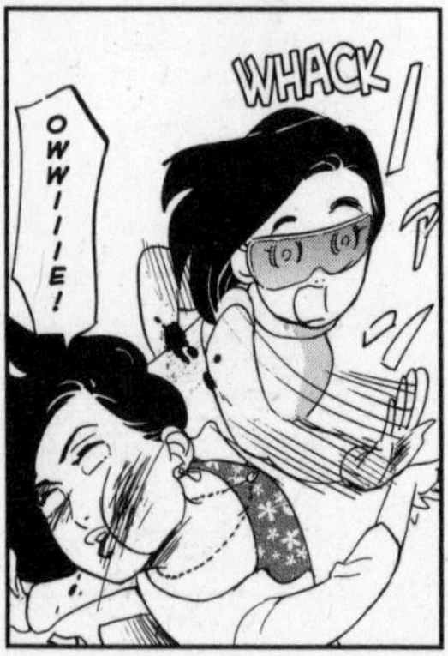
WHACK
OWWIIIIE!

Owie!, page 50
In the Japanese version, Rinko cries out, "hidebu," a nonsense word screamed by the victims of the progatonist's martial arts attacks in the manga and anime *Fist of the North Star*.

The What-A-Waste Ghosts, page 53
A reference to a series of TV public service announcements released by the Japan Ad Council in the early 1980s centered around ghosts that appear when characters waste things like food, causing them to behave better.

Chu-hi, page 127
A canned version of Chuhai, an alcoholic beverage traditionally made with shochu and carbonated water flavored with lemon, though vodka and other liquors, as well as other mixers/flavorings can be used in modern versions.

The It Happens Expedition Party, page 135
An act from the early 2000s by the comedy duo "Regular" in which the two point out little things everyone has been through (or, sometimes for laughs, things that have happened to no one) to a song and dance.

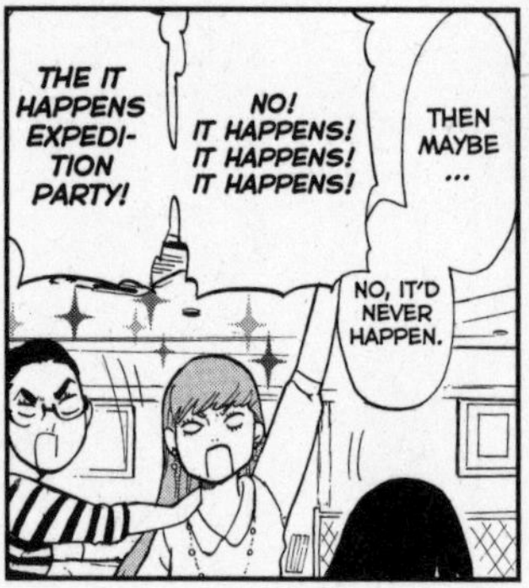
THEN MAYBE ...
NO! IT HAPPENS! IT HAPPENS! IT HAPPENS!
THE IT HAPPENS EXPEDITION PARTY!
NO, IT'D NEVER HAPPEN.

Anmitsu, page 138
A dessert made with agar jelly and *azuki* bean paste, with boiled and chilled peas, *gyuhi* (soft mochi), fruit, and a sweetened syrup to top it with. Cream anmitsu is served with whipped cream or ice cream.

Ajillo mushrooms, karasumi, iberico de Bellota, page 145

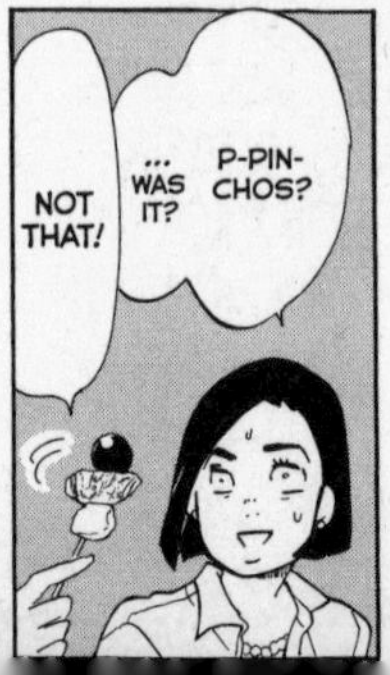
P-PINCHOS?
... WAS IT?
NOT THAT!

Ajillo mushrooms are mushrooms with a garlic sauce. Karasumi is a delicacy made by drying salted mullet roe in the sun. Iberico de Bellota is cured pork made from black Iberian pigs that were fed only acorns.

Pinchos, page 146
Small snacks typically eaten socially in bars, consisting of various ingredients held together with a toothpick and skewered on a piece of bread.

Akiko Wada, page 167
A Japanese singer and performer who is very cooperative with reporters.

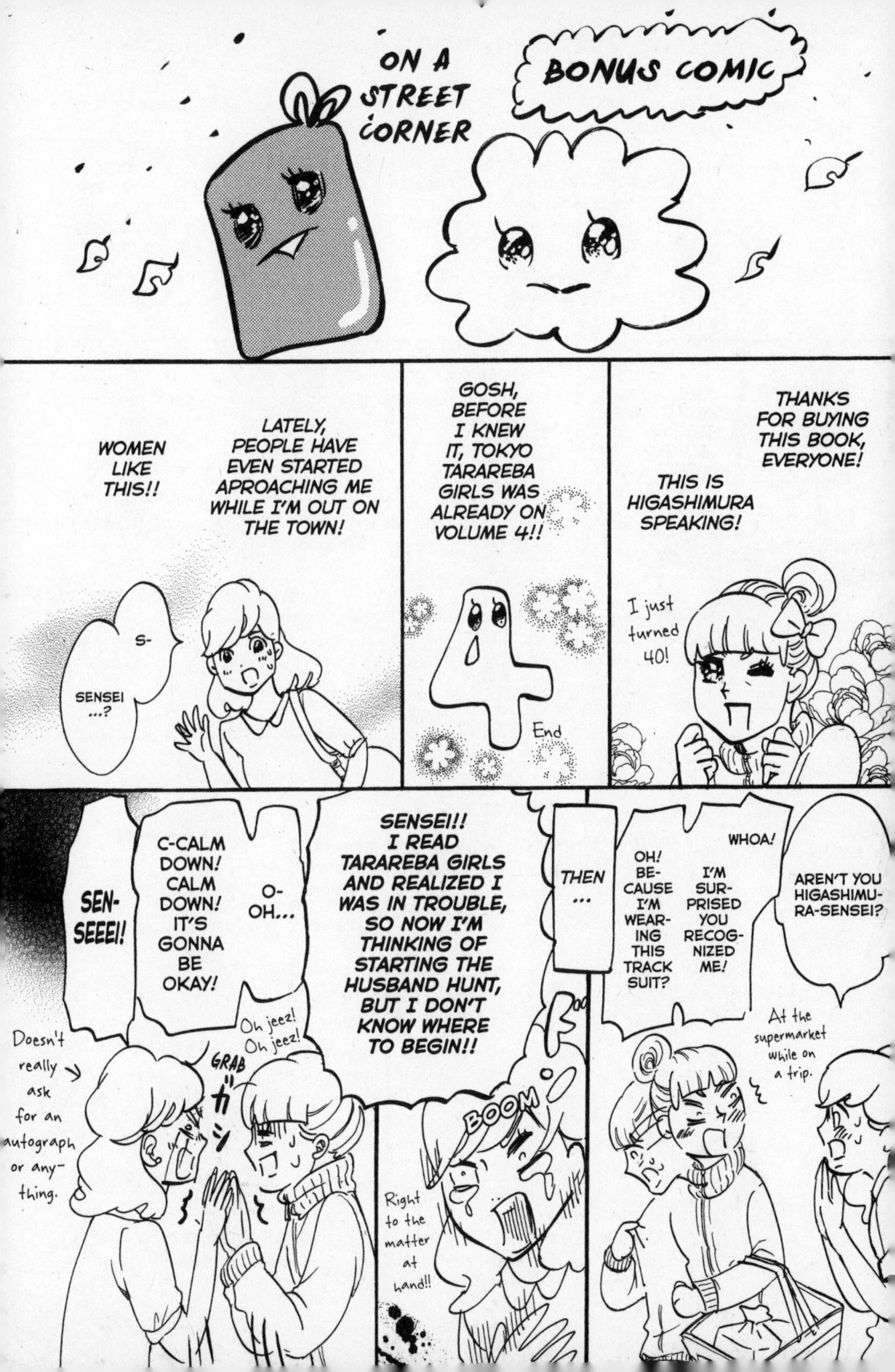
BONUS COMIC
ON A STREET CORNER
THANKS FOR BUYING THIS BOOK, EVERYONE!
THIS IS HIGASHIMURA SPEAKING!
I just turned 40!
GOSH, BEFORE I KNEW IT, TOKYO TARAREBA GIRLS WAS ALREADY ON VOLUME 4!!
End
LATELY, PEOPLE HAVE EVEN STARTED APROACHING ME WHILE I'M OUT ON THE TOWN!
WOMEN LIKE THIS!!
S- SENSEI ...?
AREN'T YOU HIGASHIMURA-SENSEI?
At the supermarket while on a trip.
WHOA! I'M SURPRISED YOU RECOGNIZED ME!
OH! BECAUSE I'M WEARING THIS TRACK SUIT?
THEN ...
SENSEI!! I READ TARAREBA GIRLS AND REALIZED I WAS IN TROUBLE, SO NOW I'M THINKING OF STARTING THE HUSBAND HUNT, BUT I DON'T KNOW WHERE TO BEGIN!!
BOOM
Right to the matter at hand!!
O-OH...
C-CALM DOWN! CALM DOWN! IT'S GONNA BE OKAY!
Oh jeez! Oh jeez!
GRAB
SEN-SEEEI!
Doesn't really ask for an autograph or anything.

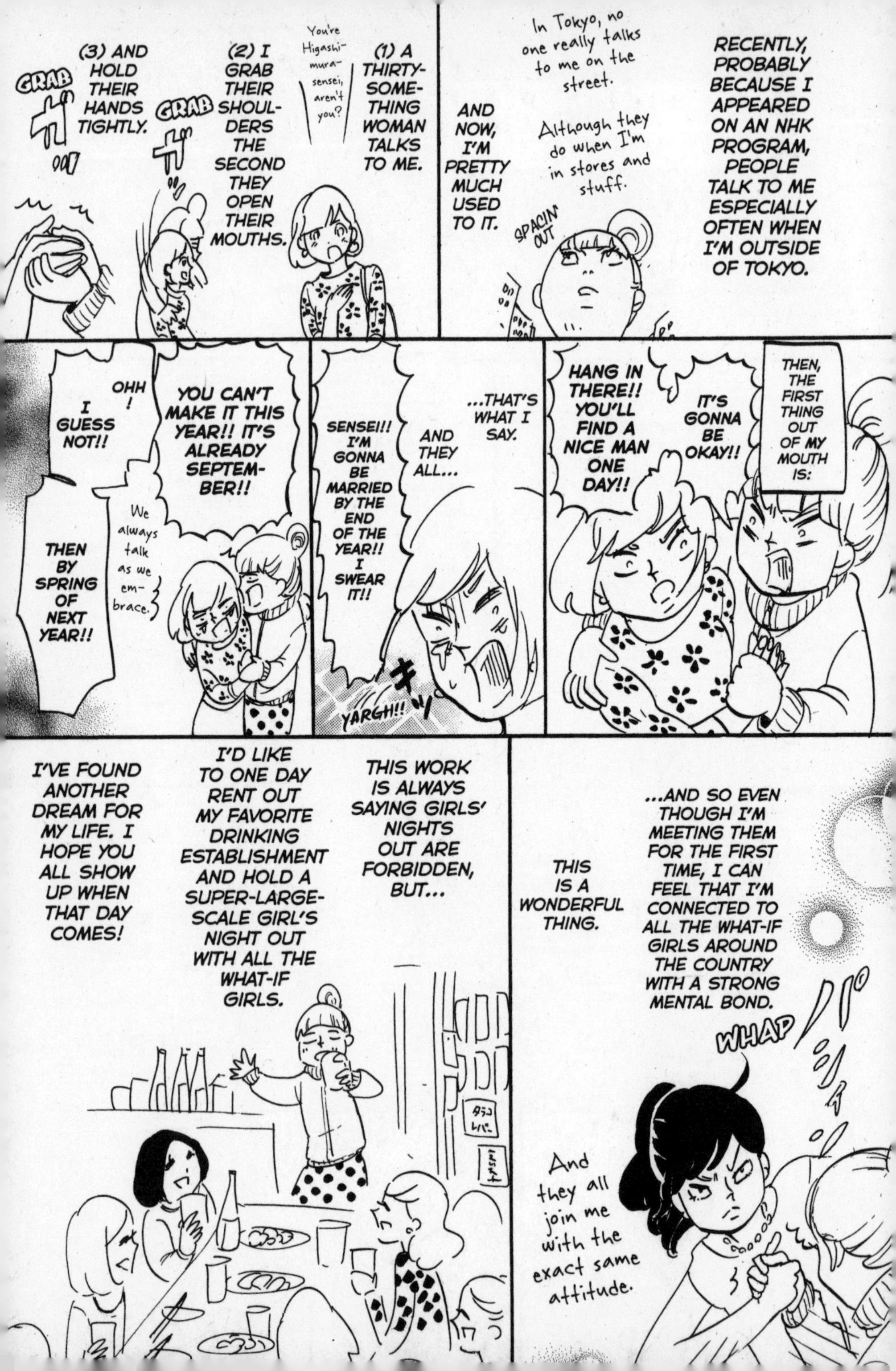
RECENTLY, PROBABLY BECAUSE I APPEARED ON AN NHK PROGRAM, PEOPLE TALK TO ME ESPECIALLY OFTEN WHEN I'M OUTSIDE OF TOKYO.
In Tokyo, no one really talks to me on the street.
Although they do when I'm in stores and stuff.
SPACIN' OUT
AND NOW, I'M PRETTY MUCH USED TO IT.
(1) A THIRTY-SOMETHING WOMAN TALKS TO ME.
You're Higashimura-sensei, aren't you?
(2) I GRAB THEIR SHOULDERS THE SECOND THEY OPEN THEIR MOUTHS.
GRAB
(3) AND HOLD THEIR HANDS TIGHTLY.
GRAB
THEN, THE FIRST THING OUT OF MY MOUTH IS:
IT'S GONNA BE OKAY!!
HANG IN THERE!! YOU'LL FIND A NICE MAN ONE DAY!!
...THAT'S WHAT I SAY.
AND THEY ALL...
SENSEI!!! I'M GONNA BE MARRIED BY THE END OF THE YEAR!! I SWEAR IT!!
YARGH!!
YOU CAN'T MAKE IT THIS YEAR!! IT'S ALREADY SEPTEMBER!!
We always talk as we embrace.
OHH!
I GUESS NOT!!
THEN BY SPRING OF NEXT YEAR!!
...AND SO EVEN THOUGH I'M MEETING THEM FOR THE FIRST TIME, I CAN FEEL THAT I'M CONNECTED TO ALL THE WHAT-IF GIRLS AROUND THE COUNTRY WITH A STRONG MENTAL BOND.
THIS IS A WONDERFUL THING.
WHAP
And they all join me with the exact same attitude.
THIS WORK IS ALWAYS SAYING GIRLS' NIGHTS OUT ARE FORBIDDEN, BUT...
I'D LIKE TO ONE DAY RENT OUT MY FAVORITE DRINKING ESTABLISHMENT AND HOLD A SUPER-LARGE-SCALE GIRL'S NIGHT OUT WITH ALL THE WHAT-IF GIRLS.
I'VE FOUND ANOTHER DREAM FOR MY LIFE. I HOPE YOU ALL SHOW UP WHEN THAT DAY COMES!

Tokyo Tarareba Girls volume 4 is a work of fiction. Names, characters, places, and incidents are the products of the author's imagination or are used fictitiously. Any resemblance to actual events, locales, or persons, living or dead, is entirely coincidental.

A Kodansha Comics Trade Paperback Original.

Tokyo Tarareba Girls volume 4 copyright © 2015 Akiko Higashimura
English translation copyright © 2018 Akiko Higashimura

All rights reserved.

Published in the United States by Kodansha Comics,
an imprint of Kodansha USA Publishing, LLC, New York.

Publication rights for this English edition arranged through Kodansha Ltd.,
Tokyo.

First published in Japan in 2015 by Kodansha Ltd., Tokyo, as *Tokyo
Tarareba Musume* volume 4.

ISBN 978-1-63236-688-7

Printed in the United States of America.

www.kodanshacomics.com

9 8 7 6 5 4 3 2 1

Translation: Steven LeCroy
Lettering: Rina Mapa and Paige Pumphrey
Editing: Sarah Tilson and Lauren Scanlan
YKS Services LLC/SKY Japan, INC.
Kodansha Comics Edition Cover Design: Phil Balsman